The Library

of

Literary History

The Library of Literary History

———◆◇◆———

A LITERARY HISTORY OF INDIA. By R. W. FRAZER, LL.B.

A LITERARY HISTORY OF IRELAND. By DOUGLAS HYDE, LL.D.

LITERARY HISTORY OF AMERICA. By BARRETT WENDELL.

Other Volumes in Preparation.

A LITERARY HISTORY OF THE JEWS. By ISRAEL ABRAHAMS.

ETC.   ETC.   ETC.

There is for every nation a history, which does not respond to the trumpet-call of battle, which does not limit its interests to the conflict of dynasties. This — the history of intellectual growth and artistic achievement — if less romantic than the popular panorama of kings and queens, finds its material in imperishable masterpieces, and reveals to the student something at once more vital and more picturesque than the quarrels of rival parliaments. Nor is it in any sense unscientific to shift the point of view from politics to literature. It is but a fashion of history which insists that a nation lives only for her warriors, a fashion which might long since have been ousted by the commonplace reflection that, in spite of history, the poets are the true masters of the earth. If all record of a nation's progress were blotted out, and its literature were yet left us, might we not recover the outlines of its lost history?

It is, then, with the literature of nations, that the present series is concerned.

Each volume will be entrusted to a distinguished scholar, and the aid of foreign men of letters will be invited whenever the perfection of the series demands it.

THE LIBRARY
OF
LITERARY HISTORY

A Literary History of America

A Literary History
of America

By

Barrett Wendell

Professor of English at Harvard College

THIRD EDITION

New York
Charles Scribner's Sons
1901

UNIVERSITY PRESS · JOHN WILSON
AND SON · CAMBRIDGE, U.S.A.

Contents

PAGE

INTRODUCTION 1

BOOK I

THE SEVENTEENTH CENTURY

   I. ENGLISH HISTORY FROM 1600 TO 1700 13

  II. ENGLISH LITERATURE FROM 1600 TO 1700 20

 III. AMERICAN HISTORY FROM 1600 TO 1700 26

 IV. LITERATURE IN AMERICA FROM 1600 TO 1700 . . . 35

  V. COTTON MATHER 44

 VI. SUMMARY 55

BOOK II

THE EIGHTEENTH CENTURY

    I. ENGLISH HISTORY FROM 1700 TO 1800 59

   II. ENGLISH LITERATURE FROM 1700 TO 1800 65

  III. AMERICAN HISTORY FROM 1700 TO 1800 70

  IV. LITERATURE IN AMERICA FROM 1700 TO 1776 . . . 78

   V. JONATHAN EDWARDS 83

  VI. BENJAMIN FRANKLIN 92

 VII. THE AMERICAN REVOLUTION 104

VIII. LITERATURE IN AMERICA FROM 1776 TO 1800 . . . 117

  IX. SUMMARY 136

CONTENTS

BOOK III

THE NINETEENTH CENTURY

PAGE

I. ENGLISH HISTORY SINCE 1800 139

II. ENGLISH LITERATURE SINCE 1800 145

III. AMERICAN HISTORY SINCE 1800 149

IV. LITERATURE IN AMERICA SINCE 1800 154

BOOK IV

LITERATURE IN THE MIDDLE STATES FROM 1798 TO 1857

I. CHARLES BROCKDEN BROWN 157

II. WASHINGTON IRVING 169

III. JAMES FENIMORE COOPER 181

IV. WILLIAM CULLEN BRYANT 192

V. EDGAR ALLAN POE 204

VI. THE KNICKERBOCKER SCHOOL 219

BOOK V

THE RENAISSANCE OF NEW ENGLAND

I. SOME GENERAL CHARACTERISTICS OF NEW ENGLAND . 233

II. THE NEW ENGLAND ORATORS 246

III. THE NEW ENGLAND SCHOLARS AND HISTORIANS . . . 260

IV. UNITARIANISM 277

V. TRANSCENDENTALISM 290

VI. RALPH WALDO EMERSON 311

VII. THE LESSER MEN OF CONCORD 328

VIII. THE ANTISLAVERY MOVEMENT 339

BOOK V (*Continued*)

		PAGE
IX.	JOHN GREENLEAF WHITTIER	358
X.	THE " ATLANTIC MONTHLY "	370
XI.	HENRY WADSWORTH LONGFELLOW	378
XII.	JAMES RUSSELL LOWELL	393
XIII.	OLIVER WENDELL HOLMES	407
XIV.	NATHANIEL HAWTHORNE	425
XV.	THE DECLINE OF NEW ENGLAND	436

BOOK VI

THE REST OF THE STORY

I.	NEW YORK SINCE 1857	449
II.	WALT WHITMAN	465
III.	LITERATURE IN THE SOUTH	480
IV.	THE WEST	500
V.	THE PRESENT TIME	514
CONCLUSION		521
AUTHORITIES AND REFERENCES		533
NOTE		555
INDEX		559

A Literary History of America

A Literary History of America

INTRODUCTION

LITERATURE, like its most excellent phase, poetry, has never
been satisfactorily defined. In essence it is too subtle, too
elusive, too vital, to be confined within the limits of phrase.
Yet everybody vaguely knows what it is. Everybody knows
that human life, in its endless, commonplace, unfathomable
complexity, impresses human beings in ways which vary not
only with individuals, but with the generations and the nations.
Somewhere in the oldest English writings there is an allegory
which has never faded. Of a night, it tells us, a little group
was gathered about the fireside in a hall where the flicker of
flame cast light on some and threw others into shadow, but
none into shadow so deep as the darkness without. And into
the window from the midst of the night flew a swallow lured
by the light; but unable by reason of his wildness to linger
among men, he sped across the hall and so out again into the
dark, and was seen no more. To this day, as much as when
the old poet first saw or fancied it, the swallow's flight remains
an image of earthly life. From whence we know not, we come
into the wavering light and gusty warmth of this world; but
here the law of our being forbids that we remain. A little we
may see, fancying that we understand, — the hall, the lords
and the servants, the chimney and the feast; more we may
feel, — the light and the warmth, the safety and the danger,
the hope and the dread. Then we must forth again, into the

voiceless, unseen eternities.   But the fleeting moments of life, like the swallow's flight once more, are not quite voiceless ; as surely as he may twitter in the ears of men, so men themselves may give sign to one another of what they think they know, and of what they know they feel.   More too ; men have learned to record these signs, so that long after they are departed, others may guess what their life meant.   These records are often set forth in terms which may be used only by those of rarely special gift and training, — the terms of architecture and sculpture, of painting and music; but oftener and more freely they are phrased in the terms which all men learn somehow to use, — the terms of language.   Some of these records, and most, are of so little moment that they are soon neglected and forgotten; others, like the fancied story of the swallow, linger through the ages.   It is to these that we give the name of literature.   Literature is the lasting expression in words of the meaning of life.

Any definition is the clearer for examples.   To make sure of ours, then, we may well recall a few names which un-doubtedly illustrate it.   The Psalms are literature, so is the Iliad, so are the Epistles of Saint Paul, so is the Æneid, and the Divine Comedy, and Don Quixote, and Hamlet.   These few names are enough to remind us not only of what literature is, but also of the fact which most distinguishes it from other arts of expression.   The lines and colours which embody architec-ture, sculpture, and painting, can be understood by anybody with eyes.   Though to people like ourselves, who have grown up amid the plastic traditions of classical antiquity and the Italian Renaissance, an Egyptian painting or a Japanese print looks odd, it remains, even to us, comprehensible.   The Psalms, on the other hand, were written in Hebrew, the Iliad and the Epistles in dialects of Greek, the Æneid was written in Latin, the Divine Comedy in Italian, Don Quixote in Spanish, and Hamlet in Elizabethan English; except through the unsatis-factory medium of translation one and all must be sealed books to those who do not know the languages native to the men who phrased them. World-old legends, after all, are the wisest; the men who fled from Babel could each see in the deserted tower a monument of impious aspiration, but this thought of each was sealed from the rest by the confusion of tongues. So to this day literature is of all fine arts the most ineradicably national.

Here again we come to a word so simple and so frequent that an important phase of its meaning is often overlooked. Nationality is generally conceived to be a question of race, of descent, of blood; and yet in human experience there is a circumstance perhaps more potent in binding men together than any physical tie. That old legend of Babel tells the story. The confusion of tongues broke every bond of common kinship; the races which should hold together through the centuries sprang afresh from men who newly spoke and newly thought and newly felt in terms of common language. For these languages which we speak grow more deeply than anything else to be a part of our mental habit who use them. It is in terms of language that we think even about the commonplaces of life, — what we shall eat, what we shall wear, whom we shall care for; in terms of language too, and in no others, we formulate the ideals which consciously, and perhaps still more unconsciously, guide our conduct and our aspirations. In a strange, subtle way each language grows to associate with itself the ideals and the aspirations and the fate of those peoples with whose life it is inextricably intermingled.

Languages grow and live and die in accordance with laws of their own, not perfectly understood, which need not now detain us. This English of ours, with which alone we are immediately concerned, may be taken as typical. Originating, one can hardly say precisely when or how, from the union and confusion of older tongues, it has struggled through the infantile diseases of dialect, each of which has left some trace, until long ago it not only had become the sole means of expression for millions of people, but also had assumed the literary form which now makes its literature in some respects the most considerable of modern times. Whatever else, this literature is the most spontaneous, the least formal and conscious, the most instinctively creative, the most free from the rankness and the debility of extreme culture, and so seemingly the most normal. Its earliest forms were artless; songs and sayings began to stray from oral tradition into written record, laws were sometimes phrased and chronicles made in the robust young terms which carried meaning to unlearned folks as well as to those versed in more polite tongues. By and by came forms of literature which at least comparatively were artistic, influenced by an impulse of writers and of readers too towards expression for expression's sake. The earliest of these which has lasted in general literary memory reached its height in the work of Chaucer. After his time came a century or more of civil disturbance, when Englishmen were too busy with wars of the Roses and the like for further progress in the arts of peace. Then, with the new national integrity which grew under the Tudors, came a fresh and stronger literary impulse, unsurpassed in vigorous spontaneity.

In 1575 there was hardly such a thing as modern English literature; in 1625 that great body of English literature which we call Elizabethan was complete. Fifty years had given us not only incomparable lyric verse and the final version of the Bible, but the work too of Spenser, of Shakspere and the other great dramatists, of Hooker, of Ralegh, of Bacon, and of all their fellows. Among these, of course, Shakspere stands supreme, just as Chaucer stood among his contemporaries whose names are now forgotten by all but special scholars; and one feature of Shakspere's supremacy is that his literary career was normal. Whoever has followed it from his experimental beginning, through the ripeness to which he brought comedy, history, and tragedy alike, to its placid close amid the growing languor of freshly established tradition, will have learned some-

thing more than even the great name of Shakspere includes, —
he will have had a glimpse of the natural law which not
only governed the course of Shakspere himself and of Elizabethan literature, but has governed in the past and will govern
in the future the growth, development, and decline of all
literature and of all fine art whatsoever. Lasting literature has
its birth when a creative impulse, which we may call imaginative, moves men to break the shackles of tradition, making
things which have not been before; sooner or later this impulse is checked by a growing sense of the inexorable limits
of fact and of language; and then creative imagination sinks
into some new tradition, to be broken only when, in time to
come, the vital force of imagination shall revive.

As English literature has grown into maturity, the working
of this law throughout its course has become evident. The
first impulse, we have seen, gave us the work of Chaucer;
the second, which came only after generations, gave us the
Elizabethan lyrics and dramas, Spenser and Shakspere, and
the final form of the English Bible. This last is probably the
greatest masterpiece of translation in the world; it has exercised on the thought and the language of English-speaking
people an influence which cannot be overestimated. As a
translation, however, it rather indicates how eager Elizabethan
Englishmen were to know the splendours of world-old literature, than reveals a spontaneous impulse towards native expression. Apart from this supreme work, the fully developed
literature of the Elizabethan period took on the whole the
form of poetry; that of the eighteenth century, on the other
hand, took on the whole the form of prose; and as English
prose literature has developed, no phase of it has developed
more highly than its fiction. Vaguely general though this
statement be, it is perhaps enough to indicate an important
general tendency. The first form in which the normal literature of any language develops is instinctively poetic; prose
comes later; and prose fiction, that intricate combination of

poetic impulse with prosaic form, comes later still.   In 1625 English literature was fully developed only in the forms of lyric and dramatic poetry.

It was about this time that the America with which we shall be concerned came into existence.   It began with a number of mutually independent settlements, each of which grew into something like political integrity.   When the Constitution of the United States was adopted, somewhat more than a hundred years ago, the sentiment of local sovereignty in the separate States was accordingly too strong to allow the federal power to assume an independent name.   As the power thus founded developed into one of the most considerable in modern history, its citizens found themselves driven by this unique fact of national namelessness to a custom which, if misunderstood, is often held presumptuous;   they called themselves Americans, a name geographically proper to all natives of the Western Hemisphere, from Canada to Patagonia.   By this time the custom thus historically established has given to the name "America" the sense in which we generally use it.   The America with whose literary history we are to be concerned is only that part of the American continent which is dominated by the English-speaking people now subject to the government of the United States.

A literary history of America, then, should concern itself with such lasting expressions in words of the meaning of life as this people has uttered during its three centuries of growingly independent existence; or, in simpler terms, with what America has contributed to the literature of the English language.

Accidents of chronology though the centuries of any era must be, they prove in such study as ours convenient divisions of time, at once easy to remember and characteristically distinct. In the history of America, at least, each century has traits of its own.   In 1600 there was no such thing as English-speaking America; in 1700 all but one of the colonies which have developed into the United States were finally established, and the English conquest of the middle colonies founded by the Dutch or the Swedes was virtually complete. In 1700 every one of the American colonies was loyally subject to the government of King William III.; in 1800 there remained throughout them no vestige of British authority. In 1800, the last complete year of the presidency of John Adams, the United States were still an experiment in government of which the result remained in doubt; the year 1900 has found them, whatever else, a power which seems as established and as important as any in the world. Clearly these three centuries of American history are at least as distinct as three generations in any race.

Again, though the political crises which decided the distinct features of these centuries were far from coincident with the centuries themselves, the typical American character of the seventeenth century differed from that of the eighteenth, and that of the eighteenth from that of the nineteenth, as distinctly as the historical limits of these centuries differed one from the other. In the seventeenth century the typical American, a man of English-speaking race, seemed to himself an immigrant hardly at home in the remote regions where his exiled life was perforce to be passed. In the eighteenth century the typical American, still English at heart, was so far in descent from the immigration that almost unawares his personal ties with the mother country had been broken. By tradition, perhaps, he knew from what part of the old world his ancestors had come, but that old home itself had probably both lost all such traditions of those ancestors and ceased to feel even curiosity about their descendants. For better or worse, this new America had become the only real home ot its natives. In the nineteenth century the typical American, politically as well as personally independent of the old world, and English only so far as the traditions inseparable from ancestral law and language must keep him so, has often felt or

fancied himself less at one with contemporary Englishmen
than with Europeans of other and essentially foreign blood.

Yet, English or not, we Americans are English-speaking
still ; and English-speaking we must always remain. An
accident of language and nothing more, this fact may seem
to many. To those who think more deeply it can hardly fail
to mean that for better or worse the ideals which underlie our
blundering conscious life must always be the ideals which
underlie the conscious life of the mother country, and which
for centuries have rectified and purified her blunders. Morally
and religiously these ideals are immortally consecrated in King
James's version of the Bible ; legally and politically these
ideals are grouped in that great legal system which, in distinction from the Canon Law or the Civil, may broadly be called
the Common Law of England. What these ideals are, every
one bred in the traditions of our ancestral language instinctively
knows ; but such knowledge is hard to phrase. Perhaps we
come as near as may be to truth when we say that in their
moral aspect the ideals which underlie our language are comprised in a profound conviction that, whatever our station or
our shortcomings, each of us is bound to do right ; and that
in their legal aspect these ideals may similarly be summarised
in the statement that we are bound on earth to maintain our
rights. But the rights contemplated by our ancestral law are
no abstract ones ; they are those which the gradually varying
custom and experience of the centuries have proved in actual
exercise to be safely favourable to the public and private welfare of men like ourselves.

Vague and general as all this may seem, it has lately come
to possess significance hardly paralleled since at the beginning
of our Christian era the imperial power, the law and the language, of Rome dominated what was then the world. Our law
and our language, our ideals and our vital energies, which had
their earliest origin in England, are at this moment struggling
for world-existence with what else in ideals, in law, and in lan-

guage have developed themselves otherwise in modern time. Yet for a century or more the two great English-speaking races, the native English and that of independent America, have been so disunited that each has often seemed to the other more hostile than many an alien. There are no feuds fiercer than the feuds of kindred. As we pursue our study, we shall perhaps see how this breach between the two branches of our race has grown. In brief, from the first settlement of Virginia until the moment when the guns of Admiral Dewey brought America unawares but fatally face to face with the problem of Asiatic empire, there has never been an instant when to native Englishmen and to English-speaking Americans the great political problems have presented themselves in the same terms. To-day at last there is little difference. To-day, then, the disunion of sympathy which for a century and more has kept Americans apart from the native English takes on world-wide significance.

An important phase of our study must accordingly be that which attempts to trace and to understand the changes in the native character of the Americans and of the English, which so long resulted in disunion of national sentiment. We can scrutinise them, however, only as they appear in literary history, and mostly in that of America. For our chief business concerns only the question of what contributions America has made, during its three centuries, to the literature of the English language.

Recurring to our rough, convenient division of native Americans into the three types which correspond to these three centuries of American history, we can instantly perceive that only the last, the Americans of the nineteenth century, have produced literature of any importance. The novelists and the historians, the essayists and the poets, whose names come to mind when American literature is mentioned, have all flourished since 1800. The greater part of our study, then, must concern the century just at an end. For all that, the two earlier centuries were not sterile; rather indeed the amount of native American writing which each produced is surprising. What is more, the American writings of the eighteenth century differed from those of the seventeenth quite as distinctly as did the American history or the American character. Of both centuries, meanwhile, two things are true : neither in itself presents much literary variety, and most of what was published in each has already been forgotten. Our task, then, is becoming plainer; it is to glance at the literary history of America during the seventeenth century and the eighteenth, and to study, with what detail proves possible, that literary history during the past hundred years.

From all this, too, an obvious method of proceeding begins to define itself. Taking each century in turn, we may conveniently begin by reminding ourselves briefly of what it contributed to the history and to the literature of England. With this in mind we may better understand a similar but more minute study of America during each of the three periods in question. When we come to the last and most important of these, the nineteenth century, we may find ourselves a little troubled by the fact that so much of it is almost contemporary with ourselves. Contemporary life is never quite ripe for history; facts cannot at once range themselves in true perspective; and when these facts are living men and women, there is a touch of inhumanity in writing of them as if we had already had the misfortune to lose them. In these straits one decision seems unavoidable, — so far as our study concerns individuals, we must confine it to those who are no longer living. Unhappily the list has so swollen that these should prove quite enough for our main purpose. For this, we should constantly remember, is chiefly to discern what, if anything, America has so far contributed to the literature of our ancestral English language.

BOOK I

THE SEVENTEENTH CENTURY

BOOK I

THE SEVENTEENTH CENTURY

I

ENGLISH HISTORY FROM 1600 TO 1700

WHATEVER else people remember about seventeenth-century England, they will pretty surely know the names of the sovereigns who came to the throne. In 1600 the reign of Queen Elizabeth was drawing to its close. After her came the pragmatic Scotchman, James I. After him came Charles I., whose tragic fate has combined with the charm of his portraits to make him at least a pathetically romantic hero. Then came Cromwell, quite as sovereign in his fleeting Commonwealth as ever king was in monarchy. Then came Charles II., with all the license of the Restoration; then James II., ousted in less than five years by the Glorious Revolution; finally came the Dutch Prince of Orange with his English Queen, royal in England only by glorious revolutionary grace. Seven sovereigns in all we find, if we count William and Mary together; and of these only six were technically royal. Of the six royalties, four were Stuarts, who came in the middle of the list; and the Stuart dynasty was broken midway by the apparition of Cromwell, the one English sovereign not of royal blood and dignity. Literally, then, Cromwell may be termed the central figure of English history during the seventeenth century.

It is in the full literary spirit of that period to remark this fantastic fact as if it were significant, saying that just as

Cromwell stands central in the list of those who during the seventeenth century of our Christian era were sovereign in Protestant England, so in the eyes of them who seek among these a fitting centre for their thoughts and meditations he proves central too. Love him or hate him, reverence or detest his memory, one fact you must grant : never before in English history had men seen dominant the type of which he is the great representative ; never since his time have they again seen that dominant type, now irrevocably vanished with the world which brought it forth, — the type of the dominant Puritan.

The Puritan character, of course, is too permanently English to be confined to any single period of English history. Throughout English records we may find it, first gathering the force which led to its momentary sovereignty, and later, even to our own time, affecting the whole course of English life and thought. In the seventeenth century, however, Puritanism for a while acquired the unique importance of national dominance, which it proved politically unable to maintain beyond the lifetime of its chief exponent. A religious system, one generally thinks it ; and rightly, for it was profoundly actuated by conscious religious motives, and by passionate devotion to that system of Christian theology which is known by the name of Calvin. A political movement, too, it often seems ; and rightly, for never in the course of English history have native Englishmen so striven to alter the form and the course of constitutional development. In such a study as ours it has both aspects ; the dominance of Puritanism may best be thought of as the period when for a little while the moral and religious ideals which underlie our language were uppermost, when for once the actuating impulse of authority was rather that the will of God should be done on earth than that any custom — however fortified and confirmed by the experience formulated in the Common Law — should for its own sake be maintained.

That the will of God should be done, on earth as it is in

Heaven, no good Englishman will ever deny. What the will of God is, on the other hand, when directly concerned with the matters of this world, even good Englishmen cannot always agree. Among the Puritans themselves there was plenty of dissension, but one thing seems fairly sure, — no good Puritan questioned the truth of Calvinism any more than good Catholics of to-day question the dogmas of an Œcumenical Council. To understand Puritanism, then, in England and in America alike, we must remind ourselves of what Calvinistic theology taught.

In the beginning, the Puritans held, God created man, responsible to Him, with perfect freedom of will. Adam, in the fall, exerted his will in opposition to the will of God; thereby Adam and all his posterity merited eternal punishment. As a mark of that punishment they lost the power of exerting their will in harmony with the will of God, without losing their hereditary responsibility to Him. But God, in His infinite mercy, was pleased to mitigate His justice. Through the mediation of Christ, certain human beings, chosen at God's pleasure, might be relieved of the just penalty of sin, and received into everlasting salvation. These were the elect; none others could be saved, nor could any acts of the elect impair their salvation. Now, there were no outward and visible marks by which the elect might be known; there was a fair chance that any human being to whom the gospel was brought might be of the number. The thing which most vitally concerned every man, then, was to discover whether he were elect, and so free from the just penalty of sin, ancestral and personal. The test of election was ability to exert the will in true harmony with the will of God, — a proof of emancipation from the hereditary curse of the children of Adam; whoever could do right, and wish to, had a fair ground for hope that he should be saved. But even the elect were infected with the hereditary sin or humanity; and, besides, no wile of the Devil was more frequent than that which deceived men into believing themselves regenerate when in truth they were not. The task of assuring one's self of election could end only with life, — a life of passionate aspirations, ecstatic enthusiasms, profound discouragements. Above all, men must never forget that the true will of God was revealed, directly or by implication, only and wholly in Scripture; incessant study of Scripture was the sole means by which any man could assure himself that his will was really exerting itself, through the mediatory power of Christ, in true harmony with the will of God.

Calvinism this creed is commonly called, in memory of the French reformer, who in modern times has been its chief exponent; but those learned in theology tell us that perhaps we might better call it the system of Saint Augustine. Augustine and Calvin alike are remembered chiefly, perhaps wholly, as theologians; and in this age, whose most characteristic energies are devoted to researches which may be confirmed by observation or experiment, theology generally seems intangibly remote from workaday life. Yet, strangely enough, the conceptions which underlie the most popular scientific philosophy of our own time have much in common with those which actuated both Augustine and Calvin. Earthly life, the modern evolutionists hold, consists in a struggle for existence wherein only the fittest can survive; for every organism which persists, myriads must irretrievably perish. In the days when Calvin pondered on the eternities, and still more in those tragic days of toppling empire when Augustine strove to imprison divine truth within the limits of earthly language, science was still to come. But what Augustine and Calvin saw, in the human affairs whence each alike inferred the systems of Heaven and Hell, was really what the modern evolutionists perceive in every aspect of Nature. Total depravity is only a theological name for that phase of life which in less imaginative times we name the struggle for existence; and likewise election is only a theological name for what our

newer fashion calls the survival of the fittest. Old-world
theology and modern science alike strive to explain facts
which have been and shall be so long as humanity casts its
shadow in the sunshine.

Now, any struggle is bound to be at its fiercest where the
struggling forces are most concentrated. In human affairs,
both good and evil struggle hardest where human beings are
most densely congregated. Augustine wrote amid the dying
throes of antiquity, in a world still formally dominated by
that imperial power of Rome whose true health and strength
were gone. Calvin wrote in the populous Europe of the
Renaissance, where at once the whole system of mediæval life
was doomed, and the pitiless pressure of economic fact was
already forcing the more adventurous spirits of every European
race to seek an outlet for their energy in the unexplored continents of our Western Hemisphere. Noble, too, though we
may find the traditions of that merry old England, which was so
vital under Queen Elizabeth, which faded under the first two
Stuarts, and which vanished in the smoke of the Civil Wars,
the plain records, both of history and of literature, show it to
have been a dense, wicked old world, whose passions ran high
and deep, and whose vices and crimes, big as its brave old
virtues, were truly such as to make the grim dogmas of the
Puritans seem to many earnest minds the only explanation of
so godless a fact as human life.

God's will be done on earth, then, the Puritans cried,
honestly conceiving this divine will to demand the political
dominance of God's elect. The society over which they
believed that these elect should make themselves politically
dominant had all the complexity which must develop itself during centuries of national and social growth; and this growth,
fortified by the uncodified, unwritten, impregnable Common
Law of England, had taken through the centuries an earthly
course at variance with what the Puritans held to be their
divinely sanctioned politics. Towards the end of Cromwell's

2

dominance, then, they tried to mend matters by giving England a written constitution.[1]   In many respects this Instrument of Government seems theoretically better than the older system which had grown under the unwritten Common Law, and which since Cromwell's time has developed after its own fashion into the Parliamentary government now controlling the British Empire.   The Instrument of Government, however, had a mortal weakness: it was not historically continuous with the past; and this was enough to prevent any historical continuity with the future.   The struggle for political existence in England was inevitably fatal to principles and ideals so little rooted in national life as those which the Puritans in their wise folly hopefully, yet hopelessly formulated.   So in England, after the momentary irruption of dominant Puritanism, the old Common Law surged back; and it has flowed on to the present day, the stronger if not the nobler of the two forces which the history of our native language compels us to admit as the ideals of our race.

By most constitutional lawyers, then, the dominance of Puritanism personified in Cromwell has been held an accidental and almost unimportant disease which may be neglected in considering the life history of the English Constitution. How far this view is right, we need not trouble ourselves to inquire; constitutional history is not within our province. What more concerns us is a fact which general readers of the social history of England during the seventeenth century can hardly fail to remark, perhaps more certainly than thorough students whose attention is rightly, but often bewilderingly, encumbered by detail.   The records which remain to us of Elizabethan England, and of the England which finally broke into civil war, seem records of a remote past.   Take, for example, almost at random, three names: those of the adventurer, Ralegh; of the soldier and courtier, Essex; and, a little later,

---

[1] The line of thought here set forth was suggested by one of Mr. A. V. Dicey's Lowell Institute lectures, in the autumn of 1898.

of that most chivalrous of autobiographers, Lord Herbert of Cherbury. All three are marked by a big, simple, youthful spontaneity, different at once from any general trait of modern times and from those which are common to every period of history. Take, equally at random, three other names which belong to the years after Cromwell's dominant Puritanism had failed; Monk, the first Duke of Albemarle; Samuel Pepys, the diarist; and John Churchill, first Duke of Marlborough. Though this last little group seem by no means contemporary with ourselves, yet, in comparison with the elder group, they seem almost modern, — old-fashioned men rather than men of an earlier type than those we live with. The contrast is deeply typical. The England which came before the dominant Puritanism of Cromwell, the England to which we may broadly give, as we often give to its literature, the name " Elizabethan," vanished when Puritan dominance broke for a while the progress of English constitutional law; the England which came afterwards, whatever its merits or its faults, lacked, as England has continued to lack ever since King Charles II. was restored, certain traits which we all feel in the old Elizabethan world.

For our purpose there is hardly anything more important than to realise, if we can, what these Elizabethan traits were, which distinguish the England before Cromwell's time from that which has come after him. Perhaps we shall have done a little to remind ourselves of what Elizabethan England possessed, when we say that in the older time we can everywhere find three characteristics which in the later time are more and more dimly discernible, — spontaneity, enthusiasm, and versatility.

II

THE social history of seventeenth-century England broadly groups itself in three parts : that which preceded the dominant Puritanism of the Commonwealth; the dominant Puritanism itself; and what came after. All three of these phases of English life found adequate expression in lasting literature. An easy way to remind ourselves of these literary types is to glance at some records of publication in England during the three distinct periods of the seventeenth century.[1] Between 1600 and 1605 appeared plays by Dekker, Ben Jonson, John Lyly, Shakspere, Marston, Middleton, Heywood, and Chapman; Fairfax's translation of Tasso, Lodge's of Josephus, and Florio's of Montaigne; "England's Helicon," Campion's "Art of English Poetry," and Davidson's "Poetical Rhapsody;" and, among many other lesser works, the last volume of Hakluyt's "Voyages." Between 1648 and 1652 appeared works by Fuller, Herrick, Lovelace, Milton, Francis Quarles, Jeremy Taylor, Baxter, Bunyan, Cowley, Hobbes, Vaughan, Davenant, Izaak Walton, and George Herbert. Finally, between 1695 and 1700 appeared plays by Colley Cibber, Southern, Congreve, Farquhar, and Vanbrugh; and works of one sort or another by Bentley, Blackmore, Defoe, Evelyn, Garth, Lord Shaftesbury, and Dryden; not to speak of Tate and Brady's version of the "Psalms." These random lists will

[1] Throughout our study, the names recorded in Ryland's "Chronological Outlines of English Literature," published by Macmillan, should suffice for such purposes as that now in mind. Though sometimes slightly inaccurate, this admirably useful book is always trustworthy enough to warrant generalisation.

define, almost as clearly as lists made with thoughtful care, the chief facts which we should now keep in mind.

In the beginning of the century, even though Elizabeth's reign was very near its end, the literature which we call Elizabethan was at its height; and as the generations have passed, we begin to see how surely its central figure, the dominant figure of all English literature, is that of Shakspere. In the middle of the century there was more confusion; yet it takes no great knowledge of English letters to feel in the first place that the Elizabethan temper was no longer strong; and in the second place, that among the men who were then writing, there was one who — if not so surely central — rose almost as superior to the rest as Shakspere was fifty years before. That man, of course, is Milton. In the last five years of the century, when the Commonwealth, the Restoration, and the Glorious Revolution had done their work, there was another group, less diverse than that of Cromwell's time, almost as homogeneous indeed as that of Elizabeth's, but as different from either of the others as the periwigs of Marlborough were from the jewelled caps of Walter Ralegh; and in this last group, as in both the others, one figure emerged from the rest. Here that figure is John Dryden, the first great maker of heroic couplets, and the first masterly writer of what has become modern English prose. It is worth our while to glance in turn at each of these literary periods, — the periods of Shakspere, of Milton, and of Dryden.

Elizabethan literature, in which Shakspere declares himself more and more supreme, is at once the first, and in many respects the greatest, of the schools or periods of letters which have come to constitute modern English literature as a whole. Marked throughout by the spontaneity, the enthusiasm, and the various versatility of the England which bred it, this period is clearly marked as well by the fact that it brought to final excellence two kinds of poetry, — the lyric, and a little later the dramatic. In thinking of Elizabethan literature, then, one is apt to forget that it includes noble work of other than poetic sort; yet no reader of English can long forget that to this same school belongs the scientific work and the final aphorisms of Bacon. It was during the first fifteen years of the seventeenth century, too, that Walter Ralegh, in the Tower, wrote his " History of the World ; " and we have only to glance back at Ryland's summaries of publication to see what masterly translations accompanied the gradual growth of that final masterpiece of translation, the English Bible of 1611. There were minor phases of literature meanwhile which posterity has been apt to forget; but the name of Hakluyt, the collector of so many records of explorations, is still familiar; and so perhaps is that of Richard Hooker, whose " Ecclesiastic Polity " remains the chief literary monument of religious controversy during the reign of Elizabeth. Poetry was first, then, and supreme; but there was fine, noble, thoughtful prose in philosophy and history alike; and not less characteristic of the time, though far less excellent as literature, was much matter of contemporary chronicle, like Hakluyt's " Voyages," and much religious controversy.

Throughout this literature there is one trait which the lapse of three centuries, with their slow, inevitable changes of language, has tended to obscure. Yet whoever grows familiar even with the work of Shakspere by himself, and still more with that of his contemporaries as well, must grow to feel it. This is a sort of pristine alertness of mind, evident in innumerable details of Elizabethan style. One may best detect it, perhaps, by committing to memory random passages of Elizabethan literature. If the trait occurred only in the work of Shakspere, one might deem it a mere fresh miracle of his genius; but you will find it everywhere. In the thinner plays, for example, of Beaumont and Fletcher, the words, the sentences, the lines, the cadences, are full of refinements of phrase, subtleties of alliteration, swift glancing varieties of allusion, flashes alike of sentiment and of wit, somehow beyond the instant perception of any English-born modern mind. Yet it is no mere juggling with words to say that the works of Beaumont and Fletcher, of Shakspere, and of all the dramatists, are truly plays; and plays are meant not for such serious study as the excellence of these has compelled from posterity, but rather to give such instant emotional pleasure as theatres afford us to-day, and as we have got best during the nineteenth century in Paris. Such literature as the Elizabethan world has left us, in short, bespeaks a public whose spontaneous alertness of mind, whose instant perception of every subtle variety of phrase and allusion, was more akin to that of our contemporary French than to anything which we are now accustomed to consider native to insular England. Elizabethan literature bears witness throughout to the spontaneous, enthusiastic versatility which the English temperament possessed in the spacious Elizabethan days.

By the middle of the century, after the convulsions of the Civil Wars, this trait had begun to fade out of English letters. Our brief list of mid-century publications revealed Milton, not as the chief of a school, but rather as the one great figure who subsisted amid a group of excellently deliberate minor poets and elaborate makers of overwrought rhetorical prose, often splendid, but never simple. Fuller, Taylor, and Walton fairly typify seventeenth-century prose; to complete our impression of it we might glance back at Burton, whose " Anatomy of Melancholy " appeared in 1621, and at Sir Thomas Browne, whose " Religio Medici " was in 1650 less than ten years old. In Milton's time, except for Milton himself, the creative impulse which had made Elizabethan literature so vital had subsided. The English imagination seemed checked by a variously developed sense of the inexorable limits of fact and of language. One term by which we may characterise this mid-century English literature, to distinguish it from the elder, is the term " deliberate." Mysteriously but certainly the old spontaneity and versatility of the Elizabethan mind had disappeared.

Deliberate, indeed, is an epithet which may help us to define the impression made by Milton himself. Throughout his poetry, even of that earlier period when in so many aspects he was still almost Elizabethan, one may often feel him tending toward his later poetic contemporaries in the conscious carefulness of his art; and surely in the great epic work of his later years, when solitary and alone he strove to give artistic expression to the dominant ideals of a Puritanism whose earthly hopes were as lost as ever Paradise was to our erring fathers, one feels amid his all but unequalled power a colossal deliberation. In the prose work which intervened between these two periods of his poetic production, there is incisive swiftness of thought and phrase, but on the whole its effect is hardly more marked by grimly passionate asperity of temper than by an almost conscious ponderousness of phrase. The literature of Cromwell's England was as different from that of Elizabeth's as Cromwell was from Walter Ralegh. The names of Shakspere and Milton tell the story.

The name of Dryden is as different from that of Milton as Milton's is from Shakspere's. Though Dryden's "Astræa Redux" was published seven years before "Paradise Lost," Dryden died in 1700 amid a literature whose poetry had cooled into something like the rational form which deadened it throughout the century to come, and whose drama had for forty years been revealing fresh phases of decadent lifelessness. For though at least the comedies of the Restoration and of the years which follow seemed to contemporaries full of wit and vitality, few bodies of literature in the world have proved more evanescent, and more corrupt, artistically as well as morally. But if poetry and the drama were for the moment sleeping, — the latter seemingly for ever, the former for well-nigh a century to come, — there were other phases of English thought, if not of English feeling, which were full of life.

Boyle had done his work in chemistry ; Newton had created a whole range of physical science ; Locke had produced his epoch-making " Essay on Human Understanding ; " and, to go no further, the works of Sir William Temple and the critical essays of Dryden himself had given English prose its most masterly, almost its final form.

In literature, just as in history, then, we find that the seventeenth century reveals in England three distinct epochs, each different from the others and all together involving such changes in the national temperament as to make the England of Dryden almost as foreign to that of Shakspere as the temper of King William III. was to Queen Elizabeth's. Like Elizabethan England, Elizabethan literature seems different from anything which we can now know in the flesh. One can hardly imagine feeling quite at home in the Mermaid Tavern with Beaumont and Ben Jonson and the rest ; but in modern London, or at least in the London of thirty years ago, one might sometimes feel that a few steps around a grimy corner should still lead to some coffee-house, where glorious John Dryden could be found sitting in robust, old-fashioned dictatorship over the laws of the language in which we ourselves think and speak and feel. For Dryden's England is not yet quite dead and gone. But dead and gone, or at least vanished from this earth, in Dryden's time almost as surely as in ours, was the elder England, whose spontaneity, whose enthusiasm, and whose versatility made Elizabethan literature the most lastingly vital record which our language shall ever phrase.

History and literature alike, then, have shown us an England of the seventeenth century wherein the great central convulsion of dominant Puritanism fatally destroyed a youthful world, and gave us at last in its place a more deliberate, permanently different new one.

III

IT was in the first quarter of this seventeenth century that the American colonies were finally established. The first lasting settlement of Virginia was made in the spring of 1607; the Pilgrims landed at Plymouth towards the end of 1620; Boston was founded less than ten years later; and from 1636 dates the oldest of native American corporations, that of Harvard College. At the latest of these dates the tragic reign of Charles I. had not half finished its course; at the earliest Queen Elizabeth had lain less than five years in Westminster Abbey; and these dates are less than a full generation apart.

From these familiar facts may instantly be inferred another which has been comparatively neglected. To speak only of New England, — for in literary history New England is far more important than the other colonies, — we may say that every leading man among the first settlers both of Plymouth and of Massachusetts Bay was born under Queen Elizabeth herself. William Bradford of Plymouth, for example, was born in 1590, the year when Spenser published the first books of the "Faerie Queene;" and Edward Winslow was born in 1595, when Shakspere had published only "Venus and Adonis" and "Lucrece." Thomas Dudley is said to have been born in 1576, some ten years before the execution of Mary Stuart. John Winthrop was born in 1588, the year of the Invincible Armada. John Cotton was born in 1585, the year before Sir Philip Sidney was killed, when for aught we know Shakspere had not yet emerged from Stratford, and when surely John Foxe, the martyrologist, was still alive. Thomas Hooker was born only a year later, in 1586. Richard Mather was only ten years younger, born in the year when Ben Jonson's first play is said to have been acted, when Ralegh published his " Discovery of Guiana," and Spenser the last three books of his " Faerie Queene." Roger Williams was born in 1600, the year which gave us the first quartos of " Henry IV.," " Henry V.," " The Midsummer Night's Dream," " The Merchant of Venice," and " Much Ado About Nothing." And what is thus shown true of New England is truer still of Virginia, founded half a generation earlier. Though the sovereigns to whom both northern and southern colonies owed their first allegiance were Stuarts, all the founders of these colonies were of true Elizabethan birth.

They were not, to be sure, quite the kind of Elizabethans who expressed themselves in poetry. The single work produced in America which by any stretch of language may be held a contribution to Elizabethan letters is a portion of George Sandys's translation of Ovid, said to have been made during his sojourn in Virginia between 1621 and 1624. In general, the settlers of Virginia were of the adventurous type which expresses itself far more in action than in words ; while the settlers of New England were too much devoted to the affairs of another world than this to have time, even if they had had taste or principle, for devotion to any form of fine art. Of Elizabethan times, all the while, as of any period in history, it remains true that in a deep sense the men of a single generation cannot help being brethren. For all their mutual detestation, Puritans and playwrights alike possessed the spontaneity of temper, the enthusiasm of purpose, and the versatility of power which marked Elizabethan England.

Broadly speaking, all our northern colonies developed from those planted in Massachusetts, and all our southern from that planted in Virginia. Questionable though this statement may seem to those who consider merely or chiefly the legal and political aspects of history, it is socially true to an extraordinary degree. The type of character which planted itself first on the shores of Massachusetts Bay displayed from the beginning a marked power of assimilating whatever came within its influence. This trait, akin to that which centuries before had made the conquered English slowly but surely assimilate their Norman conquerors, the Yankees of our own day have not quite lost. An equal power of assimilation marked the less austere type of character which first planted itself on the James River. Vague and commonplace as this statement may seem, it is really important. In modern America no fact is more noteworthy than that, for all the floods of immigration which have seemed to threaten almost every political and social landmark, our native type still absorbs the foreign. The children of immigrants insensibly become natives. The irresistible power of a common language and of the common ideals which underlie it still dominates. This tendency declared itself almost from the moments when Jamestown and Plymouth were settled. North and South alike, then, may broadly be regarded as regions finally settled by native Elizabethan Englishmen, whose ardent traits proved strong enough to impress themselves on posterity and to resist the immigrant influences of other traditions than their own.

Were our study of American history general, it would be our business to consider the southern and central colonies quite as much as those of New England; but in literary history New England is so predominant that, at least for the moment, we may neglect the other portions of the country. Plymouth and Massachusetts Bay were both settled by devout Calvinists, slightly different perhaps in some matter of religious discipline, certainly different at first in their theoretical relation to the ancestral Church of England, but still so much alike that it is hardly by misuse of language that both are now generally called Puritan. Both colonies were governed from the beginning by written charters, things which, except for Cromwell's Instrument of Government, remain foreign to the politi-

struggles of the native Indians to maintain their existence in the presence of the invading race which has long ago swept them away.

The history of seventeenth-century New England, in brief, is that of a dominant Puritanism, twenty years older than Cromwell's and surviving his by forty years more. Amid the expanding life of a still unexplored continent, Puritanism was disturbed by no such environment as impeded it in England and fatally checked it so soon. Rather, the only external fact which affected New England Puritanism at all, was one which strengthened it, — the threatening growth near by of a system as foreign to every phase of English thought as it was to Puritanism itself.

From this state of affairs resulted a general state of social character which may best be understood by comparing the historical records of New England during the hundred years now in question. The earliest history of Plymouth is that of Governor Bradford, sometimes so blunderingly called the " Log of the ' Mayflower; ' " and the earliest history of Massachusetts is that of Governor Winthrop. Winthrop, born in 1588, died in 1649; and Bradford, born in 1590, died in 1657. Both were born under Queen Elizabeth; both emigrated before English Puritanism was dominant; and neither survived to see the Restoration. The state of life and feeling which they record, then, must clearly belong to the first period of the seventeenth century, — the period when mature men were still of Elizabethan birth. In 1652, three years after Winthrop died and five years before the death of Bradford, Samuel Sewall was born in England. In 1661, four years after Bradford's death, he was brought to Massachusetts, where he lived all his life, becoming Chief Justice of the Superior Court. From 1674 to 1729 he kept a diary, which has been published by the Massachusetts Historical Society. He died in 1730. Sewall's life, then, mostly passed in Massachusetts, was contemporary with the English literature between Walton's "Complete

Angler" and Pope's "Dunciad." Both Winthrop and Bradford, on the other hand, were born before Shakspere was
certainly known as a popular playwright. Yet a hasty comparison of Bradford's writing or Winthrop's with Sewall's will
show so many more points of resemblance than of difference,
both in actual circumstance and in general mood, that it is
hard to realise how when Sewall began his memoranda — not
to speak of when he finished them — the generation to which
Winthrop and Bradford belonged was almost extinct. The
three books impress one as virtually contemporary.

How different this social pause was from the social progress
of seventeenth-century England may be felt by similarly comparing two familiar English records of the period. Lord
Herbert of Cherbury, born in 1582 and dead in 1648, was
almost exactly contemporary with Winthrop; his autobiography, written in his last years, is among the most characteristic records of social temper in our language. Fifteen
years before Lord Herbert's death, and ten before he began
his autobiography, Samuel Pepys was born, whose celebrated
diary runs from 1660 to 1669. Pepys stopped writing five
years before Sewall began, and so far as age goes he might
personally have known Lord Herbert. Yet the whole temper
of Herbert is so remote from that of Pepys as to make their
writing seem of distinctly different epochs; the fact that their
lives overlapped seems half incredible.

Almost any similar comparison you choose will tell the
same story. Compare, for example, your impressions of Essex and of Ralegh with those of Monk and of Marlborough;
compare Bacon with Newton, and Elizabeth with William
III. Then hastily name to yourself some of the worthies
who are remembered from seventeenth-century America.
Bradford and Winthrop, we have named already; Winslow
and Dudley, too. Add to them Standish, Endicott, Roger
Williams, and John Eliot, the apostle to the Indians; John
Cotton and Richard Mather; Increase Mather, son of the

one and son-in-law of the other; Cotton Mather, who combined the blood of the two immigrant ministers; Sir William Phips; and Sewall, who with Stoughton and the rest sat in judgment on Salem witchcraft. You can hardly help admitting that, though the type of character in America could not remain quite stationary, the change there between the earlier years of the seventeenth century and its close was surprisingly less marked than was the change in England. A little thought will speedily show what this means. Although the type of character which planted itself in New England during the first quarter of the seventeenth century was very Puritan and therefore, from the point of view of its contemporary English literature, very eccentric, it was truly an Elizabethan type. One conclusion seems clear: the native Yankees of 1700 were incalculably nearer their Elizabethan ancestors than were any of their contemporaries born in the mother country.

In this fact, — a fact rarely emphasised, but once perceived hardly to be denied, — we come to a consideration worth pondering. Such historical convulsions as those which declared themselves in the England of the seventeenth century result from the struggling complexity of social and political forces in densely populated regions. Such stagnation of social evolution as marks the seventeenth century in New England is humanly possible only under conditions where the pressure of external fact, social, political, and economic, is relaxed, — under conditions, in short, where the individual type is for a while stronger than environment. Such changes as the course of history brought to seventeenth-century England, which it found in the full vigour of Elizabethan life and left under the constitutional sway of King William III., are changes which must result to individuals just as much as to nations themselves in something which, for want of a more exact word, we may call experience. Such lack of change as marks the America of the seventeenth century indicates the absence of this. Yet even in the America of the seventeenth century

3

a true nation, the nation of which we modern Americans are ourselves a part, was growing towards a maturity which in our time is beginning to reveal itself. Though the phrase seem paradoxical, it is surely true that our national life in its beginnings was something hardly paralleled in other history, — a century of untrammelled national inexperience.

IV

AN instructive impression of the character of literature in America during the seventeenth century may be derived from a glance at the titles recorded in Mr. Whitcomb's "Chronological Outlines." [1] Speaking roughly, — and in considerations like this minute precision is of little importance, — we may say that out of about two hundred and fifteen of these titles one hundred and ten deal with matters which may unquestionably be described as religious, and that of these all but one name books produced in New England. The next most considerable class of writings includes matters which may be called historical or biographical, beginning with "The True Relation" of Captain John Smith, — a work hardly to be included in any classification of American literature which should not equally include M. de Tocqueville's study of our democracy and Mr. Bryce's of our contemporary commonwealth; this list also includes such biographies as those of Cotton Mather, whose main purpose was quite as religious as it was biographical. Out of fifty-five titles thus comprehensively grouped, thirty-seven are of New England origin; the other eighteen, including the separate works of Captain John Smith, come either from Virginia or

---

[1] Throughout our consideration of literature in America, Whitcomb's "Chronological Outlines of American Literature," also published by Macmillan, will prove as generally useful as we shall find Ryland's "Outlines" concerning English literature. For the history of literature in America during the seventeenth and eighteenth centuries, Professor M. C. Tyler's books, published by Putnam of New York, are indispensable. The extracts from the writers of these centuries in Stedman and Hutchinson's "Library of American Literature" are adequate for all general purposes.

from the middle colonies.   Twenty of Mr. Whitcomb's titles, including such things as "The Freeman's Oath," of 1639, said to have been the first product of the press in the United States, may be called political; only three of these twenty are not from New England.   Of nineteen other titles, including almanacs and works of scientific character, which may best be classified with miscellanies, all but two originated in this same region.   Finally there are nine titles to which the name of literature may properly be applied, if under the head of literature one include not only the poems of that tenth Muse, Mrs. Anne Bradstreet, but the "Bay Psalm Book," and so pervasively theological a poem as Michael Wigglesworth's "Day of Doom," and the first version of the "New England Primer."   Of the nine books thus recorded only Sandys's translation of Ovid did not proceed directly from New England.

Though the precise numbers of this hasty count may be inexact, and the classification itself questionable, the main facts which the classification shows can hardly be denied. In the first place, the intellectual activity of New England so far exceeded that of any other part of the country that in literary history other regions may be neglected. In the second place, the intellectual activity of New England expressed itself chiefly in a religious form; and next in a form which, if the term "history" include diaries and the like, may broadly be described as historical.   Out of two hundred and fifteen titles all but forty-eight fall under one or the other of these heads; and of these remaining forty-eight only nine may by any stretch of classification be held pure literature.   Meanwhile more than half of Whitcomb's titles are incontestably religious in character; and at least the New England publications which we have hastily classified under the heads of history, politics, miscellany, and even literature itself, are considerably impregnated with religious material.

Contrasting this impression with our hasty summary of English literature during this seventeenth century, — the century in which England added to literature the names of Shakspere, of Milton, and of Dryden, — it seems at first as if America produced no literature at all. Glancing at our English summary a shade more carefully, however, we may observe a brief mention that in Elizabethan England along with supreme poetry there was also both lasting prose, like that of Hooker, of Bacon, and of Ralegh, and such minor prose records and annals as are typified by Hakluyt's "Voyages," together with a good deal of now forgotten religious writing. In English literature, these last sorts of writing are unimportant; they were generally produced not by men of letters, but either by men of action or by earnest, uninspired men of God. Now, the men who founded the colonies of Virginia and of New England were on the one hand men of action, and on the other, men of God. It is precisely such matter as their Elizabethan prototypes left in books now remembered only as material for history that the fathers of America produced throughout the first century of our national inexperience.

If we seek in New England for traces of pure literature during the seventeenth century, indeed, we shall find our attention sadly or humorously attracted by such work as the "Bay Psalm Book," produced under the supervision of Richard Mather, Thomas Welde, and John Eliot, in 1640, the year which in England saw the publication of Carew's "Poems," and of Izaak Walton's "Life of Donne." An extract from the preface and from the Nineteenth Psalm will give a sufficient taste of its quality : —

"If therefore the verses are not alwayes so smooth and elegant as some may desire or expect; let them consider that God's Altar needs not our pollishings: Ex. 20. for wee have respected rather a plaine translation, then to smooth our verses with the sweetness of any paraphrase, and soe have attended Conscience rather then Elegance,

fidelity rather than poetry, in translating the hebrew words into english language, and Davids poetry into english meetre ; that soe we
may sing in Sion the Lords songs of prayse according to his owne
will; untill hee take us from hence, and wipe away all our teares, &
bid us enter into our masters ioye to sing eternall Halleluiahs."

   •   •   •   •   •   •   •   •

"PSALME XIX

To the chiefe Musician a psalme of David

The heavens doe declare
   the majesty of God :
also the firmament shews forth
   his handy-work abroad.
2 Day speaks to day, knowledge
   night hath to night declar'd.
3 There neither speach nor language is,
   where their voyce is not heard.
4 Through all the earth their line
   is gone forth, & unto
the utmost end of all the world,
   their speaches reach also :
A Tabernacle hee
   in them pitcht for the Sun.
5 Who Bridegroom like from 's chamber goes
   glad Giants-race to run.
6 From heavens utmost end,
   his course and compassing ;
to ends of it, & from the heat
   thereof is hid nothing."

The King James version of the same psalm, finally phrased not
quite thirty years before, was perfectly familiar to the men who
hammered out this barbarous imitation of a metre similarly
used by Henry VIII.'s Earl of Surrey. This fact should give
sufficient impression of the literary spirit which controlled the
Puritan fathers.

Twenty-two years later, in 1662, — the year when Fuller's
" Worthies " was published, the year after Davenant's final
version of " The Siege of Rhodes," and the year before the
first part of Butler's " Hudibras," Cowley's " Cutter of
Colman Street," and Dryden's " Wild Gallant," — Michael

Wigglesworth, then minister of Malden, published his "Day of Doom, or, A Poetical Description of the Great and Last Judgment," which retained its popularity in New England for about a century. Of this the "Plea of the Infants," still faintly remembered, is example enough : —

"Then to the Bar, all they drew near
   Who dy'd in infancy,
And never had or good or bad
   effected pers'nally.
But from the womb unto the tomb
   were straightway carried,
(Or at the least e'er they transgrest)
   who thus began to plead :

Reprobate Infants plead for themselves. Rev. 20. 12, 15, compared with Rom. 5. 12. 14, & 9. 11, 13. Ezek. 18. 2.

"If for our own transgression,
   or disobedience,
We here did stand at thy left hand
   just were the Recompence :
But Adam's guilt our souls hath spilt,
   his fault is charg'd on us :
And that alone hath overthrown,
   and utterly undone us.

"Not we, but he ate of the Tree,
   whose fruit was interdicted :
Yet on us all of his sad Fall,
   the punishment's inflicted.
How could we sin that had not been
   or how is his sin our
Without consent which to prevent,
   we never had a pow'r ? "

The plea extends to several stanzas more; then the Lord takes up the argument at great length, concluding as follows : —

"Am I alone of what's my own,
   no Master or no Lord?

Mat. 20. 15.

Or if I am, how can you claim
   what I to some afford?
Will you demand Grace at my hand,
   and challenge what is mine?
Will you teach me whom to set free,
   and thus my grace confine?

Psl. 58. 3.
Rom. 6. 23.
Gal. 3. 10.
Rom. 8. 29, 30,
& 11. 7.
Rev. 21. 27.
Luk. 12. 4, 8.
Mat. 11. 22.
The wicked
all convinced
and put to si-
lence.
Rom. 3. 19,
Mat. 22. 12,
Behold the
formidable
state of all
the ungodly,
as they stand
hopeless and
helpless be-
fore an im-
partial Judge,
expecting
their final
sentence.
Rev. 6. 16, 17.

"You sinners are, and such a share
    as sinners may expect,
Such you shall have; for I do save
    none but my own Elect.
Yet to compare your sin with their
    who lived a longer time,
I do confess yours is much less,
    though every sin 's a crime.

"A Crime it is, therefore in bliss
    you may not hope to dwell;
But unto you I shall allow
    the easiest room in Hell.
The glorious King thus answering,
    they cease and plead no longer:
Their Consciences must needs confess
    his reasons are the stronger."

Such work as this is more characteristic of seventeenth-century America than the sporadic, avowedly literary verse of Mrs. Anne Bradstreet, daughter of the elder Governor Dudley, whom Professor Tyler calls the first professional poet of New England. She died in 1672, — the year when Addison was born, and the year which gave to English literature, among other things, Dryden's "Conquest of Grenada" and "Marriage à la Mode," with his "Preface of Heroic Plays," Sir William Temple's "Observations on the Netherlands," and William Wycherly's "Love in a Wood." A few verses from her posthumous volume published in 1678, — the year which gave us the "Pilgrim's Progress," the third part of "Hudibras," Dryden's "All for Love," Lee's "Mithridates," and South's "Sermons," — will show her at her best:—

"I heard the merry grasshopper then sing,
    The black-clad cricket bear a second part,
They kept one tune, and played on the same string,
    Seeming to glory in their little art.
Shall creatures abject thus their voices raise?
And in their kind resound their Maker's praise:
Whilst I, as mute, can warble forth no higher lays.

"When I behold the heavens as in their prime,
  And then the earth (though old) still clad in green,
The stones and trees, insensible of time,
  Nor age nor wrinkle on their front are seen;
If winter come, and greenness then do fade,
A Spring returns, and they more youthful made;
But man grows old, lies down, remains where once he 's laid.

" By birth more noble than those creatures all,
  Yet seems by nature and by custom curs'd,
No sooner born, but grief and care makes fall
  That state obliterate he had at first:
Nor youth, nor strength, nor wisdom spring again,
Nor habitations long their name retain,
But in oblivion to the final day remain.

"O Time, the fatal wrack of mortal things,
  That draws oblivion's curtains over kings,
Their sumptuous monuments, men know them not,
  Their names without a record are forgot,
Their parts, their ports, their pomp 's all laid in th' dust,
Nor wit nor gold, nor buildings 'scape time's rust;
But he whose name is grav'd in the white stone
Shall last and shine when all of these are gone."

Mrs. Bradstreet's family, as the career of her brother, Governor Joseph Dudley, indicates, kept in closer touch with England than was common in America; and besides she was clearly a person of what would nowadays be called culture. Partly for these reasons her work seems neither individual nor indigenous. In seventeenth-century New England, indeed, she stands alone, without forerunners or followers; and if you compare her poetry with that of the old country, you will find it very like such then antiquated work as the " Nosce Teipsum" of Sir John Davies, published in 1599, the year which gave us the final version of " Romeo and Juliet." In its own day, there seems little doubt, the little pure literature of seventeenth-century New England was already archaic.

Apart from this, New England produced only annals, records, and far more characteristically writings of the class which may be grouped broadly under theology. Just as our glance at the history of seventeenth-century America revealed no central convulsion like the Commonwealth, dividing an old epoch from a new, so our glance at the American publications of this century reveals no central figure like Milton's standing between the old Elizabethan world which clustered about Shakspere, and the new, almost modern, school of letters which gathered about Dryden.

A fact perhaps more characteristic of seventeenth-century America than any publication was the foundation in 1636 of Harvard College, intended to preserve for posterity that learned ministry which was the distinguishing glory of the immigrant Puritans. From the very beginning, the history of Harvard reveals the liberalism which still distinguishes the college. Intended as a conservative force, its general tendency has constantly proved radical. One can see why. The English traditions of the ministers who founded it had been passionately Protestant; but, once secure in their New England isolation, these Puritans would have erected a dominant priesthood. Their purpose is nowhere better stated than in that passage of Cotton Mather's " Magnalia " which records the first political efforts of his grandfather Cotton, the first minister of the First Church of Boston. On his arrival, " he found the whole country in a perplexed & a divided state, as to their *civil constitution;* " and being requested to suggest convenient laws " from the laws wherewith God governed his ancient people," he recommended among other things " that none should be *electors,* nor *elected,* . . . except such as were *visible subjects* of our Lord Jesus Christ, personally *confederated* in our churches. In these & many other ways, he propounded unto them an endeavor after a *theocracy,* as near as might be, to that which was the glory of Israel." Now the essence of theocratic authority, which in simple English means the rule of God himself, is that it is absolute; and nothing is more fatally foreign to Protestantism than the conception of a government which should needlessly limit individual liberty. Harvard has always been Protestant to the core. Dunster, the first president, lost his seat because he could not conscientiously free himself from Baptist heresy; to-day the unsectarian religion of the college combines with its elective system to prove Harvard for two centuries and a half faithful to the Protestant traditions of its Puritan founders.

In the history of Harvard College during the seventeenth century the most conspicuous individuals were probably President Increase Mather and his son Cotton, both of whom wasted some of the best energies of their passionately active lives in an effort to make our ancestral seat of learning rather a treasury of priestly tradition than a seminary of Protestant enthusiasm. The younger of these was a very prolific writer. His first publication was apparently a sermon which saw the light in 1686; before he died, on the 13th of February, 1728, he had published more than four hundred separate titles. In these forty-two years of literary activity, however, he never changed either his style or his temper; his work falls chiefly though not wholly under the two heads of religion and history, which with him were so far from distinct that it is often hard to say under which a given work or passage should be grouped. These heads are the same which we have seen to include most American writings of the seventeenth century. Cotton Mather's work, in short, may be taken as typical of all the American publications of his time. A little study of this prolific and representative writer will serve as well as more extended observation to define for us what seventeenth-century writing in America really was.

V

COTTON MATHER

COTTON MATHER, born in Boston on the 12th of February, 1663, was the son of Increase Mather, a minister already eminent, and the grandson of John Cotton and of Richard Mather, two highly distinguished ministers of the immigration. In 1678 he took his degree at Harvard College. Only three years later, in 1681, he became associated with his father as minister of the Second Church in Boston, where he preached all his life.

To understand both his personal history and his literary work, we must never forget that the Puritan fathers had believed New England charged with a divine mission to show the world what human society might be when governed by constant devotion to the revealed law of God. This is nowhere better stated than by Cotton Mather himself in the general introduction to his " Magnalia " : —

" In short, the *First Age* was the *Golden Age:* To return unto *That*, will make a Man a *Protestant*, and I may add, a *Puritan*. 'T is possible, that our Lord Jesus Christ carried some Thousands of *Reformers* into the Retirement of an *American Desart*, on purpose, that with an opportunity granted unto many of his Faithful Servants, to enjoy the precious *Liberty* of their *Ministry*, tho' in the midst of many *Temptations* all their days, He might there *To* them first, and then *By* them, give a *Specimen* of many good Things, which he would have His Churches elsewhere aspire and arise unto: And *This* being done, He knows not[1] whether there be not *All Done*, that *New England* was planted for; and whether the Plantation may not, soon after this, *Come to Nothing*."

[1] Mather's rare *Errata* bid us " blot out NOT."

Whatever the political disturbances of Massachusetts under the original charter, the period between the foundation of the colony and the revocation of this charter was on the whole one of theocracy. Toward the end of this period Cotton Mather entered upon his ministry and the extreme activity of his life. At that very moment the charter was in danger; four years later it was revoked. To advocates of the old order the ensuing troubles seemed the most critical which New England had ever known. In few words the question was whether under some new government the old domination of the ministry should persist or whether the ministry must relinquish temporal power. Increase Mather hastened to England, where he hoped he might do something toward securing a restoration of the charter. Cotton Mather, still almost a boy, was left virtually at the head of the conservative party in Boston, devoting himself with untiring enthusiasm both in public acts and in private devotions to the maintenance in New England of the ancestral policy of theocracy. In 1692 came news that King William had granted a new charter which secured to Massachusetts a government as free as any in the civilised world, and that the first royal governor appointed thereunder was Sir William Phips, a devout, old-fashioned New England Calvinist, and a member of the very church over which the Mathers presided.

Cotton Mather believed that this triumphant answer to his prayers demanded on his part some peculiar act for the service of God. He looked about to see what service God most needed, and discovered thickening in the air about him a storm of occultism. Nowadays we call such things spiritualism, or hypnotism; in the seventeenth century they were called witchcraft, and were believed to be literally the work of the Devil himself. Beyond doubt Cotton Mather was among the chief leaders of the attack on this mysterious evil which ended in the memorable tragedy at Salem; but posterity, which will never forget that the witches were hanged, has long forgotten the legal point on which their hanging turned. No one dreamt of denying the devilish fact of witchcraft, — acknowledged by the law of the period as a capital crime. The only doubt was how it might legally be proved. A question arose whether what was called spectral evidence should be accepted; that is, whether the testimony of bewitched persons, concerning what they saw and felt in the paroxysms of their possessions, was valid against the accused. Cotton Mather's personal records declare that he warned the court against the dangers of spectral evidence in cases of life and death ; but that when against his protest the court decided to accept it, he felt bound, believing witchcraft diabolical, not publicly to oppose the decision. It was mostly on spectral evidence that the witches were hanged; when spectral evidence was rejected, the prosecutions soon came to an end. Then arose that deep revulsion of feeling which posterity has so bitterly cherished. For two hundred years, there has been little mercy shown the theocratic ministers who devotedly urged on the prosecution of the witches ; and, whatever his actual responsibility, Cotton Mather, the least forgotten of these ministers, has borne the brunt of all the evil which tradition has fixed on the period.

The collapse of the witch trials in 1692 may be said to mark the end of theocracy in New England. Nine years later, in 1701, the orthodox party in the church had another blow. Increase Mather, after sixteen years' incumbency as President of Harvard College, was finally removed to be replaced by a divine of more liberal tendencies. This really ended the public career of both father and son. In the public life of New England, as in that of the mother country, we may say, the ideal of the Common Law finally supplanted the biblical ideal of the Puritans, and at the oldest of New England seminaries the ideal of Protestantism finally vanquished that of priesthood.

Cotton Mather lived on until 1728, preaching, writing numberless books, and doing much good scientific work;

among other things, he was the first person in the English-speaking world to practise inoculation for small-pox. Untiringly busy, hoping against hope for well on to thirty years, he died at last with the word *Fructuosus* on his lips as a last counsel to his son. Undoubtedly he was eccentric and fantastic, so reactionary in temper that those who love progress have been apt to think him almost as bad as he was queer. For all his eccentricity, however, and perhaps on account of the exaggeration of his traits in general, he seems on the whole the most complete type of the oldest-fashioned divine of New England. He was born in Boston, and educated at Harvard College; he lived in Boston all his life, never straying a hundred miles away. Every external influence brought to bear on him was local. Whatever else his life and work means, then, it cannot help expressing what human existence taught the most intellectually active of seventeenth-century Yankees.

Here, of course, we are concerned with him only as a man of letters. His literary activity was prodigious. Sibley's "Harvard Graduates" records some four hundred titles of his actual publications; besides this, he wrote an unpublished treatise on medicine which would fill a folio volume; and his unpublished "Biblia Americana" — an exhaustive commentary on the whole Bible — would fill two or three folios more. He left behind him, too, many sermons, not to speak of letters and of diaries, which have never seen print. Until one actually inspects the documents, it seems incredible that in forty-five years any single human being could have penned so many words as we thus see to have come from the hand of one of the busiest ministers, one of the most insatiable scholars and readers, and one of the most active politicians whom America has ever known.

To discuss in detail such a mass of work is out of the question; but, though many of Cotton Mather's writings were published after 1700, his most celebrated and considerable book, the "Magnalia," which was made toward the middle of his life and which includes reprints of a number of brief works published earlier, typifies all he did as a man of letters, before or afterwards. It was begun, his diary tells us, in 1693; and although not published until 1702, it was virtually finished in 1697. These dates throw light on what the book really means; they come just between the end of those witchcraft trials which broke the political power of the clergy, and the final defeat of the Mathers in their endeavour to retain the government of Harvard College. Though Harvard tradition still holds this endeavour to have been chiefly a matter of personal ambition, whoever comes intimately to know the Mathers must feel that to them the question seemed far otherwise. What both had at heart was a passionate desire, based on fervent, unshaken faith, that New England should remain true to the cause of the fathers, which both believed indubitably the cause of God. In the years when the " Magnalia " was writing, there seemed a chance that if contemporary New England could awaken to a sense of what pristine New England had been, all might still go well. Despite the fact that the " Magnalia " is professedly a history, then, it may better be regarded as a passionate controversial work. Its true motive was to excite so enthusiastic a sympathy with the ideals of the Puritan fathers that, whatever fate might befall the civil government, their ancestral seminary of learning should remain true to its colours.

At the time when the " Magnalia " was conceived, the New England colonies were about seventy years old. Broadly speaking, there had flourished in them three generations, — the immigrants, their children, and their grandchildren. The time was come, Cotton Mather thought, when the history of these three generations might be critically examined; if this examination should result in showing that there had lived in New England an unprecedented proportion of men and women and children whose earthly existence had given signs that they were among the elect, then his book might go far to prove that the pristine policy of New England had been especially favoured of the Lord. For surely the Lord would choose His elect most eagerly in places where life was conducted most according to His will.

In this mood the " Magnalia " was written. Its first sentence sounds the key-note of the whole : —

" I write the *Wonders* of the *Christian Religion*, flying from the Depravations of *Europe*, to the *American Strand:* And, assisted by the Holy Author of that *Religion*, I do, with all Conscience of *Truth*, required therein by Him, who is the *Truth* it self, report the *Wonderful Displays* of His Infinite Power, Wisdom, Goodness, and Faithfulness, wherewith His Divine Providence hath *Irradiated* an *Indian Wilderness*."

So it proceeds through its hundreds of pages, dwelling most on those traits of New England which Cotton Mather believed especially to indicate the favour of God. He tells first the story of the colonies, giving little space to what he thinks the evil side of it : —

" Though I cannot approve the conduct of Josephus ; (whom Jerom not unjustly nor inaptly calls ' the Greek Livy,') when he had left out of his Antiquities, the story of the *Golden Calf*, and I don't wonder to find Chamier, and Rivet, and others, taxing him for his partiality towards his country-men ; yet I have left unmentioned some censurable occurrences in the story of our Colonies, as things no less unuseful than improper to be raised out of the grave, wherein Oblivion hath now buried them; lest I should have incurred the *pasquil* bestowed upon Pope Urban, who, employing a committee to rip up the old errors of his predecessors, one clapped a pair of spurs upon the heels of the statue of St. Peter ; and a label from the statue of St. Paul opposite thereunto, upon the bridge, asked him, ' Whither he was bound ? ' St. Peter answered, ' I apprehend some danger in staying here ; I fear they 'll call me in question for denying my Master.' And St. Paul replied, ' Nay then I had best be gone too, for they question me also for persecuting the Christians before my conversion.' "

Cotton Mather's scale of values, then, considerably differs from that of a critical modern historian. In his general narrative, for example, he hardly mentions the Antinomian controversy, and has little to say of such subsequently famous personages as Roger Williams or Mrs. Anne Hutchinson.   On the other hand, he details at loving length, first the lives of those governors and magistrates who seemed especial servants of the Lord, from Bradford and Winthrop and Theophilus Eaton to Sir William Phips; and next the lives and spiritual experiences of a great number of the immigrant clergy and of their successors in the pulpit.   He recounts the history of Harvard College during its first sixty years; and he lays down with surprising lucidity the orthodox doctrine and discipline of the New England churches.   These matters fill five of the seven books into which the " Magnalia " is divided.   The last two books portray the reverse of the picture; one deals with " Remarkable Mercies and Judgments on many particular persons among the people of New England," and the other with " The Wars of the Lord — the Afflictive Disturbances which the Churches of New England have suffered from their various adversaries; and the Wonderful Methods and Mercies, whereby the Churches have been delivered."   Full of petty personal anecdote, and frequently revealing not only bigoted prejudice but grotesque superstition, these last two books have been more generally remembered than the rest.   One commonly hears the " Magnalia " mentioned in terms which seem to assert these least admirable parts of it to be the most characteristic of work and writer alike.   Characteristic they are, but little more so than the Clown in " Hamlet " is of Shakspere; no one but their author could have written them, yet in the whole body of his work they are a minor feature.   For whoever grows familiar with the " Magnalia " must feel that it goes far toward accomplishing the purpose which Cotton Mather intended.

The prose epic of New England Puritanism it has been called, setting forth in heroic mood the principles, the history, and the personal characters of the fathers.   The principles, theologic and disciplinary alike, are stated with clearness, dignity, and fervour. The history, though its less welcome phases are often lightly emphasised, and its details are hampered by no deep regard for minor accuracy, is set forth with a sincere ardour which makes its temper more instructive than that of many more trustworthy records. And the life-like portraits of the Lord's chosen, though full of quaintly fantastic phrases and artless pedantries, are often drawn with touches of enthusiastic beauty.

A few sentences from his life of the apostle Eliot, whose Indian Bible is remembered as the first complete version of scripture printed in New England, will typify Mather's fantastic vein : —

" I know not what thoughts it will produce in my Reader, when I inform him, that once finding that the *Daemons* in a possessed young Woman, understood the *Latin* and *Greek* and *Hebrew* Languages, my Curiosity led me to make Trial of this *Indian* language, and the *Daemons* did seem as if they did not understand it. This tedious Language our *Eliot* (the Anagram of whose name was Toile) quickly became a Master of; he employ'd a pregnant and witty *Indian*, who also spoke *English* well, for his Assistance in it ; and compiling some Discourses by his Help, he would single out a *Word*, a *Noun*, a *Verb*, and pursue it through all its variations : Having finished his Grammar, at the close he writes, *Prayers and Pains thro' Faith in Christ Jesus will do any thing !* And being by his *Prayers* and *Pains* thus furnished, he set himself in the year 1646 to preach the Gospel of our Lord Jesus Christ, among these Desolate Outcasts."

The last paragraph of the life of Theophilus Eaton, first Governor of New Haven, will show the dignity of Mather's best narrative : —

" Thus continually he, for about a Score of Years, was the *Glory* and *Pillar* of *New-Haven* Colony. He would often say, *Some count it a great matter to* Die *well, but I am sure 'tis a great matter to* Live *well. All our Care should be while we have our Life to use it well, and so when Death puts an end unto that, it will put an end unto all our Cares.* But having Excellently managed his *Care* to *Live well*, God would have him to *Die well*, without any room or time then given to take any *Care* at all; for he enjoyed a Death *sudden* to everyone but himself ! Having worshipped God with his Family after his usual manner, and upon some Occasion with much Solemnity charged all the Family to carry it well unto their Mistress who was now confined by Sickness, he Supp'd, and then took a turn or two abroad for his Meditations.   After that he came in to bid his Wife *Good-night,* before he left her with her *Watchers;* which when he did, she said, *Methinks you look sad!*   Whereto he reply'd, *The Differences risen in the Church of Hartford make me so;* she then added, *Let us e'en go back to our Native Country again;* to which he answered, *You may,* (and so she did) *but I shall die here.*   This was the last Word that ever she heard him speak; for now retiring unto his Lodging in another Chamber, he was overheard about midnight fetching a *Groan;* and unto one, sent in presently to enquire how he did, he answered the Enquiry with only saying, *Very Ill!* And without saying any more, he fell *asleep in Jesus:*   In the Year 1657 *loosing Anchor from New-Haven* for the better."

Finally, the last clause of a ponderous sentence from his life of Thomas Shepard, first minister of Cambridge, is far more characteristic of Mather than are many of the oddities commonly thought of when his name is mentioned : —

" As he was a very *Studious* Person, and a very lively Preacher; and one who therefore took great Pains in his *Preparations* for his Publick Labours, 'which Preparations he would usually finish *on Saturday,* by two a Clock in the Afternoon ; with Respect whereunto he once used these Words, *God will curse that Man's Labours, that lumbers up and down in the World all the Week, and then upon Saturday, in the afternoon goes to his Study; whereas God knows, that Time were little enough to pray in and weep in, and get his Heart into a fit Frame for the Duties of the approaching Sabbath;* So the Character of his daily Conversation, was *A Trembling Walk with God.*"

" A trembling walk with God," — you shall look far for a nobler phrase than that, or for one which should more truly characterise not only Thomas Shepard, but the better life of all the first century of New England.   In old New England there were really more such characters as the Puritans deemed marked for God's elect than are recorded of almost any other society of equal size and duration in human history. For this fact we can account in modern terms which would have been strangely unwelcome to Cotton Mather and the godly personages whose memories he has preserved. In their New England, the pressure of external fact was politically and socially relaxed ; except with the brute forces of nature the struggle for existence was less fierce than in almost any other region now remembered. Individuals could there progress from cradle to grave with less distortion than must always be worked by such social struggles as changed the England of Elizabeth through that of Cromwell into that of William III., and as have steadily altered and developed the course of European history ever since. Relax the pressure which a dense society brings upon human life, and the traits of human nature which will reveal themselves in a simpler world are generally traits which those who love ideals are apt to call better. Such relaxation of pressure blessed pristine New England ; the results thereof the " Magnalia " records.

These it records with an enthusiasm which, in spite of the pedantic queerness of Mather's style, one grows to feel more and more vital. What is more, amid all his vagaries and oddities, one feels too a trait which even our few extracts may perhaps indicate. Again and again, Cotton Mather writes with a rhythmical beauty which recalls the enthusiastic spontaneity of Elizabethan English, so different from the English which came after the Civil Wars. And though the " Magnalia " hardly reveals the third characteristic of Elizabethan England, no one can read the facts of Cotton Mather's busy, active life without feeling that this man himself, who wrote with enthusiastic spontaneity, and who in his earthly life was minister, politician, man of science, scholar, and constant organiser of innumerable good works, embodied just that kind of restless versatility which characterised Elizabethan England and which even to our own day has remained characteristic of New England Yankees.

For if the lapse of seventy years had not left New England unchanged, it had altered life there far less than men have supposed. The " Magnalia " was published two years after

Dryden died ; and even the few extracts at which we have been able to glance will show that it groups itself not with such work as Dryden's, but rather with such earlier work as that of Fuller or even of Burton. As a man of letters, Cotton Mather, who died in the reign of George II., had more in common with that generation of his ancestors which was born under the last of the Tudors than with any later kind of native Englishmen.

VI

SUMMARY

OUR hasty glance at the literary history of America during the seventeenth century has revealed some facts worth remembering. In 1630, when Boston was founded, the mature inhabitants of America, like their brethren in England, were native Elizabethans. In 1700 this race had long been in its grave. In densely populated England, meanwhile, historical pressure — social, political, and economic alike — had wrought such changes in the national character as are marked by the contrast between the figures of Elizabeth and of King William III. The dominant type of native Englishmen had altered: national experience was steadily accumulating. In America there had been no such external pressure; and though the immigrant Puritans had long been no more, and though isolation was making the inhabitants of New England more and more provincial, they had preserved to an incalculable degree the spontaneous, enthusiastic, versatile character of their immigrant ancestors. In literature seventeenth-century England had expressed itself in at least three great and distinct moods, of which the dominant figures were Shakspere, Milton, and Dryden. Though America had meanwhile produced hardly any pure letters, it had continued, long after Elizabethan temper had faded from the native literature of England, to keep alive with little alteration those minor phases of Elizabethan thought and feeling which had expressed the temper of the ancestral Puritans. In history and in literature alike, the story of seventeenth-century America is a story of unique national inexperience.

BOOK II

THE EIGHTEENTH CENTURY

BOOK II

THE EIGHTEENTH CENTURY

I

ENGLISH HISTORY FROM 1700 TO 1800

WHEN the eighteenth century began, the reign of William III. was about as near its close as that of Elizabeth was a hundred years before. In 1702 William was succeeded by Queen Anne. In 1714 George I. followed her, founding the dynasty which still holds the throne. George II. succeeded him in 1727; and in 1760 came George III., whose reign extended till 1820. The names of these sovereigns instantly suggest certain familiar facts, of which the chief is that during the first half of the century the succession remained somewhat in doubt. It was only in 1745, when the reign of George II. was more than half finished, that the last fighting with Stuart pretenders occurred on British soil. On British soil, but not on English: there has been no actual warfare in England since in 1685 the battle of Sedgmoor suppressed the Duke of Monmouth's rebellion against James II. These obvious facts indicate historical circumstances which have had profound effect on English character.

Continental nations are now and again disposed to call the English a nation of shopkeepers; and certainly during the past two centuries the commercial prosperity of England has exceeded that of most other countries. An imperative condition of such prosperity is peace and domestic order. Good business demands an efficient police, and in general a state of life which permits people to devote themselves to their own affairs, trusting politics to those whose office it is to govern. Under such circumstances people have small delight in civil wars and disputed successions. Many eighteenth-century Englishmen, no doubt, who in the perspective of a hundred and fifty years look romantically attractive, thought the divine right of the Stuarts unquestionable, and the Georges usurpers; but parliamentary government could give England what divine right could no longer give it, — prosperous public order. In the course of the eighteenth century, then, there steadily grew a body of public opinion, at last overwhelming, which with all the tenacity of British unreason maintained the actual state of the constitution. The whole force of social and political history in England tended slowly but surely to the maintenance of established institutions.

During this eighteenth century we accordingly find in England no such radical changes as marked the preceding. Though George III. survived William of Orange far longer than William had survived Queen Elizabeth, we can feel between the Prince of Orange and his native English successor no such contrast as we felt between William and the last Tudor queen. For all that, the century was not stagnant; and perhaps our simplest way of estimating its progress is to name four English battles which are still enough remembered to be recorded in the brief historical summaries of Ryland's "Outlines of English Literature." In 1704 was fought the battle of Blenheim; in 1745, that of Fontenoy; in 1759 Wolfe fell victorious at Quebec; and in 1798 Nelson won the first of his great naval victories — the battle of the Nile.

Whatever else these battles have in common, all four were fought against the French, — the one continental power whose coast is in sight of England. Throughout the century, then, the English Channel was apt to be an armed frontier; the geographical isolation of England was tending toward that international isolation which until our own time has been so marked. A second fact about these four battles is almost as obvious. However important the questions at issue, people nowadays have generally forgotten what Blenheim and Fontenoy were fought about. Of Blenheim, indeed, we remember, along with the great name of Marlborough, only the poem by Southey, where old Caspar, his work done, tells little Peterkin, who is rolling about the skulls just turned up by the ploughshare, how these were the fruits of the famous victory; and when Peterkin inquires what the dead soldiers died for, all old Caspar can tell him is that Marlborough was there, and Prince Eugene, and that the victory was famous. Southey doubtless intended this poem as a protest against war; it now seems rather an unwitting satire on historic tradition. For though this tradition has preserved the names of Blenheim and of Marlborough and of Eugene, it has quite forgotten why Englishmen and Frenchmen were struggling to the death in 1704. So of Fontenoy: tradition keeps surely alive only a doubtful anecdote that when the French and English were face to face, some French officer pulled off his hat with a polite bow and civilly invited the enemy to fire first. The other two battles which we have called to mind, those of Quebec and of the Nile, were fought in the second half of the century; and of these tradition still remembers the objects. The battle of Quebec finally assured the dominance in America of the English Law. The battle of the Nile began to check that French revolutionary power which under the transitory empire of Napoleon had seemed about to conquer the whole civilised world, and which met its final defeat seventeen years later at Waterloo.

The names of Blenheim and the Nile suggest one more fact: each of these battles gave England a national hero. Marlborough we have already glanced at, — a soldier of the closing seventeenth century as well as of the dawning eighteenth, whose career asserted that in the political struggles of continental Europe England could never be left out of

account. Nelson, whose name is almost as familiarly associated with the battle of the Nile as with his victorious
death at Trafalgar, stood for even more; he embodied not
only that dominion of the sea which since his time England
has maintained, but also that imperial power — for in his
time England was already becoming imperial — which was
able to withstand and to destroy the imperial force of France
incarnate in Napoleon. Imperial though Nelson's victories
were, however, Nelson himself was almost typically insular.
It is hardly a play on words to say that as we compare
Marlborough, the chief English hero of the opening century,
with Nelson, the chief English hero of its close, Marlborough seems a European and Nelson an Englishman.
This fact implies the whole course of English history in
the eighteenth century. Just as the internal history of
England tended to a more and more conservative preservation of public order, so her international history tended more
and more to make Englishmen a race apart.

Before the century was much more than half done, this
insular English race had on its hands something more than
the island where its language, its laws, its traditions, and its
character had been developed; something more, besides, than
those American colonies whose history during their first century we have already traced. As the name of Quebec has
already reminded us, the wars with the French had finally
resulted in the conquest by the English Law of those American regions which had threatened to make American history
that of a ceaseless conflict between English institutions and
those of continental Europe. The same years which had
brought about the conquest of Canada had also achieved the
conquest of that Indian Empire which still makes England
potent in Asia. In 1760, when George III. came to the
throne, imperial England, which included the thirteen colonies
of North America, seemed destined to impose its image on the
greatest continents of both hemispheres.

Twenty years later the American Revolution had broken all political union between those regions in the old world and in the new which have steadily been dominated by English Law. That on both sides of the Atlantic the Common Law has been able to survive this shock is perhaps the most conclusive evidence of vitality in its long and varied history. The Revolution itself we shall consider more closely later : one fact about it we may remark here. Until the Revolution, America, like England, had considered France a traditional enemy. Open warfare with England naturally brought America and France together; without French aid, indeed, our independence could hardly have been established. A very few years, then, awoke among Americans a general sentiment, which their tradition has steadily maintained, of strong nominal sympathy with the French. At the moment when this declared itself, as any one can now see, France, regardless of any such impediment to freedom of thought as might lurk in the facts of human experience, was vigorously, blindly developing that abstract philosophy of human rights which less than twenty years later resulted in the tragic convulsions of the French Revolution. The fascinating commonplaces of this philosophy were eagerly welcomed in America, where they have been popularly repeated ever since. From that time to this, indeed, American talk has been so radical that comparatively few appreciate how slightly all these glittering generalities have really distorted American conduct from the good old principle that true human rights are those which experience has proved beneficial. In no way, however, has America evinced its English origin more clearly than by the serenity with which it has forbidden logic to meddle with the substantial maintenance of legal institutions.

But our concern now is with England, who found herself, when the French Revolution came, the chief conservative power of Europe. The conservatism for which she stood, and has stood ever since, is of the kind which defends tradition against the assaults of untested theory. Without ignoring human rights, it maintains that the most precious human rights are those which have proved humanly feasible; abstract ideals of law and government, however admirable on paper, it regards with such suspicion as in daily life practical men feel concerning the vagaries of plausible thinkers who cannot make both ends meet. The conservatism of eighteenth-century England, in short, defended against untested philosophy the experience embodied in the unwritten Common Law; it defended custom, which at worst had proved tolerable, against theory, which had never been put to proof. So in this closing struggle of the eighteenth century, which continued for half a generation after the century ended, external forces combined with internal ones, — with a full century of domestic peace, and the final settlement of the royal succession, — to develop in England that isolated, deliberate, somewhat slow-witted character which foreigners now suppose permanently English.

The typical Englishman of modern caricature is named John Bull. What he looks like is as familiar to any reader of the comic papers as is the "austerely sheepish" countenance of Stuart's Washington. There is a deep significance, then, in the fact that the costume still attributed to John Bull is virtually that of the English middle classes in 1800. No date better marks the moment when external forces and internal had combined to make typical of England the insular, vigorous, intolerant character embodied in that familiar and portly figure. Whatever else John Bull may be, he is not spontaneous in his reactions to fresh impressions; he is not enthusiastic, except in irascibility; and he is about as far from versatile as any human being who ever trod the earth.

ENGLISH LITERATURE FROM 1700 TO 1800

THE English literature of the eighteenth century is very different from that of the century before. The contrast may conveniently be considered by comparing the two periods as they began, as they proceeded, and as they closed. The three literary periods of the seventeenth century were dominated by three great figures, — those of Shakspere, of Milton, and of Dryden. While no such eminence as theirs marks the literary history of the century with which we are now concerned, three typical figures of its different periods may conveniently be called to mind, — Addison, Johnson, and Burke. The very mention of these names must instantly define the contrast now worth our attention. The seventeenth century was one of decided literary development, or at least of change. In comparison the eighteenth century was one of marked monotony.

The literature of its beginning is traditionally associated with the name of Queen Anne almost as closely as that of a hundred years before is with the name of Queen Elizabeth. In 1702, when Anne came to the throne, neither Addison, Steele, Swift, Defoe, nor Pope had attained full reputation; in 1714, when she died, all five had done enough to assure their permanence, and to fix the type of literature for which their names collectively stand. Prose they had brought to that deliberate, balanced, far from passionate form which it was to retain for several generations; poetry they had cooled into that rational heroic couplet which was to survive in America until the last days of Dr. Holmes. They had brought into being meanwhile a new form of publication, —

the periodical, — destined to indefinite development. From the time when the first "Tatler" appeared in 1709 to the present day, a considerable part of our lasting literature has been published in periodicals; and periodicals bespeak, before all things else, a permanent and increasing literary public. If any one name can imply all this, it is surely that of the urbane Joseph Addison.

In the middle of the century, when the reign of George II. was two-thirds over, English literature was producing a good many works which have survived. Between 1748 and 1752, for example, there were published, to go no further, Richardson's "Clarissa Harlowe," Smollett's "Roderick Random" and "Peregrine Pickle," Thomson's "Castle of Indolence," Fielding's "Tom Jones" and "Amelia," Johnson's "Vanity of Human Wishes" and a considerable portion of the "Rambler," Gray's "Elegy in a Country Churchyard," and Goldsmith's "Life of Nash." Sterne's work and Goldsmith's more famous writing came only a little later; and during these same five years appeared Wesley's "Plain Account of the People Called Methodists," Hume's "Inquiry into the Human Understanding," — and his "Inquiry concerning the Principles of Morals" and "Political Discourses." Though the works of Wesley and of Hume are something else than mere literature, they deserve our notice because Wesley's name recalls that strenuous outburst against religious formalism which has bred the most potent body of modern English Dissenters, and Hume's that rational tendency in philosophy which during the eighteenth century was far more characteristic of France than of England. Putting these aside, we may find in the literary record of this mid-century a state of things somewhat different from that which prevailed under Queen Anne. Another considerable form of English literature had come into existence, — the prose novel, whose germs were already evident in the character sketches of the "Spectator," and in the characterless but vivacious fictions of Defoe. Poetry, preserving studied correctness of form, was beginning to tend back toward something more like romantic sentiment; the prose essay had grown heavier and less vital. For the moment the presiding genius of English letters was Dr. Johnson, throughout whose work we can feel that the formalism which under Queen Anne had possessed the grace of freshness was becoming traditional. In conventional good sense his writings, like those which surrounded them, remained vigorous; but their vigour was very unlike the spontaneous, enthusiastic versatility of Elizabethan letters.

About twenty-five years later comes a date so memorable to Americans that a glance at its literary record in England can hardly help being suggestive. The year from which our national independence is officially dated came at the height of Burke's powers, and just between Sheridan's "Rivals," published the year before, and his "School for Scandal," of the year after. In the record of English publications, 1776 is marked by no important works of pure literature; but in that year Hume died, Jeremy Bentham published his "Fragment on Government," Gibbon the first volume of his "Decline and Fall of the Roman Empire," Adam Smith his "Wealth of Nations," and Thomas Paine his "Common Sense;" the second edition of the "Encyclopedia Britannica," too, appeared in ten volumes. In 1776, it seems, things literary in England, as well as things political in the British Empire, were taking a somewhat serious turn.

In the last ten years of the century, the years when the French Revolution was at its fiercest, there appeared in England works by Burke and by Mrs. Radcliffe, Boswell's "Johnson," Cowper's "Homer," Paine's "Rights of Man," Rogers's "Pleasures of Memory," poems by Burns, two or three books by Hannah More, the first poems of Wordsworth, Coleridge, Southey, Scott, and Landor, Godwin's "Caleb Williams," Lewis's "Monk," Miss Burney's "Camilla," Roscoe's "Life of Lorenzo the Magnificent," and Charles Lamb's "Rosamund

Gray." A curious contrast this shows to the state of things in contemporary France. Though in political matters the French had broken away from every tradition, their literature had to wait thirty years more for enfranchisement from the tyranny of conventional form. England meanwhile, more tenacious of political tradition than ever before, had begun to disregard the rigid literary tradition which had been dominant since the time of Dryden. Burns, to this day the greatest British poet of the people, died in 1796. The " Lyrical Ballads " of Wordsworth and Coleridge, which may be regarded in literature as declaring the independence of the individual spirit, appeared in 1798, the year when Nelson fought the battle of the Nile. Fiction at the same time seemed less vital. In the hands of Richardson, Fielding, and Smollett it had reached high development. Compared with the masterpieces of forty years before, Mrs. Radcliffe's " Mysteries of Udolpho," Lewis's " Monk," and in some aspects even Godwin's " Caleb Williams," look more like the vagaries of an outworn affectation than like the heralds of what a few years later was to prove a great romantic period. In the last decade of the eighteenth century, though formal tradition was clearly broken, the renewed strength which was to animate English literature for the next thirty years was not yet quite evident. At the moment, too, no figure in English letters had even such predominance as that of Addison in Queen Anne's time, far less such as Johnson's had been in the later years of George II. Of the elder names mentioned in our last hasty list the most memorable seems that of Burke.

These names of Addison, Johnson, and Burke prove quite as significant of English literature in the eighteenth century as those of Shakspere, Milton, and Dryden proved of that literature a century before. Shakspere, Milton, and Dryden seem men of three different epochs; at least comparatively, Addison, Johnson, and Burke seem men of a single type. The trait which most distinguishes them from one another, indeed, seems that Johnson's temper was rather more serious than that of Addison, and Burke's than Johnson's. After all, the mere names tell enough. Think of Shakspere and Dryden together, and then of Addison and Burke. Think of Milton as the figure who intervenes between the first pair, and of Johnson similarly intervening between the second. You can hardly fail to perceive the trend of English letters. In 1600 these letters were alive with the spontaneity, the enthusiasm, and the versatility of the Elizabethan spirit. By Dryden's time this was already extinct; throughout the century which followed him it showed little symptom of revival. The romantic revival which in Burke's time was just beginning, had, to be sure, enthusiasm; but this was too conscious to seem spontaneous. And although the names of Rogers, Wordsworth, Coleridge, Lamb, Landor, and Moore, who had all begun writing before 1800, suggest something like versatility, it is rather variety. They differ from one another, but compared with the Elizabethan poets each seems limited, inflexible. Taken together, their works combine in complicated orchestral harmonies. To the end, however, you can hardly imagine any of them as master of more than a single instrument. Versatility can hardly be held to characterise any English man of letters who came to maturity in the eighteenth century.

So far as literature is concerned, then, that century seems more and more what the commonplaces of the school-books call it, a century of robustly formal tradition; rational, sensible, prejudiced, and towards the end restless; admirable and manly in a thousand ways, but further, if so may be, from the spontaneous, enthusiastic versatility of Elizabethan days than was the period of Dryden. Above all, throughout this eighteenth century, English literature, like English history, seems more and more marked by that kind of insular temper which nowadays we unthinkingly believe always to have characterised the English.

III

IN broad outline the history of America during the eighteenth century seems as different from that of England as was the case a century earlier. Two facts which we remarked in seventeenth-century America remained unchanged. In the first place no one really cared much who occupied the throne. To any American, the question of who was sent out as governor was generally more important than that of who sent him. In the second place, the absorptive power of the native American race remained undiminished, as indeed it seems still to remain. Though there was comparatively less immigration to America in the eighteenth century than in the seventeenth or the nineteenth, there was enough to show our surprising power of assimilation.

In another aspect, the history of America during the eighteenth century is unlike that of the century before. Until 1700, at least in New England, the dominant English ideal had been rather the moral than the political, — the tradition of the English Bible rather than that of the Common Law. The fathers of New England had almost succeeded in establishing " a theocracy as near as might be to that which was the glory of Israel." The story of the Mathers shows how this theocratic ambition came to grief. Church and State in America tended to separate with true Protestant antagonism. Once separate, the State was bound to control in public affairs; and so the Church began to decline into such formalism as later times, mistaking the lifeless rigidity of Puritan decline for the whole story, have been apt to believe all Puritanism.

So, speaking very generally, we may call the eighteenth century in America one of growing material prosperity, under the chief guidance no longer of the clergy, but rather of that social class to whose commercial energy this prosperity was chiefly due.

It is to the eighteenth century, indeed, and to the pre-revolutionary part of it, that New England families owe most of the portraits which still attest their ancestral dignity, now so often a thing of the past. The best of these portraits were painted by the father of the celebrated Lord Lyndhurst. This was John Singleton Copley, a native of Boston who emigrated to England about the time of the Revolution and remained there for the rest of his life. Whoever knows Copley's American portraits will recognise in the people he painted a type of native Americans which had hardly developed in the seventeenth century and which hardly survived the Revolution.

These old New England worthies were mostly merchants who owed their fortune to their own ability. To take a single family, for example, there lived in Cambridge during the seventeenth century a presumably God-fearing man in no way related to the dominant clerical class or to the families conspicuous in the government of the colony. He was in some small way of trade, he married four times, and he left a great many children. One of these removed to Boston, where he so prospered as to be able in his last years to present to the Second Church, then under the ministry of Cotton Mather, a silver communion cup. His son, a grandson of the prolific tradesman of Cambridge, became a merchant of local eminence, whose affairs brought him into correspondence not only with England, but with France, Portugal, and the Indies. He married a lady whose family from the earliest days of the colony had maintained the dignity of what old Yankees used to call quality. And Copley painted them both; and very stately old figures they are; and their silver bears a fine coat of arms.

So far the story is quite like that of prosperous people in the old country. The difference lies in the fact that when this old Boston worthy had made his fortune he found himself in a society where there was neither a nobility nor a landed gentry to deprive him of social distinction. The state of personal feeling which ensued, familiar throughout American history, was different from what any man of just this class has generally felt in England, and more like that of the grander merchants of Venice. As a prosperous man of affairs, he felt all the unquestioning sense of personal dignity which everywhere marks the condition of a gentleman. Superficially, perhaps in consequence, his manners seem to have become rather more like those of fashionable England than had been common in earlier America. A fragment from a letter addressed him during the Revolution by the minister of the church where he was for years a deacon will tell something of his temper. The reverend gentleman was travelling in the Middle States, where he had been impressed by the Moravian settlement at Bethlehem, Pennsylvania; and he commented on it as follows : —

" The Nunnery, as they call it, is an object of curiosity. A picture of diligence, but as I could not but observe, much to the ruining of their health & to the destruction of the social disposition. About sixty or more girls kept entirely to work without any recreation or amusement & without any intercourse with men, under the strict orders of an *Old Maid Governess*. Judge how miserable must be their condition! — Their complexions are sallow, & discontentment is painted on every countenance. More ordinary people I never saw. A remark struck me when I heard an Old Man praise the conduct of our soldiers when they were in Bethlehem. He said there was no one instance where they attempted the chastity of their women, which I could impute to another cause besides their love of virtue. For No woman need have against a Man any other armour than her ugliness, & the Girls at Bethlehem are well equipped with *this Coat of Mail*."

It is doubtful whether such words would have been apt to proceed in eighteenth-century England from a devout dissenting minister to a bell-wether of his flock. They read more like the correspondence of men of the world. The Revolution destroyed the fortunes and the social leadership of this class. To find such people again in America, we must probably wait until after the Civil War.

But, after all, this development of a small class into full contemporary vigour did not much affect what is often called the bone and the sinew of the American commonwealth, nor indeed did it result in any serious social breach. Our mercantile aristocracy was not hereditary; if fortune failed, its members reverted almost immediately to the sound old native type, and able people were continually making their way into that fortunate class whose prosperity the Revolution brought to an end.

Meanwhile throughout the first half of our eighteenth century, external affairs constantly took a pretty definite form. Increased commercial prosperity and superficial social changes could not alter the fact that until the conquest of Canada the English colonies in America were constantly menaced by disturbances which Yankee tradition still calls the French and Indian wars. These began before the seventeenth century closed. In 1690 Sir William Phips captured Port Royal, now Annapolis, in Nova Scotia; later in the year he came to grief in an expedition against Quebec itself; in 1704 came the still remembered sack of Deerfield in the Connecticut valley; in 1745 came Sir William Pepperell's somewhat fortuitous conquest of Louisbourg; in 1755 came Braddock's defeat; in 1759 came Wolfe's final conquest at Quebec. The whole story is excellently told in the works of Francis Parkman. As we have seen before, these really record the struggle which decided the future of America. When the eighteenth century began, — as the encircling names of Quebec, Montreal, Chicago, St. Louis, and New Orleans may still remind us, — it was doubtful whether the continent which is now the United States should ultimately be controlled by the traditions of England or by those of continental Europe. Throughout the first half of the eighteenth century this question was still in doubt, — never more so, perhaps, than when Braddock fell in what is now Western Pennsylvania. The victory on the Plains of Abraham settled the fate of a hemisphere. Once for all, the continent of America passed into the control of the race which still maintains there the traditions of the English Law.

In the second quarter of the eighteenth century, there declared itself throughout British America a movement which throws a good deal of light on American temperament. As we saw in our glance at English literature, one of the writers still busy in 1750 was John Wesley, the founder of that great dissenting sect commonly called Methodist. This originated in a fervent evangelical protest against the corrupt, unspiritualised condition of the English Church during the reign of George II. Though Methodism made permanent impression on the middle class of England, however, it can hardly be regarded in England as a social force of the first historical importance. Nor were any of its manifestations there salient enough to attract the instant attention of people who consider general English history. In America the case was different. During the earlier years of the eighteenth century the Puritan churches had begun to stiffen into formalism. Though this never went so far as to divorce religion from life, or to let native Yankees long forget the main tenets of Calvinism, there was such decline of religious fervour as to give the more earnest clergy serious ground for alarm.

In 1738 George Whitefield, perhaps the most powerful of English revivalists, first visited the colonies. In that year he devoted himself to the spiritual awakening of Georgia. In 1740 he came to New England. The Great Awakening of religion during the next few years was largely due to his preaching. At first the clergy were disposed ardently to welcome this revival of religious enthusiasm. Soon, however, the revival took a turn of which we may best form a conception by supposing that half the respectable classes of New England should fervently abandon their earthly affairs, and, enrolling themselves under the banners of the Salvation Army, should proceed to camp-meetings of the most enthusiastic disorder.

The more conservative clergy were alarmed; in 1744 Harvard College formally protested against the excesses of Whitefield, and in 1745 Yale followed this example. The religious enthusiasm which possessed the lower classes of eighteenth-century America, in short, grotesquely outran the gravely passionate ecstasies of the immigrant Puritans. So late as Cotton Mather's time, the devout of New England were still rewarded with mystic visions, wherein divine voices and heavenly figures revealed themselves to prayerful keepers of fasts and vigils. The Great Awakening which expressed itself in mad shoutings and tearing off of garments was more like what the earlier Puritans had deemed the diabolical excesses of Quakerism. The personal contrast between the immigrant Puritans and Whitefield typifies the difference. The old ministers had entered on their duties with all the authority of scholars from English universities; Whitefield began his career as an inspired potboy who emerged from a tavern of the lower kind. Seventeenth-century Puritanism was a profound and lasting spiritual power; Whitefield's revival was rather an outburst of ranting excess. Yet for all this excess the Great Awakening testifies to one lasting fact, — a far-reaching spontaneity and enthusiasm among the humble classes of America, which, once aroused, could produce social phenomena much more startling than Methodism produced in King George II.'s England.

The people who had been so profoundly stirred by this Great Awakening were the same who in 1776 declared themselves independent of the mother country. The American Revolution is important enough for separate consideration. Before speaking of that, we had best consider the literary expression of America up to 1776. Here, then, we need only recall a few dates. The Stamp Act was passed in 1765, the year in which Blackstone published the first volume of his " Commentaries on the Law of England." Lexington, Concord, and Bunker Hill came in 1775, the year in which Burke delivered his masterly speech on " Conciliation with America." On the Glorious Fourth of July, 1776, the Declaration of Independence was signed. American independence was finally acknowledged by the peace of 1783. The Constitution of the United States was adopted in 1789. In 1800 the presidency of John Adams was drawing to a close, and Washington was dead. Now, very broadly speaking, the forces which expressed themselves in these familiar facts were forces which tended in America to destroy the mercantile class whom Copley painted, and to substitute as the ruling class throughout the country one more like that which had been stirred by the Great Awakening. In other words, the Revolution once more brought to the surface of American life the sort of natives whom the Great Awakening shows so fully to have preserved the spontaneity and the enthusiasm of earlier days.

A trifling anecdote may perhaps define this somewhat vague generalisation. In the Museum of Fine Arts at Boston is a room which contains a number of portraits by Copley, representing the mercantile aristocracy of the town a few years before the American Revolution. To this room, not long ago, there chanced to stray a gentleman eminent in the political and social life of a modern English colony. A shrewd man, of wide experience, he had found the United States a little puzzling. The sight of these Copley portraits was to him as a burst of light. He laughed, and pointing to the wall which their dignity adorns, exclaimed : " Why, that's the sort of people we are ! " The sort of people whom Copley painted, in short, still socially and politically control the British colonies. Except for the Revolution, they might still have controlled America.

During the eighteenth century, then, America seems slowly

to have been developing into an independent nationality as conservative of its traditions as England was of hers, but less obviously so because American traditions were far less threatened. The geographical isolation of America combined with the absorptive power of our native race to preserve the general type of character which America had displayed from its settlement. In the history of native Americans, the seventeenth century has already defined itself as a period of untrammelled inexperience. The fact that American conditions changed so little until the Revolution implies that this national inexperience persisted. Inexperience leaves character far less altered than can be the case when experience accumulates. In many superficial aspects, no doubt, particularly if of the prosperous class, the native Americans of 1776 appeared to be men of the eighteenth century. In personal temper, however, Thomas Hutchinson and Samuel Adams were far more like John Winthrop and Roger Williams than Chatham and Burke were like Bacon and Burleigh. One inference seems clear: the Americans of the revolutionary period retained to an incalculable degree qualities which had faded from ancestral England with the days of Queen Elizabeth.

IV

LITERATURE IN AMERICA FROM 1700 TO 1776

UNTIL 1728, when Cotton Mather died, the general state of literature in America remained unaltered. Between 1729 and 1776, the titles recorded by Whitcomb indicate decided change both in the character of the publications and in their distribution. Out of some two hundred and thirty of these titles, only thirty-seven are precisely religious ; thirty-eight are historical ; forty-seven are political ; forty-eight — though none have survived in literature — are at least as literary as the verses of Wigglesworth or of Mrs. Bradstreet ; and the rest — including scientific works, almanacs, periodicals, and the like — can be classed only as miscellaneous. In religious writing, New England remained more prolific than the rest of the country ; but the most memorable religious work of this period, that of Jonathan Edwards, was produced not in eastern Massachusetts, but in the Connecticut valley, — in other words, under the influence not of Harvard College but of Yale. Each of the other classes of publication — historical, political, literary, and miscellaneous — appeared in slightly greater numbers elsewhere than in New England. These rough memoranda indicate two significant facts. As the material prosperity of America increased, it tended to develop the middle colonies ; during the greater part of the eighteenth century the most important town in America was not Boston, but Philadelphia. And though in purely religious writing New England kept the lead, the centre of its religious thought had shifted from the shore of Massachusetts Bay to that of Long Island Sound.

Some familiar dates in the history of American education emphasise these facts. Yale College, founded in 1700, began its career under King William III., until whose reign the only established school of higher learning in America had been Harvard College, founded under Charles I. The avowed purpose of the founding of Yale was to maintain the orthodox traditions threatened by the constantly growing liberalism of Harvard. Under George II., three considerable colleges were founded in the middle colonies. In 1746, Princeton College was established to maintain an orthodoxy as stout as that of Yale. In 1749, partly under the auspices of the American Philosophic Society which had lately been founded by Franklin, the University of Pennsylvania began an academic history which more than any other in America has kept free from entanglement with dogma. In 1754, King's College was founded at New York, where, under the name of Columbia, it still maintains admirable traditions of learning in friendly relation with the ancestral Church of England. Meanwhile Harvard College had done little more than preserve its own prudently liberal traditions, with no marked alteration in either character or size. The higher intellectual activity of America was clearly tending for a while to centralise itself elsewhere than in those New England regions where the American intellect had first been active.

During the first half of the eighteenth century, too, there had rapidly grown up in America a profusion of periodical publications. We had no " Tatler," to be sure, or " Spectator ; " but from 1704, when the " Boston News Letter " was established, we had a constantly increasing number of newspapers. A dozen years before the Revolution these had everywhere become as familiar and as popular, in a country where technical illiteracy was rare, as were those annual almanacs which had already sprung up in the seventeenth century, and of which the most highly developed example was the " Poor Richard's Almanac," begun by Franklin in 1733. Pretty clearly, this eighteenth century was a period of growing intellectual activity and curiosity among the whole people of America; and these same people were showing disposition to concern themselves rather with the affairs of this world than with those of the next.

In the Middle Colonies there was meanwhile developing an aspect of religion very different from that which commended itself to the orthodox Calvinism of New England. Undoubtedly the most important religious writing in America at the period with which we are now concerned was that of Jonathan Edwards. But the memory of another American, of widely different temper, has tended, during a century and more, to strengthen in the estimation of those who love comfortable spiritual thought expressed with fervid simplicity. John Woolman was a Quaker farmer of New Jersey, born in 1720, who became in 1746 an itinerant preacher, who began to testify vigorously against slavery as early as 1753, and who died during a visit to England in 1772. His record of a vision will show at once why he held himself bound to oppose slavery, and how the eternities presented themselves to American Quakers of the eighteenth century :—

"In a time of sickness with the pleurisy, . . . I was brought so near the gates of death that I forgot my name. Being then desirous to know who I was, I saw a mass of matter of a dull, gloomy colour, between the south and the east; and was informed that this mass was human beings in as great misery as they could be and live; and that I was mixed in with them, and that henceforth I might not consider myself as a distinct or separate being. In this state I remained several hours. I then heard a soft, melodious voice, more pure and harmonious than any I had heard with my ears before; I believed it was the voice of an angel, who spake to the other angels. The words were; 'John Woolman is dead.' I soon remembered that I once was John Woolman, and being assured that I was alive in the body, I greatly wondered what that heavenly voice could mean. . . .

" I was then carried in spirit to the mines, where poor, oppressed people were digging rich treasures for those called Christians, and heard them blaspheme the name of Christ, at which I grieved, for his name to me was precious.

"Then I was informed that these heathen were told that those who oppressed them were the followers of Christ ; and they said amongst themselves, if Christ directed them to use us in this sort, then Christ is a cruel tyrant.

"All this time the song of the angel remained a mystery ; and in the morning my dear wife and some others coming to my bedside, I asked them if they knew who I was ; and they telling me I was John Woolman, thought I was light-headed, for I told them not what the angel said, nor was I disposed to talk much to any one, but was very desirous to get so deep that I might understand this mystery.

"My tongue was often so dry that I could not speak till I had moved it about and gathered some moisture, and as I lay still for a time, at length I felt divine power prepare my mouth that I could speak, and then I said : 'I am crucified with Christ, nevertheless I live ; yet not I, but Christ that liveth in me ; and the life I now live in the flesh is by faith in the Son of God, who loved me, and gave himself for me.'

"Then the mystery was opened, and I perceived there was joy in heaven over a sinner who had repented, and that the language — 'John Woolman is dead' — meant no more than the death of my own will."

According to the Quaker faith, in brief, man was not essentially lost, nor was God the grimly just autocrat of Calvinism. The Quakers, to quote one of themselves, " drank in the truth of the universal love of God to all men in Christian, Jewish, or Pagan lands, that God so *loved* the *world* that He sent His Son, that Christ died for *all* men, and that His atonement availed for all who in every land accepted the light with which He enlightened their minds and consciences, and who listening to His still small voice in the soul turned in any true sense toward God, away from evil and to the right and loving." If we choose, these Quakers held, we may save ourselves by voluntarily accepting Christ — by willing attention to the still small voice of the Holy Spirit.

Though words like Woolman's throw light on a growing phase of American sentiment, however, they are not precisely literature. Neither was such political writing as we shall consider more particularly when we come to the Revolution ; nor yet was the more scholarly historical writing of which the prin-

6

cipal example is probably Thomas Hutchinson's " History of
the Colony of Massachusetts Bay." The first volume of this
appeared in 1764. Neglected by reason of the traditional
unpopularity which sincere, self-sacrificing Toryism brought
on the last native governor of provincial Massachusetts, this
remains an admirable piece of serious historical writing, not
vivid, picturesque, or very interesting, but dignified, earnest,
and just. In the history of pure literature, however, it has
no great importance.

Further still from unmixed literature seems the work of the
two men of this period who for general reasons now deserve
such separate consideration as we gave Cotton Mather. They
deserve it as representing two distinct aspects of American
character, which closely correspond with the two ideals most
inseparable from our native language. One of these ideals
is the religious or moral, inherent in the lasting tradition of
the English Bible ; the other is the political or social, equally
inherent in the equally lasting tradition of the English Law.
In the pre-revolutionary years of our eighteenth century, the
former was most characteristically expressed by Jonathan
Edwards ; and the kind of national temper which must always
underlie the latter was incarnate in Benjamin Franklin. Before
considering the Revolution and the literature which came with
it and after it, we may best attend to these men in turn.

V

JONATHAN EDWARDS

JONATHAN EDWARDS, son of a minister who had been educated at Harvard, was born at East Windsor, Connecticut, on October 5, 1703. In 1720 he took his degree at Yale, where he was a tutor from 1724 to 1726. In 1727 he was ordained colleague to his grandfather, Solomon Stoddard, minister of Northampton, Massachusetts. Here he remained settled until 1750, when his growing austerities resulted in his dismissal from that ministry. The next year he became a missionary to the Stockbridge Indians, in a region at that time remote from civilisation. In 1757 he was chosen to succeed his son-in-law, Burr, as President of Princeton College. He died at Princeton, in consequence of inoculation for small-pox, on March 22, 1758.

Beyond doubt, Edwards has had more influence on subsequent thought than any other American theologian. In view of this, the uneventfulness of his life, so utterly apart from public affairs, becomes significant of the condition of the New England ministry during his lifetime. He was born hardly two years after Increase Mather, the lifelong champion of theocracy, was deposed from the presidency of Harvard College; and as our glance at the Mathers must have reminded us, an eminent Yankee minister of the seventeenth century was almost as necessarily a politician as he was a divine. Yet Edwards, the most eminent of our eighteenth-century ministers, had less to do with public affairs than many ministers of the present day. A more thorough divorce of church and state than is indicated by his career could hardly exist.

Nothing less than such separation from public affairs could have permitted that concentration on matters of the other world which makes the work of Edwards still potent. From his own time to ours his influence has been so strong that almost all discussions of him are concerned with the question of how far his systematic theology is true. For our purposes this question is not material, nor yet is that of what his system was in detail. It is enough to observe that throughout his career, as preacher and writer alike, he set forth Calvinism in its most uncompromising form, reasoned out with great logical power to extreme conclusions. As for matters of earthly fact, he mentioned them only as they bore on his theological or philosophical contentions.

Early in life, for example, he fell in love with Sarah Pierrepont, daughter of a New Haven minister, and a descendant of the great emigrant minister Thomas Hooker, of Hartford. Accordingly this lady presented herself to his mind as surely among God's elect, an opinion which he recorded when she was thirteen years old and he was twenty, in the following words : —

" They say there is a young lady in New Haven who is beloved of that great Being who made and rules the world, and that there are certain seasons in which this great Being, in some way or other invisible, comes to her and fills her mind with exceeding sweet delight, and that she hardly cares for anything except to meditate on Him ; that she expects after a while to be received up where he is, to be raised up out of the world and caught up into heaven; being assured that he loves her too well to let her remain at a distance from Him always. There she is to dwell with Him, and to be ravished with His love and delight for ever. Therefore, if you present all the world before her, with the richest of its treasures she disregards and cares not for it, and is unmindful of any pain or affliction. She has a strange sweetness in her mind, and singular purity in her affections; is most just and conscientious in all her conduct; and you could not persuade her to do anything wrong or sinful, if you would give her the whole world, lest she should offend this great Being. She is of a wonderful calmness, and universal benevolence of mind; especially after this great God has manifested himself to her mind. She will sometimes go about from place to place singing sweetly; and seems to be always full of joy and pleasure, and no one knows for what. She loves to be alone, walking in the fields and groves, and seems to have some one invisible always conversing with her."

The spiritual gifts of this chosen vessel of the Lord, who in 1727 became Mrs. Edwards, in no way interfered with her attention to human duties. During the twenty-three years of her husband's ministry at Northampton she bore him eleven children, one of whom married the Reverend Aaron Burr, first President of Princeton College, and became the mother of that other Aaron Burr whose political and social career was among the most scandalous of our opening nineteenth century.

That little record of Edwards's innocent love, which felt sure that its object enjoyed the blessings of God's elect, has a certain charm. What tradition has mostly remembered of him, however, is rather the unflinching vigour with which he set forth the inevitable fate of fallen man. His most familiar work is the sermon on "Sinners in the Hands of an Angry God," of which one of the least forgotten passages runs thus : —

"O sinner! consider the fearful danger you are in : it is a great furnace of wrath, a wide and bottomless pit, full of the fire of wrath, that you are held over in the hand of that God, whose wrath is provoked and incensed as much against you, as against many of the damned in hell : — you hang by a slender thread, with the flames of divine wrath flashing about it, and ready every moment to singe it and burn it asunder ; and you have no interest in any Mediator, and nothing to lay hold of to save yourself, nothing to keep off the flames of wrath, nothing of your own, nothing that you ever have done, nothing that you can do, to induce God to spare you one moment. . . .

"It is everlasting wrath. It would be dreadful to suffer this fierceness and wrath of Almighty God one moment ; but you must suffer it to all eternity : there will be no end to this exquisite, horrible misery : when you look forward you shall see a long for ever, a boundless duration before you, which will swallow up your thoughts and amaze your soul ; and you will absolutely despair of ever having any deliverance, any end, any mitigation, any rest at all ; you will know certainly that you must wear out long ages, millions of millions of ages, in wrestling and conflicting with this Almighty merciless vengeance ; and then, when you have so done, when so many ages have actually been spent by you in this manner, you will know that all is but a point to what remains."

In view of such doctrine as this, his last sermon to the church of Northampton, delivered on June 22, 1750, becomes very grim. His final trouble with his parishioners arose from a decay in church discipline which by that time had grown conspicuous. In the New England churches there had early arisen something called the Half Way Covenant, by which those who had received baptism in infancy might in turn present their own children for baptism. At first, however, no one was admitted either to the Lord's Supper or to the voting privileges of a church without performing some personal act of public consecration. As time went on, and discipline relaxed, many ministers, among them Edwards's grandfather Stoddard, began to administer the communion to those who were consecrated to the Lord by the Half Way Covenant only. The chief ground of Edwards's dispute with his congregation was his refusal of the sacrament to persons who had not formally joined the church. And here are some of the words in which he bade his flock farewell : —

" My work is finished which I had to do as a minister: You have publicly rejected me, and my opportunities cease.

" How highly therefore does it now become us, to consider of that time when we must meet one another before the chief Shepherd? When I must give an account of my stewardship, of the service I have done for, and the reception and treatment I have had among the people he sent me to : And you must give an account of your conduct toward me, and the improvement you have made of these three and twenty years of my ministry. There is nothing covered that shall not be revealed, nor hid which shall not be known; all will be examined in the searching, penetrating light of God's omniscience and glory, and by him whose eyes are as a flame of fire; and truth and right shall be made plainly to appear, being stripped of every veil; and all error, falsehood, unrighteousness and injury shall be laid open, stripped of every disguise; every specious pretense, every cavil, and all false reasoning shall vanish in a moment, as not being able to bear the light of that day. . . . Then every step of the conduct of each of us in this affair, from first to last, and the spirit we have exercised in all shall be examined and manifested, and our own consciences shall speak plain and loud, and each of us shall be convinced, and the world shall know; and never shall there be any more mistake, misrepresentation, or misapprehension of the affair to eternity."

This unflinching insistence on sin and its penalty has impressed people so deeply that they have been apt to hold it comprehensive of Edwards's theological system. Really this is far from the case. He stoutly defended the divine justice of his pitiless doctrine, to be sure, with characteristically impregnable logic : —

" God is a being infinitely lovely, because he hath infinite excellency and beauty. To have infinite excellency and beauty, is the same thing as to have infinite loveliness. He is a being of infinite greatness, majesty, and glory; and therefore he is infinitely honourable. He is infinitely exalted above the greatest potentates of the earth, and highest angels in heaven; and therefore is infinitely more honourable than they. His authority over us is infinite; and the ground of his right to our obedience is infinitely strong; for he is infinitely worthy to be obeyed in himself, and we have an absolute, universal, and infinite dependence upon him.

" So that sin against God, being a violation of infinite obligations, must be a crime infinitely heinous, and so deserving of infinite punishment."

Yet in spite of all this, he held, God now and again shows unmerited mercy, which may by chance be granted to any one of us. We have seen already how surely he believed this vouchsafed to the lady who became his wife. Here is another of his infrequent statements of fact, recording how divine grace came to one Phebe Bartlet, a child of Northampton, born in March, 1731 : —

" On Thursday, the last day of July (1735), the child being in the closet, where it used to retire, its mother heard it speaking aloud, which was unusual, and never had been observed before; and her voice seemed to be as of one exceeding importunate and engaged, but her mother could distinctly hear only these words, (spoken in her childish manner, but seemed to be spoken with extraordinary earnestness, and out of distress of soul) Pray *Bessed Lord* give me salvation ! *I pray, beg* pardon all my sins ! When the child had done prayer, she came out of the closet, and came and sat down by her mother, and cried out aloud. Her mother very earnestly asked her several times, what the matter was, before she would make any answer, but she continued exceeding crying, and wreathing her body to and fro, like one in anguish of spirit. Her mother then asked her whether she was afraid that God would not give her salvation. She then answered yes, I am afraid I shall go to hell! Her mother then endeavoured to quiet her, and told her that she would not have her cry . . . she must be a very good girl, and pray every day, and she hoped God would give her salvation. But this did not quiet her at all . . . but she continued thus earnestly crying and taking on for some time, till at length she suddenly ceased crying and began to smile, and presently said with a smiling countenance. . . . Mother the kingdom of heaven is come to me! Her mother was surprised at the sudden alteration, and at the speech, and knew not what to make of it, but at first said nothing to her. The child presently spake again, and said, there is another come to me, and there is another . . . there is three; and being asked what she meant, she answered . . . One is, thy will be done, and there is another . . . enjoy him for ever; by which it seems that when the child said, there is three come to me, she meant three passages of its catechism that came to her mind."

Hideous as this picture of Puritan infancy must seem in certain moods, there are others, and moods which to Edwards would have seemed much more rational, in which it takes on an aspect of ecstatic beauty. According to the system from which he never wavered, the misery and the subsequent joy of this little child meant that, for no merit of her own, God had been mercifully pleased to receive her into the fellowship of the saints, wherein she was destined to enjoy for ever such peace as his own words shall describe : —

"The peace of the Christian infinitely differs from that of the worldling, in that it is unfailing and eternal peace. That peace which carnal men have in the things of this world is, according to the foundation it is built upon, of short continuance; like the comfort of a dream, 1 John ii. 17, 1 Cor. vii. 31. These things, the best and most durable of them, are like bubbles on the face of the water; they vanish in a moment, Hos. x. 7.

"But the foundation of the Christian's peace is everlasting; it is what no time, no change, can destroy. It will remain when the body dies; it will remain when the mountains depart and the hills shall be removed, and when the heavens shall be rolled together as a scroll.

The fountain of his comfort shall never be diminished, and the stream shall never be dried. His comfort and joy is a living spring in the soul, a well of water springing up to everlasting life."

In plain truth, what people commonly remember of Edwards is merely one extreme to which he reasoned out his consistent system. Like the older theology of Calvin and of Augustine, it all rests on the essential wickedness of the human will, concerning which Edwards's great treatise is still held a strong bit of philosophising. He asserts something like an utter fatalism, a universality of cause affecting even our volition, quite beyond human control. This fatal perversion of human will he believes to spring from that ancestral curse which forbids any child of Adam to exert the will in true harmony with the will of God. Reconciliation he holds possible only when superhuman power comes, with unmerited grace, to God's elect.

Once accept Edwards's premises, and you will be at pains to avoid his conclusions. Yet it is hardly too much to say that long ago American posterity has generally rejected both, more absolutely indeed than it may come to reject them in the future. One can see why. In his American world, so relieved from the pressure of external fact that people generally behaved much better than is usual in earthly history, Edwards, whose personal life was exceptionally removed from anything practical, reasoned out with unflinching logic, to extreme conclusions, a kind of philosophy which is justified in experience only by such things as occur in densely populated, corrupt societies. Augustine wrote amid the corruption of decadent Rome, whose ruined amphitheatres still testify to the brutish riots of pleasure which could subsist amid what seemed civilisation, and whose fashionable vices had run in men and women alike to more than Neronic excess. Calvin reiterated this theology in a Europe where the most potent family was the Medici, the Florentine race whose blood combined with that of degenerate Stuarts to complete the degradation of royalty in Charles II., and James, and the Pretenders. And, a century and more later, this Jonathan Edwards tried logically to extend Calvinism in a world where there were few more dreadful exhibitions of human depravity than occasional cheating, the reading of eighteenth-century novels, — which Edwards is said to have held dangerously obscene, — and such artless merry-making and moonlight flirtation as have always gladdened youth in the Yankee country. Whoever knew American life in the middle of the eighteenth century and honestly asked himself whether its manifestations were such as the theology of Edwards would explain, could hardly avoid a deeper and deeper conviction that even though he was traditionally accustomed to accept the premises which so clearly involved Edwards's conclusions, somehow these conclusions were not so.

By the middle of the eighteenth century, in short, religious thought in America had divorced itself from life almost as completely as from politics. The slow result was certain. In 1857, nearly a hundred years after the death of Edwards, the most familiar and unanswerable comment on his system appeared. Often misunderstood, generally thought no more than a piece of comic extravagance, Dr. Holmes's "One-Hoss Shay" is really among the most pitiless satires in our language. Born and bred a Calvinist, Holmes, who lived in the full tide of Unitarian hopefulness, recoiled from the appalling doctrines which had darkened his youth. He could find no flaw in their reasoning, but he would not accept their conclusions. In a spirit as earnest, then, as his words seem rollicking, he wrote of Edwards thus : —

> " Little of all we value here
> Wakes on the morn of its hundredth year
> Without both feeling and looking queer.
> In fact, there 's nothing that keeps its youth,
> So far as I know, but a tree and truth.
> (This is a moral that runs at large ;
> Take it. — You 're welcome. — No extra charge.)

"FIRST OF NOVEMBER, — the Earthquake-day, —
There are traces of age in the one-hoss shay,
A general flavour of mild decay,
But nothing local as one may say.
There could n't be, — for the Deacon's art
Had made it so like in every part
That there was n't a chance for one to start.
For the wheels were just as strong as the thills,
And the floor was just as strong as the sills,
And the panels just as strong as the floor,
And the whipple-tree neither less nor more,
And the back-crossbar as strong as the fore,
And spring and axle and hub *encore*.
And yet, *as a whole*, it is past a doubt
In another hour it will be *worn out!*

" First of November, 'Fifty-five!
This morning the parson takes a drive.
Now, small boys, get out of the way!
Here comes the wonderful one-hoss shay,
Drawn by a rat-tailed, ewe-necked bay.
'Huddup!' said the parson. — Off went they.
The parson was working his Sunday's text, —
Had got to *fifthly*, and stopped perplexed
At what the — Moses — was coming next.
All at once the horse stood still,
Close by the meet'n'-house on the hill.
First a shiver, and then a thrill,
Then something decidedly like a spill, —
And the parson was sitting upon a rock,
At half past nine by the meet'n'-house clock, —
Just the hour of the Earthquake shock!
What do you think the parson found,
When he got up and stared around?
The poor old chaise in a heap or mound,
As if it had been to the mill and ground!
You see, of course, if you 're not a dunce,
How it went to pieces all at once, —
All at once, and nothing first, —
Just as bubbles do when they burst.

" End of the wonderful one-hoss shay.
Logic is logic. That 's all I say."

VI

THE contemporary of Edwards who best shows what American human nature had become, is Benjamin Franklin. Unlike the persons at whom we have glanced, this man, who before he died became more eminent than all the rest together, sprang from socially inconspicuous origin. The son of a tallow chandler, he was born in Boston, on January 6, 1706. As a mere boy, he was apprenticed to his brother, a printer, with whom he did not get along very well. At seventeen he ran away, and finally turned up in Philadelphia, where he attracted the interest of some influential people. A year later he went to England, carrying from these friends letters which he supposed might be useful in the mother country. The letters proved worthless; in 1726, after a life in England for which vagabond is hardly too strong a word, he returned to Philadelphia. There he remained for some thirty years. He began by shrewdly advancing himself as printer, publisher, and shopkeeper; later, when his extraordinary ability had drawn about him people of more and more solid character, he became a local public man and proved himself also an admirable self-taught man of science. About the time of Washington's birth, he started that " Poor Richard's Almanac " whose aphorisms have had such lasting vogue. It is Poor Richard who told us, among other things, that " Early to bed and early to rise, makes a man healthy, wealthy, and wise; " that " God helps them that help themselves; " and that " Honesty is the best policy." After fifteen years Franklin's affairs had so prospered that he could retire from shopkeeping and give himself over to scientific work. He made numerous inventions: the lightning-rod, for example; the stove still called by his name; and double spectacles, with one lens in the upper half for observing distant objects, and another in the lower half for reading. In 1755 he was made Postmaster-General of the American colonies; and the United States post-office is said still to be conducted in many respects on the system he then established. So he lived until 1757, the year before Jonathan Edwards died.

In 1757 he was sent to England as the Agent of Pennsylvania. There he remained, with slight intervals, for eighteen years, becoming agent of other colonies too. In 1775 he returned home, where in 1776 he was a signer of the Declaration of Independence. Before the end of that year he was despatched as minister to France, where he remained until 1785. Then he came home and was elected President of Pennsylvania. In 1787 he was among the signers of the Constitution of the United States. On the 17th of April, 1790, he died at Philadelphia, a city to which his influence had given not only the best municipal system of eighteenth-century America, but also, among other institutions which have survived, the American Philosophical Society and the University of Pennsylvania.

The Franklin of world tradition, the great Franklin, is the statesman and diplomatist who from 1757 until 1785 proved himself both in England and in France to possess such commanding power. But the Franklin with whom we are concerned is rather the shrewd native American whose first fifty years were spent in preparation for his world-wide career. He was born, we have seen, a Yankee of the lower class, not technically a gentleman. How significant this fact was in the middle of the eighteenth century may be seen by a glance at any Quinquennial Catalogue of Harvard College. In this, from the beginning until 1772, the names of the graduates are arranged not in alphabetical order, but in that of social precedence. The sons of royal governors and of king's counsellors come first, then sons of ministers and magistrates, and so on; and the records of the College show that an habitual form of discipline during this period was to put a man's name in his class-list beneath the place to which his birth entitled him. To spirited American youths social inferiority is galling; the effect of it on Franklin's career appeared in several ways. For one thing he always hated Harvard College, and had small love for anything in Massachusetts; for another, he instinctively emigrated to a region where he should not be hampered by troublesome family traditions; for a third, with the recklessness which is apt to endanger youth in such a situation, he consorted during his earlier life with men who though often clever were loose in morals. Before middle life, however, his vagabond period was at an end. By strict attention to business and imperturbable good sense, he steadily outgrew his origin. By the time he was fifty years old his studies in electricity had gained him European reputation; and in all the American colonies there was no practical public man of more deserved local importance.

In the course of this career he had written and published copiously. None of his work, however, can be called exactly literary. Its purpose was either to instruct people concerning his scientific and other discoveries and principles; or else, as in "Poor Richard's Almanac," — perhaps his nearest approach to pure letters, — to influence conduct. But if Franklin's writings were never precisely literature, his style was generally admirable. His account in the "Autobiography" of how, while still a Boston boy, he learned to write, is at once characteristic of his temper and conclusive of his accomplishment: —

"About this time I met with an odd volume of the 'Spectator.' It was the third. I had never before seen any of them. I bought it, read it over and over, and was much delighted with it. I thought the writing excellent, and wished, if possible, to imitate it. With this

view I took some of the papers, and, making short hints of the sentiment in each sentence, laid them by a few days, and then, without
looking at the book, try'd to compleat the papers again, by expressing
each hinted sentiment at length, and as fully as it had been expressed
before, in any suitable words that should come to hand. Then I
compared my 'Spectator' with the original, discovered some of my
faults, and corrected them. But I found I wanted a stock of words,
or a readiness in recollecting and using them, which I thought I
should have acquired before that time if I had gone on making
verses; since the continual occasion for words of the same import,
but of different length, to suit the measure, or of different sound for
the rhyme, would have laid me under a constant necessity of searching for variety, and also have tended to fix that variety in my mind,
and make me master of it. Therefore I took some of the tales and
turned them into verse; and, after a time, when I had pretty well forgotten the prose, turned them back again. I also sometimes jumbled
my collection of hints into confusion, and after some weeks endeavoured to reduce them into the best order, before I began to form the
full sentences and compleat the paper. This was to teach me method
in the arrangement of thoughts. My time for these exercises and for
reading was at night, after work or before it began in the morning, or
on Sundays, when I contrived to be in the printing-house alone, evad-
ing as much as I could the common attendance on public worship
which my father used to exact of me when I was under his care, and
which indeed I still thought a duty, though I could not, as it seemed
to me, afford time to practice it."

Sound eighteenth-century English this, though hardly of
Addisonian urbanity. Even more characteristic than the
English of this passage, however, is Franklin's feeling about
religion, implied in its last sentence. The Boston where this
printer's boy stayed away from church to teach himself how to
write was the very town where Increase and Cotton Mather
were still preaching the dogmas of Puritan theocracy; and a
few days' journey westward Jonathan Edwards, only three years
older than Franklin, was beginning his lifelong study of the
relation of mankind to eternity. To the religious mind of
New England, earthly life remained a mere fleeting moment.
Life must always end soon, and death as we see it actually
seems unending. With this solemn truth constantly in mind,
the New England Puritans of Franklin's day, like their devout

ancestors, and many of their devout descendants, bent their whole energy toward eternal welfare as distinguished from anything temporal. Yet in their principal town Franklin, a man of the plain people, exposed to no influences but those of his own day and country, was coolly preferring the study of earthly accomplishment to any question which concerned matters beyond human life.

Another extract from his " Autobiography " carries his religious history a little further : —

" My parents had early given me religious impressions, and brought me through my childhood piously in the Dissenting way. But I was scarce fifteen, when, after doubting by turns of several points, as I found them disputed in the different books I read, I began to doubt of Revelation itself. Some books against Deism fell into my hands; they were said to be the substance of sermons preached at Boyle's Lectures. It happened that they wrought an effect on me quite contrary to what was intended by them ; for the arguments of the deists, which were quoted to be refuted, appeared to me much stronger than the refutations ; in short, I soon became a thorough Deist. My arguments perverted some others, particularly Collins and Ralph; but, each of them having afterwards wrong'd me greatly without the least compunction, and recollecting Keith's conduct towards me (who was another free-thinker), and my own towards Vernon and Miss Read, which at times gave me great trouble, I began to suspect that this doctrine, tho' it might be true, was not very useful."

" Not very useful : " the good sense of Franklin tested religion itself by its effects on every-day conduct.

Later still in his " Autobiography " he tells how he was impressed by the ministrations of the only Presbyterian minister in Philadelphia, to whose services he paid the willing tribute of annual subscription : —

" He used to visit me sometimes as a friend, and admonish me to attend his administrations, and I was now and then prevailed on to do so, once for five Sundays successively. Had he been in my opinion a good preacher, perhaps I might have continued, notwithstanding the occasion I had for the Sunday's leisure in my course of study ; but his discourses were chiefly either polemic arguments, or explications of the peculiar doctrines of our sect, and were all to me very dry, un·

interesting, and unedifying, since not a single moral principle was inculcated or enforc'd, their aim seeming rather to make us Presbyterians than good citizens."

The spiritual life thus begun, if spiritual it may be called, developed as might have been expected. Years afterward, it excited painful apprehension in the mind of the great George Whitefield, to whom in 1764 Franklin wrote thus : —

"Your frequently repeated wishes for my eternal, as well as my temporal happiness, are very obliging, and I can only thank you for them and offer you mine in return. I have myself no doubt, that I shall enjoy as much of both as is proper for me. That Being, who gave me existence, and through almost threescore years has been continually showering his favours upon me ; whose very chastisements have been blessings to me; can I doubt that he loves me ? And, if he loves me, can I doubt that he will go on to take care of me, not only here but hereafter? This to some may seem presumption; to me it appears the best grounded hope; hope of the future built on experience of the past."

The personal relations with Whitefield attested by this letter had begun in 1739, when the revivalist first came to Philadelphia. Here

"he was at first permitted to preach in some of our churches; but the clergy, taking a dislike to him, soon refused him their pulpits, and he was obliged to preach in the fields. The multitudes of all sects and denominations that attended his sermons were enormous, and it was matter of speculation to me, who was one of the number, to observe the extraordinary influence of his oratory on his hearers, and how much they admired and respected him, notwithstanding his common abuse of them, by assuring them they were naturally *half beasts and half devils.* It was wonderful to see the change soon made in the manner of our inhabitants. From being thoughtless or indifferent about religion, it seem'd as if all the world were growing religious, so that one could not walk thro' the town in an evening without hearing psalms sung in different families of every street."

Franklin, who was employed as printer on many of Whitefield's sermons, soon came to have a high opinion of the Methodist's personal honesty. Of his prudence, the shrewd Yankee had more doubt; but at least once Whitefield's preaching, with its "wonderful power over the hearts and the purses of his hearers," carried him away. The revivalist wished to establish in Georgia a charitable orphanage, which Franklin thought impracticable.

"I therefore refused to contribute," writes Franklin. "I happened soon after to attend one of his sermons, in the course of which I perceived he intended to finish with a collection, and I silently resolved he should get nothing from me. I had in my pocket a handful of copper money, three or four silver dollars, and five pistoles in gold. As he proceeded I began to soften, and concluded to give the coppers. Another stroke of his oratory made me asham'd of that, and determined me to give the silver; and he finished so admirably, that I empty'd my pocket wholly into the collector's dish, gold and all."

Generally, however, Franklin kept his head better. The cool scientific temper with which on another occasion he attended to one of Whitefield's impassioned public discourses is more characteristic : —

"He preach'd one evening from the top of the Court-house steps, which are in the middle of Market-street, and on the west side of Second-street, which crosses it at right angles. Both streets were filled with hearers to a considerable distance. Being among the hindmost in Market-street, I had the curiosity to learn how far he could be heard, by retiring backwards down the street towards the river; and I found that his voice was distinct till I came near Front-street, when some noise in that street obscur'd it. Imagining then a semicircle, of which my distance should be the radius, and that it were filled with auditors, to each of whom I allowed two square feet, I computed that he might well be heard by more than thirty thousand. This reconcil'd me to the newspaper accounts of his having preached to twenty-five thousand people in the fields, and to ancient histories of generals haranguing whole armies, of which I had sometimes doubted."

Far more in this vein is Franklin's friendly record of their personal relations : —

"The following instance will show something of the terms on which we stood. Upon one of his arrivals from England at Boston, he wrote to me that he should come soon to Philadelphia, but knew not where he could lodge when there, as he understood his old friend and host, Mr. Benezet, was removed to Germantown. My answer was, ' You know my house; if you can make shift with its scanty accommodations, you will be most heartily welcome.' He reply'd, that if I made that kind offer for Christ's sake, I should not miss of a reward. And I returned, '*Don't let me be mistaken; it was not for Christ's sake, but for your sake.*' One of our common acquaintances jocosely remark'd that, knowing it to be the custom of the saints, when they received any favour, to shift the burden of the obligation from off their own shoulders, and place it in heaven, I had contriv'd to fix it on earth."

To Franklin, indeed, things on earth were of paramount importance. He never denied the existence of God, but he deemed God a beneficent spirit, abundantly able to take care of himself and to take care of us too; so long then, as men behave decently, they may confidently leave to God the affairs of heaven and of hell, if perchance there be one. Franklin's God, in short, was much more like that Supreme Being to whom Voltaire in his last days erected a classical temple in the grounds of Ferney, than like the orthodox God of New England, — Him whom in the midst of Franklin's lifetime Jonathan Edwards so fervently described as holding sinners for a moment above eternal fires into which His angry hand should presently drop them. Of earthly morality, meanwhile, so far as it commended itself to good sense, Franklin was shrewdly careful. No passage in his " Autobiography " is more familiar than the list of virtues which he drew up and endeavoured in turn to practise. The order in which he chose to arrange them is as follows: Temperance, Silence, Order, Resolution, Frugality (under which his little expository motto is very characteristic : " Make no expense but to do good to others or yourself "), Industry, Sincerity (under which he directs us to " Use no hurtful deceit "), Justice, Moderation, Cleanliness, Tranquillity, Chastity, and finally one which he added later as peculiarly needful to him, — Humility. The injunction placed under this last is perhaps the most characteristic of all : " Imitate Jesus and Socrates."

Now though all this is sound practical morality of a kind which should at once advance a man's earthly prosperity and incidentally benefit society, it is about as far from the passionate morality which should save souls as it is from vice itself. The most familiar saying of Poor Richard, " Honesty is the best policy," is typical of this. Very likely honesty will bring you to heaven, but for the moment that question is immaterial; if you are honest in this world, you will get on here better than if you are not. A profound truth this, by the way, particularly for English-speaking people. Compared with races of Latin or Greek origin, ours is not intellectually alert. Now if you act honestly and tell the truth, you play your part in exact accordance with life as you see it. On the other hand, begin to cheat, to act dishonestly, or to lie, and you have set up such contradiction of fact as you must constantly support by fresh and various misrepresentation. To alert-minded people a frequent demand for mendacious ingenuity often seems stimulating. To people of our sluggish race it is rather bewildering; English-speaking people are the least successful liars in the world. Very good: we are of English tradition; the part of good sense, then, is to lie as little as possible, to " use no hurtful deceit," to be honest. " Honesty is the best policy." So far as conduct goes, worldly wisdom brings us nearly into accord with the dogmatic morality of Christianity. In other words, such common sense as Franklin's ultimately makes human beings behave in a manner so far from superficially damnable that you might be at pains to distinguish them from God's own elect.

The deliberate good sense with which Franklin treated matters of religion and morality, he displayed equally in his scientific writings; and, a little later, in the public documents and correspondence which made him as eminent in diplomacy and statecraft as he had earlier been in science and in local affairs. His examination before the House of Commons in 1766 shows him as a public man at his best. A letter to a London newspaper, written the year before, shows another phase of his mind, less frequently remembered. It is a bantering comment on ignorant articles concerning the American colonies which appeared at about this time in the daily prints : —

" I beg leave to say, that all the articles of news that seem improbable are not mere inventions. The very tails of the American sheep are so laden with wool, that each has a little car or wagon on four little wheels, to support and keep it from trailing on the ground. Would they caulk their ships, would they even litter their horses with wool, if it were not both plenty and cheap? And what signifies the dearness of labor when an English shilling passes for five-and-twenty? Their engaging three hundred silk throwsters here in one week for New York was treated as a fable, because, forsooth, they have 'no silk there to throw.' Those, who make this objection, perhaps do not know, that, at the same time the agents from the King of Spain were at Quebec to contract for one thousand pieces of cannon to be made there for the fortification of Mexico, and at New York engaging the usual supply of woollen floor carpets for their West India houses, other agents from the Emperor of China were at Boston treating about an exchange of raw silk for wool, to be carried in Chinese junks through the Straits of Magellan.

"And yet all this is as certainly true, as the account said to be from Quebec, in all the papers of last week, that the inhabitants of Canada are making preparations for a cod and whale fishery 'this summer in the upper Lakes.' Ignorant people may object, that the upper Lakes are fresh, and that cod and whales are salt water fish ; but let them know, Sir, that cod, like other fish when attacked by their enemies, fly into any water where they can be safest ; that whales, when they have a mind to eat cod, pursue them wherever they fly ; and that the grand leap of the whale in the chase up the Falls of Niagara is esteemed, by all who have seen it, as one of the finest spectacles in nature."

This passage is noteworthy as an early instance of what we now call American humour, — the grave statement, with a sober face, of obviously preposterous nonsense. Though its style is almost Addisonian, its substance is more like what in our own days has given world-wide popularity to Mark Twain.

The character of Franklin is too considerable for adequate treatment in any such space as ours ; but perhaps we have

seen enough to understand how human nature tended to develop in eighteenth-century America, where for a time economic and social pressure was so relaxed. This relaxation,
indeed, is incidentally attested by two stray passages from
Franklin's writings. One is in a letter to his wife from
London, dated the 27th of June, 1760 : —

"The accounts you give me of the marriages of our friends are very
agreeable. I love to hear of everything that tends to increase the
number of good people. You cannot conceive how shamefully the
mode here is a single life. One can scarce be in the company of a
dozen men of circumstance and fortune, but what it is odds that you
find on inquiry eleven of them are single. The great complaint is the
excessive expensiveness of English wives."

The other is from his celebrated examination before the
House of Commons in 1766 : —

"*Q.* What do you think is the reason that the people in America
increase faster than in England?
"*A.* Because they marry younger, and more generally.
"*Q.* Why so?
"*A.* Because any young couple, that are industrious, may easily
obtain land of their own, on which they can raise a family.
"*Q.* Are not the lower ranks of the people more at their ease in
America than in England?
"*A.* They may be so, if they are sober and diligent, as they are
better paid for their labour."

From these very lower ranks Franklin himself sprung. Undoubtedly he was what we call great; his qualities were on a
larger scale than is common anywhere; but the question of
scale does not affect that of character. Devoting himself
with unceasing energy, common-sense, and tact to practical
matters, and never seriously concerning himself with eternity,
he developed into a living example of such rational, kindly
humanity as the philosophy of revolutionary France held attainable by whoever should be freed from the distorting influence of accidental and outworn institutions. In Jonathan
Edwards we found theoretical Puritanism, divorced from life,

proclaiming more uncompromisingly than ever that human nature is damnable. In such temper we find on a grand scale something akin to the petty enthusiasm of our own day, which now and again maintains that whoever takes a glass of wine shall sleep in a drunkard's grave, or that whoever smokes a cigarette shall smoke for it in hell. All the while we see about us godly smokers the better for rational stimulant. And all the while when Edwards was preaching his unflinching Calvinism, Franklin, by living as well and as sensibly as he could, was demonstrating that, at least in America, unaided human nature could develop into an earthly shape which looked quite as far from damnable as that of any Puritan parson.

The America which in the same years bred Jonathan Edwards and Benjamin Franklin bred too the American Revolution.

VII

THE AMERICAN REVOLUTION

LIKE Calvinism, the American Revolution has generally been discussed so passionately that in eagerness to prove one side right historians have hardly been able to consider the questions which arose as matters of mere historic fact. And as Professor Tyler's " Literary History " shows, the tradition of the Revolution which commonly prevails in the United States is a remarkable distortion of a familiar truth. The war which began at Lexington and ended six years later with the surrender of Cornwallis at Yorktown has been talked about in public places and taught about in schools as if it had been a rising against a foreign invader, like the old Spanish wars in the Netherlands, or those more recent wars in which the Austrians were expelled from what is now united Italy. No error could be much graver. Up to 1760 the colonies of America were as loyal to the crown of England as Australia or Canada is to-day. England, of course, was separated from America by the Atlantic Ocean; and, so far as time goes, the North Atlantic of the eighteenth century was wider than the equatorial Pacific is to-day. But the people of the American colonies were as truly compatriots of Englishmen as the citizens of our Southern States in 1860 were compatriots of New England Yankees. The Revolution, in short, was a civil war, like the wars of Cavaliers and Round-heads a century before in England, or the war in our own country between 1861 and 1865. Both of those other civil wars, the older English and the newer American, have already faded into a past where one can feel them, for all their tragedy, to have something of the character of family quarrels which have ended in fresh family concord. What distinguishes the American Revolution from other civil wars is the fact that the quarrel which produced it a century and a quarter ago has never been truly settled or forgotten.

Already in 1780 American feeling toward England had become consciously foreign. Consciously foreign it remains; there are plenty of sensible Americans to-day who really feel less strange in Paris than in London. In modern Boston the unaltered King's Chapel of the royal governors, surrounded by the tombs of colonial worthies, seems almost as much a relic of some mysterious past as the ruins of Stonehenge seem on Salisbury Plain. Yet one has but to land at Halifax to see a surviving image of what Boston was in 1775; Canada to-day is English in the sense in which Boston was English when George III. ascended the throne. The political frontier which divides Canada from New England, however, remains as distinct as it was when Canada was French; for New England now is not English but American. The American Revolution was a civil war whereof the end is not yet, and indeed may never be.

To those Americans who most cherish our deep national ideal of union, this fact has an aspect which may well qualify our just pride of independence. This ideal of union means that, however much men of common race, language, and principles may differ, it is best that they devote their energies to neglecting, or at worst to compromising, their differences, and to working in common for ends in which all believe, trusting that from such common effort better things shall ensue for mankind. It needs no great effort of imagination, and as time passes it will probably need less and less, to see that this ideal of union applies as fully to the events of 1776 as to those of 1861. Had the Southern States succeeded in their heroic attempt at secession, our country to-day, whatever its condition, must have been politically so weak as to make impossible the imperial questions now affecting our politics. If the American colonies had failed in their heroic attempt to assert independence of England, there can be little question that by this time the imperial dominance of our language, our law, and our ideals would be assured throughout the world. The American Revolution, then, disuniting the English-speaking race, has had on history an effect which those who cherish the moral and political heritage of our language may well grow to feel in some sense tragic.

To modern scholars of the critical kind, too, the Revolution is becoming more of a puzzle than it used to be. The distortion of tradition which has represented it rather as a war against an alien invader than as a civil war, is not our only popular error. American writings, in general, tell only one side of the story ; and we have been accustomed to accept their *ex parte*, though sincere, assertions as comprehensive. So much is this the case that few remember the origin of a phrase which from a political letter written by Rufus Choate in 1856 has passed into idiomatic use. This phrase, " glittering generality," is commonly used of empty rhetoric : Mr. Choate used it of a piece of rhetoric which American tradition is apt to believe the least empty in our history. His words were : " The glittering and sounding generalities of natural right which make up the Declaration of Independence." Now, to describe the Declaration of Independence as a tissue of glittering generalities is by no means to tell its whole story; but so to describe it is probably as near the truth as to accept it for a sober statement of historic fact. Not that Jefferson, who wrote it, or his compatriots who signed it, were insincere ; the chances are that they believed what they said. But the fact that in a moment of high passion a man believes a thing does not make it true. And when under the cool scrutiny of posterity fervid convictions prove somewhat mistaken, the vital question is from what they arose.

Professor Tyler collects and arranges as never before

material which may help one to hazard an answer to this question. Although in pure literature the Revolution has left no more permanent record than was left by the century and a half which came before, it was almost as fruitful of publication bearing on contemporary fact as were those Civil Wars of England which resulted in the execution of King Charles I. and the momentary dominance of Cromwell's Puritanism. Professor Tyler is a thoroughly patriotic American citizen; this does not prevent him from setting forth with full sympathy a fact which any one who reads the long-neglected writings of the American loyalists must be brought to acknowledge. Right or wrong, these loyalists were sincerely patriotic, too, and willing, when the crucial moment came, to sacrifice fortune and home to the principles which they held as devoutly as ever revolutionist held his. What is more, as one considers to-day the arguments of the loyalists, it is hard to feel them legally weaker than those which finally prevailed. Rather one begins to feel that the two sides misunderstood one another more profoundly than has yet been realised. They used the same terms, but they assumed them to mean widely different things.

Take, for example, one of the best-remembered phrases of the period, — " no taxation without representation." What does this really mean ? To the American mind of to-day, as to the mind of the revolutionary leaders in King George's colonies, it means that no constituency should be taxed by a legislative body to which it has not actually elected representatives, generally resident within its limits. To the English mind of 1770, more than sixty years before the first Reform Bill, it meant something very different. In England to this day, indeed, the notion that a representative should be resident in his constituency is as strange as to any American it is familiar. Not only was this the case in eighteenth-century England, but many boroughs which returned members to Parliament had hardly any residents; while some of the chief cities in the kingdom returned no members at all. In King

George's England, we see, the question of representation had little to do with actual suffrage. What no taxation without representation meant there, was that no British subject should be taxed by a body where there was not somebody to represent his case. This view, the traditional one of the English Common Law, was held by the loyalists of America. When the revolutionists complained that America elected no representatives to Parliament, the loyalists answered that neither did many of the most populous towns in the mother country ; that the interests of those towns were perfectly well cared for by members elected elsewhere ; and that if anybody should inquire what members of Parliament were protecting the interests of the American colonies, the answer would instantly satisfy any complaint. This contention is really strong. Among the men who defended the American cause in the House of Commons were the elder Pitt, Fox, and Burke. It is doubtful whether New England or Virginia could have exported to Parliament representatives in any respect superior.

But the argument of the American loyalists — Tories, we have called them for the last century or so, but a truer name were Imperial Unionists — had no effect on the revolutionists, — patriots, Imperial Secessionists. The course of the equally sincere arguments of this party may be typified in two brief extracts from the utterances of one of their first heroes, — James Otis. In February, 1761, having resigned the office of Advocate-General because he would not support an application to the Superior Court for writs of assistance, he appeared against them, and among other things spoke as follows : —

"I shall not think much of my pains in this cause, as I engaged in it from principle. I was solicited to argue this cause as advocate-general ; and because I would not, I have been charged with desertion from my office. To this charge I can give a very sufficient answer. I renounced that office, and I argue this cause, from the same principle ; and I argue it with the greater pleasure, as it is in favour of British liberty, at a time when we hear the greatest monarch upon earth declaring from his throne that he glories in the name of Briton, and that the privileges of his people are dearer to him than the most valuable prerogatives of his crown; and as it is in opposition to a kind of power, the exercise of which, in former periods of English history, cost one king of England his head, and another his throne. . . . The writ prayed for in this petition, being general, is illegal. . . .

"Let us see what authority there is for it. Not more than one instance can be found in all our law books; and that was in the zenith of arbitrary power, namely, in the reign of Charles II., when star-chamber powers were pushed to extremity by some ignorant clerk of the exchequer. But had this writ been in any book whatsoever, it would have been illegal. All precedents are under control of the principles of law. Lord Talbot says it is better to observe these than any precedents. . . . No acts of Parliament can establish such a writ. . . . An act against the constitution is void."

Otis, in short, a trained lawyer, argued this case on grounds of strict legal precedent. A year later this same James Otis published a pamphlet entitled "The Vindication of the House of Representatives," wherein the basis of his argument is as remote from Common Law temper as it is agreeable to the abstract philosophy of Revolutionary France: —

"1. God made all men naturally equal. 2. The ideas of earthly superiority, pre-eminence, and grandeur are educational; — at least acquired, not innate. 3. Kings were, — and plantation governors should be, — made for the good of the people, and not the people for them. 4. No government has a right to make hobby-horses, asses, and slaves of the subjects, nature having made sufficient of the two former, . . . but none of the last, — which infallibly proves they are unnecessary. 5. Though most governments are 'de facto' arbitrary, and consequently the curse and scandal of human nature, yet none are 'de jure' arbitrary."

The latter of these utterances by Otis is doubtless the more characteristic of our revolutionary temper, and perhaps of what has since been the native temper of America. In the former case his argument, like that of any sound lawyer, is concerned with the question of what the law is; in the latter, his argument is concerned with a very different question, extremely foreign to the legal traditions of England, — namely, what the law ought to be. At least in New England, one

can see why the latter kind of reasoning proved so agreeable
to general sentiment. A century and a half of incessant
theological discussion had made the native Yankee mind far
more accessible to moral arguments than to legal. By the
middle of the eighteenth century, then, native Americans
were more affected by general principles than were the native
English.

Again, as the Great Awakening of 1740 showed, the
American temper of revolutionary times was more explosive
than the English, just as American temper remains to-day.
No living creature, to be sure, is more tenacious of rights than
an Englishman, but until you meddle with him he is not very
apt to trouble himself about what you say. To this day, on the
other hand, Americans get highly excited about mere phrases
with which they happen not to agree. So it was in the last
days of British dominion here. At the time of the Stamp
Act the house of Thomas Hutchinson, Lieutenant-Governor
of Massachusetts, and a thoroughly patriotic New Englander,
was sacked by a mob; and his library and collection of historical papers were destroyed as ruthlessly as were his mirrors
and his furniture. In 1764 the house of Martin Howard, a
Tory gentleman of Newport, who had ventured to answer
the pamphlets of James Otis, was similarly destroyed. In
1775 Samuel Seabury, afterwards the ancestral bishop of the
Protestant Episcopal Church of the United States, was subjected, together with his family, to a brutal mob violence,
which only stopped short of outrage and murder. He was
believed to be the author of some strong loyalist arguments
signed "A Westchester Farmer;" and though he was an
admirably devoted parish priest, nothing could protect him,
an advocate of unpopular principles, from the explosive
violence of the Connecticut mob. By 1775, in short, the
misunderstanding between the temper of native America and
that of the mother country had got beyond the point of
argument.

The fact that Seabury was a clergyman of the Church of England, though it had little to do with his uncomfortable experience, recalls a half-forgotten phase of New England temper which freshly illustrates this honest international misunderstanding of what seem the simplest terms.[1] As is well known, no clergyman of the Church of England can receive orders except at the hands of a bishop. In the American colonies there were no bishops. Any American who desired to become a clergyman of what is now our Episcopal Church, then, was compelled to go abroad for ordination. Chiefly to avert this hardship, certain churchmen, both in England and in America, began a movement for the establishment of bishoprics in the American colonies. Whoever has followed the history of Anglican episcopacy from the time of Charles II. onward will feel pretty sure that such bishoprics would have had no more political effect than have those of our present Episcopal Church. In colonial times, however, even among Americans of high intelligence, the mere word " bishop " revived in pristine fervour not only all the hatred, but all the dread which had been excited in the minds of the ancestral Puritans by the persecutions of Laud. An innocent desire that devout American Episcopalians might obtain holy orders without crossing the Atlantic was honestly regarded by hundreds of other Americans as an effort to impose upon the religious freedom of the colonies the absolute domination of an intolerant and persecuting established Church. At least in ecclesiastical matters, the instinctive temper of revolutionary Americans remained surprisingly like that of their immigrant ancestors born under Queen Elizabeth.

The American Revolution, we begin to see, which resulted in imperial disunion, sprang from a deep temperamental misunderstanding between the native English and their American

[1] This line of thought was suggested by the thesis for which Dr. Cross was awarded the degree of Ph.D. and the Toppan Prize at Harvard University in 1899.

compatriots. Of this symptoms may be found on all sides.
Professor Tyler shows, more definitely than has ever been
shown before, what extraordinary power of political pamphleteering developed here during the revolutionary period. In the
contemporary England, of course, there was plenty of such
pamphleteering. Those masterpieces which were signed by
the name of Junius were hardly a dozen years old; and Dr.
Johnson himself was, among other things, a writer of political
pamphlets. In native English literature, however, the most
salient period of political pamphleteering is probably the reign
of Queen Anne, when, to go no further, so much of the
work of Arbuthnot, of Defoe, and of the masterly Swift took
this form. If one looks further back, too, one may find England flooded with political pamphlets during the civil wars of
Cavaliers and Roundheads. The political pamphlets of revolutionary America, of course, like the impassioned outbursts
of Otis and of Patrick Henry and of the other orators whose
names are preserved in our manuals of patriotic elocution,
were phrased in the style of the eighteenth century. Whatever their phrasing, nevertheless, these pamphlets indicate in
our country a kind of intellectual activity which in England
had displayed itself most characteristically a hundred years
earlier. More and more, one begins to think, the secret of
the American Revolution may be found in the fact that while
under the influence of European conditions the English temperament had steadily altered from that of spontaneous, enthusiastic, versatile Elizabethans to that of stubborn, robust
John Bull, the original American temper, born under Elizabeth
herself, had never deeply changed.

What the difference was, to be sure, may long remain a
matter of dispute; but before the end of the eighteenth century, native Americans had begun to feel it. Francis Hopkinson, a remarkably vivacious and spirited writer, was among
the first to specify the fact. A Philadelphia gentleman
born in 1737, he saw something of good society in England

between 1766 and 1768. He was a signer of the Declaration of Independence; and he died United States District Judge for Pennsylvania in 1791. His only familiar work is his satirical poem, "The Battle of the Kegs;" but his writings in general are entertaining; and in the posthumous collection of his works is a passage, apparently written during the revolutionary period, which shows beyond question that he felt as distinctly as people feel to-day how different the temperaments of England and of America had become: —

"This infatuated [English] people have wearied the world for these hundred years with loud eulogiums upon liberty and their constitution; and yet they see that constitution languishing in a deep decay without making any effort for its recovery. Amused with trifles, and accustomed to venality and corruption, they are not alarmed at the consequences of their supineness. They love to talk of their glorious constitution because the idea is agreeable, and they are satisfied with the idea; and they honour their king, because it is the fashion to honour the king. . . .

"The extreme ignorance of the common people of this civilised country can scarce be credited. In general they know nothing beyond the particular branch of business which their parents or the parish happened to choose for them. This, indeed, they practise with unremitting diligence; but never think of extending their knowledge farther.

"A manufacturer has been brought up a maker of pin-heads; he has been at this business forty years and, of course, makes pin-heads with great dexterity; but he cannot make a whole pin for his life. He thinks it is the perfection of human nature to make pin-heads. He leaves other matters to inferior abilities. It is enough for him that he believes in the Athanasian creed, reverences the splendour of the court, and makes pin-heads. This he conceives to be the sum-total of religion, politics and trade. He is sure that London is the finest city in the world; Blackfriars Bridge the most superb of all possible bridges; and the river Thames, the largest river in (the) universe. It is vain to tell him that there are many rivers in America, in comparison of which the Thames is but a ditch; that there are single provinces there larger than all England; and that the colonies formerly belonging to Great Britain, now independent states, are vastly more extensive than England, Wales, Scotland and Ireland, taken all together — he cannot conceive this. He goes into his best parlour, and looks on a map of England, four feet square; on the other side of the room he sees a map of North and South America,

8

not more than two feet square, and exclaims;—'How can these things be? It is altogether impossible.' He has read the Arabian Nights' Entertainment, and he hears this wonderful account of America;— he believes the one as much as the other. . . .

"It is not so in America. The lowest tradesman there is not without some degree of general knowledge. They turn their heads to everything; their situation obliges them to do so. A farmer there cannot run to an artist upon every trifling occasion. He must make and mend and contrive for himself. This I observed in my travels through that country. In many towns and in every city they have public libraries. Not a tradesman but will find time to read. He acquires knowledge imperceptibly. He is amused with voyages and travels and becomes acquainted with the geography, customs, and commerce of other countries. He reads political disquisitions and learns the great outlines of his rights as a man and as a citizen. He dips a little into philosophy, and knows that the apparent motion of the sun is occasioned by the real motion of the earth. In a word, he is sure that, notwithstanding the determination of the king, lords, and commons to the contrary, two and two can never make five.

"Such are the people of England, and such the people of America."

It is worth while to compare with this sketch of Hopkinson's a passage concerning Americans written a little later by a Frenchman, named Crèvecœur, who resided near New York from 1754 to 1780:—

"What then is the American, this new man? He is either a European or a descendant of a European, hence that strange mixture of blood, which you will find in no other country. I could point out to you a family whose grandfather was an Englishman, whose wife was Dutch, whose son married a French woman, and whose present four sons have now four wives of different nations. *He* is an American, who leaving behind him all his ancient prejudices and manners, receives new ones from the new mode of life he has embraced, the new government he obeys, the new rank he holds. He becomes an American by being received in the broad lap of our great Alma Mater.

"Here individuals of all nations are melted into a new race of men, whose labours and posterity will one day cause great changes in the world. Americans are the western pilgrims, who are carrying along with them that great mass of arts, sciences, vigour, and industry which began long since in the East; they will finish the great circle. The Americans were once scattered all over Europe; here they are incorporated into one of the finest systems of population which has ever appeared, and which hereafter will become distinct by the power of the different climates they inhabit. The American is a new man, who acts upon new principles ; he must therefore entertain new ideas, and form new opinions. From involuntary idleness, servile dependence, penury, and useless labour, he has passed to toils of a very different nature, rewarded by ample subsistence. — This is an American."

The contrast between these two passages is sharp. Hopkinson's American is, after all, a human being ; Crèvecœur's American is no more human than some ideal savage of Voltaire ; and yet, in Crèvecœur's time and since, it has been the fashion to suppose that the French understand us better than our true brothers, the English.

For this there is a certain ground. Englishmen are not accessible to general ideas ; and they are not explosive. The French are both ; and so, like the subjects of Queen Elizabeth, are the native Americans. Since 1775, then, America has often seemed more nearly at one with France than with England. Suggestive evidence of a deeper truth may be found in the career of the national hero whom the French cherish in common with ourselves, — Lafayette. Stirred by enthusiasm for the rights of man, he offered his sword to those rebellious colonies whom he believed to be fighting for mere abstract principles ; and he had warrant for his belief, in the glittering generalities of the Declaration of Independence. He saw our Revolution triumphant. He went back to France, and saw the Revolution there end in tragic failure. To the last he could never guess why the abstract principles which had worked so admirably in America would not work in France. The real truth he never perceived. Whatever reasons the revolutionary Americans gave for their conduct, their underlying impulse was one which they had inherited unchanged from their immigrant ancestors ; namely, that the rights for which men should die are not abstract but legal. The abstract phrases of the American Revolution, deeply as they have affected the surface of American thought, remain superficial. By 1775, however, the course of American history had made our conception of legal rights different from that of the English. We had developed local traditions of our own, which we believed as immemorial as ever were the local traditions of the mother country. The question of representation, for example, was not abstract; it was one of established constitutional practice; but when we came to discussing it, we did not understand each other's terms. Misunderstanding followed, a family quarrel, a civil war, and world disunion. Beneath this world disunion, all the while, is a deeper fact, binding America and England at last together at heart, — each really and truly believed itself to be asserting the rights which immemorial custom had sanctioned. Revolutionary France, on the other hand, tried to introduce into human history a system of abstract rights different from anything which ever flourished under the sun. Naturally it came to grief. And Lafayette, who never even in his dreams suspected the force and vitality of that Common Law tradition which is instinctively cherished by every English-speaking race, never understood what either revolution really signified.

Slight, vague, and cursory as our consideration has been, we can now perhaps begin to see what the American Revolution means. By 1775, the national experience which had been accumulating in England from the days of Queen Elizabeth had brought the temper of the native English to a state very remote from what this native temper had been under the Tudor sovereigns. In that same year the lack of economic pressure to which we have given the name of national inexperience had kept the original American temper singularly unaltered. When at last, on the accession of George III., legal and constitutional questions were presented in the same terms to English-speaking temperaments on different sides of the Atlantic, these temperaments had been forced, by mere historic circumstance, so far apart that they honestly could not understand each other. Neither of them, then, would have been true to the deepest traditions of their common race, had anything less than the Revolution resulted.

VIII

LITERATURE IN AMERICA FROM 1776 TO 1800

THE first six chapters of Mr. Henry Adams's "History of the United States" admirably set forth the stagnation of mental life in America between the close of the Revolution and the beginning of the nineteenth century. For half a generation or more our newly independent country was adrift; the true course of our national life was slow in declaring itself. Until the very end of the eighteenth century, then, we remained without trace of lasting literature. But just as in earlier periods there had been writing which a study like ours cannot quite neglect, so during the last quarter of this eighteenth century there was a good deal of publication at which we must glance.

One fact is instantly salient. No one who has written of our literary expression during the period in question has made much distinction between public men and those who for courtesy's sake may be styled pure men of letters. It is doubtful whether anything could much more have surprised Washington, or John Adams, or Jefferson, or Madison, or Hamilton, or the rest, than to find themselves discussed in the literary history of their country much as their eminent contemporary Dr. Johnson is discussed in the literary history of England. Without doubt, however, the father of our country, together with that eminent band of political obstetricians who cooperated at its birth, not only displayed practical skill, but also wrote memorably about the matters which engaged their attention. So, for want of any memorable literature during our early years of independence, our literary historians have been glad to treat our elder public men as men of letters too.

In this the historians have been right. During the last quarter of the eighteenth century our public men wrote in admirable style. They were earnestly thoughtful; they had strong common sense; they were far-sighted and temperate; and they expressed themselves with that dignified urbanity which in their time marked the English of educated people. In purely literary history, however, they can hardly be regarded as much more important than Blackstone is in the literary history of England.

This kind of American writing reached its acme in 1787 and 1788, when Hamilton, Madison, and John Jay supported the still unaccepted Constitution of the United States in a remarkable series of political essays, named the "Federalist." As a series of formal essays, the "Federalist" groups itself roughly with the "Tatler," the "Spectator," and those numerous descendants of theirs which fill the literary records of eighteenth-century England. It differs, however, from all these, in both substance and purpose. The "Tatler," the "Spectator," and their successors dealt with superficial matters in a spirit of literary amenity: the "Federalist" deals, in an argumentative spirit as earnest as that of any Puritan divine, with political principles paramount in our history; and it is so wisely thoughtful that one may almost declare it the permanent basis of sound thinking concerning American constitutional law. Like all the educated writing of the eighteenth century, too, it is phrased with a rhythmical balance and urbane polish which give it claim to literary distinction. After all, however, one can hardly feel it much more significant in a history of pure letters than are the opinions in which a little later Judge Marshall and Judge Story developed and expounded the constitutional law which the "Federalist" commented on. Its true character appears when we remember the most important thing published in England during the same years, — the poetry of Robert Burns. The contrast between Burns and the "Federalist" tells the whole literary story. Just as in the seventeenth century the only serious literature of America was a phase of that half-historical, half-theological sort of work which had been a minor part of English literature generations before; so in the eighteenth century the chief product of American literature was an extremely ripe example of such political pamphleteering as in England had been a minor phase of letters during the period of Queen Anne. Pure letters in America were still to come.

Even during the seventeenth century, however, as we saw in our glance at the "Tenth Muse," Mrs. Anne Bradstreet, there had been in America sporadic and consciously imitative efforts to produce something literary. So there were during the eighteenth century. We had sundry writers of aphoristic verse remotely following the tradition of Pope; and we had satire, modelled on that of Charles Churchill, a popular contemporary writer, now remembered mostly because some of our ancestors paid him the compliment of imitation. Toward the end of the eighteenth century, however, a little group of clever and enthusiastic men made a serious attempt to establish a native literature; and though the results of this effort were neither excellent nor permanent, the effort was earnest and characteristic enough to deserve attention.

To understand its place in our literary records we must recall something of our intellectual history. This may be said to have begun with the foundation of Harvard College as a seminary of scholarly tradition in 1636. Throughout the seventeenth century, Harvard, then the only school of the higher learning in America, remained the only organised centre of American intellectual life. Cotton Mather, we remember, was a Harvard graduate, a member of the Board of Overseers and of the Corporation, and an eager aspirant for the presidency of the college. Long before his busy life was ended, however, the tendency toward liberalism which has remained characteristic of Harvard had swerved it from the old Puritan tradition; and Yale College, the stronghold of New England orthodoxy, had consequently been established in New Haven. It was from Yale that Jonathan Edwards emerged. The fact that the centre of American intellectual life was no longer on the shores of Boston Bay was again attested by the career of Franklin, who, though born in Boston, lived mostly in what during his time was the principal city of America,— Philadelphia. In what we said of the " Federalist," too, the same trend was implied. Boston bred revolutionary worthies, of course : James Otis was a Massachusetts man, so were John and Samuel Adams, so earlier was Thomas Hutchinson, so later was Fisher Ames. But of the chief writers of the " Federalist," Hamilton and Jay were from New York; and Madison was one of that great school of Virginia public men which included Patrick Henry and Jefferson and Washington, and Marshall, and many more. In the American perspective of the eighteenth century, Eastern Massachusetts does not loom so large in the foreground as Massachusetts tradition would have us believe.

It is not surprising, then, that the highest literary activity of the later eighteenth century in America had its origin at Yale College. The most eminent of the men of letters then developed there was Timothy Dwight, a grandson of Jonathan Edwards. He took his degree in 1769, and remained a tutor at Yale until 1777. He then became for a year a chaplain in the Continental Army. While tutor at Yale he co-operated with his colleague, John Trumbull, in the production of some conventional essays modelled on the "Spectator." While chaplain in the army he wrote a popular song entitled "Columbia." Of this the last of its six stanzas is a sufficient example; the last couplet repeats the opening words of the poem : —

> "Thus, as down a lone valley, with cedars o'erspread,
> From war's dread confusion I pensively strayed —

The gloom from the face of fair heaven retired;
The winds ceased to murmur; the thunders expired;
Perfumes, as of Eden, flowed sweetly along,
And a voice, as of angels, enchantingly sung;
' Columbia, Columbia, to glory arise,
The queen of the world, and the child of the skies.' "

In 1783 Dwight became minister of Greenfield, Connecticut. In 1795 he was made President of Yale College, an office which he held to his death in 1817; and certainly until the time of President Woolsey his name was the most distinguished in the academic annals of Yale. As President, he wrote his posthumously published " Travels in New England and New York," which record experiences during a number of summer journeys and remain an authority on the condition of those regions during his time. He did some sound work in theology too; but by this time Calvinistic theology belongs apart from pure letters even in America. In 1788, however, he expressed some of his ecclesiastical views in a poem entitled " The Triumph of Infidelity," of which one passage is well worth our notice.

To appreciate what it means we must again glance for a moment at Boston. Here for a century the pulpits had been steadily tending toward liberalism. Among the chief churches of Boston was, and remains, King's Chapel, the official place of worship of the royal governors, who were generally members of the Church of England. At the time of the Revolution the ministers of this communion, whose ordination vows bound them to personal allegiance just as firmly as to the thirty-nine articles, generally emigrated. So in 1785 King's Chapel found itself in charge of an excellent native divine named James Freeman, who was not in formal communion with the English Church. For legal reasons, said to be connected with endowments, it was essential that the services of King's Chapel should be conducted in accordance with the Anglican liturgy; but in view of the new state of sovereignty in America this liturgy obviously required amendment. Dr. Freeman took occasion to amend it pretty radically. In the liturgy which has been employed at King's Chapel from his time to our own, although the general form of the episcopal service is preserved rather more nearly than the episcopal service preserves that of the Church of Rome, there is occasional avoidance of the Holy Ghost. In consequence, the publication of the King's Chapel liturgy has sometimes been held the beginning of the Unitarian movement in New England. Certainly, too, along with this insistence on the unity of God, as distinguished from the mysteries of Trinity, Dr. Freeman's teaching tended to agree with that which has since been fashionable in Boston, by emphasising the more amiable as distinguished from the more terrible aspects of Deity. As we shall see later, the theology of nineteenth-century Massachusetts has occupied itself in so thickly freezing over the Calvinistic hell that to this day those who slide about on its surface, particularly in the neighbourhood of Harvard College, are disposed to deny that there were ever any brimstone fires at all.

To the orthodoxy of Yale this tendency was abhorrent; and Dwight's "Triumph of Infidelity" thus attacks the type of ecclesiastic who was to develop into such eminent spiritual leaders as Channing, Emerson, and Phillips Brooks:—

> "There smiled the smooth Divine, unused to wound
> The sinner's heart, with hell's alarming sound.
> No terrors on his gentle tongue attend;
> No grating truths the nicest ear offend.
> That strange new-birth, that methodistic grace,
> Nor in his heart nor sermons found a place.
> Plato's fine tales he clumsily retold,
> Trite, fireside, moral seesaws, dull as old;
> His Christ and Bible placed at good remove,
> Guilt hell-deserving, and forgiving love.
> 'T was best he said, mankind should cease to sin:
> Good fame required it: so did peace within.
> Their honours, well he knew, would ne'er be driven;
> But hoped they still would please to go to heaven.
> Each week he paid his visitation dues;
> Coaxed, jested, laughed; rehearsed the private news;

> Smoked with each goody, thought her cheese excelled;
> Her pipe he lighted, and her baby held.
> Or placed in some great town, with lacquered shoes,
> Trim wig, and trimmer gown, and glistening hose,
> He bowed, talked politics, learned manners mild ;
> Most meekly questioned, and most smoothly smiled ;
> At rich men's jests laughed loud, their stories praised ;
> Their wives' new patterns gazed, and gazed, and gazed ;
> Most daintily on pampered turkeys dined ;
> Nor shrunk with fasting nor with study pined ;
> Yet from their churches saw his brethren driven,
> Who thundered truth, and spoke the voice of heaven,
> Chilled trembling guilt, in Satan's headlong path,
> Charmed the feet back, and roused the ear of death.
> ' Let fools,' he cried ' starve on, while prudent I
> Snug in my nest shall live, and snug shall die.' ''

Good sound eighteenth-century satire this of Dwight's, expressing vigorous theologic conservatism, but written, as any one can see, in the traditional manner of the early English eighteenth century, and published in a year signalised in England by a collected edition of the poems of Burns. American literature still lagged behind that of the mother country. Dwight also wrote a poem called "Greenfield Hill," of which the name is remembered. It is long, tedious, formal, and turgid; but it indicates, like the good President's travels, that he was touched by a sense of the beauties of nature in his native country.

Toward the end of the century the literary group of which President Dwight is the most memorable figure developed into a recognised little company, designated as the " Hartford Wits ; " for most of them, though graduates of Yale, lived at one time or another in the old capital of colonial Connecticut. In Stedman and Hutchinson's " Library of American Literature " a special section is given to these " Hartford Wits," of whom the chief are said to have been : John Trumbull, Lemuel Hopkins, David Humphreys, Joel Barlow, Theodore Dwight, M. F. Cogswell, and E. H. Smith. Of these names only two, those of Trumbull and Barlow, now survive even in tradition.

Trumbull was on the whole the more important. He was two years older than President Dwight, and graduated at Yale in 1767, two years before him. In 1769 he co-operated with him in publishing that series of essays in the manner of the "Spectator." From 1771 to 1773 he was a tutor at Yale; afterwards he practised law in New Haven and in Boston; and in 1781 he went to Hartford, where he remained as lawyer and later as Judge of the Superior Court until 1819. From 1825 until his death in 1831 he lived at Detroit in Michigan. Trumbull's principal works are two long poems in the manner of "Hudibras." The first, entitled the "Progress of Dulness," and written between 1772 and 1774, satirises the state of clerical education in a manner of which the following extract will give a sufficient example : —

> " Our hero's wit and learning now may
> Be proved by token of diploma,
> Of that diploma, which with speed
> He learns to construe and to read;
> And stalks abroad with conscious stride,
> In all the airs of pedant pride,
> With passport signed for wit and knowledge
> And current under seal of college.
> Few months now past, he sees with pain
> His purse as empty as his brain;
> His father leaves him then to fate,
> And throws him off, as useless weight;
> But gives him good advice, to teach
> A school at first, and then to preach.
> Thou reason'st well; it must be so;
> For nothing else thy son can do.
> As thieves of old, t' avoid the halter,
> Took refuge in the holy altar,
> Oft dulness flying from disgrace
> Finds safety in that sacred place;
> There boldly rears his head, or rests
> Secure from ridicule or jests;
> Where dreaded satire may not dare
> Offend his wig's extremest hair;
> Where scripture sanctifies his strains,
> And reverence hides the want of brains."

Trumbull's other Hudibrastic work is a mock epic entitled
" M'Fingal," written between 1774 and 1782, which satirises
the follies of his countrymen, particularly of the Tory persua-
sion. The poem had great popularity; it is said to have
passed through more than thirty editions. A taste of it may
be had from the following description of how M'Fingal, a
caricatured Tory, was punished by a patriot mob for cutting
down a Liberty pole : —

> " Forthwith the crowd proceed to deck
> With halter'd noose M'Fingal's neck,
> While he in peril of his soul
> Stood tied half-hanging to the pole;
> Then lifting high the ponderous jar,
> Pour'd o'er his head the smoking tar.
> With less profusion once was spread
> Oil on the Jewish monarch's head,
> That down his beard and vestments ran,
> And covered all his outward man.
> As when (so Claudian sings) the Gods
> And earth-born Giants fell at odds,
> The stout Enceladus in malice
> Tore mountains up to throw at Pallas;
> And while he held them o'er his head,
> The river, from their fountains fed,
> Pour'd down his back its copious tide,
> And wore its channels in his hide :
> So from the high-raised urn the torrents
> Spread down his side their various currents;
> His flowing wig, as next the brim,
> First met and drank the sable stream;
> Adown his visage stern and grave
> Roll'd and adhered the viscid wave;
> With arms depending as he stood,
> Each cup capacious holds the flood;
> From nose and chin's remotest end
> The tarry icicles descend;
> Till all o'erspread, with colors gay,
> He glittered to the western ray,
> Like sleet-bound trees in wintry skies,
> Or Lapland idol carved in ice.
> And now the feather-bag display'd
> Is waved in triumph o'er his head,

> And clouds him o'er with feathers missive,
> And down upon the tar, adhesive :
> Not Maia's son, with wings for ears,
> Such plumage round his visage wears,
> Nor Milton's six-wing'd angel gathers
> Such superfluity of feathers.
> Now all complete appears our Squire,
> Like Gorgon or Chimæra dire ;
> Nor more could boast on Plato's plan
> To rank among the race of man,
> Or prove his claim to human nature,
> As a two-legg'd unfeather'd creature."

Now, clearly, this is not " Hudibras," any more than John Trumbull, the respectable and scholarly Connecticut lawyer of the closing eighteenth century, was Samuel Butler, the prototype of Grub Street in Restoration London.   Most historians of American literature who have touched on Trumbull have accordingly devoted themselves to emphasising the difference between " M'Fingal " and " Hudibras."   For our purposes the likeness between the poems seems more significant. Butler died, poor and neglected, in 1680 ; Trumbull was prosperously alive one hundred and fifty years later; and yet an intelligent reader might easily mistake many verses of the latter for verses of the former.   Trumbull's are less clever, more decent, and doubtless distinguishable in various more profound ways; but the two poems are so much alike as to indicate in the cleverest American satirist of the closing eighteenth century a temper essentially like that of the cleverest English satirist of a century before.   Butler was born less than ten years after Queen Elizabeth died, and Trumbull only ten years before the accession of King George III.   It is hardly unreasonable to find in these facts a fresh indication of how nearly the native temper of America remained like that of the first immigration.

Joel Barlow, the other Hartford Wit who is still faintly remembered, was rather more erratic.   He was born in 1754. While a Yale undergraduate he served in the Continental

Army, in which he was afterward a chaplain, from 1780 to 1783. In 1786 he became a lawyer at Hartford, where he was later the editor of a weekly newspaper; and in 1787 he published an epic poem entitled "The Vision of Columbus," which by 1807 had been elaborated into "The Columbiad." Here is a bit of it:—

> "Based on its rock of Right your empire lies,
>   On walls of wisdom let the fabric rise;
>   Preserve your principles, their force unfold,
>   Let nations prove them and let kings behold.
>   EQUALITY, your first firm-grounded stand;
>   Then FREE ELECTION ; then your FEDERAL BAND;
>   This holy Triad should forever shine
>   The great compendium of all rights divine,
>   Creed of all schools, whence youths by millions draw
>   Their themes of right, their decalogues of law;
>   Till men shall wonder (in these codes inured)
>   How wars were made, how tyrants were endured."

Even in its first form this turgid epic, which few mortals now living have more than glanced at, was the most ambitious attempt at serious literature which had appeared in the United States. To this day, furthermore, a quarto edition of "The Columbiad" is among the most impressive books to look at in the world. It brought Barlow political influence. He went abroad, first as a sort of business agent, and had something to do with politics in both France and England. From 1795 to 1797 he was United States Consul at Algiers. From 1797 to 1805 he lived in Paris; from 1805 to 1811 in Washington. In 1811 he was made United States minister to France, in which character he journeyed to meet Napoleon in Russia; becoming involved in the retreat from Moscow, he died from exhaustion at a Polish village on Christmas Eve, 1812.

Though "The Columbiad" was Barlow's most serious work, his most agreeable was a comic poem entitled "The Hasty Pudding." This, written while he was abroad in 1793, is a humorous lament that Europe lacks a delicacy of the table which, with the Atlantic between them, he remembered tenderly. A few lines will sufficiently exemplify his rather heavy humour : —

> " There is a choice in spoons.   Though small appear
> The nice distinction, yet to me 't is clear,
> The deep bowl'd Gallic spoon, contrived to scoop
> In ample draughts the thin diluted soup,
> Performs not well in those substantial things,
> Whose mass adhesive to the metal clings;
> Where the strong labial muscles must embrace,
> The gentle curve and sweep the hollow space.
> With ease to enter and discharge the freight,
> A bowl less concave, but still more dilate,
> Becomes the pudding best.   The shape, the size,
> A secret rests, unknown to vulgar eyes.
> Experienced feeders can alone impart
> A rule so much above the lore of art.
> These tuneful lips that thousand spoons have tried,
> With just precision could the point decide.
> Though not in song; the muse but poorly shines
> In cones, in cubes, and geometric lines;
> Yet the true form, as near as she can tell,
> Is that small section of a goose egg shell,
> Which in two equal portions shall divide
> The distance from the centre to the side.
> Fear not to slaver; 't is no deadly sin : —
> Like the free Frenchman, from your joyous chin
> Suspend the ready napkin; or like me,
> Poise with one hand your bowl upon your knee;
> Just in the zenith your wise head project,
> Your full spoon, rising in a line direct,
> Bold as a bucket, heed no drops that fall,
> The wide mouth'd bowl will surely catch them all ! "

Such was Barlow at his best.   The other Hartford Wits may be judged by an extract from " The Political Green-house," written by Alsop, Theodore Dwight, and Hopkins, in 1799; they apostrophised Bonaparte as follows : —

> " Ambitious Chief ! in dust laid low,
> Behold the honours of thy brow,

The laurels culled on Egypt's shore
Shall wither ere the day be o'er;
Thy armies thinned, reduced thy force,
Fell ruin waits thine onward course,
While of thy country's aid bereft,
No safety but in flight is left,
And victory's self but seals thy doom,
And brings thee nearer to the tomb.
I see destruction wing her way,
I see the eagles mark their prey,
Where pent in Cairo's putrid wall,
In heaps thy dying soldiers fall;
Or, mid the desert's burning waste,
Smote by the Samiel's fiery blast;
Or pressed by fierce Arabian bands,
With thirst they perish on the sands.
While Bonaparte's dreaded name
Shall shine a beacon's warning flame,
To point to times of future date
Unprincipled ambition's fate."

Certainly prophetic of what twelve or fifteen years later befell Napoleon, who at this time was just beginning his imperial career, this extract, together with those which we have considered from Dwight, Trumbull, and Barlow, may suffice to exemplify the first literary efflorescence of our country; and a good Harvard man, not free from some of the prejudices which are the price of a Harvard education, lately remarked in speaking of the Hartford Wits that they represent the only considerable efflorescence of Yale. Perhaps they do; and very clearly they contribute nothing memorable to the wisdom of the eternities. The answer which was made to that complacent Harvard man is nevertheless true: at the time when the Hartford Wits wrote, no Harvard man had produced literature half so good as theirs. They made an intensely spirited effort, serious in purpose even if sometimes light in form, to create in our new country a literature which should assert national independence as surely as that independence had been asserted in politics. The result was patriotic,

9

it was not without humour, it had all sorts of qualities of which one may speak respectfully; and they did their very best. This best, however, proved thoroughly imitative, and at the same time full of indications that its writers lacked that peculiar fusion of thought and feeling which made English character in the eighteenth century such as could fitly be expressed by the kind of literature which the Hartford Wits so courageously attempted. An heroic, patriotic effort they stand for, and one made with enthusiasm, wit, and courage. Nobody can fairly hold them to blame for the fact that their America still lacked national experience ripe for expression in a form which should be distinctive.

Contemporary with the Hartford Wits was a much less eminent man, until lately almost forgotten, whose memory is now beginning to revive. In one or two of his poems, it now seems probable, we can find more literary merit than in any other work produced in America before the nineteenth century. His name was Philip Freneau. Of French-Huguenot descent, the son of a New York wine merchant, he was born in that city on the 2d of January, 1752. He was educated at Princeton, and having taken to the sea, was captured by the British during the Revolution and passed some time on a prison ship near New York. After the Revolution he resumed his mercantile career. In 1791 he became the editor of a very radical newspaper in Philadelphia. In 1798 he took to the sea again; and the rest of his life has no significance for us. He died in New Jersey in 1832.

Freneau was a man of strong feeling, ardently in sympathy with the Revolution, and intensely democratic. As a journalist, then, he was a sharp and bitter opponent of any attempt on the part either of England or of the more prudent class in his own country to assert authority; and a considerable part of his poetry, of which he supervised at least four separate editions between 1786 and 1815, consists of rather reckless satire, not conspicuously better or worse than much other satire of the period. Our bare outline of his life, however, which omits many details, — for one thing, he resided for a while in the West Indies, where he was much stirred by the horrors of slavery, — indicates one characteristic fact. The son of a New York man of business, educated at a thoroughly respectable college, he became both a practical sailor and a journalist. Now, in George III.'s England a man who was either scholar, sailor, or journalist was apt to be nothing else; but in America to this day such a career as Freneau's remains far from unusual. Far from unusual, too, it would have been in the England of Queen Elizabeth, — of which probably the most typical personage was Walter Ralegh, soldier, sailor, statesman, adventurer, chemist, historian, coloniser, poet, and a dozen things else. Ralegh's career was one of unsurpassed magnificence; Freneau's in comparison seems petty. In both, however, one can see the common fact that a man whose life was intensely and variously busy found himself instinctively stirred to poetic expression.

The greater part of Freneau's poetry, to be sure, was occasional. On his satires we have touched already. Here is an example of his patriotic verse: —

> "At Eutaw Springs the valiant died:
>   Their limbs with dust are covered o'er;
> Weep on, ye springs, your tearful tide;
>   How many heroes are no more!

Here is another, from a poem " On Barney's Victory over the Ship ' General Monk ' " : —

> "Lo! I see their van appearing —
>   Back our top-sails to the mast!
> They toward us full are steering
>   With a gentle western blast:
> I 've a list of all their cargoes,
>   All their guns, and all their men:
> I am sure these modern Argo's
>   Can't escape us one in ten:

> " Yonder comes the Charming Sally
>   Sailing with the General Greene —
> First we 'll fight the Hyder Ally,
>   Taking her is taking them :
> She intends to give us battle,
>   Bearing down with all her sail —
> Now, boys, let our cannon rattle !
>   To take her we cannot fail."

However interesting such verse may be historically, it is not of the kind which rises above the dust of the centuries. Now and then, however, Freneau struck a note different from this, and different on the whole from any which had previously been sounded in America. His most generally recognised poem is that on " The Indian Burying-Ground," to which attention has been called by the fact that Thomas Campbell, in " O'Connor's Child," stole one of its lines. Campbell's verse runs as follows : —

> " Bright as the bow that spans the storm,
>   In Erin's vesture clad,
> A son of light, a lovely form,
>   He comes and makes her glad.
> Now on the grass-green turf he sits,
>   His tasselled horn beside him laid ;
> Now o'er the hills in chase he flits —
>   The hunter and the deer — a shade."

Freneau's poem is worth quoting in full : —

> " In spite of all the learned have said,
>   I still my old opinion keep ;
> The posture that we give the dead
>   Points out the soul's eternal sleep.

> " Not so the ancients of these lands ; —
>   The Indian, when from life released,
> Again is seated with his friends,
>   And shares again the joyous feast.

> " His imaged birds, and painted bowl,
>   And venison, for a journey dressed,
> Bespeak the nature of the soul,
>   Activity, that wants no rest.

" His bow for action ready bent,
　　And arrows, with a head of stone,
Can only mean that life is spent,
　　And not the old ideas gone.

" Thou, stranger, that shalt come this way,
　　No fraud upon the dead commit, —
Observe the swelling turf, and say,
　　They do not *lie*, but here they *sit*.

" Here still a lofty rock remains,
　　On which the curious eye may trace
(Now wasted half by wearing rains)
　　The fancies of a ruder race.

" Here still an aged elm aspires,
　　Beneath whose far projecting shade
(And which the shepherd still admires)
　　The children of the forest played.

" There oft a restless Indian queen
　　(Pale Shebah with her braided hair)
And many a barbarous form is seen
　　To chide the man that lingers there.

" By midnight moons, o'er moistening dews,
　　In habit for the chase arrayed,
The hunter still the deer pursues,
　　The hunter and the deer — a shade !

" And long shall timorous Fancy see
　　The painted chief and pointed spear.
And Reason's self shall bow the knee
　　To shadows and delusions here."

In the genuineness and simplicity of these verses, there is true beauty. In the opening thought, that it were better for the alert dead to sit than to lie drowsing, — that *Hic sedet* were a better epitaph than *Hic jacet*, — there is something really imaginative. And in the pensive melancholy with which Freneau records the rock-tracings of the vanished natives of America, there is likeness to the motive of a poem which twelve years before Freneau died permanently enriched English literature. This is John Keats's " Ode to a Grecian Urn," published in 1820 : —

> " Heard melodies are sweet, but those unheard
> Are sweeter; therefore, ye soft pipes, play on;
> Not to the sensual ear, but, more endear'd,
> Pipe to the spirit ditties of no tone :
> Fair youth, beneath the trees, thou canst not leave
> Thy song, nor ever can those trees be bare;
> Bold Lover, never, never canst thou kiss,
> Though winning near the goal — yet, do not grieve;
> She cannot fade, though thou hast not thy bliss,
> For ever wilt thou love, and she be fair ! "

Here, of course, is no such plagiarism as that of Campbell, who stole a whole line of Freneau's; no such plagiarism, either, as that of Sir Walter Scott, who stole another ; nor yet such as that still more unprincipled one which Professor Tyler records, where an English lady printed as her own a poem of Freneau in full. It may fairly be doubted whether Keats ever saw a line of Freneau's, or ever heard his name. The contrast between Freneau's " Indian Burying-Ground " and Keats's " Grecian Urn " is worth our attention only because both poets had a similar motive. Freneau expressed it simply, directly, and even beautifully ; Keats expressed it immortally. The contrast is one between good literature and great, between the very best that America had produced in the closing years of the eighteenth century and one of the many excellent things which England produced during the first twenty years of the century that followed. Taken by itself, " The Indian Burying-Ground " may fairly excite our patriotic enthusiasm to an excessive degree ; a comparison with the " Grecian Urn " may recall our patriotism to the limits of common-sense.

The literature produced in this country between the outbreak of the American Revolution and the close of the eighteenth century may fairly be typified, if not precisely summarised, by what we have glanced at, — the writings of those orators and public men who reached their highest expression in the " Federalist," the conscious and imitative effort of the Hartford Wits, and the sporadic poetry of Philip Freneau.

IX

SUMMARY

WE have now glanced at the literary history of America during the first two centuries of American existence. In the seventeenth century, the century of immigration, when Americans felt themselves truly to be emigrant Englishmen, they expressed themselves only in such theological and historical work as may be typified by the " Magnalia " of Cotton Mather. During the eighteenth century, the century of independence, when Americans felt themselves still Englishmen, but with no personal ties to England, America produced in literature a theology which ran to metaphysical extremes, such vigorous common sense as one finds in the varied works of Franklin, and such writings as we have glanced at since. These two centuries added to English literature the names of Shakspere, Milton, Dryden, Swift, Addison, Pope, Johnson, and Burns. To match these names in America we can find none more eminent than those of Cotton Mather, Edwards, Franklin, the writers of the " Federalist," the Hartford Wits, and Freneau. As we have seen, the history of England during these two centuries was that of a steadily developing and increasing national experience. In comparison, the history of America reveals national inexperience. There is no need for further emphasis on the commonplace that lack of experience does not favour literary or artistic expression.

BOOK III

THE NINETEENTH CENTURY

BOOK III

THE NINETEENTH CENTURY

I

ENGLISH HISTORY SINCE 1800

In 1800 King George III., who had been forty years on the throne, was lapsing into that melancholy madness in which his sixty years of royalty closed. The last ten years of his reign were virtually part of his successor's, the Prince Regent, afterward George IV. In 1830 King William IV. succeeded his brother; his reign lasted only seven years. Since 1837 the sovereign of England has been Queen Victoria. During the nineteenth century, then, only three English sovereigns came to the throne. It chances that each of these represents a distinct phase of English history.

The Regency, under which general name we may for the moment include also the reign of George IV., was the time when the insular isolation of England was most pronounced. In 1798 Nelson won the battle of the Nile. No incident more definitely marks the international position of England as the chief conservative defender of such traditions as for a while seemed fatally threatened by the French Revolution becoming incarnate in Napoleon. During the first fifteen years of the nineteenth century the conflict persisted, more and more isolating England and emphasising English conservatism. In 1805, Trafalgar, which finally destroyed the sea power of Napoleon, made the English Channel more than ever a frontier separating England from the rest of Europe.

It was not until ten years later, in 1815, that Waterloo, finally overthrowing Napoleon, made room for the reaction which overran continental Europe for thirty years to come; and only then could England begin to relax that insularity which the Napoleonic wars had so developed in English temper.   England is the only country of civilised Europe where Napoleon never succeeded in planting his power; only English soil remained free from his invasion; and during the first part of the nineteenth century the price which England paid for this freedom was an unprecedented concentration of her own life within her own bounds.   This era of dogged resistance to the French Revolution finally developed the traditional type of John Bull.

To suppose that England remained unmoved by revolutionary fervour, however, would be a complete mistake.   Two years after William IV. ascended the throne, there occurred in English politics an incident as revolutionary as any which ever took place in France.   The results of it have long since altered the whole nature of English life, social and political. Although revolutionary in purpose, however, and in ultimate effect rather more successfully revolutionary than any convulsion of continental Europe, the Reform Bill of 1832 was carried through in England by formally constitutional means. This Bill permanently altered the theory and practice of suffrage in England, establishing the broadly democratic principle that representation in the House of Commons shall be apportioned to the population.   To the conservative temper of the time nothing could have been more abhorrent than parliamentary reform.   The fact that under the old system the House of Commons had worked admirably seemed reason enough why there should be no change; the principles on which reform was urged involved something like recognition of those abstract rights which even to the present day remain foreign to the most characteristic temper of England.   Undoubtedly the consequent opposition of the better classes was

blindly prejudiced. The reformed Parliaments, newly reformed more than once since 1832, have worked far better
than the opponents of reform expected; but in the minds of
many competent judges it is still an open question whether as
agents of government they have worked so well as the Parliaments which came before. The old system, where a great
gentleman often carried half a dozen boroughs in his pocket,
made it easy to find a seat in the House for any young man
of promise; to go no further, it was to this system that we
owe the parliamentary career of Burke. There can be little
doubt that with the progress of democratic temper in England
the House of Commons has tended personally to deteriorate.
No doubt there are aspects in which the new system seems
more just than the old; but there are aspects, too, in which
the old seems to have been the safer. Such speculations as
this, however, are fruitless; the Reform Bill is a fact; and the
thing for us to remark about it is that this virtual revolution
in England was accomplished constitutionally. In brief, what
happened was this. The House of Lords, the more conservative chamber of Parliament, was unprepared to pass the
Reform Bill; the House of Commons, representing, it believed,
the ardent conviction of the country, was determined that the
Bill should be passed. Thereupon the King was persuaded
to inform the Lords that in case they persisted in voting
against the measure he should create new peers enough to
make a majority of the House. This threat brought the conservative peers to terms. They did not vote for the measure,
but under the leadership of the Duke of Wellington they
walked out of the house in silent protest. A revolutionary
threat on the part of the King had accomplished under constitutional forms a peaceful revolution.

Five years later King William IV. was dead. Then began
the reign of the most tenderly human sovereign in English
history. For sixty-two years, in the full blaze of public life,
she has unfalteringly done what she has deemed her duty.

This devoted conscientiousness has strengthened English royalty beyond words. Through sixty years of growing democracy the fact that the throne of England has been filled by Queen Victoria has gone far to re-establish in popular esteem a form of government which it is the fashion to call a thing of the past.

In general this Victorian era has been peaceful, but still one which is best typified by the newest title of its sovereign. For during the last sixty years of the nineteenth century England has been quietly asserting itself no longer as an isolated kingdom, but as a world-empire. This imperialism of England seems different from any other which has declared itself since the pristine empire of Rome. It stands not for the assertion of central and despotic authority, but rather for the maintenance of those legal traditions which evince the elasticity of still unbroken vitality. For, speaking broadly, the English Common Law is a system, not of rules, but of principles. Its fundamental notion is that the world should be governed by established custom. So long as its influence was confined to the island where it was developed, to be sure, it still seemed impracticably rigid. The American Revolution, however, taught England a lesson which has been thoroughly learned, — that when English authority asserts itself in foreign regions, the true spirit of the Common Law should recognise and maintain all local customs which do not conflict with public good. In India, for example, local custom sanctioned many things essentially abominable, — murder, self-immolation, and the like. Such crimes against civilisation the English power has condemned and repressed. Harmless local custom, on the other hand, — freedom of worship, peculiarities of land tenure, and whatever harmonises with public order, — the English government has maintained as strenuously as in England itself it has maintained the customs peculiar to the mother country. So in Canada it has maintained a hundred forms of old French law ancestral to those provinces. So in

Australia it has maintained many new systems and customs which have grown up in a colony settled since the American Revolution. Its modern state is typified by the fact that in the judicial committee of the Privy Council — whose functions resemble those of the Supreme Court of the United States — there are now regularly members from Canada, from India, from Australia, to pronounce in this court of appeal on questions referred to the mother country from parts of the empire where the actual law differs from that of England herself.

The Victorian epoch, then, has begun to explain the true spirit of the English law : whatever the letter, this spirit maintains that throughout the empire, and all the places where the imperial influence extends, the whole force of England shall sustain the differing rights and traditions which have proved themselves, for the regions where they have grown, sound, safe, and favourable to civilised prosperity. The growing flexibility of English government has tended to make dominant in many parts of the world the language and the ideals which we share with England. The progress of imperial England, then, frequently misrepresented, as though it were mere selfish aggression, is really a phase of a world-conflict which the acceleration of intercommunication — steam travel and the electric telegraph — has at last made inevitable. Beyond doubt war is terrible; one of our own generals in the Civil War is said to have declared that " War is Hell." At least to the traditional American mind, however, hell hardly yet presents itself as a thing which unaided human ingenuity can certainly avoid ; and when war means that the progress of the moral, legal, and political ideals which we share with England either must be checked or must dominate by armed force, minds loyal to our ancestral traditions may fairly begin to question whether tame peace is not worse still.

Historically, then, England began the century as an isolated conservative power. In the reign of King William IV. it underwent a revolution which its ancestral legal forms proved strong and flexible enough to accomplish without convulsion or bloodshed ; and during the long reign of Queen Victoria it has been more and more widely asserting the imperial dominion of the flexibly vital traditions of our Common Law.

ENGLISH LITERATURE SINCE 1800

So we come to the literature of England during the nineteenth century. By chance several dates which we have named for other purposes are significant in literary history as well as in political. In 1798, when Nelson fought the battle of the Nile, Wordsworth and Coleridge published their famous volume of "Lyrical Ballads." This little book is commonly regarded as the first important expression of that romantic outburst of poetry which substituted for the formal literary traditions of the eighteenth century those traditions of individual artistic freedom which have persisted until the present time. In brief, the literary emancipation of England, amid blind political conservatism, was almost as marked as the literary conservatism of France, amid revolutionary political changes. The spirit of revolution was everywhere abroad; but in England it more profoundly influenced phrase than conduct, while in France the case was just the reverse. In 1832, the year of the Reform Bill, Scott died; Byron, Shelley, and Keats were already dead; so was Miss Austen; and every literary reputation contemporary with theirs was finally established.

Broadly speaking, the period of English literature which began with the "Lyrical Ballads" and ended with the death of Scott may be divided at 1815, the year of Waterloo. The chief expression which preceded this was a passionate outburst of romantic poetry, maintaining in widely various forms the revolutionary principle that the individual, freed from accidental and conventional trammels, may be trusted to tend toward righteousness; that human nature is not essentially evil but excellent; and that sin, evil, and pain are brought into being

by those distortions of such human nature which are wrought
by hampering, outworn custom and superstition. Though this
philosophy may never have been precisely or fully set forth
by any one of the English poets who flourished between
1800 and 1815, it pervades the work of all ; and this work
taken together is the most memorable body of poetry in our
language, except the Elizabethan. So far as one can now tell,
this school distinguishes itself from the Elizabethan, and from
almost any other of equal merit in literary history, by the
eclectic variety of its individual members ; their passionate
devotion to the ideal of freedom in both thought and phrase
made these new poets differ from one another almost as conspicuously as the poets of the eighteenth century were alike.
For all this, as one reads them now, a trait common throughout their work grows salient. Despite the fervour of their
revolutionary individualism, Wordsworth and Coleridge and
Byron and Shelley and the rest agreed in eagerly looking forward to an enfranchised future in which this world was to be
incalculably better and nobler than in the tyrant-ridden past.
This was the dominant sentiment of English literature from
the battle of the Nile to that of Waterloo.

Between Waterloo and the Reform Bill, which was passed
in the year when Scott died, a new phase of feeling dominated
the literature of England. Though something of this elder
spirit of hope lingered, the most considerable fact was the
publication of all but the first two of the Waverley Novels.
The contrast between these and the preceding poetry is strongly
marked. What gave them popularity and has assured them
permanence is the fervour with which they retrospectively assert the beauty of ideals which even in their own time had
almost vanished. If the first outburst of English literature in
the nineteenth century was a poetry animated by aspiration
toward an ideal future, the second period of that literature,
embodied in the novels of Sir Walter Scott, dwelt in carelessly
dignified prose on the nobler aspects of a real past.

These two phases of English literature roughly correspond with the Regency and the reign of William IV. The literature which has ensued will probably be known to the future as Victorian; and it is still too near us for any confident generalisation. But although there has been admirable Victorian poetry, of which the most eminent makers seem to have been Tennyson and the Brownings; and although in its own time serious Victorian prose, of which perhaps the most eminent makers were Ruskin and Carlyle, has seemed of paramount interest, — there is probability that posterity may find the most characteristic feature of Victorian literature to have been that school of fiction which brought the English novel to a point of development comparable with that of the Elizabethan drama. It is almost literally to the reign of Queen Victoria that we owe the work of Dickens, Thackeray, George Eliot, and the numberless lesser novelists and story-tellers whose work has been the chief reading of the English-speaking world, down to the days of Stevenson and Rudyard Kipling.

The first and the most widely popular of Victorian novelists was Dickens, whose work began less than five years after Scott's ended. The contrast between them is among the most instructive in literary history. Scott's ideal was always that of a gentleman; Dickens's, with equal instinctive honesty of feeling, was that of the small trading classes. Whatever merits Dickens had, and these were great and lasting, he fatally lacked one grace which up to his time the literature of his country had generally preserved, — that of distinction. The other novelists who soon arose differed from Dickens in many ways, often possessing a sense of fact far more true than his, and sympathies more various. At least in their comparative lack of distinction, however, they have been more like him than like the men of letters of any preceding period. They have generally dealt, too, with matters of nearly contemporary fact. In brief, the dominant note of Victorian fiction, which is probably the dominant fact of Victorian literature, is a note of triumphant democracy.

Broadly speaking, then, we may say that up to the time of the Reform Bill the English literature of the nineteenth century expressed itself first in that body of aspiring poetry which seems the most memorable English utterance since Elizabethan times, and secondly in those novels of Sir Walter Scott, which, dealing romantically with the past, indicate the accomplishment of a world revolution; and that since the Reform Bill decidedly the most popular phase of English literature has been prose fiction dealing with contemporary life. It is beyond our purpose to emphasise the growth of science meanwhile, a growth which has corresponded with such material changes as are typified by the use of steam and electricity. But many now think that in time to come the most lasting name of the Victorian epoch will, after all, be that of Charles Darwin.

Slight as this sketch of English literature in the nineteenth century has been, it is sufficient for our purpose, which is only to remind ourselves of what occurred in England during the century when something which we may fairly call literature developed in America.

III

AMERICAN HISTORY SINCE 1800

MR. HENRY ADAMS shows how amid the constant growth of democracy, amid practical assertion of the power which resides in the uneducated classes, and which our Constitution made conscious, our national life began with bewildering confusion. To the better classes, embodied in the old Federalist party, this seemed anarchical; the election of Mr. Jefferson they honestly believed to portend the final overthrow of law and order. Instead of that, one can see now, it really started our permanent progress. Among the early incidents of this progress was the purchase of Louisiana, which finally established the fact that the United States were to dominate the North American continent. So complete, indeed, has our occupation of this continent become that it is hard to remember how in 1800 the United States, at least so far as they were settled, were almost comprised between the Alleghanies and the Atlantic. In less than one hundred years we have colonised, and to a considerable degree civilised, the vast territory now under our undisputed control; and the fact that the regions which we have colonised have chanced to be contiguous to the regions which were first under our sovereignty has only concealed without altering the truth that the United States have proved themselves the most successful colonising power in modern history.[1]

Our colonial growth, or expansion, — call it what you will, — began with the purchase of Louisiana. Nine years later,

[1] See an article by Mr. A. Lawrence Lowell in the "Atlantic" for February, 1899.

under President Madison, came that second war with England which, while unimportant in English history, was very important in ours. The War of 1812 asserted our independent nationality, our ability to maintain ourselves against a foreign enemy, and, above all, our fighting power on the sea, of which fresh evidence was given during the brief but crucial war with Spain in 1898. The War of 1812, besides, the only foreign war in our history except this recent Spanish one, did much to revive and strengthen the Revolutionary conviction of our essential alienation from England. Before that war broke out there were times when it seemed almost as likely to arise with France. It was an incident, we can now see, of that death-grapple wherein England was maintaining against continental Europe incarnate in Napoleon those traditions of Common Law which we share with her. America had felt the arbitrary insolence of Napoleon, as well as that of England; neutrality proved impossible. We chanced to take the French side. Thereby, whatever we gained, — and surely our strengthened national integrity is no small blessing, — we certainly emphasised and prolonged that misunderstanding with the mother country which still keeps disunited the two peoples who preserve the Common Law.

The next critical fact in our history was the assertion in 1823 of the Monroe Doctrine. In brief, this declares that the American continent is no longer a region where foreign powers may freely colonise; that from the Arctic Ocean to Cape Horn American soil is as fully controlled by established governments as is Europe itself; that the chief political power in America is the United States; and that any attempt on the part of a foreign power to establish colonies in America, or to interfere with the governments already established there, will be regarded by the United States as an unfriendly act. This virtual declaration of imperial dominance in a whole hemisphere has generally been respected. Except for the transitory empire of Maximilian in Mexico, established during the most troublous period of our Civil War by that filibustering French emperor who deliberately embodied continental as distinguished from English ideals, the integrity of the American continent has remained unthreatened since President Monroe's famous message.

During the next thirty-five years developed that inevitable national disunion which culminated in the Civil War of 1861. The economic and social systems of North and of South were radically different: generation by generation they naturally bred men less and less able to understand each other. As we shall see later, the Southern temper lagged behind the Northern somewhat as for two centuries the native temper of America lagged behind that of England. The Southerners of the fifties were far more like their revolutionary ancestors than were the Northerners. General Washington and General Lee, for example, have many more points of resemblance than have President Washington and President Lincoln; and Lee was really as typically Southern in his time as Lincoln in those same days was typically Northern. The Civil War involved deep moral questions, concerning the institution of slavery and national union; but at last we can begin to see that it was a moral struggle on both sides. So the generation now in its prime, to whom the Civil War is a matter not of experience but of history, is coming to understand that what ultimately makes it so superbly heroic a tradition is the fact that on both sides men ardently gave their lives for what they believed to be the truth. The conflict was truly irrepressible; social and economic conditions had developed the different parts of our country in ways so different that nothing but force could prevent disunion.

Disunion did not ensue. Instead of it, after a troubled interval, has come a union constantly stronger. Our history since the Civil War is too recent for confident generalisation. Two or three of its features, however, are growing salient. Long before the Civil War certain phases of material prosperity had begun to develop in this country,—the great cotton-growing of the South, for one thing, and for another, the manufactures of New England. Since the Civil War some similar economic facts have produced marked changes in our national equilibrium. One has been the opening of the great lines of transcontinental railway. Along with these has developed the enormous growth of bread-stuffs throughout the West, together with incalculable increase of our mineral wealth. These causes have effected the complete settlement of our national territory. At the close of the Civil War a great part of the country between the Mississippi and California remained virtually unappropriated. At present almost every available acre of it is in private ownership. The Spanish War of 1898, then, indicates something more than the political accidents or intrigues which superficially seemed to cause it. Just as truly as the Revolution or the Civil War, the Spanish War probably marked a critical fact in American history. Our continent is finally settled. Such freedom as our more adventurous spirits used to find in going West they must now find, if at all, in emigrating, like our English cousins, to regions not politically under our control. There they must face a serious question. Shall they submit themselves, in the regions where their active lives must pass, to legal and political systems foreign to their own ; or shall they assert in those regions the legal and political principles which, for all the superficial materialism of their lives, the fact of their ancestral language makes them believe ideal? There is an aspect, which future years may prove profoundly true, wherein what we call imperialism seems a blundering awakening to the consciousness that if our language and our law are to survive, they must survive by unwelcome force of conquest.

So for the first time since the settlement of Virginia and New England we come to a point where the history of England and that of America assume similar aspects. For nearly three centuries the national experience of England and the national inexperience of America have tended steadily to diverge. Our inexperience is fast fading. At the close of our first century of independent existence we find ourselves as a nation unexpectedly and regretfully face to face with the question which during the reign of her present Majesty has been the most important before the mother country. The growth of population during the nineteenth century, the incredible improvement of intercommunication by steam and electricity, and the immense consequent development of trade, are placing before us an unavoidable dilemma. Shall our language, with its ideals of law and of conduct, dominate; or shall it recede and yield to others? This same question presses on England, too. In this final historical fact of common experience there appears some chance of such future union of our ancestral language and ideals as the disuniting influence of three hundred years long placed almost beyond the range of hope.

IV

IT is only during this nineteenth century, as we have seen, that literature in America has advanced to a point where it deserves detached study. By chance its various phases, though not exactly like those of contemporary English literature, fall into chronologic groups very like those which we noted in the literature of the mother country. During the first thirty years of this century the chief development of literature in America took place in the Middle States, centring — as the life of the Middle States tended more and more to centre — in the city of New York. The literary prominence of this region roughly corresponds with those years between 1798 and 1832 which produced the poets of the Regency and the "Waverley Novels." Meanwhile, as we shall see later, New England, which for a century past had been less conspicuous in American intellectual life than at the beginning, was gathering the strength which finally expressed itself in the most important literature hitherto produced in our country. Broadly speaking, this literature was contemporary with the Victorian. In 1837, when her Majesty came to the throne, it was hardly in existence; before 1881, when George Eliot, the third of the great Victorian novelists, died, it was virtually complete. To-day it may be regarded as a thing of the past. What has succeeded it is too recent for historical treatment; at this we shall only glance. For in a study like ours to discuss living men seems more and more to be as far from wisdom as to sensitive temper it must seem from decency. In the chapters to come, then, we shall consider these three literary epochs in turn : first, the prominence of the Middle States; next, the Renaissance of New England; and, finally, what has followed.

BOOK IV

LITERATURE IN THE MIDDLE STATES FROM 1798 to 1857

BOOK IV

LITERATURE IN THE MIDDLE STATES FROM 1798 to 1857

I

CHARLES BROCKDEN BROWN

DURING the last quarter of the eighteenth century the Hartford Wits were far from alone in their vigorously patriotic effort to create a national literature for America. A glance through the pages of Stedman and Hutchinson's " Library of American Literature" will show how considerable in quantity, though not in quality, was the fruitless literary activity of the period. Decidedly before 1800 a great many Americans were trying to write, and were founding on all sides newspapers, magazines, reviews, and the like, usually ephemeral. The numerous printing-presses which thus came into existence began meantime to place at public disposal, for surprisingly low prices, the masterpieces of that English literature which our patriotic men of letters were endeavouring to emulate or to surpass. In New York, a little later, appeared an admirably printed series of British Classics in something like a hundred volumes; and a characteristic example of what occupied the leisure of country printers, whose chief business was to produce weekly newspapers, may be found in a pretty little pocket edition of Boswell's " Life of Johnson," printed in 1824 at Bellows Falls, Vermont.

Among other abortive phases of literary activity during the period of the Hartford Wits, was an effort to create a native American drama. In fact, up to the present time, the Ameri-

can theatre has produced no more permanent work than that
of John Howard Payne, who is remembered only as the
author of " Home, Sweet Home," a song from an otherwise
forgotten opera.   In life, however, Payne was not a solitary
figure; he belonged to the later period of that school of
American theatrical writing whose chief founder is sometimes
said to have been William Dunlap.   Of late years the Dunlap
Society of New York has revived his name and has tried to
revive his plays.   This pious act has succeeded only in justi-
fying the oblivion which long ago overtook writer and work
alike.   Yet in the course of Dunlap's literary career he produced one book worth our attention.   The man himself, son
of an Irish officer who had settled in New Jersey after the
capture of Quebec, was a person whose general character
may be inferred from the fact that, having lost the sight of
his right eye, he devoted himself to the art of painting, in
which he so far succeeded as to become a founder of the
National Academy of Design.   His career as artist and
dramatist was at its height in New York at the beginning of
the nineteenth century.   The work which makes him worth
our momentary attention came a little later; it is his two-
volume book, published in 1815, which remains the principal
authority concerning the life of Charles Brockden Brown.

Dunlap's Life of Brown is unintentionally comic.   It runs
through its two long volumes with never a chapter from
beginning to end; it has neither table of contents nor index;
and the diffuse pomposity of its style may be inferred from the
sentence with which, after above two pages of generalities, he
finally attacks his subject : —

" Brown is one of those names which belongs to so great a portion
of those who descend from English parentage that it ceases to identify
an individual.   Brockden is a happy addition which was derived from
a distant relation."

Incidentally Dunlap introduces such copious extracts from
Brown's writings, and in so confused a way, that except as a

matter of style you would often be at a loss to know which of
the two you were reading. His temper, too, is as far from
critical as that of the Mr. Weems who gave us the story of
Washington and the cherry-tree. For all its faults, however,
Dunlap's book is honestly admiring, affectionately sympathetic,
and artless enough to produce, along with exasperating
bewilderment, a growing sense of the artistic and literary environment from which our first professional man of letters
emerged.

For Brockden Brown, though for years almost forgotten,
was really so memorable that in 1834, when Jared Sparks
began his " Library of American Biography," a Life of Brown
by Prescott, the future historian, deservedly appeared in the
first volume. Charles Brockden Brown was born in Philadelphia, of respectable Quaker parentage, on January 17,
1771. For a while he studied law ; but, finding himself
irresistibly interested in literature, he turned to letters as a
means of support at the age of about twenty-five. Before
1796 he had contributed essays to the " Columbus Magazine."
In 1797 he published a work on marriage and divorce entitled
" The Dialogue of Alcuin." In the following year, — the year
of the " Lyrical Ballads," — he produced his first novel,
" Wieland," which had popular success. Within three years
he had published five other novels. In 1799 he became
editor of the " Monthly Magazine and American Review,"
which lasted only a few months. For five years after 1803
he edited " The Literary Magazine and American Register."
The names of these periodicals, like that of the " Columbus
Magazine " to which he had contributed years before, are
worth mention only because we are always in danger of forget-
ting what weedy crops of such nature had long ago sprung up
and withered in our country. The greater part of Brown's
literary life was passed in New York. He died of consumption on the 22d of February, 1810.

Brown's mature years came during that period, between the

Revolution and the War of 1812, when the nationally independent feeling of America was most acutely conscious. For the first time Europeans were becoming aware that America existed. Native Americans were consequently possessed by an impulse, not yet wholly past, to declare to all mankind, and particularly to Europeans, that Americans are a race of remarkable merit. This impulse — the " American brag " so frequently remarked by foreigners — is clearly evident in the works of Brown; it is more so still in the books which Dunlap and Prescott wrote about him. These biographers were disposed not only to speak of him in such superlative terms as occasionally make one fear lest the American vocabulary may lose the positive degree of adjectives; but also to maintain as his chief claim to eminence that his work, being purely American, must of course be thoroughly original.

The most cursory glance at Brown's English contemporaries should have reminded them that no claim could be much worse founded. During the last ten years of the eighteenth century, English literature was not particularly rich. Among its most conspicuous phases was a kind of darkly romantic novel, which probably reached highest development in the more extravagant work of Germany when Germans were obese and romantic and sentimental. Half a century before, English fiction had produced masterpieces, — " Clarissa Harlowe," for example, " Tom Jones," " Tristram Shandy," and " The Vicar of Wakefield." Between 1790 and 1800 English fiction was in that apparently decadent and really abortive condition manifested by such books as Lewis's " Monk," Mrs. Radcliffe's " Mysteries of Udolpho," and Godwin's more significant " Caleb Williams."

Godwin is partly remembered because of his great influence on Shelley, which resulted in the poet's application to the philosopher's own family of those principles concerning love and marriage which Godwin so coolly set forth. Really, however, the man had power enough to be remembered for himself; deeply influenced by the rationalistic philosophy of the eighteenth century, he devoted himself both in such direct writings as his "Political Justice," and in such medicated fiction as "Caleb Williams," to expounding deeply revolutionary ideas. "Caleb Williams" is a story written to demonstrate how hopelessly the artificial conditions of society and law may distort a normally worthy character. The hero has committed a murder, morally justifiable, but legally a capital crime. To avert the legal consequence of his act, he is driven to a course of deceit and falsehood which finally changes him into an utter villain. We are left to infer that when law and morals happen not to coincide, law is a monstrous evil. Incidentally "Caleb Williams" is written in what is meant to be a thrillingly mysterious style. The crimes and the distortion of character with which it deals are dark and horrible. At least in manner and temper, then, the book has something in common with such sensational, meaningless novels as the "Mysteries of Udolpho," which were then at the height of their popularity.

Though this kind of literature has happily proved abortive, it deeply affected several men properly eminent in English literature. If Shelley had written only such trivial fiction as "Zastrozzi," however, and De Quincey nothing more significant than "Klosterheim," neither name would now be remembered. The masterpiece of this school is probably Mrs. Shelley's deeply imaginative "Frankenstein," published in 1817; its last manifestations in England may perhaps be found among the earlier and more ridiculous works of Bulwer Lytton. Nowadays all this seems so lifelessly antiquated that one is prone to forget how slight were the indications in 1798 that the main current of English letters was so soon to take another and more wholesome direction.

Were there no direct evidence that Brockden Brown was consciously influenced by Godwin, the fact might be inferred

from the discussion of marriage in the " Dialogue of Alcuin,"
from which Dunlap gives copious extracts : —

" Marriage," writes Brown, who is believed to have lived a blameless private life, "is an union founded on free and mutual consent.
It cannot exist without friendship. It cannot exist without personal
fidelity. As soon as the union ceases to be spontaneous, it ceases to
be just. This is the sum. If I were to talk for months I could add
nothing to the completeness of the definition."

Brown's admiration of Godwin might equally be inferred
from the general character of his style; but for their historical
relation we have better authority still. While Dunlap insists
so strongly on Brown's individuality, he actually quotes words
of Brown's which assert that he deliberately made Godwin his
model : —

" What is the nature or merit of my performance ? — When a mental
comparison is made between this and the mass of novels, I am inclined to be pleased with my own production. But when the objects
of comparison are changed, and I revolve the transcendent merits of
' Caleb Williams,' my pleasure is diminished, and is preserved from a
total extinction only by the reflection that this performance is the
first."

The truth is that, at least in his philosophical speculations
and his novels, Brockden Brown, honestly aspiring to prove
America highly civilised, was instinctively true to the American temper of his time in attempting to prove this by conscientious imitation. What he happened to imitate was a
temporarily fashionable phase of stagnant English fiction.
Nothing better marks the difference between English literature
and American in 1798 than that this year produced both the
" Lyrical Ballads " and "Wieland." The former first expressed a new literary spirit in England; the latter, the first
serious work of American letters, was as far from new as
Wordsworth's verses and the " Ancient Mariner " were from
conventional. Beyond doubt one's first impression is that the
novels of Brown are merely imitative.

After a while, however, one begins to feel, beneath his conscientious imitative effort, a touch of something individual. In that epoch-making " Wieland," the hero is a gentleman of Philadelphia, who in the midst of almost ideal happiness is suddenly accosted by a mysterious voice which orders him to put to death his superhumanly perfect wife and children. The mysterious voice, which pursues him through increasing moods of horror, declares itself to be that of God. At last, driven to madness by this appalling command, Wieland obeys it and murders his family. To this point, in spite of confusion and turgidity, the story has power. The end is ludicrously weak; the voice of God turns out to have been merely the trick of a malignant ventriloquist. The triviality of this catastrophe tends to make you feel as if all the preceding horrors had been equally trivial. Really this is not the case. The chapters in which the mind of Wieland is gradually possessed by delusion could have been written only by one who had genuinely felt a sense of what hideously mysterious things may lie beyond human ken. Some such sense as this, in terribly serious form, haunted the imagination of Puritans. In a meretricious form it appears in the work of Poe. In a form alive with beauty it reveals itself throughout the melancholy romances of Hawthorne. In Poe's work and in Hawthorne's, it is handled with something like mastery, and few men of letters have been much further from mastery of their art than Charles Brockden Brown; but the sense of horror which Brown expressed in " Wieland " is genuine. To feel its power you need only compare it with the similar feeling expressed in Lewis's " Monk," in the " Mysteries of Udolpho," or even in " Caleb Williams " itself.

In two of Brown's later novels, " Ormond " and " Arthur Mervyn," there are touches more directly from life which show another kind of power. Among his most poignant personal experiences was the terrible fact of epidemic yellow fever. During a visitation of this scourge Brown was in New York, where he was on intimate terms with one Dr. Smith, a young physician of about his own age. An Italian gentleman, arriving in town with an introduction to Dr. Smith, was taken with the plague and refused lodging in any respectable hotel. Smith found him, terribly ill, in a cheap lodging-house, whence he took him home. There the Italian died; and Smith, who contracted the disease, died too. Brockden Brown was with them all the while; he came to know the pestilence appallingly well. In both " Ormond " and " Arthur Mervyn " there are descriptions of epidemic yellow fever almost as powerful as Defoe's descriptions of the London plague. The passage in " Arthur Mervyn," for example, which describes a yellow fever hospital is hideously vivid: —

"After a time I opened my eyes, and slowly gained some knowledge of my situation. I lay upon a mattress, whose condition proved that an half decayed corpse had recently been dragged from it. The room was large, but it was covered with beds like my own. Between each, there was scarcely the interval of three feet. Each sustained a wretch, whose groans and distortions bespoke the desperateness of his condition. . . .

" You will scarcely believe that, in this scene of horrors, the sound of laughter should be overheard. While the upper rooms of this building are filled with the sick and the dying, the lower apartments are the scenes of carousals and mirth. The wretches who are hired, at enormous wages, to tend the sick and convey away the dead, neglect their duty and consume the cordials, which are provided for the patients, in debauchery and riot. A female visage, bloated with malignity and drunkenness, occasionally looked in. Dying eyes were cast upon her, invoking the boon, perhaps, of a drop of cold water, or her assistance to change a posture which compelled him to behold the ghastly writhings or dreadful *smile* of his neighbour.

" The visitant had left the banquet for a moment, only to see who was dead. If she entered the room, blinking eyes and reeling steps showed her to be totally unqualified for ministering the aid that was needed. Presently she disappeared and others ascended the staircase, a coffin was deposited at the door, the wretch, whose heart still quivered, was seized by rude hands, and dragged along the floor into the passage."

The power, indicated in descriptions like that, of setting his scenes in a vividly real background again distinguishes Brown from his English contemporaries. His characters, meanwhile, are lifelessly conventional. In " Ormond," for example, the villanous seducer who out-Lovelaces Lovelace in a literal Philadelphia is irretrievably " make believe ; " and so is the incredibly spotless Constantia Dudley, who, oddly enough, is said to have impressed Shelley as the most perfect creature of human imagination. There is a funny touch in " Ormond," which brings out as clearly as anything the contrast between Brown's true backgrounds and his tritely fictitious characters. Constantia Dudley, with a blind father on her hands, in the midst of epidemic yellow fever, is persecuted by her seducer at a moment when the total resources of the family amount to about five dollars. Old Mr. Dudley — who incidentally and for no reason has once been a drunkard, but has now recovered every paternal excellence — has travelled all over the world. In the course of his journeys in Italy he has remarked that the people of that country live very well on *polenta*, which is nothing but a mixture of Indian meal and water, resembling the Hasty Pudding so dear to the heart of Joel Barlow. In Philadelphia at that time Indian meal could be purchased very cheaply. With about two dollars and three quarters, then, Constantia procures meal enough to preserve the lives of her father, herself, and their devoted servant for something like three months, thereby triumphantly protecting her virtue from the assaults of wealthy persecution. Now, it is said that these facts concerning the price and the nutritive qualities of Indian meal are as true as were the horrors of yellow fever. Constantia and her father, meanwhile, and the wicked seducer, whose careers were so affected by these statistics, are rather less like anything human than are such marionettes as doubtless delighted the Italian travels of Mr. Dudley.

The veracity of Brown's backgrounds appears again in " Edgar Huntley." The incidents of this story are unimportant, except as they carry a somnambulist into the woods and caves of the Pennsylvanian country. These, despite some theatrically conventional touches, are almost as real as the somnambulist is not. Such incongruities cannot blend harmoniously; Brown's incessant combination of reality in nature with unreality in character produces an effect of bewildering confusion.

Nor is this confusion in Brown's novels wholly a matter of conception. Few writers anywhere seem at first more hopelessly to lack constructive power. Take " Arthur Mervyn," for example : the story begins in the first person; the narrator meets somebody in whose past history he is interested; thereupon the second personage begins to narrate his own past, also in the first person; in the course of this narrative a third character appears, who soon proceeds to begin a third autobiography; and so on. As one who is bewildered by this confusion, however, pauses to unravel it or to wonder what it means, a significant fact presents itself. Whoever tries to write fiction must soon discover one of his most difficult problems to be the choice and maintenance of a definite point of view. To secure one, this device of assuming the first person is as old as the " Odyssey," where Odysseus narrates so many memorable experiences to the king of the Phæacians. In brief, a resort to this world-old device generally indicates a conscious effort to get material into manageable form. Paradoxical as it seems, then, these inextricable tangles of autobiography, which make Brockden Brown's construction appear so formless, probably arose from an impotent sense that form ought to be striven for; and, indeed, when any one of his autobiographic episodes is taken by itself, it will generally be found pretty satisfactory.

When we come to the technical question of style, too, the simple test of reading aloud will show that Brockden Brown's sense of form was unusual. Of course his work shows many of the careless faults inevitable when men write with undue haste; and his vocabulary is certainly turgid;

and consciously trying to write effectively, he often wrote absurdly; but the man's ear was true. In reading any page of his aloud, you will find your voice dwelling where the sense requires it to dwell. Critics have remarked that if you wish to distinguish between the style of Addison and that of Steele, all you need do is to apply a vocal test. Addison's ear was so delicate that you require little art to bring out the emphasis of his periods; Steele wrote more for the eye. In other words, Steele comparatively lacked a trait which Addison and Brockden Brown possessed — an instinctive sense of formal phrasing.

If we regard Brockden Brown only as an imitator, — and as such he is perhaps most significant, — we may instructively remark that the literature of America begins exactly where the pure literature of a normally developed language is apt to leave off. A great literature, originating from the heart of the people, declares itself first in spontaneous songs and ballads and legends; it is apt to end in prose fiction. With laboured prose fiction our American literature begins. The laboured prose fiction of Brown has traits, however, which distinguish it from similar work in England. To begin with, the sense of horror which permeates it is not conventional but genuine. Brockden Brown could instinctively feel, more deeply than almost any native Englishman since the days of Elizabeth, what mystery may lurk just beyond human ken. In the second place, Brown's work, for all its apparent confusion, proves confused chiefly by impotent, futile attempt to assure his point of view by autobiographic device. In the third place he reveals on almost every page an instinctive sense of rhythmical form.

Brown's six novels are rather long, and all hastily written; and in his short, invalid life he never attempted any other form of fiction. As one considers his work, however, one may well incline to guess that if he had confined his attempts to single episodes, — if he had had the originality, in short, to invent the short story, — he might have done work favourably comparable with that of Irving or Poe or even Hawthorne. Brockden Brown, in brief, never stumbled on the one literary form which he might have mastered; pretty clearly that literary form was the sort of romantic short story whose motive is mysterious; and since his time that kind of short story has proved itself the most characteristic phase of native American fiction.

II

THE name of Washington Irving reminds us rather startlingly how short is the real history of American letters. Although he has been dead for a little more than forty years, many people still remember him personally ; and when in 1842 he went as President Tyler's minister to Spain, he passed through an England where Queen Victoria had already been five years on the throne, and he presented his credentials to Queen Isabella II., who, although long exiled from her country, is still a not very old lady in Paris. Yet in one sense this Irving, who has not yet faded from living memory, may be called, more certainly than Brockden Brown, the first American man of letters. At least, he was the first whose work has remained popular ; and the first, too, who was born after the Revolution had made native Americans no longer British subjects but citizens of the United States. His parents, to be sure, were foreign, his father Scotch, his mother English ; but he himself was born in New York in 1783. He was not very strong; his early habits were rather desultory and his education irregular ; he studied law and was admitted to the bar, but never practised much; and at the age of twenty-one he was sent abroad for his health. There he remained two years.

His distinctly American character first becomes salient during this trip abroad, at that time an unusual experience. He was of simple origin ; his family were in respectable trade. Born in England, he might have been as accomplished and agreeable as he ever became, but he could hardly have been received on equal terms by the polite society of Europe. Going abroad, as an American citizen, however, he took from the beginning a social position there which he maintained to the end. He was cordially received by people of rank, and incidentally had little to do with those of the station which would have been his had his family never emigrated to this side of the Atlantic. He was among the first, in short, of that distinguished body of Americans, of whom later examples are such men as Ticknor, Everett, Sumner, Motley, and Lowell, who have proved during the nineteenth century the social dignity of American letters.

In 1806, Irving returned home; the next year, in company with one or two kinsmen, he began writing a series of essays called the "Salmagundi Papers." Only his subsequent eminence has preserved from blameless oblivion these conventional survivals of the eighteenth century. About this time occurred an episode which deeply influenced his whole life: he fell in love with a young girl whose death at seventeen almost broke his heart. When she died he was at her bedside; and throughout his later life he could not bear to hear her name mentioned. The tender melancholy which one recognises all through his writings was probably due to this bereavement; and the intense simplicity and faithfulness of his pure and ideal love is characteristic not only of the man but of his country.

In 1809 he published his first considerable book, — the "Knickerbocker History of New York." Shortly thereafter he devoted himself to business; and in 1815 he went abroad in connection with his affairs. There, after a few years, commercial misfortune overtook him. In 1819 he brought out his "Sketch Book;" from that time forth he was a professional man of letters. He remained abroad until 1832, spending the years between 1826 and 1829 in Spain, and those between 1829 and 1832 as Secretary to the American Legation in London. Coming home, he resided for ten years at Tarrytown on the Hudson, in that house " Sunnyside " which has become associated with his name. From 1842 to 1846 he was Minister to Spain. He then finally returned home, crowning his literary work with his " Life of Washington," of which the last volume appeared in the year of his death, 1859.

Irving was the first American man of letters to attract wide attention abroad. The " Knickerbocker History " was favourably received by contemporary England; and the " Sketch Book " and " Bracebridge Hall," which followed it, were from the beginning what they have remained, — as popular in England as they have been in his native country. The same, on the whole, is true of his writings about Spain; and, to somewhat slighter degree, of his " Life of Goldsmith " and his " Life of Washington." The four general classes of work here mentioned followed one another in fairly distinct succession through his half-century of literary life. We may perhaps get our clearest notion of him by considering them in turn.

The " Knickerbocker History of New York " has properly lasted. The origin of this book resembles that of Fielding's " Joseph Andrews " some seventy years before, and of Dickens's " Pickwick Papers " some twenty-five years later. All three began as burlesques and ended as independent works of fiction, retaining of their origin little more trace than occasional extravagance. In 1807 one Dr. Samuel Latham Mitchill had published " A Picture of New York," said to be ridiculous, even among works of its time, for ponderous pretentiousness. The book had such success, however, that Irving and his brother were moved to write a parody of it. Before long Irving's brother tired of the work, which was left to Irving himself. As he wrote on, his style and purpose underwent a change. Instead of burlesquing Mitchill, he found himself composing a comic history of old New York, and incidentally introducing a good deal of personal and polit-

ical satire, now as forgotten as that which lies neglected in
" Gulliver's Travels." His style, which began in deliberately
ponderous imitation of Dr. Mitchill's, passed almost insensibly
into one of considerable freedom, evidently modelled on that
of eighteenth-century England. Most of the book, then,
reads like some skilful bit of English writing during the generation which preceded the American Revolution. The
substance of the book, however, is distinctly different from
what was then usual in England.

Assuming throughout the character of Diedrich Knickerbocker, an eccentric old bachelor who typifies the decaying
Dutch families of New York, Irving mingles with many actual
facts of colonial history all manner of unbridled extravagance.
The governors and certain other of his personages are historical; the wars with New Englanders are historical wars; and
historical, too, is the profound distaste for Yankee character
which Washington Irving needed no assumed personality to
feel. But throughout the book there mingles with these historical facts the wildest sort of sportive nonsense. Wouter
Van Twiller, to take a casual example, was an authentic Dutch
governor of New Amsterdam; and here is the way in which
Irving writes about him : —

"In his council he presided with great state and solemnity. He
sat in a huge chair of solid oak, hewn in the celebrated forest of the
Hague, fabricated by an experienced timmerman of Amsterdam, and
curiously carved about the arms and feet, into exact imitations of
gigantic eagle's claws. Instead of a sceptre he swayed a long Turkish pipe, wrought with jasmin and amber, which had been presented
to a stadtholder of Holland, at the conclusion of a treaty with one of
the petty Barbary powers. In this stately chair would he sit, and
this magnificent pipe would he smoke, shaking his right knee with
constant motion, and fixing his eye for hours together upon a little
print of Amsterdam, which hung in a black frame against the opposite wall of the council chamber. Nay, it has even been said that
when any deliberation of extraordinary length and intricacy was on the
carpet, the renowned Wouter would shut his eyes for full two hours
at a time, that he might not be disturbed by external objects — and at
such times the internal commotion of his mind was evinced by certain

regular guttural sounds, which his admirers declared were merely the noise of conflict, made by his contending doubts and opinions."

More than possibly the chair here mentioned was some real chair which Irving had seen and in which an old Dutch governor might have sat. Conceivably the Turkish pipe may have been at least legendarily true. The rest of the passage is utter extravagance; yet you will be at a little pains to say just where fact passes nonsense.

Though this kind of humour is not unprecedented, one thing about it is worth attention. When we were considering the work of Franklin, we found in his letter to a London newspaper concerning the state of the American colonies a grave mixture of fact and nonsense, remarkably like the American humour of our later days. In Irving's "Knickerbocker History" one finds something very similar. The fun of the thing lies in frequent and often imperceptible lapses from sense to nonsense and back again. Something of the same kind, expressed in a far less gracious manner than Irving's, underlies Mark Twain's comic work and that of our latest journalistic humourist, Mr. Dooley. This deliberate confusion of sense and nonsense, in short, proves generally characteristic of American humour; and although the formal amenity of Irving's style often makes him seem rather an imitator of the eighteenth-century English writers than a native American, one can feel that if the "Knickerbocker History" and Franklin's letter could be reduced to algebraic formulæ, these formulæ would pretty nearly coincide both with one another and with that of the "Innocents Abroad." The temper of the "Knickerbocker History," may, accordingly, be regarded as freshly American. The style, meanwhile, is rather like that of Goldsmith. When the "Knickerbocker History" was published, Goldsmith had been dead for thirty-five years. In Irving, then, we find a man who used the traditional style of eighteenth-century England for a purpose foreign at once to the century and the country of its origin.

It was ten years before Irving again appeared as a serious man of letters. Then came the "Sketch Book," which contains his best-known stories, — "Rip Van Winkle" and "The Legend of Sleepy Hollow." The book is a collection of essays and short stories, written in a style more like Goldsmith's than ever. The year in which it appeared was that which gave to England the first two cantos of "Don Juan," Hazlitt's "Lectures on the Comic Writers," Leigh Hunt's "Indicator," Scott's "Bride of Lammermoor" and "Legend of Montrose," Shelley's "Cenci," and Wordsworth's "Peter Bell." There can be little doubt that in formal style the "Sketch Book" is more conscientious than any of these. Its prose, in fact, has hardly been surpassed, if indeed it has been equalled, in nineteenth-century England. This prose, however, is of that balanced, cool, rhythmical sort which in England flourished most during the mid years of the eighteenth century.

In the "Sketch Book," too, there are many papers and passages which might have come straight from some of the later eighteenth-century essayists. On the other hand, there are many passages, such as "Rip Van Winkle," which could hardly have appeared in Goldsmith's England. Though Goldsmith's England, of course, was becoming sentimental, it never got to that delight in a romantic past which characterised the period of which the dominant writer was Sir Walter Scott. By 1819, however, Scott had attained his highest development. In his work there was far more passion and meaning than in the romantic stories of Irving; in technical form, on the other hand, it is comparatively careless, nor on the whole is it more genuinely permeated with the romantic sentiment of the nineteenth century. The story of Rip Van Winkle, for example, is a legend which exists in various European forms. Whether Irving adopted it from such old German tales as that of the sleeping Barbarossa, or from some Spanish story such as he later told when he described the sleep of enchanted

Moors, or whether in his time the legend itself had migrated to the Hudson Valley, makes no difference. He assumed that it belonged in the Catskills. He placed it, as a little earlier Brockden Brown placed his less significant romances, in a real background; and he infused into it the romantic spirit which was already characteristic of European letters, and soon to be almost more so of American. He enlivened the tale, meanwhile, with a subdued form of such humour as runs riot in the "Knickerbocker History;" and all this modern sentiment, he phrased as he had phrased his first book, in terms modelled on the traditional style of a generation or two before. The peculiar trait of the "Sketch Book," in short, is its combination of fresh romantic feeling with traditional Augustan style.

The passages of the "Sketch Book" which deal with England reveal so sympathetic a sense of old English tradition that some of them, like those concerning Stratford and Westminster Abbey, have become almost classical; just as Irving's later work, "Bracebridge Hall," is now generally admitted to typify a pleasant phase of country life in England almost as well as Sir Roger de Coverley typified another, a century earlier. There are papers in the "Sketch Book," however, which from our point of view are more significant. Take those, for example, on "John Bull" and on "English Writers concerning America." Like the writing of Hopkinson at the time of the American Revolution, these reveal a distinct sense on the part of an able and cultivated American that the contemporary English differ from our countrymen. The eye which observed John Bull in the aspect which follows, is foreign to England : —

"Though really a good-hearted, good-tempered old fellow at bottom, yet he is singularly fond of being in the midst of contention. It is one of his peculiarities, however, that he only relishes the beginning of an affray; he always goes into a fight with alacrity, but comes out of it grumbling even when victorious; and though no one fights with more obstinacy to carry a contested point, yet, when the battle is over, and he comes to the reconciliation, he is so much taken up with the mere shaking of hands, that he is apt to let his antagonist pocket all that they have been quarrelling about. It is not, therefore, fighting that he ought so much to be on his guard against, as making friends. It is difficult to cudgel him out of a farthing; but put him in a good humour, and you may bargain him out of all the money in his pocket. He is like a stout ship, which will weather the roughest storm uninjured, but roll its masts overboard in the succeeding calm.

"He is a little fond of playing the magnifico abroad; of pulling out a long purse; flinging his money bravely about at boxing matches, horse races, cock fights, and carrying a high head among 'gentlemen of the fancy;' but immediately after one of these fits of extravagance, he will be taken with violent qualms of economy; talk desperately of being ruined and brought upon the parish; and, in such moods, will not pay the smallest tradesman's bill, without violent altercation. He is in fact the most punctual and discontented paymaster in the world; drawing his coin out of his breeches pocket with infinite reluctance; paying to the uttermost farthing, but accompanying every guinea with a growl.

"With all his talk of economy, however, he is a bountiful provider, and a hospitable housekeeper. His economy is of a whimsical kind, its chief object being to devise how he may afford to be extravagant; for he will begrudge himself a beef-steak and pint of port one day, that he may roast an ox whole, broach a hogshead of ale, and treat all his neighbours on the next."

In "Bracebridge Hall" and the "Tales of a Traveller," works which followed the "Sketch Book," Irving did little more than continue the sort of thing which he had done in the first. Perhaps his most noteworthy feat in all three books is that he made prominent in English literature a literary form in which for a long time to come Americans excelled native Englishmen, — the short story. During our century, of course, England has produced a great school of fiction; and except for Cooper and one or two living writers, America can hardly show full-grown novels so good even as those of Anthony Trollope, not to speak of the masterpieces of Dickens, Thackeray, and George Eliot. Certainly until the time of Robert Louis Stevenson, however, no English-speaking writer out of America had produced many short stories of such merit as anybody can recognise in the work of Hawthorne and Poe and Irving. In this fact there is something akin to that other fact which we have just remarked, — the formal superiority of Irving's style to that of contemporary Englishmen. The English novel, whatever its merits, runs to interminable length, with a disregard of form unprecedented in other civilised literature. A good short story, on the other hand, must generally have complete and finished form. Now, during the nineteenth century American men of letters have usually had a more conscious sense of form than their English contemporaries. The American conscience, in fact, always a bit overdeveloped, has sometimes seemed evident in our attempts at literary art. No one who lacks artistic conscience can write an effective short story; and it is doubtful whether any one troubled with much artistic conscience can write in less than a lifetime a three-volume novel. The artistic conscience revealed in the finish of Irving's style and in his mastery of the short story, then, may be called characteristic of his country.

Equally characteristic of America, in the somewhat different manner foreshadowed by " Bracebridge Hall " and the " Tales of a Traveller," are the series of Irving's writings, between 1828 and 1832, which deal with Spain. He was first attracted thither by a proposition that he should translate a Spanish book concerning Columbus. Instead of so doing, he ended by writing his " Life of Columbus," which was followed by his " Conquest of Granada " and his " Tales of the Alhambra." For Americans, Spain has sometimes had more romantic charm than all the rest of Europe put together. In the first place, as the very name of Columbus should remind us, its history is inextricably connected with our own. In the second place, at the very moment when this lasting connection between Spain and the New World declared itself, the eight hundred years' struggle between Moors and Spaniards had at length ended in the triumph of the Christians; and no other conflict of the whole European past involved a contrast

of life and of ideals more vivid, more complete, more varied,
or more prolonged.   In the third place, the decline of Spain
began almost immediately ; so in the early nineteenth century
Spain had altered less since the middle ages than any other
part of Europe.   Elsewhere an American traveller could find
traces of the picturesque, romantic, vanished past.   In Spain
he could find a state of life so little changed from olden time
that he seemed almost to travel into that vanished past itself.

Now, as the American character of the nineteenth century has declared itself, few of its æsthetic traits are more
marked than eager delight in olden splendours.   Such delight,
of course, has characterised the nineteenth century in Europe
as well as among ourselves.   A modern Londoner, however,
who can walk in a forenoon from Westminster Abbey to the
Temple Church and so to the Tower, can never dream of
what such monuments mean to an imagination which has
grown up amid no grander relics of antiquity than King's
Chapel or Independence Hall, than gray New England farm-
houses and the moss-grown gravestones of Yankee burying-
grounds.   To any sensitive nature, brought up in nineteenth-
century America, the mere sight of anything so immemorially
human as a European landscape must have in it some touch
of that stimulating power which the Europe of the Renaissance found in the fresh discovery of classical literature and art.
Americans can still feel the romance even of modern London
or Paris; and to this day there is no spot where our starved
craving for human antiquity can be more profusely satisfied
than amid the decaying but not vanished monuments of Christian and of Moorish Spain.   No words have ever expressed
this satisfaction more sincerely or more spontaneously than the
fantastic stories of old Spain which Irving has left us.

His later work was chiefly biographical.   His " Life of
Goldsmith " and his " Life of Washington " alike are written
with all his charm and with vivid imagination.   Irving, how-

ever, was no trained scholar. He was far even from the critical habit of the New England historians, and further still from such learning as is now apt to make history something like exact science. It may be doubted whether Irving's Goldsmith or his Washington can be accepted as the Goldsmith or the Washington who once trod the earth; yet his Goldsmith and Washington, and the other personages whom he introduced into their stories, are at least living human beings. His work is perhaps halfway between history and fiction; imaginative history is perhaps the best name for it. As usual, he was preoccupied almost as much with a desire to write charmingly as with a purpose to write truly; but in itself this desire was beautifully true. Throughout, one feels, Irving wrote as well as he could, and he knew how to write better than almost any contemporary Englishman.

No doubt a great deal of English work contemporary with Irving's is of deeper value. Our hasty glance at his literary career has perhaps shown what this first of our recognised men of letters — the first American who in his own lifetime established a lasting European reputation — really accomplished. His greatest merits, which nothing can abate, are pervasive artistic conscience, admirable and persistent sense of form, and constant devotion to his literary ideals. If we ask ourselves, however, what he used his admirable style to express, we find in the first place a quaintly extravagant sort of humour growing more delicate with the years; next we find romantic sentiment set forth in the beautifully polished phrases of a past English generation whose native temper had been rather classical than romantic; then we find a deeply lasting delight in the splendours of an unfathomably romantic past; and finally we come to pleasantly vivid romantic biographies. One thing here is pretty clear: the man had no message. From beginning to end he was animated by no profound sense of the mystery of existence. Neither the solemn eternities which stir philosophers and theologians, nor the actual lessons as dis-

tinguished from the superficial circumstances of human experience, ever much engaged his thought.   Delicate, refined,
romantic sentiment he set forth in delicate, refined classic
style.   One may often wonder whether he had much to say ;
one can never question that he wrote beautifully.

This was the first recognised literary revelation of the New
World to the Old.   In a previous generation, Edwards had
made American theology a fact for all Calvinists to reckon
with.   The political philosophers of the Revolution had made
our political and legal thought matters which even the Old
World could hardly neglect.   When we come to pure literature, however, in which America should at last express to
Europe what life meant to men of artistic sensitiveness living
under the conditions of our new and emancipated society,
what we find is little more than greater delicacy of form than
existed in contemporary England.   Irving is certainly a permanent literary figure.   What makes him so is not novelty or
power, but charming refinement.

III

In 1820, American literature, at least so far as it has survived even in tradition, consisted of the work of Brockden Brown, then ten years dead, and of Irving's "Sketch Book," the first edition of which had appeared the year before. Apart from these works, what had been produced in this country was so obviously imitative as to express only a sense on the part of our numerous writers that they ought to copy the eminent authors of England. In 1820 appeared the first work of a new novelist, soon to attain not only permanent reputation in America, but also a European recognition more general than Irving's, if not so critically admiring. This was James Fenimore Cooper.

He was born in New Jersey in 1789. When he was about a year old his father, a gentleman of means, migrated to that region in the wilderness of Central New York where Cooperstown now preserves his name. Here the father founded and christened the settlement where for the rest of his life he maintained a position of almost feudal superiority. Here, in a country so wild as to be almost primeval, Cooper was brought up. Before he was fourteen years old he went to Yale College, then in charge of its great President, Timothy Dwight; but some academic trouble brought his college career to a premature end. The years between 1806 and 1810 he spent at sea, first as a kind of apprentice on a merchant vessel, afterward as an officer in the navy. In 1811, having married a lady of the Tory family of De Lancey, he resigned his commission.

After several years of inconspicuous life — he was living at the time in the country near New York City — he read some now forgotten but temporarily fashionable English novel ; and stirred by the notion that he could write a better, he rapidly produced a story, now almost as forgotten as its model, entitled " Precaution." This, published in 1820, was a tale of fashionable life in England, of which at the time Cooper knew very little. It had a measure of success, being mistaken for the anonymous work of some English woman of fashion. In the following year Cooper produced " The Spy," an historical novel of the American Revolution, then less than fifty years past. In 1823 came " The Pioneers," the first in publication of his Leather-Stocking tales ; and just at the beginning of 1824 appeared " The Pilot," the first of his stories of the sea. " The Last of the Mohicans," perhaps his masterpiece, was published in 1826. In that year he went abroad, where he remained for seven years. He then came home, and resided for most of the rest of his life on the ancestral estate at Cooperstown, where he died in 1851. Peculiarities of temper kept him throughout his later years in chronic quarrels with the public, with his neighbours, and with almost everybody but some of his personal friends, who remained strongly attached to him.

At the age of thirty, as we have seen, Cooper had never published anything ; he died at the age of sixty-two ; and in the incomplete list of his writings appended to Professor Lounsbury's biography of him there are some seventy entries. Of these hastily written works a number dealt with matters of fact ; for one thing, with characteristic asperity and lack of tact, he wrote books about both America and England, in which, when discussing either country, he seemed chiefly animated by a desire to emphasise those truths which would be least welcome to the people concerned. He wrote, too, a considerable history of the American Navy which generously contributed to his personal difficulties. For years there had been a dispute among naval people as to the comparative merit in the battle of Lake Erie of Perry, whose name is permanently associated with that victory, and his second in command, a subsequently distinguished officer named Elliott. In his account of this battle, Cooper reserved his opinion, simply stating facts; he was consequently held by the partisans both of Elliott and of Perry to have been what they certainly became, — venomously libellous. And long before the naval history appeared, he was already prosecuting newspaper after newspaper for personal criticisms, which but for these prosecutions — technically successful, by the way, — would long ago have been forgotten.

A glance at Professor Lounsbury's bibliography, however, will show that with one exception all of Cooper's works which fall into this invidious class were written after the year in which Sir Walter Scott died, 1832; and that meantime, between 1820 and that date, he had produced at least ten novels which have maintained their position in literature. What is more, these novels almost immediately attained worldwide reputation; they were translated not only into French, but also into many other languages of continental Europe, in which they preserve popularity. Great as was his success at home and in England, indeed, it is sometimes said to have been exceeded by that which he has enjoyed throughout continental Europe. For this there is a reason which has been little remarked. The mere number and bulk of Cooper's works bear evidence to the fact that he must have written with careless haste. He had small literary training and little more tact in the matter of style than he displayed in his personal relations with people who did not enjoy his respect. Cooper's English, then, is often ponderous and generally clumsy. An odd result follows. His style is frequently such as could hardly be altered except for the better. A translator into whatever language can often say what Cooper said in a form more readable and agreeable than Cooper's own. Many of the minor passages in his writings seem more felicitous in French translation than in his own words.

Yet his own words, though even in his best work impaired by clumsiness and prolixity, are well worth reading. He has been called the American Scott, and indeed was so called in his own time, for his reputation was literally contemporary with Sir Walter's. " The Spy " appeared in the same year with " Kenilworth " and " The Pirate ; " " The Pilot " in the year of " Quentin Durward." Now, Scott and Cooper really belong to different categories of merit. Scott, saturated with the traditions of a brave old human world, was gifted with an imagination so robust as to have invented in the historical novel a virtually new form of literature, and to have enlivened it with a host of characters so vital that among the creatures of English imagination his personages rank almost next to Shakspere's. When Cooper began to write, " Waverley " was already about six years old. In a certain sense, then, he may be said to have imitated Scott ; it is doubtful, however, whether he was by any means so conscious of his model as Brockden Brown was of Godwin, or Irving of Goldsmith. The resemblance between Cooper and Scott lies chiefly in the fact that each did his best work in fiction dealing with the romantic past of his own country. By just so much, then, as the past of Cooper's America was a slighter, less varied, less human past than that of Scott's England or Scotland, Cooper's work must remain inferior to Scott's in human interest. Partly for the same reason, the range of character created by Cooper is at once less wide and far less highly developed than that brought into being by Sir Walter. Cooper, indeed, as the very difficulties of his later life would show, was temperamentally narrow in sympathy. It happened, for example, that he was an Episcopalian ; consequently, if for no other reason, he detested the New England Puritans. Now and again he introduced them into his novels ; and although he was too honest intentionally to misrepresent them, malignant caricature could hardly have strayed much further from the truth. And so on; to compare Cooper with Scott, indeed, except for the matter of popularity, in which they have often been neck and neck, is needlessly to belittle Cooper. Here we may better consider him in connection with his American contemporaries.

When " The Spy " was published, the novels of Brockden Brown were already almost forgotten; and Irving had produced only " The Knickerbocker History " and the admirable essays of his " Sketch Book." " The Spy " is an historical novel of the American Revolution, often conventional, but at the same time set in a vivid background; for Cooper, actually living in the country where he laid his scenes, sincerely endeavoured not only to revive the fading past, but to do full justice to both sides in that great conflict which disunited the English-speaking races. In " The Pilot " we have a somewhat similar state of things; but here, instead of laying the scene on American soil, Cooper lays it for the first time in literature aboard an American ship. " The Pilot " is very uneven. The plot is conventionally trivial; and most of the characters are more so still. But Long Tom Coffin is a living Yankee sailor; and when we come to the sea, with its endless variety of weather, and to sea-fights, such as that between the " Ariel " and the " Alacrity," it is hardly excessive to say that there is little better in print. If the plot and the characters had been half so good as the wonderful marine background in which they are set, the book would have been a masterpiece.

Something similar may be said of the Leather-Stocking stories, of which " The Last of the Mohicans," published in 1826, is probably the best. The trivially conventional plots concern characters not particularly like anything recorded in human history. Lowell's comment on them in the " Fable for Critics " is not unfair; after declaring Natty Bumppo vital enough to be named in the same breath with Parson

Adams, and doing surprisingly scant justice to Long Tom
Coffin, he proceeds thus : —

> " All his other men-figures are clothes upon sticks,
> The *dernière chemise* of a man in a fix,
> (As a captain besieged, when his garrison 's small,
> Sets up caps upon poles to be seen o'er the wall) ;
> And the women he draws from one model don't vary,
> All sappy as maples and flat as a prairie.
> When a character 's wanted, he goes to the task
> As a cooper would do in composing a cask ;
> He picks out the staves, of their qualities heedful,
> Just hoops them together as tight as is needful,
> And, if the best fortune should crown the attempt, he
> Has made at the most something wooden and empty."

Cooper's noble Indians, in fact, are rather more like the
dreams of eighteenth-century France concerning aboriginal
human nature than anything critically observed by ethnology ;
and Natty Bumppo himself is a creature rather of romantic
fancy than of creative sympathy with human nature. The
woods and the inland waters, on the other hand, amid which
the scenes of these stories unroll themselves, are true American
forests and lakes and streams. It is hardly too much to say
that Cooper introduced to human recognition certain aspects
of Nature unknown to literature before his time, and of a kind
which could have been perceived and set forth only by an
enthusiastic native of that newest of nations to which he was
so devotedly attached.

For, in spite of his later quarrels with his countrymen,
Cooper was an intensely patriotic American. He chanced,
however, to be of a temper not generally characteristic of
our country, and partly to be accounted for by his personal
origin. His father had been something like a feudal lord in
the savage country where Cooper's boyhood was passed ;
and the son could not help inheriting a certain instinct of personal superiority, or at least of personal independence, peculiarly foreign to that sensitive consciousness of majorities which

has often made Americans so slow to express unpopular opinions. Cooper, too, had strong prejudices ; and when brought face to face with anything he did not like, he was given to expressing disapprobation with a vigour more characteristic of the English than of ourselves. Though he thoroughly loved his country, he saw in it traits which by no means delighted him. So in his " Notions of the Americans Picked up by a Travelling Bachelor," published in 1828, when his popularity was at its height, he expressed concerning our countrymen views which may be summarised in the statement that Americans, though full of energy and other admirable qualities, have a blind passion for money-seeking, an undue respect for popular opinion, and an irrepressible tendency to brag. For this he was called Anglomaniac ; his Anglo-mania did not prevent him from writing just as frankly about the English, of whom his published views may similarly be summarised in the statement that the English are not only the most efficiently powerful nation in the world, but also by far the most snobbish. Both nations resented such comments. Some notion of the amenities of criticisms sixty years ago may be gained from a few phrases which were consequently bestowed upon Cooper both in England and in America. In 1838 the " New Yorker" wrote of him as follows : " He is as proud of blackguarding as a fishwoman is of Billingsgate. It is as natural to him as snarling to a tomcat or growling to a bull-dog. . . . He has the scorn and contempt of every well-informed American. The superlative dolt." A little later " Fraser's Magazine " called him a " bilious braggart," a " liar," a " full jackass," an " insect," a " grub," and a " reptile."

The troubles in which he thus involved himself during his last twenty years were enhanced not only by those which sprang from his honest effort to be fair in his History of the Navy, but by quarrels with neighbours at Cooperstown, concerning the public use of some land to which he held a clear title, and by various infirmities of temper. Intensely aristocratic in personal feeling, he cherished the most democratic general sentiments, believing equally in the rights of man and in the vileness of any actual populace. In politics he was a Democrat, but he hated free trade as blindly as Tory squire ever loved the Corn Laws; and so on. One can begin to see why, after what he must have felt to be a lifetime of misunderstanding and vexation, he wished no biography of him made.

Yet, after all, now that he has been half a century in his grave, little memory is left of his foibles or his troubles. The Cooper who persists and who will persist in popular memory is the author of those wholesome novels of sea and of forest which were the first American writings to win and to keep a truly wide popularity. In touching on them a little while ago, we remarked the extraordinary truthfulness of their background; and this, probably, is the trait which gives them their highest positive value. It is hardly to so unusual a quality, however, that they have owed their popular vitality. Their plots, though conventional, are put together with considerable skill. In spite of prolixity one constantly feels curious to know what is coming next. In spite even of lifeless characters, this skilful handling of plot makes one again and again feel unexpected interest concerning what these personages are going to do or what is going to happen to them. As we have seen already, too, crucial episodes, such as the wreck of the " Ariel " in " The Pilot," possess, in spite of careless phrasing, a vividness and a bravery sure to appeal to broad human temper.

Cooper's plots, then, if commonplace, are often interesting enough to atone for their prolixity; and whatever the conventionality of his characters, the spirit of his books is vigorously brave and manly. Excellent as these traits are, however, they are not specifically American. Another trait of Cooper's work, less salient, but just as constant, may fairly be regarded as national. From beginning to end of his writings there is hardly a passage which anybody would hesitate to put into the hands of a child or of a young girl; nor is this pervasive purity apparently deliberate. The scenes of his novels are often laid in very rough places, and as a natural consequence many of his characters and incidents are of a rough, adventurous kind; but, with a freedom from pruriency as instinctive as his robustness, the man avoids those phases of rough human life which recent " decadence " has generally tended either to overemphasise or so studiously to neglect that the neglect amounts to emphasis. Cooper's temper was unaffectedly pure; and purity of temper is probably still characteristic of American letters.

Cooper lived until 1851, and Irving lived eight years longer. Both men wrote until they died. In a certain way, then, their work might be held to extend to a distinctly later period than that in which we are considering them; for here we have treated them as almost contemporary with Brockden Brown, who died in 1810. In another aspect, however, they belong very early in the history of American letters. In 1798, we remember, the year when Wordsworth and Coleridge published the " Lyrical Ballads," appeared also Brockden Brown's " Wieland," the first American book which has survived. In 1832 the death of Sir Walter Scott brought to an end that epoch of English letters which the " Lyrical Ballads " may be said to have opened. In that year, of course, Brown had long been dead; and both Irving and Cooper had still some years to write. The reputation of each, however, was virtually complete. Irving had already published his " Knickerbocker History," his " Sketch Book," his " Bracebridge Hall," his " Tales of a Traveller," his " Life of Columbus," his " Fall of Granada," and his "Alhambra; " nothing later materially increased his reputation. Cooper had published " The Spy," " The Pioneers," " The Pilot," " Lionel Lincoln," " The Last of the Mohicans," " The Prairie," the " Red Rover," the " Wept of Wish-ton-Wish,"

" The Water Witch," and the " Bravo."   When Scott died, then, Cooper, too, had produced enough to make his reputation permanent; nothing which he wrote later much enhanced it.

The three writers whom we have considered — Brockden Brown, Irving, and Cooper — were the only Americans who between 1798 and 1832 achieved lasting names in prose. Though they form no school, though they are very different from one another, two or three things may be said of them in common.   They all developed in the Middle States; the names of all are associated with the chief city of that region, New York.   The most significant work of all assumed a form which in the general history of literatures comes not early but late, — prose fiction.   This form, meantime, happened to be on the whole that which was most popular in contemporary England.   Again, in the previous literature of America, if literature it may be called, two serious motives were expressed. In the first place, particularly in New England, there was a considerable development of theologic thought; the serious Yankee mind was centred on the eternities.   A little later, partly in New England, but more in Virginia and in New York, there was admirable political writing.   These two motives — the one characteristic of the earliest type of native American, the second of that second type which politically expressed itself in the American Revolution — may be regarded as expressions in this country of the two ideals most deeply inherent in our native language, — those of the Bible and of the Common Law.   Whatever the ultimate significance of American writing during the seventeenth or the eighteenth centuries, then, such of it as now remains worthy of attention is earnest in purpose, dealing either with the eternal destinies of mankind or with deep problems of political conduct.   In our first purely literary expression, on the other hand, a different temper appears.   Neither Brown nor Irving nor Cooper has left us anything profoundly significant.   All three are properly remembered as writers of wholesome fiction; and the object of wholesome fiction is neither to lead men heavenward nor to teach them how to behave on earth; it is rather to please. There is a commonplace which divides great literature into the literature of knowledge, which enlarges the intellect, and that of power, which stimulates the emotions until they become living motives. Such work as Brockden Brown's or Irving's or Cooper's can hardly be put in either category. Theirs is rather a literature of wholesome pleasure. Nor can one long look at them together without tending to the conclusion that the most apt of the forms in which their peculiar literature of wholesome pleasure was cast is that short story which the American Irving first perfected in English.

This prose on which we have now touched was the most important literature produced in New York, or indeed in America, during the period which was marked in England by everything between the "Lyrical Ballads" and the death of Scott. Even in America, however, the time had its poetry. At this we must now glance.

IV

In the early summer of 1878 there died at New York, from a sunstroke received just after delivering a speech at the unveiling of a monument in Central Park, William Cullen Bryant, by far the most eminent man of letters in our chief city. The circumstances of his death show how thoroughly he retained his vitality to the end; and his striking personal appearance combined with the extreme physical activity which kept him constantly in the streets to make him a familiar local figure. To any one who can remember New York twenty-five years ago, then, the memory of Bryant must be so vivid as to make startling the truth that if he had lived till now he would have been well past his century.

In his later years the younger generation of Americans who were beginning to feel interest in literature had a way of rather deriding him. They were told that he was a great poet; and turning to the numerous collections of his works, they found little which impressed them as better than respectably commonplace. The prolonged life of the man, in fact, had combined with his unusual physical vitality to make people forget that his first published work — a very precocious one, to be sure, — had appeared before Brockden Brown died, in the same year with Scott's "Marmion;" and that this remote 1808 had seen the "Quarterly Review" founded in England, and Andover Seminary in Massachusetts. They forgot that Bryant's "Thanatopsis," presented to them as the work of a contemporary and vigorous man of letters, had been printed in 1817, the year in which Byron wrote "Manfred,"

in which Jane Austen died, in which Coleridge produced his
" Biographia Literaria," and Keats the first volume of his
poems, and Mrs. Shelley her " Frankenstein," and Moore his
" Lalla Rookh." They forgot that a collected edition of
Bryant's poems had appeared in 1821, the year when Keats
died, when the first version of De Quincey's " Opium-Eater "
came into existence, when Scott published " Kenilworth " and
the " Pirate," and Shelley " Adonais." And incidentally they
forgot what Bryant's general bearing rather encouraged them
to forget, that besides being what he preferred to think himself, a poet, he was the most admirably successful journalist
whom America has yet produced. For a full half-century he
was at the head of the New York " Evening Post," which
brought him the rare reward of a considerable personal fortune
earned by a newspaper in which from beginning to end the
editor could feel honest pride. As a journalist, indeed, Bryant
belongs almost to our own time. As a poet, however,—and
it is as a poet that we are considering him here, — he belongs
to the earliest period of our native letters.

He was born, the son of a country doctor, at Cumming-
ton, a small town of Western Massachusetts, in 1794. At
that time a country doctor, though generally poor, was, like
the minister and the squire, an educated man, and so a person
of local eminence; and Dr. Bryant, who was occasionally
a member of the General Court at Boston, came to have a
considerable acquaintance among the better sort of people in
Massachusetts. The son was extremely precocious. When
he was only thirteen years old, verses of his were printed in a
country newspaper; and a year later, in 1808, his satire on
President Jefferson, " The Embargo," was brought to Boston
by his admiring father and actually published. The only particular merit of this poem is accuracy of rhyme and metre, a
trait of deliberate excellence which Bryant preserved until the
end. For a year or so the boy went to Williams College,
but as his father was too poor to keep him there, he soon

13

entered a lawyer's office.   Law, however, proved by no means congenial to him; he wanted to be a man of letters. In this aspiration his father sympathised; and when the son was twenty-three years of age, the father took to Boston a collection of his manuscripts among which was "Thanatopsis," already six years old.

These manuscripts Dr. Bryant submitted to Mr. Willard Phillips, one of the three editors of the "North American Review," then lately founded.   Delighted with the verses, Phillips showed them to his colleagues, Mr. Richard Henry Dana and Professor Edward Tyrrell Channing.   The story of the way in which these gentlemen received the poems throws light on the condition of American letters in 1817. According to Mr. Parke Godwin's biography of Bryant, "they listened attentively to his reading of them, when Dana, at the close, remarked with a quiet smile : ' Ah! Phillips, you have been imposed upon; no one on this side of the Atlantic is capable of writing such verses.' "   Four years later, in 1821, Bryant delivered before the Phi Beta Kappa Society of Harvard College a poem, "The Ages," which remains his longest; and in the same year he published in pamphlet form eight poems.   There were only forty-four pages in all; but among the poems were both "The Waterfowl" and "Thanatopsis."   The life of a country lawyer becoming more and more distasteful to him, he determined to move to town. He thought seriously of going to Boston, — a city with which at that time his affiliations were stronger than with any other; but instead he cast in his lot with New York, to which he finally removed in 1825.

At that time Brockden Brown had been dead for fifteen years, and the reputations of Irving and of Cooper were established.   At that time, too, there was in New York a considerable literary activity of which the results are now pretty generally forgotten.   Whoever is curious to know something about it may turn to one or two works which may be found in any considerable public library. One is Rufus Wilmot Griswold's "Poets and Poetry of America," published in 1842; it was followed within ten years by his "Prose Writers of America" and his "Female Poets of America;" and in 1856 came the first edition of Evert Augustus Duyckinck's "Cyclopedia of American Literature." A comparison of these with Stedman and Hutchinson's "Library of American Literature" will surprisingly reveal how much has been written in this country which even so catholic a taste as that of these latest editors has already been compelled to reject. Almost the only survival of New York poetry before Bryant came there, indeed, is Samuel Woodworth's accidentally popular "Old Oaken Bucket." The mere name of James Kirke Paulding, to be sure, who was associated with Irving in the "Salmagundi Papers," and who subsequently wrote a number of novels, and other prose, is still faintly remembered; and so are the names rather than the actual work of two poets, Joseph Rodman Drake and Fitz-Greene Halleck.

Drake, born in 1795, had died in 1820. He was a gentleman and a man of taste. He wrote several pretty things, among them a poem published after his death, entitled "The Culprit Fay." This conventional tale of some tiny fairies, supposed to haunt the Hudson River, is so much better than American poetry had previously been that one is at first disposed to speak of it enthusiastically. An obvious comparison puts it in true perspective. Drake's life happened nearly to coincide with that of Keats. Both left us only broken fragments of what they might have done, had they been spared; but the contrast between these fragments tells afresh the story of American letters. Amid the full fervour of European experience Keats produced immortal work; Drake, whose whole life was passed amid the national inexperience of New York, produced only pretty fancies. When he tried heroics he could make no better verses than such as these from his poem on "The American Flag": —

> " When Freedom from her mountain height
>   Unfurled her standard to the air,
> She tore the azure robe of night,
>   And set the stars of glory there.
> She mingled with its gorgeous dyes,
> The milky baldric of the skies,
> And striped its pure celestial white
> With streakings of the morning light;
> Then from his mansion in the sun
> She called her eagle bearer down,
> And gave into his mighty hand
> The symbol of her chosen land.
>
> .   .   .   .   .   .
>
> " Flag of the free heart's hope and home!
>   By angel hands to valour given;
> Thy stars have lit the welkin dome,
>   And all thy hues were born in heaven.
> Forever float that standard sheet!
>   Where breathes the foe but falls before us,
> With Freedom's soil beneath our feet,
>   And Freedom's banner streaming o'er us? "

Fitz-Greene Halleck, five years older, survived Drake by
forty-seven years. If we except his Campbell-like " Marco
Bozzaris," however, which was published in 1825, his only
surviving lines are comprised in the first stanza of his poem on
the death of Drake, written in 1820 : —

> " Green be the turf above thee,
>   Friend of my better days!
> None knew thee but to love thee,
>   Nor named thee but to praise."

In 1811, Halleck and Drake contributed to the New York
" Evening Post " a series of poetical satires entitled " The
Croaker Papers; " and Halleck published a mildly satirical
poem entitled " Fanny," which may be described as a dilution
of Byron with Croton water. In 1827 he brought out " Aln-
wick Castle " and other poems. In 1832 his poetic career
was virtually closed by his acceptance of a clerical position in
the employ of Mr. John Jacob Astor. The general insig-
nificance of New York letters at the time when Bryant first

came to the town is in no way better typified than by the fact
that literary work so inconsiderable as Halleck's has been
deemed worthy of a bronze statue, still sitting cross-legged
in the Grand Alley of Central Park.

Compared with such work as this, there is no wonder that
poems like " Thanatopsis " and " The Waterfowl " seemed to
the early editors of the " North American Review " too good
to be native; and, as we have seen, Bryant's life and activity
were so prolonged that it is hard to remember how nearly his
poetical work was accomplished at the beginning of his career.
It was not all produced at once, of course; but, as is often
the case with precocious excellence, — with men, for example,
like his contemporaries, Landor and Whittier, — even though
he rarely fell below his own first level, he hardly ever surpassed it. This is clearly seen if we compare the familiar
concluding lines of " Thanatopsis," written before he was
twenty-seven, with a passage of about equal length from
" Among the Trees," published after he was seventy. The
former lines run thus : —

> " So live, that when thy summons comes to join
> The innumerable caravan, which moves
> To that mysterious realm, where each shall take
> His chamber in the silent halls of death,
> Thou go not, like the quarry-slave at night,
> Scourged to his dungeon, but, sustained and soothed
> By an unfaltering trust, approach thy grave,
> Like one who wraps the drapery of his couch
> About him, and lies down to pleasant dreams."

The latter lines are these : —

> " Ye have no history. I ask in vain
> Who planted on the slope this lofty group
> Of ancient pear-trees that with spring-time burst
> Into such breadth of bloom. One bears a scar
> Where the quick lightning scorched its trunk, yet still
> It feels the breath of Spring, and every May
> Is white with blossoms. Who it was that laid
> Their infant roots in earth, and tenderly

Cherished the delicate sprays, I ask in vain,
Yet bless the unknown hand to which I owe
The annual festival of bees, these songs
Of birds within their leafy screen, these shouts
Of joy from children gathering up the fruit
Shaken in August from the willing boughs."

The former of these passages is the work of an inexperienced country boy; the latter, by the same hand, is the work
of an old man who had made a fortune as the most successful
journalist in New York; but, so far as internal evidence goes,
the latter might almost have been written first. Beyond doubt,
as an American poet Bryant really belongs to the generation
contemporary with Sir Walter Scott.

In the year of Scott's death, indeed, the same 1832 which
saw in England the passage of the Reform Bill and in America the Nullification Act of South Carolina and President
Jackson's Bank Veto, Bryant had already been for four years
at the head of the "Evening Post," and the first considerable
edition of his poems appeared both in England and in America.
Nothing which he wrote later, except perhaps his translations,
— some admirable versions of Spanish lyrics, which are said
to have attracted many young eyes to fascinating romantic
vistas, and far later his well-known rendering of Homer —
will much alter the impression produced by this early
volume. The lifelong evenness of his work seems to justify
reference at this point to what he wrote about poetry many
years later. In 1871 he became editor of a "Library of
Poetry and Song," — one of those innumerable anthologies
which are from time to time inflicted on the public, either
for sale by country book agents or for unacceptable Christmas presents. To this "library" Bryant contributed an
introduction in which he stated at considerable length what
he conceived to be the most important qualities of lasting
poetry. The trait which on the whole he most valued appears
to be luminosity: "The best poetry," he says, — "that which
takes the strongest hold on the general mind, not in one age

only but in all ages, — is that which is always simple and always luminous."

Simple and luminous Bryant was from beginning to end. For this simple luminosity he paid the price of that deliberate coolness which Lowell so pitilessly satirised in the "Fable for Critics," of 1848 : —

> "There is Bryant, as quiet, as cool, and as dignified,
> As a smooth, silent iceberg, that never is ignified,
> Save when by reflection 't is kindled o' nights
> With a semblance of flame by the chill Northern Lights.
> He may rank (Griswold says so) first bard of your nation
> (There 's no doubt he stands in supreme iceolation),
> Your topmost Parnassus he may set his heel on,
> But no warm applauses come, peal following peal on, —
> He 's too smooth and too polished to hang any zeal on;
> Unqualified merits, I 'll grant, if you choose, he has 'em,
> But he lacks the one merit of kindling enthusiasm ;
> If he stir you at all, it is just, on my soul,
> Like being stirred up with the very North Pole."

If Bryant's careful attention to luminosity, however, prevented him from ever being passionate, and gave his work the character so often mistaken for commonplace, it never deprived him of tender delicacy. Take, for example, "The Death of the Flowers," of which the opening line —

> "The melancholy days are come, the saddest of the year" —

is among his most familiar. The last two stanzas run as follows : —

> "And now, when comes the calm mild day, as still such days will come,
> To call the squirrel and the bee from out their winter home;
> When the sound of dropping nuts is heard, though all the trees are still,
> And twinkle in the smoky light the waters of the rill,
> The south wind searches for the flowers whose fragrance late he bore,
> And sighs to find them in the wood and by the stream no more.

" And then I think of one who in her youthful beauty died,
   The fair meek blossom that grew up and faded by my side.
   In the cold moist earth we laid her, when the forests cast the leaf,
   And we wept that one so lovely should have a life so brief;
   Yet not unmeet it was that one, like that young friend of ours,
   So gentle and so beautiful, should perish with the flowers."

To a generation familiar with all the extravagances of nineteenth-century romanticism, a feeling so restrained, so close to sentimentality, as this — expressed, too, with such deliberate luminosity, — may well seem unimpassioned. But one cannot dwell on these lines without feeling genuine sweetness of temper, or without finally discerning, in what at first seems chilly deliberation of phrase, what is rather a loving care for every syllable.

The allusion in the last stanza is to the early death from consumption of Bryant's sister. Only a few years before, his father had died of the same disease. So he had personal reason for melancholy. As one looks through his work, however, one is apt to wonder whether, even if his life had been destitute of personal bereavement, his verse might not still have hovered sentimentally about the dead. His most successful poem, " Thanatopsis," was apparently written before death had often come near him ; and it is hardly excessive to say that if a single name were sought for his collected works, from beginning to end, a version of that barbarous Greek title might be found suitable, and the whole volume fairly entitled " Glimpses of the Grave." Of course he touched on other things; but he touched on mortality so constantly as to make one feel regretfully sure that whenever he felt stirred to poetry his fancy started for the Valley of the Shadow of Death. In this, of course, he was not peculiar. The subject had such fascination for eighteenth-century versifiers that in 1751 Gray's " Elegy " made of it a masterpiece; and we need only remember those mortuary memorials wherein the hair of the departed is woven into the weeping willows of widowed brooches, to be reminded how general this kind of sentimentality has been. This underlying impulse of Bryant's poetry, however, was most general in the eighteenth century ; and Bryant's style — distinctly affected by that of Cowper, and still more by that of Wordsworth — belongs rather to the nineteenth. A contemporary of Irving, then, he reverses the relation of substance to style which we remarked in Irving's prose. Irving, imbued with nineteenth-century romantic temper, wrote in the classical style of the century before; Bryant, writing in the simply luminous style of his own century, expressed a somewhat formal sentimentality which had hardly characterised vital work in England for fifty years.

Always simple and always luminous, then, tenderly sentimental, melancholy and sweet, given to commonplace didactic moralising and coolly careful metre and rhyme, Bryant, a far from prolific poet, had done, when he came to New York at the age of thirty-one, as good work as he was ever destined to do. In New York he lived for fifty-three years ; and during those years most of what is now called American literature came into existence. His life, indeed, is really coeval with the letters of his country. As a matter of fact, the chief development of these letters centred in Boston. Had Bryant yielded to his first impulse, and gone not to New York, but to the chief city of his native New England, the chances are that his eminence would have suffered. In New York, however, throughout his residence there, it became clearer and clearer that he was not only the most eminent of local journalists, but also the only resident poet of distinction. That accidental word calls to mind a trait which any one who ever saw Bryant must remember. Whatever one thought of his literary merit, — and the great changes in literary fashion which occurred during his lifetime often made his younger contemporaries deem him less of a poet than calm reflection makes him seem now, — there can be no question that his aspect was remarkably distinguished.

Partly, of course, this was a matter of mere personal appearance. His firm old features, encircled by a cloud of snowy hair and beard, would have impressed anybody; but in the distinction of Bryant's appearance there was something more than accident of feature, and something far more significant in the history of literary America. One does not remember his manner as in the least assertive. Rather to those who, without knowing him, saw him at a distance his aspect was gentle, kindly, calmly venerable. But it had not the simplicity of unconsciousness. Whatever he really felt, he looked like a man who felt himself considerable; and certainly the qualities for which he most valued himself were not those which as journalist and man of business had made him a man of fortune. The thing for which he most respected himself was his work as a poet; and beyond question it was his work as a poet which the public most willingly recognised. The distinction he may have felt, — the distinction which he certainly received from his contemporaries, and which came to be so embodied in his personal appearance, — was wholly due to his achievement as a man of letters.

In this fact there is something characteristic of America at the time when Bryant's best work was done. Ours was a new country, at last conscious of its national independence. It was deeply and sensitively aware that it lacked a literature. Whoever produced writings which could be pronounced admirable was accordingly regarded by his fellow-citizens as a public benefactor, a great public figure, a personage of whom the nation should be proud. Bryant, fully recognised in early middle life, retained to the end that gracious distinction of aspect which comes from the habit of personal eminence.

Such was the eldest of our nineteenth-century poets, the first whose work was recognised abroad. In the nature of things he has never been widely popular; and in the course of a century whose poetry has been chiefly marked by romantic passion, he has tended to seem more and more commonplace. But those of us who used to think him commonplace forgot his historical significance; we forgot that his work was really the first which proved to England what native American poetry might be. The old world was looking for some wild manifestation of this new, hardly apprehended, western democracy. Instead, what it found in Bryant, the one poetic contemporary of Irving and Cooper whose writings have lasted, was fastidious over-refinement, tender sentimentality, and pervasive luminosity. Refinement, in short, and conscious refinement, groups Bryant with Irving, with Cooper, and with Brockden Brown. In its beginning the American literature of the nineteenth century was marked rather by delicacy than by strength, by palpable consciousness of personal distinction rather than by any such outburst of previously unphrased emotion as on general principles democracy might have been expected to excite.

V

EDGAR ALLAN POE

IN April, 1846, Edgar Allan Poe published in "Godey's Lady's Book" a considerable article on William Cullen Bryant. In the six following numbers of the same periodical, whose colored fashion-plates are said to have been highly acceptable to the contemporary female public, appeared that series of comments on the literary personages of the day which has been collected under the name of the "Literati." The personal career of Poe was so erratic that one can hardly group him with any definite literary school. It seems, however, more than accidental that his principal critical work concerned the contemporary literature of New York; and though he was born in Boston and passed a good deal of his life in Virginia, he spent in New York rather more of his literary years than anywhere else. On the whole, then, this seems the most fitting place to consider him.

Erratic his career was from the beginning. His father, the son of a Revolutionary soldier, had gone wrong and brought up on the stage; his mother was an English actress of whom little is known. The pair, who chanced to be in Boston when their son was born, in 1809, died when he was still a little child. At the age of two, he was adopted by a gentleman of Richmond, Virginia, named Allan, who soon took him to Europe, where he remained from 1815 to 1820. In 1826 he was for a year at the University of Virginia, where his career was brought to an end by a gambling scrape, which in turn brought almost to an end his relations with his adopted father. In 1827 his first verses were published,

a little volume entitled "Tamerlane and Other Poems."
Then he drifted into the army, and a temporary reconciliation
with Mr. Allan got him into the Military Academy at West
Point, from which in 1831 he managed to get himself dismissed. After that he always lived from hand to mouth,
supporting himself as a journalist and as a contributor to
numberless periodicals which flourished in his day and have
long since disappeared. The unedifying question of his personal habits need not seriously concern us. Beyond doubt
he was occasionally drunk, and he probably took more or
less opium; at the same time there is no evidence that he
was abandoned to habitual excesses. His " Manuscript found
in a Bottle," published in 1833, procured him for a while
the editorship of the " Southern Literary Messenger," published
at Richmond and for many years the most successful literary
periodical of the South. In 1835 he secretly married a
charming but penniless girl, a relative of his own; he married
her again openly in 1836. In 1839 and 1840 he edited the
" Gentleman's Magazine " in Philadelphia; from 1840 to
1842 he edited " Graham's Magazine " in New York; his
general career was that of a literary hack. In 1847, after a
life of distressing poverty, his wife died; two years later Poe
himself died under circumstances which have never been quite
clear. He had certainly alleviated his widowhood by various
flirtations, and it is said that he was about to marry again.
The story goes that he was passing through Baltimore, either
on his way to see his betrothed or on his way from a visit to
her. In that city an election was about to take place; and
some petty politicians in search of " repeaters " picked him
up, got him drunk, and made him vote all over town. Having thus exhausted his political usefulness, they left him in the
gutter from whence he found his way to the hospital, where
he certainly died.

Born fifteen years later than Bryant and dead twenty-nine
years earlier, Poe, now fifty years in his grave, seems to

belong to an earlier period of our letters; but really, as we
have seen, Bryant's principal work was done before 1832.
At that time Poe had published only three volumes of verse;
his lasting prose came somewhat later; in fact, the permanent
work of Poe may be said to coincide with the first twelve
years of the Victorian epoch.   In 1838, the year of "Arthur
Gordon Pym," Dickens was at work on "Oliver Twist" and
"Nicholas Nickleby;" and Carlyle's "French Revolution"
was a new book.   In 1849, when Poe died, Thackeray's
"Vanity Fair" and the first two volumes of Macaulay's
"History" had lately appeared; Dickens was publishing
"David Copperfield," and Thackeray "Pendennis;" and
Ruskin brought out his "Seven Lamps of Architecture."
Had Poe survived to Bryant's years, he would have outlived
not only Bryant himself, but Emerson and Hawthorne and
Longfellow and Lowell, and indeed almost every literary con-
temporary except Holmes.

The very mention of these names is enough to call to
mind a distinction between the career of Poe and that of
almost every other American whose literary reputation has
survived from the days when he was writing.   The men on
whom we have already touched were socially of the better
sort, either by birth or by achieved position.   So in general
were the chief men of letters who made the Renaissance of
New England the most important fact in American literary
history.   Poe, on the other hand, was always a waif and a stray,
essentially a Bohemian.   There was in his nature something
which made futile the effort of that benevolent Virginian gentleman to adopt him into the gentler social classes of America.
In his lifetime, then, Poe must have seemed personally inferior
to most of his eminent contemporaries in American letters.   Yet
now that all are dead, he begins to seem quite as important as
any.   In 1885 Mr. William Minto, writing of him in the
"Encyclopedia Britannica," called him "the most interesting
figure in American literature."   Superlatives, of course, are

dangerous; and Poe's writings could never obtain such general, uncritical popularity as Cooper's; but, to turn only to the bibliography in the last volume of Stedman and Woodberry's admirable edition of Poe, it appears that between 1890 and 1895 there were at least ten translations from his works into various foreign languages, among others Swedish, something which looks like Bohemian, Italian, Danish, and South American Spanish. Certainly among the literary classes of Europe no American author has attracted more attention than Poe, whose influence still seems extending.

Fifty years after his death, then, we find his reputation familiar throughout the civilised world; and such a reputation obscures the fact that in life the man who has won it was of doubtful repute. The accident that his first published work bears almost the same name as that of the first tragedy of Christopher Marlowe suggests a real analogy. Poe and Marlowe alike were men of extraordinary power and of reckless personal habit; alike they produced work which will always enrich the literature of the language in which it was written. In their own times, however, neither was an admirably solitary man of genius; each was only one of a considerable group of writers, now mostly forgotten but undeniably more presentable than the artists whom time has proved greater. Both, after troublesome, irregular careers, died miserably in public places; it is only as each has receded into tradition that his earthly immortality has become assured.

The historical position of Poe in American letters can be seen by glancing at his already mentioned papers, the "Literati." These, we remember, followed in "Godey's Lady's Book" on a lengthy criticism of Bryant. It is worth while to name the thirty-eight persons, then mostly living in New York and certainly contributing to the New York periodicals of the moment, whom Poe thought considerable and interesting enough for notice. Here is the list: George Bush, George H. Colton, N. P. Willis, William M.

Gillespie, Charles F. Briggs, William Kirkland, John W. Francis, Anna Cora Mowatt, George B. Cheever, Charles Anthon, Ralph Hoyt, Gulian C. Verplanck, Freeman Hunt, Piero Maroncelli, Laughton Osborn, Fitz-Greene Halleck, Ann S. Stephens, Evert A. Duyckinck, Mary Gove, James Aldrich, Thomas Dunn Brown, Henry Cary, Christopher Pearse Cranch, Sarah Margaret Fuller, James Lawson, Caroline M. Kirkland, Prosper M. Wetmore, Emma C. Embury, Epes Sargent, Frances Sargent Osgood, Lydia M. Child, Elizabeth Bogart, Catherine M. Sedgwick, Lewis Gaylord Clark, Anne C. Lynch, Charles Fenno Hoffman, Mary E. Hewitt, and Richard Adams Locke. In this list there is one name which we have already found worthy of a glance, — that of Fitz-Greene Halleck. There is another which we have mentioned, — that of Evert A. Duyckinck. There are two at which we shall certainly glance later, — those of N. P. Willis and Sarah Margaret Fuller. And there are two or three which we may conceivably mention, — those of Mrs. Child, of Miss Sedgwick, of Lewis Gaylord Clark, and of Charles Fenno Hoffman. The very names of the other " Literati " are mostly forgotten : they lived ; they flourished ; they died ; and they are so thoroughly buried, some in the pages of Griswold or of Duyckinck, that even such generous editors as Stedman and Hutchinson have found no room for mention of a full sixteen of the thirty-eight. It seems almost cruel to disturb the peace of such untroubled, untroublesome dead.

Our chief reason for recalling these forgotten people is not to remind ourselves of what they happened to be publishing when Poe's best work was done ; it is rather to point out why a considerable part of Poe's best work has itself been forgotten. His critical writings, collected in the sixth, seventh, and eighth volumes of Stedman and Woodberry's edition of his works, are the only ones in which he shows how he could deal with actual fact ; and in dealing with actual fact he proved himself able. Though some of the facts he dealt with, however, were worthy of his pen, — he was among the first, for example, to recognise the merit of Tennyson and of Mrs. Browning, — most of them in the course of fifty years have proved of no human importance. For all this, they existed at the moment. Poe was a journalist, who had to write about what was in the air; and he wrote about it so well that in certain aspects this critical work seems his best. He dabbled a little in philosophy, of course, particularly on the æsthetic side; but he had neither the seriousness of nature — spiritual insight, one might call it, — which must underlie serious philosophising, nor yet the scholarly training which must precede lasting, solid thought. What he did possess to a rare degree was the temper of an enthusiastic artist, who genuinely enjoyed and welcomed whatever in his own art, of poetry, he found meritorious. No doubt he was more than willing to condemn faults; whoever remembers any of his critical activity, for example, will remember how vigourously he attacked Longfellow for plagiarism. We ought to recall with equal certainty how willingly Poe recognised in this same Longfellow those traits which he believed excellent. Poe's serious writing does not concern the eternities as did the elder range of American literature, nor yet does it touch on public matters. True or not, indeed, that grotesque story of his death typifies his relation to political affairs. His critical writing, all the same, deals with questions of fine art in a spirit which if sometimes narrow, often dogmatic, and never scholarly, is sincere, fearless, and generally eager in its impulsive recognition of merit.

Take, for example, a stray passage from the " Literati," — his enthusiastic criticism of Mrs. Frances Sargent Osgood, a lady whose work never fulfilled the promise which Poe discerned in it : —

"Whatever be her theme, she at once extorts from it its whole essentiality of grace. Fanny Ellsler has been often lauded: true poets have sung her praises; but we look in vain for anything written

14

about her, which so distinctly and vividly paints her to the eye as the
. . . quatrains which follow : —

> " ' She comes — the spirit of the dance !
>   And but for those large eloquent eyes,
> Where passion speaks in every glance,
>   She 'd seem a wanderer from the skies.

> " ' So light that, *gazing breathless there !*
>   *Lest the celestial dream should go,*
> *You 'd think the music in the air*
>   *Waved the fair vision to and fro ;*

> " *Or that the melody's sweet flow*
>   *Within the radiant creature played,*
> *And those soft wreathing arms of snow*
>   *And white sylph feet the music made.*' [1]

"This is indeed poetry — and of the most unquestionable kind —
poetry truthful in the proper sense — that is to say, breathing of
Nature. There is here nothing forced or artificial — no hardly sustained enthusiasm. The poetess speaks because she feels, and what
she feels ; but then what she feels is felt only by the truly poetical."

This passage deserves our attention both as containing an
unusually good fragment of the long-forgotten poetry produced
in New York sixty years ago, and as indicating the temper in
which Poe approached contemporary literature. To his mind
the only business of a poet was to make things of beauty.
If in what professed to be poetry he found ugly things, he
unhesitatingly condemned them; if he found anything which
seemed beautiful, nobody could welcome it more eagerly. His
enthusiasm, indeed, often led him into superlative excess; in
the case of these pleasantly pretty lines of Mrs. Osgood's, it
certainly did so ; but if we neglect the superlatives, we can
admit that what he felt to be beautiful was at least good, just
as what he condemned was almost always abominable. However meretricious, — and surely there are aspects enough in
which he seems very meretricious indeed, — Poe really loved
his art ; and whatever his lack of training, he had a natural,
instinctive, eager perception of beauty. This, too, he set

---

[1] The italics are Poe's.

forth in a style always simple and clear, always free from affectation or mannerism, and always marked by a fine sense of rhythm. All these merits appear saliently in those portions of his work which deal with actual fact.

When it comes to his philosophical writings, the whole thing seems more suspicious. As everybody remembers, one of Poe's feats as a journalist was to publish a successful hoax concerning the passage of the Atlantic by a balloon, in which, along with other persons, the minor novelist, Harrison Ainsworth, was said to have journeyed from England to the Carolinas. The tendency to humbug typified by this harmless journalistic feat was deeply characteristic of Poe. When you read such papers as his " Poetic Principles," his " Rationale of Verse," or his " Philosophy of Composition," it is hard to feel sure that he is not gravely hoaxing you. On the whole, he probably was not. In his work of this kind one feels intense ingenuity and unlimited scholarly ignorance. One feels, too, more and more constantly, that his temper was far from judicial. The man who would set forth a lastingly serious study of poetry must do so with deliberation, weighing all questions which present themselves, and arriving at conclusions slowly and firmly. It is one thing to delight in what is good ; it is quite another critically to understand the reasons for such pleasure. The former power is a matter of temperament ; the latter is rather one of thoughtful scholarly training. The traits which make Poe's occasional criticisms excellent are only swiftness of perception and fineness of taste ; these are matters not of training but of temperament.

Temperament, indeed, of a markedly individual kind is what gives lasting character and vitality to the tales and the poems by which he has become permanently known. Both alike are instantly to be distinguished from the critical work at which we have glanced by the fact that they never deal with actualities, be those actualities of this world or of the next. Poe's individual and powerful style, to be sure, full of what

seems like vividness, constantly produces "that willing sus-
pension of disbelief for the moment which constitutes poetic
faith;" but one has only to glance at the attempts to illustrate
his work in the excellent edition of Stedman and Woodberry
to feel the full resurgent rush of suspended disbelief.

Take, for example, a passage which has been chosen for
illustration in " The Fall of the House of Usher " : —

"As if in the superhuman energy of his utterance there had been
found the potency of a spell, the huge antique panels to which the
speaker pointed threw slowly back, upon the instant, their ponderous
and ebony jaws. It was the work of the rushing gust — but then
without those doors there *did* stand the lofty and enshrouded figure
of the lady Madeline of Usher. There was blood upon her white
robes, and the evidence of some bitter struggle upon every portion of
her emaciated frame. For a moment she remained trembling and
reeling to and fro upon the threshold — then, with a low moaning cry,
fell heavily inward upon the person of her brother, and, in her violent
and now final death-agonies, bore him to the floor a corpse, and a
victim to the terrors he had anticipated."

Compare with this the grotesque picture at the beginning of
the tale in Stedman and Woodberry's volume. The trouble
is not chiefly that the draughtsman, however skilful, has not
been gifted with genius, nor yet that he has so far departed
from the text as to depict a man who has just sprung
"furiously to his feet" pensively seated in a very uncomfortable armchair; it is rather that fictions even so vivid as
Usher and the Lady Madeline and the unearthly house of
their doom are things which no one can translate into visual
terms without demonstrating their unreality.

It is just so with Poe's most familiar poems. " The Raven "
cannot be credibly visualised, any more than the uninspired
draughtsman who tried to compose a frontispiece for the poem
could make the lost Lenore anything but ridiculous. The picture which illustrates " Annabel Lee," in its attempt at real-
ism, brings out the trait more clearly still. And take the
opening stanzas of " Ulalume " : —

" The skies they were ashen and sober ;
　　The leaves they were crispèd and sere,
　　The leaves they were withering and sere ;
　It was night in the lonesome October
　　Of my most immemorial year ;
　It was hard by the dim lake of Auber,
　　In the misty mid region of Weir :
　It was down by the dank tarn of Auber,
　　In the ghoul-haunted woodland of Weir.

" Here once, through an alley Titanic
　　Of cypress, I roamed with my soul —
　　Of cypress, with Psyche, my Soul.
　These were days when my heart was volcanic
　　As the scoriac rivers that roll,
　　As the lavas that restlessly roll
　Their sulphurous currents down Yaanek
　　In the ultimate climes of the pole,
　That groan as they roll down Mount Yaanek
　　In the realms of the boreal pole."

You can hardly read this over without becoming conscious of two facts : for all the vividness of impression there is no actuality about these images ; and yet there hovers around them a mood, a temper, an impalpable but unmistakable quality, which could never have emanated from any other human being than Edgar Allan Poe.

This individuality of his is hard to define. One or two things about it, however, seem clear. In tales and poems alike he is most characteristic when dealing with mysteries ; and though to a certain point these mysteries, often horrible, are genuinely mysterious, they reveal no trace of spiritual insight. They indicate a sense that human perception is inexorably limited, but no vital perception of the eternities which lie beyond it. Excellent in their way, one cannot but feel their way to be melodramatic. The very word " melo-dramatic " recalls to us the strolling stage from which Poe almost accidentally sprung in that Boston lodging-house ninety years ago. From beginning to end his temper had the inextricable combination of meretriciousness and sincerity which

marks the temperament of typical actors.   Theirs is a strange
trade, wherein he does best who best shams.   At its noblest
the stage rises into tragedy or broadens into comedy ; but
in our century it has probably appealed most generally to
the public when it has assumed its less poetical and more
characteristic form of melodrama.   Poe, at least temperamentally, seems to have been a melodramatic creature of
genius.

For genius he certainly had, and to no small degree in that
excellent form which has been described as " an infinite
capacity for taking pains."   In his tales, now of melodramatic
mystery, again of elaborate ingenuity, one feels not only that
constant power of imagination peculiar to him ; one feels also
masterly precision of touch.   Take, for example, a familiar
passage from " The Fall of the House of Usher " : —

" I have just spoken of that morbid condition of the auditory nerve
which rendered all music intolerable to the sufferer, with the exception of certain effects of stringed instruments.   It was, perhaps, the
narrow limits to which he thus confined himself upon the guitar,
which gave birth, in great measure, to the fantastic character of his
performances.   But the fervid *facility* of his impromptus could not be
so accounted for.   They must have been, and were, in the notes, as
well as in the words of his wild fantasias (for he not infrequently
accompanied himself with rhymed verbal improvisations), the result
of that intense mental collectedness and concentration to which I
have previously alluded as observable only in particular moments of
the highest artificial excitement.   The words of one of these rhap-
sodies I have easily remembered.   I was, perhaps, the more forcibly
impressed with it, as he gave it, because, in the under or mystic current of its meaning, I fancied that I perceived, and for the first time,
a full consciousness, on the part of Usher, of the tottering of his lofty
reason upon her throne.   The verses, which were entitled ' The
Haunted Palace,' ran very nearly, if not accurately, thus : —

I

" In the greenest of our valleys
By good angels tenanted,
Once a fair and stately palace —
Radiant palace — reared its head.

In the monarch Thought's dominion,
    It stood there;
Never seraph spread a pinion
    Over fabric half so fair.

II

" Banners yellow, glorious, golden,
    On its roof did float and flow,
(This — all this — was in the olden
    Time long ago)
And every gentle air that dallied,
    In that sweet day,
Along the ramparts plumed and pallid,
    A winged odor went away.

III

" Wanderers in that happy valley
    Through two luminous windows saw
Spirits moving musically
    To a lute's well-tuned law,
Round about a throne where, sitting,
    Porphyrogene,
In state his glory well befitting,
    The ruler of the realm was seen.

IV

" And all with pearl and ruby glowing
    Was the fair palace door,
Through which came flowing, flowing, flowing,
    And sparkling evermore,
A troop of Echoes whose sweet duty
    Was but to sing,
In voices of surpassing beauty,
    The wit and wisdom of their king.

V

" But evil things, in robes of sorrow,
    Assailed the monarch's high estate ;
(Ah, let us mourn, for never morrow
    Shall dawn upon him desolate !)
And round about his home the glory
    That blushed and bloomed
Is but a dim-remembered story
    Of the old time entombed.

VI

"And travellers now within that valley
    Through the red-litten windows see
Vast forms that move fantastically
    To a discordant melody;
While, like a ghastly rapid river,
    Through the pale door
A hideous throng rush out forever,
    And laugh — but smile no more."

Here we chance to have side by side his prose and his verse. It is hardly excessive to say that as you read both over and over again, particularly if you read aloud, you will feel more and more that almost every vowel, every consonant, and more surely still every turn of rhythm which places the accent so definitely where the writer means it to fall, indicates not only a rare sense of form, but unusual technical mastery.

They indicate more than this, too. Whether the things which Poe wished to express were worth his pains is not the question. He knew what they were, and he unfeignedly wished to express them. He had almost in perfection a power more frequently shown by skilful melodramatic actors than by men of letters, — the power of assuming an intensely unreal mood and of so setting it forth as to make us for the moment share it unresistingly. This power one feels perhaps most palpably in the peculiar melody of his verse. That "Haunted Palace" may be stagey as you like; but there is something in its lyric quality — that quality whereby poetry impalpably but unmistakably performs the office best performed by pure music — which throws a reader into a mood almost too subtle for words. A morbid mood, to be sure, this of Poe's, and perhaps a meretricious; plenty of things may be said against it; but the mood is distinct from any other into which literature has taken us.

A little while ago we reminded ourselves of a certain analogy between Poe's career and that of Marlowe, the Elizabethan tragic dramatist, who came to his end just as

Shakspere's serious work was beginning. Between Poe's work and Marlowe's there is another analogy which has historically proved more characteristic of literature in America than in England. Marlowe's life, like Poe's, was ugly, sinful, and sordid; yet hardly a line of Marlowe's tragedies is morally corrupt. For this, indeed, there was good reason. Marlowe chanced to belong to the period when English literature was first springing into conscious life, with all the force of unhampered imaginative vitality. In literature, as in human existence, a chief grace of normal youth is freedom from such baseness as time must make familiar to maturity. In the case of Poe a similar contrast between life and work appears. Here, however, this normal reason for it did not exist. The very fact that Poe's work has been eagerly welcomed by continental Europe is evidence enough, if one needed evidence, that his temper was such as the cant of the present day calls decadent. Now the decadent literature which has prevailed in recent England, and far more that which has prevailed elsewhere in Europe, is pruriently foul, obscenely alive with nameless figures and incidents, and with germ-like suggestions of such decay as must permeate a civilisation past its prime. In Poe's work, on the other hand, for all the decadent quality of his temper, there is a singular cleanness, something which for all the thousand errors of his personal life seems like the instinctive purity of a child. He is not only free from any taint of indecency; he seems remote from fleshliness of mental habit.

In the strenuousness of his artistic conscience we found a trait more characteristic of America than of England, — a trait which is perhaps involved in the national self-consciousness of our country. In this instinctive freedom from lubricity, so strongly in contrast with the circumstances of his personal career, and yet to all appearances so unaffected, one feels a touch still more characteristic of his America. It is allied, perhaps, with that freedom from actuality which we have seen to characterise his most apparently vivid work. The world which bred Poe was still a world to whose national life we may give the name of inexperience.

Intensely individual, then, and paradoxically sincere in all his histrionic malady of temper, Poe set forth a peculiar range of mysterious though not significant emotion. In the fact that this emotion, even though insignificant, was mysterious, is a trait which we begin to recognise as characteristically American, at least at that moment when American life meant something else than profound human experience. There is something characteristically American, too, in the fact that Poe's work gains its effect from artistic conscience, an ever present sense of form. Finally, there is something characteristically American in Poe's freedom from either conventional or real fleshly taint. Though Poe's power was great, however, his chief merits prove merits of refinement. Even through a time so recent as his, refinement of temper, conscientious sense of form, and instinctive neglect of actual fact remained the most characteristic traits, if not of American life, at least of American letters.

VI

In the course of our glances at Poe we had occasion to recognise the existence of an extensive, though now forgotten, periodical literature, — " Godey's Lady's Books," " Southern Literary Messengers," " Graham's Magazines," and the like, — which carried on the impulse toward periodical publication already evident in the time of Brockden Brown. Throughout the older regions of America such things sprung up, flourished for a little while, and withered, in weed-like profusion. A year or two ago, Dr. W. B. Cairns, of the University of Wisconsin, published an admirable pamphlet, " On the Development of American Literature from 1815 to 1833," in which this ephemeral phase of it is thoroughly set forth. So far as the periodicals were literary, they were intensely conventional and sentimental, often in the manner of which Mrs. Rowson's once popular novel, " Charlotte Temple," may be taken as a comically extravagant example. In brief, as Dr. Cairns displays them, they are another proof, if proof were needed, of what inevitable luxuriance of insignificant waste must accompany any period of artistic achievement, even when the achievement itself is so far from amazing as was that of America during the years now in question.

In 1833, the year when Dr. Cairns brings his study to a close, there was founded in New York the magazine in which this phase of literary activity may be said to have culminated. This " Knickerbocker Magazine," then, deserves more attention than its positive merit would warrant. It was founded the year after Bryant brought out the first consider-

able collection of his poems,—that 1832 which was marked
in English history by the Reform Bill and in English literature by the death of Scott.   The chief founder of the
" Knickerbocker Magazine" is said to have been Charles
Fenno Hoffman, a gentleman of New York whom Poe
recorded among the Literati of 1846, who published a number of novels and poems, and whose career sadly closed with
an insanity which, beginning in 1849, kept him for a full
thirty-five years in the seclusion where he died.   During its
thirty years or so of existence the " Knickerbocker Magazine "
became not only the most conspicuous, but also the oldest
periodical of its class in the United States.   Though Poe's
Literati were not all contributors to it, their names fairly
typify the general character of its staff, toward the end of
the 40's.

In 1854 its editor was a gentleman named Lewis Gaylord
Clark, whose actual contributions to literature were not important enough to have been found worthy of a place in Stedman and Hutchinson's generously comprehensive " Library."
He had a slightly more eminent twin-brother, Willis Gaylord
Clark, who died young; Stedman and Hutchinson print one
of the latter's poems, " A Witch Song," of which masterpiece
of the Clark genius the following stanza may give an adequate
notion : —

> " Our boat is strong, its oars are good,
>   Of charnel bones its ribs are made;
> From coffins old we carved the wood
>   Beneath the gloomy cypress shade;
> An ignis-fatuus lights the prow, —
>   It is a felon's blood-shot e'e,
> And it shineth forth from his skeleton brow
>   To light our way o'er the Hexen Zee."

As the twenty-fifth anniversary of the founding of the
magazine was approaching, somebody proposed that "the
surviving writers for the 'Knickerbocker' should each furnish, gratuitously, an article, and that the collection should be

published in a volume of tasteful elegance, of which the entire proceeds should be devoted to the building, on the margin of the Hudson, of a cottage, suitable for the home of a man of letters, who, like Mr. Clark, is also a lover of rural life." The book, which is entitled the " Knickerbocker Gallery," was published early in 1855.

In general aspect it is a rather comical relic of obsolete taste. It is a fat volume of about five hundred gilt-edged pages, bound in some imitation of morocco, heavily overlaid with gilt roses and conventional designs. In the middle of the cover is a rough image of the proposed Knickerbocker cottage, a pseudo-Gothic structure with a regular American piazza, almost heraldically supported on either side by a small tree, one apparently a pine, the other perhaps a maple, and neither quite reaching to the second-story windows. The interior of the book corresponds with its inviting external aspect. There are fifty-five contributions by fifty-four separate men of letters. For some reason which does not appear, no women seem to have been invited to co-operate in the benevolent scheme. In general, the contributions are such as pervaded the sentimental annuals and gift-books which during the second quarter of the nineteenth century delighted the reading public in England and in America alike. Forty-seven of the articles are enriched by portraits of the writers engraved on steel. The most characteristic of these is perhaps a gently smirking vignette of Bryant, whose chin beard, shaven upper lip, and poetically bald forehead, dividing unkempt locks, emerge from the broad velvet collar of a much befrogged dressing-gown. Among the faces thus immortalised was that of Irving, whose portrait is taken not from a daguerreotype, but from a togaed bust by Ball Hughes. He contributed some notes from a commonplace book of the year 1821. Bryant sent some verses on " A Snow Shower; " and Halleck a poetical " Epistle to Clark." There are also contributions from several duly portrayed literary men of New England: Holmes sent a

four-page poem entitled " A Vision of the Housatonic ; "
Fields sent an " Invitation to our Cottage Home," in sixteen lines of innocent blank verse; Longfellow contributed a poem, " On the Emperor's Bird's Nest ; " and Lowell,
whose portrait does not appear, sent his verse on " Massac-
cio's Paintings in the Brancacci Chapel " at Florence.   The
other contributors were mostly either resident in New York
or closely associated with that city.   At least three, Mr. Donald Grant Mitchell, Mr. Charles Godfrey Leland, and Mr.
Richard Henry Stoddard, are still surviving and writing in
the year 1900.   The remainder may be taken as fairly typical
of that phase in the letters of New York which has sometimes
been called the Knickerbocker School.   Some of their names
have survived; those, for example, of George Henry Boker,
of Bayard Taylor, of John G. Saxe, of Henry Theodore
Tuckerman, of George William   Curtis, and — an unexpected person to find in such company — of William H.
Seward.   Many of their names are completely forgotten ;
those, for example, of William Pitt Palmer, John W. Francis,
Thomas Ward, J. L. McConnell, Alfred B. Street, and more.
Of all the names and faces in the book, the most characteristic
of the literary period which produced it in New York are
those of Nathaniel Parker Willis.

In the Riverside edition of Lowell's " Fable for Critics,"
a poem originally published seven years before the " Knickerbocker Gallery," when Willis was at the height of his popularity, there are two full pages of tripping verses which
characterise Willis admirably.   And in the paper entitled
" The New Portfolio," with which in 1885 Dr. Holmes
opened his " Mortal Antipathy," is a less familiar passage
about Willis, worth reading in full : —

" Nathaniel Parker Willis was in full bloom when I opened my
first Portfolio.   He had made himself known by his religious poetry,
published in his father's paper, I think, and signed ' Roy.'   He had
started the ' American Magazine,' afterwards merged into the ' New

York Mirror.' He had then left off writing scripture pieces, and taken to lighter forms of verse. He had just written

> " ' I 'm twenty-two, I 'm twenty-two, —
> They idly give me joy,
> As if I should be glad to know
> That I was less a boy.'

" He was young, therefore, and already famous. He came very near being very handsome. He was tall; his hair, of light brown colour, waved in luxuriant abundance; his cheek was as rosy as if it had been painted to show behind the footlights; he dressed with artistic elegance. He was something between a remembrance of Count D'Orsay and an anticipation of Oscar Wilde. There used to be in the gallery of the Luxembourg a picture of Hippolytus and Phædra, in which the beautiful young man, who had kindled a passion in the heart of his wicked step-mother, always reminded me of Willis, in spite of the shortcomings of the living face as compared with the ideal. The painted youth is still blooming on the canvas, but the fresh-cheeked, jaunty young author of the year 1830 has long faded out of human sight. I took the leaves which lie before me as I write, from his coffin, as it lay just outside the door of St. Paul's Church, on a sad, overclouded winter's day, in the year 1867. At that earlier time, Willis was by far the most prominent young American author."

When the " Knickerbocker Gallery " appeared, Willis was so ill that he could contribute only a jaunty apology, of which the closing sentence is typical : —

Well, success to you ! — only don't be so prosperous as to stagger our faith in your other deservings — and among those who will " take stock " in you (as long as you continue " well-requited ") put me down for a share or two, and believe me,

Yours truly,   N. P. WILLIS.

In fact, he was approaching the laborious and melancholy end of a career whose earlier phases had been full of careless gaiety. He was born at Portland, Maine, in 1807. His father, a professional journalist, was an ardent member of the old Congregational communion to which the dialect of New England long gave the name of " orthodox." When the son was a mere boy, the father removed to Boston, where he ultimately founded that remarkably successful children's paper, — now circulating by hundreds of thousands, — the " Youth's Companion." A more significant fact to his son was that the godly old gentleman became a deacon of the Park Street Church. As we shall see later, this office involved social isolation. In Boston, Unitarianism had swept away the pristine religious traditions. Among the older churches only the Old South had stuck by its original Calvinistic colours, and its members generally remained orthodox at the expense of their visiting lists. The Park Street Church, still so conspicuous from Boston Common, had been founded as a new citadel of Calvinism; and it had maintained its principles so bravely as to win for itself in local slang the hardly yet forgotten name of " Brimstone Corner." In the Boston of Willis's youth, then, its members were socially in a position similar to that of contemporary English Dissenters. They are said to have consoled themselves, as indeed orthodox Yankees sometimes do still, by thoughts of what would happen beyond the grave to the triumphant religious liberals who on earth rarely invited them to dinner.

Born and bred amid such surroundings as this, Willis, whose temper was among the most frivolously adventurous of his time, began life in a state of edifying religious conviction. He was sent to school at that stronghold of orthodoxy, Andover, which was still trying to defend the old faith so completely routed by Unitarianism at Harvard College. From Andover, instead of going to Harvard — in orthodox opinion the gate of the broad road to perdition — he was sent to complete the salvation of his soul at Yale. At the prayer meetings which refreshed school-boy life at Andover, he had displayed unusual gifts of exhortation. The creative powers thus evinced found later expression in diluted narrative poetry which dealt with Old Testament stories in a temper somewhat like that of Leigh Hunt, and which is said long to have remained among the favourite edifications of devout old persons in New England. But even Yale orthodoxy failed to keep Willis within the fold. He was handsome; women, particularly older than he, were apt to fall in love with him. He had an instinctive aptitude for gaiety, and when he came back to Boston from college, this son of a Park Street deacon was the most elaborate fop who had ever been seen on the shores of Massachusetts Bay. In spite of considerable religious backsliding, however, he was unable in Boston to overcome the social traditions which kept his family apart from fashion. He tried a little editorial work there, with small success; and he ended by quitting the town in disgust, hating it for life, and returning only for burial nearly forty years later.

In New York he found things more to his taste. Before 1831 he had become associated with one George P. Morris, — now remembered only as the author of a once popular sentimental poem beginning " Woodman, spare that tree," — in the conduct of a periodical called the New York " Mirror." Between them they hit upon a plan of sending Willis abroad, from whence he should write regular European letters; so to Europe he went at the age of twenty-five. His career there for the next five years seems incredible. His pecuniary resources are said to have been limited to ten dollars a week, which Morris agreed to send him; so, of course, he never really knew how his bills were to be paid. But he somehow got letters of introduction; he managed nominally to attach himself to an American legation ; and, before long, there was little fashionable society in Europe where he was not cordially and even intimately received. When toward the end of his stay abroad he went to Dublin, it is recorded that he took to the Lord-Lieutenant of Ireland a letter of introduction from a near relative of that functionary, who described him as an eminent young American likely to attain the Presidency. Soon afterward he married an English heiress, daughter of a general in the army, to whom his financial condition was perfectly well known. Meanwhile he supported himself by regular correspondence with the New York " Mirror." His letters are better than tradition has represented them. At least in New England, people have been apt to fancy that Willis forced his way on false pretences into European society, and then wrote home for publication no end of things which came to his knowledge in private, and which ought to have been recorded, if at all, only in posthumously printed diaries. In this charge there is a grain of truth ; but whoever will read Willis's letters must feel that although in his day there may have been a certain impropriety in publishing any record of private life, he wrote not only pleasantly, but with tactful good-humour. Superficial as you like, his letters are vivid, animated, and carefully reticent of anything which might justly have displeased the persons concerned. If personal journalism is ever to be tolerated, Willis's may be taken as a model of it.

The circumstances of his later career need not be detailed. In brief as set forth in Professor Beers's biography of him, they were constantly more to his credit. His first wife died, and he married again. He got into various money troubles, and he worked unremittingly to support himself and his family honourably, until the disease came upon him which ended his life at the age of sixty-one. By that time the literary fashion which he exemplified was generally outworn ; but the " Home Journal," which he founded, continues to this day its weekly career of chatty personal journalism.

In Willis's palmy days, he was the most popular American writer out of New England. He dashed off all sorts of things with great ease, — not only such descriptions of life and people as formed the staple of his contributions to the " Mirror," but poems and stories, and whatever else belongs to occasional periodical writing. Throughout, his prose style had the provoking kind of jaunty triviality evident in the little sentence which closed his letter to Clark for the " Knickerbocker Gallery." The following poem is perhaps his highest achievement in serious verse : —

"UNSEEN SPIRITS.

" The shadows lay along Broadway,
    'T was near the twilight-tide —
And slowly there a lady fair
    Was walking in her pride.
Alone walked she; but, viewlessly,
    Walked spirits at her side.

" Peace charmed the street beneath her feet,
    And Honour charmed the air;
And all astir looked kind on her,
    And called her good as fair —
For all God ever gave to her,
    She kept with chary care.

" She kept with care her beauties rare,
    From lovers warm and true,
For her heart was cold to all but gold,
    And the rich came not to woo —
But honoured well are charms to sell
    If priests the selling do.

" Now walking there was one more fair —
    A slight girl, lily-pale;
And she had unseen company
    To make the spirit quail;
'Twixt Want and Scorn she walked forlorn,
    And nothing could avail.

" No mercy now can clear her brow
    For this world's peace to pray;
For, as love's wild prayer dissolved in air,
    Her woman's heart gave way ! —
But the sin forgiven by Christ in heaven
    By man is cursed alway ! "

Work so slight may seem hardly worth emphasis. As time passes, however, Willis appears more and more the most characteristic New York man of letters after the year 1832, — the most typical of the school which flourished throughout the career of the " Knickerbocker Magazine." The earlier writers whom we have considered were all imitative, or at least their work seems reminiscent. Brockden Brown is reminiscent of Godwin, Irving of Goldsmith, Cooper of Scott, Bryant of Cowper and Wordsworth, and so on. In a similar way Willis may be said to remind one of Leigh Hunt, and perhaps here and there of Benjamin Disraeli, and Bulwer. The contrast of these last names with those of the earlier models tells the story. As men of letters, Godwin and Goldsmith and Scott and Cowper and Wordsworth are distinctly more important than Bulwer and Disraeli and Leigh Hunt. The merits of the former group are solid ; those of the latter are meretricious ; and when you undertake to dilute Leigh Hunt and Disraeli and Bulwer with Croton water, you get a stimulant hardly strong enough sensibly to affect heads seasoned to draughts of sound old literature. As a descriptive journalist, Willis did work which is still worth reading. His letters from abroad give pleasant and vivid pictures of European life in the 30's ; his letters " from Under a Bridge " give pleasant pictures of country life in our Middle States a little later ; but when it comes to anything like literature, one can hardly avoid the conviction that he had nothing to say.

In the work of the earlier New York school, and even in the work of Poe, we have already remarked, nothing was produced which touched seriously on either God's eternities or the practical conduct of life in the United States. The literature of Brockden Brown, of Irving, of Cooper, and of Poe is only a literature of pleasure, possessing, so far as it has excellence at all, only the excellence of conscientious refinement. Willis, too, so far as his work may be called literature, made nothing higher than literature of pleasure ; and for all the bravery with which he worked throughout his later life, one cannot help feeling in his writings, as well as in some of the social records of his earlier years, a palpable falsity of taste. He was a man of far wider social experience than Bryant or Cooper, probably indeed than Irving himself; and those who personally knew him remember him, as Dr. Holmes did, pleasantly and kindly. Yet, after all, one feels in him rather the quality of a dashing adventurer, of an amiably honourable Bohemian, than such secure sense of personal distinction as marked Bryant and Irving and their contemporaries in New England. A school of letters in which a man of Willis's quality could attain the eminence which for years made him conspicuous was certainly declining.

The "Knickerbocker Magazine," which came to an end in 1864, began to fade about 1857. In that year the "Atlantic Monthly" was started in Boston, and in New York "Harper's Weekly." Both persist; this date, then, two years after the "Knickerbocker Gallery" was published, is a convenient one at which to close our first survey of the literature produced in the Middle States. There are certain names which we might have mentioned; Mrs. Kirkland, for example, whom Poe records among the Literati, wrote some sketches of life in the Middle West which are still vivid, and although of slight positive merit, decidedly interesting as history. Hermann Melville, with his books about the South Seas, which Robert Louis Stevenson is said to have declared the best ever written, and with his novels of maritime adventure, began a career of literary promise, which never came to fruition. Certain writers, too, who reached maturity later had already made themselves known, — Bayard Taylor, for example, and George William Curtis; and in regular journalism Horace Greeley had made the "New York Tribune" already a strong and important ally of the reforms which were strenuously declaring themselves in New England. But certainly between 1833 and 1857 the "Tribune," even with Margaret Fuller and later with George Ripley as its literary critics, had not in New York perspective such characteristic importance as had the "Knickerbocker Magazine." What the "Tribune" stood for, was rather an offshoot of some New England energies which we shall consider later.

The truth is, that the school of letters which began in 1798 with the work of Brockden Brown and persisted throughout the lifetime of Sir Walter Scott in the writings of Irving, of Cooper, and of Bryant, never dealt with deeply significant matters. Almost from the time when Bryant first collected his poems, the literature made in New York and under its influence became less and less important. New York newspapers, to be sure, of which the best examples are the " Evening Post " and the " Tribune," were steadily gaining in merit and influence; but literature pure and simple was not. If we may hold Poe to have belonged to the general phase of American literary activity which we have been considering, — the only phase which during the first half of the nineteenth century developed itself outside of New England, — we may say that this literary activity reached its acme in the work of Poe, itself for all its merit not deeply significant. And even in Poe's time, and still more surely a little later, the literature of which he proves the most important master declined into such good-humoured trivialities as one finds in the " Knickerbocker Gallery " and in the life and work of Willis. By the middle of the nineteenth century, in fact, the literary impulse of the Middle States had proved abortive. For the serious literature of America we must revert to New England.

BOOK V

THE RENAISSANCE OF NEW ENGLAND

BOOK V

THE RENAISSANCE OF NEW ENGLAND

I

SOME GENERAL CHARACTERISTICS OF NEW ENGLAND

FROM the time, shortly after 1720, when Franklin left Boston, where Increase and Cotton Mather were still preaching, we have paid little attention to that part of the country. For during the seventy-two years which intervened between Cotton Mather's death and the nineteenth century, Boston was of less literary importance than it was before or than it has been since. To understand its revival, we must call to mind a little more particularly some general characteristics of New England.

A glance at any map will show that Boston, whose geographical position has obviously made it the principal city of that region, may be distinguished from most American cities by the fact that, comparatively speaking, it is not on the way anywhere. The main line of travel from abroad to-day comes to the port of New York. People bound thence for Washington proceed through Philadelphia and Baltimore; people bound westward are pretty sure to tend toward Chicago; people going southwest pass through St. Louis or New Orleans; people going around the world generally sail from San Francisco; but the only people who are apt to make the excursion from New York to Boston and return are those who do so on purpose. Of course, the ease of intercommunication nowadays combines with several other causes to disguise this isolation of the capital city of New

England. All the same, an isolation, socially palpable to any one who lives there, really characterises not only the city, but the whole region of which it is the natural centre.

This physical isolation was somewhat less pronounced when the English-speaking settlements in America were confined to the fringe of colonies along the Atlantic seaboard. Even then, however, a man proceeding by land from Boston to Philadelphia had to pass through New York; and so one proceeding from New York to Virginia or the Carolinas had to pass through Philadelphia; but the only people who needed to visit Boston were people bound thither. It had happened, meanwhile, that the regions of Eastern Massachusetts, although not literally the first American colonies to be settled, were probably the first to be politically and socially developed. Sewall's " Diary," for example, is an artless record of busy life in and about Boston, from 1674 to 1729. In spite of the many archaic passages which make it so quaintly vivid, it has few more remarkable traits than the fact that the surroundings and in many respects the society which it represents are hardly yet unfamiliar to people born and bred in Eastern New England.

In the first place, the whole country from the Piscataqua to Cape Cod, and westward to the Connecticut River, was almost as settled as it is to-day. Many towns of Sewall's time, to be sure, have been divided into smaller ones; but the name and the local organisation of almost every town of his time still persist; in two hundred years the municipal outlines of Massachusetts have undergone hardly more change than any equal space of England or of France. In Sewall's time, again, the population of this region, though somewhat different from that which at present exists, was much like that which was lately familiar to anybody who can remember the New England country forty years ago. It was homogeneous, and so generally native that any inhabitants but born Yankees attracted attention; and the separate towns were so distinct that any one who knew much of the country could probably infer from a man's name just where he came from. So isolated a region, with so indigenous a population, naturally developed a pretty rigid social system.

Tradition has long supposed this system to have been extremely democratic, as in some superficial aspects it was. The popular forms of local government which were early established, the general maintenance of schools in every town at public expense, and the fact that almost any respectable trade was held a proper occupation for anybody, have gone far to disguise the truth that from the very settlement of New England certain people there have enjoyed an often recognised position of social superiority. This Yankee aristocracy, to be sure, has never been strictly hereditary; with almost every generation old names have socially vanished and new ones appeared until it is now asserted that only one family of Boston has maintained itself without marked vicissitude from the settlement of the town to the present day. Until well into the nineteenth century, however, two facts about New England society can hardly be questioned: at any given time there was a tacitly recognised upper class, whose social eminence was sometimes described by the word "quality;" and although in the course of time most families had their ups and downs, the changes in this respect were never so swift or so radical as materially to alter the general social structure. Names may have changed, but not traditions or ideals; and no matter how fallen in fortune, people who had once been of good stock rarely forgot the fact and rarely suffered it to be forgotten.

In the beginning, as Cotton Mather's old word "theocracy" asserted, the socially and politically dominant class was the clergy. Until 1885, indeed, a relic of this fact survived in the Quinquennial Catalogues of Harvard College, where the names of all graduates who became ministers were still distinguished by italics. In the same catalogues the names of graduates who became governors or judges, or in certain other offices attained public distinction, were printed in capital letters.   These now trivial details indicate how the old social hierarchy of New England was based on education, public service, and the generally acknowledged importance of the ministry.   When the mercantile class of the eighteenth century grew rich, it enjoyed in Boston a similar social distinction, maintained by pretty careful observance of the social traditions which by that time had become immemorial.   And as the growing complexity of society in country towns developed the learned professions of law and medicine, the squire and the doctor were almost everywhere recognised as persons of consideration.   From the beginning, meanwhile, there had been in New England two other kinds of people, tacitly felt to be of lower rank; the more considerable were those plain folks who, maintaining personal respectability, never rose to intellectual or political eminence, and never made more than enough money to keep decently out of debt; the other comprised those descendants of immigrant servants and the like whose general character resembled that of the poor whites of the South.   Just as the local aristocracy of fifty years ago provided almost every Yankee village with its principal people, so this lowest class contributed to almost every village a recognised group of village drunkards.

The political forms which governed this isolated population were outwardly democratic; the most characteristic were the town meetings of which so much has been written.   The population itself, too, was nowhere so large as to allow any resident of a given town to be a complete stranger to any other; but as the generations passed, the force of local tradition slowly, insensibly increased until, long before 1800, the structure of New England society had become extremely rigid.   Sewall, as we have seen, preserves an unconscious picture of this society in the closing years of the seventeenth century and the beginning of the eighteenth. In more deliberate literature there are various more conscious pictures of it later. To mention only a few, Mrs. Stowe's " Oldtown Folks" gives an admirably vivid account of the Norfolk County country about 1800,; Whittier's " Snow-Bound " preserves in " Flemish pictures" the Essex County farmers of a few years later; and Lowell's papers on " Cambridge Thirty Years Ago" and on " A Great Public Character" — Josiah Quincy — give more stately pictures of Middlesex County at about the same time. The incidental glimpses of life in Jacob Abbott's Rollo Books are artlessly true of Yankee life in the 40's; Miss Lucy Larcom's " New England Girlhood " and Dr. Edward Everett Hale's more cursory " New England Boyhood " carry the story from a little earlier to a little later. Miss Alcott's " Little Women " does for the '60's what " Rollo " does for the '40's. And the admirable tales of Miss Mary Wilkins and of Miss Sarah Orne Jewett portray the later New England country in its decline. In all these works, and in the many others of which we may take them as typical, you will find people of quality familiarly mingling with others, but tacitly recognised as socially superior almost like an hereditary aristocracy.

A characteristic example of the family discipline which ensued is preserved in the diary of a Boston merchant who was born before the Revolution and died at about the time when the "Knickerbocker Gallery " enriched the literature of New York. After the good old Yankee fashion, this gentleman had a very large family. One of his younger sons had fallen out of favour; and five of his elder children, all married and in respectably independent positions, desired to intercede for their erring brother. They were afraid, it appears, to broach the subject in conversation; so meeting together with their husbands and wives, they drew up a paper signed by all ten, praying in diplomatically formal terms for parental leniency. This paper was gravely presented without comment to the head of the family. He received it with dignified surprise, and kept it under prayerful consideration for a number of days. Finally, having deliberately made up his mind that paternal authority must not be questioned even by adult children, he sent for the signers one by one, to demand that the signatures be separately erased; and apparently all but one of the signers regretfully but dutifully obeyed. Doubtless an excessive incident of the patriarchal rigidity of New England life about 1830, this is not unique; and it is clearly a thing which could have occurred only in a society of which the structural traditions were immemorially fixed.

Such fixity of social structure, developed during two centuries of geographical and social isolation, could not help resulting in characteristic ways of thinking and feeling. There can be little doubt that the deepest traits of Yankee character had their origin in the intense religious convictions of the immigrants. The dominant class of pristine New England were the clergy, whose temper so permeated our seventeenth-century literature. Their creed was sternly Calvinistic; and Calvinism imposes upon whoever accepts it the duty of constant, terribly serious self-searching. The question before every individual who holds this grim faith is whether he can discern within himself the signs which shall prove him probably among the elect of God. The one certain sign of his regeneration may be found in spontaneous consciousness of ability to use his will in accordance with that of God; in other words, the elect, and no one else, can be admitted by unmerited divine grace into something like spiritual communion with God himself. God himself embodies absolute right and absolute truth. What the strenuously self-searching inner life of serious Yankees aimed to attain, then, was immutable conviction of absolute truth.

This it sought under the guidance of a tyrannically dominant priestly class. Till long after 1800, the orthodox clergy of New England maintained their formal eminence almost unbroken. In every village the settled minister, who usually held his office for life, was a man apart; but he was in constant correspondence with his fellows elsewhere. If by any chance a New England parson happened to go away from home, he naturally put up at the minister's in every town where he passed a night. As Dr. Holmes once put the case, the Yankee clergy formed something like a Brahmin caste, poor in the goods of this world, but autocratic in power.

A fact about them which is often forgotten, however, profoundly influenced New England life. Once in office, they exercised tyrannical authority; but to exercise this, they had to get into office and to stay there. In most parts of the world a dominant hierarchy is self-perpetuating: it is the central authority of the Roman Church, for example, which appoints priests all over the world; it is the distortion of this system effected in England by the Reformation which allows the English gentry still to nominate the rectors of parishes adjacent to their estates. In New England, on the other hand, the congregations themselves called their ministers from the beginning, just as they do still. At first, to be sure, the only actual members of New England churches were people who had satisfied the clergy that they were probably elect; but once church members, they had a right to choose their minister by majority vote. The elect of God, as somebody has phrased it, became the electors of God's chosen. So even if the clergy were so conspicuously the chosen vessels of the Lord, the members of the New England churches may be described as the potters by whose hands the Lord was content to see modelled the vessels of his choice.

From this state of things resulted a palpable check on the power of the old Yankee ministers. In one aspect they were autocratic tyrants; in another they were subject to the tyrannical power of an irresponsible majority vote. The kind of thing which sometimes resulted has always been familiar in America. The first President of Harvard College was compelled to resign his office because he believed in baptism by immersion; after twenty years of service, Jonathan Edwards was deposed from the pulpit of Northampton at the instance of a disaffected congregation; and there were plenty of more fleshly troubles which brought about similar results. The second John Cotton, for example, the son of the first minister of Boston and himself minister of Plymouth, was forced to leave his pulpit under circumstances which may have suggested to Hawthorne the story of "The Scarlet Letter," and though he asserted his innocence to the end, he died obscurely in the Carolinas. If the old New England clergy, in fact, felt bound to watch and guard their congregations, whose errors they denounced with all the solemnity of divine authority, the congregations from the beginning returned the compliment. They watched, they criticised, they denounced errors of the clergy almost as strenuously as the clergy watched and criticised and denounced theirs.

One can see why this state of things was unavoidable. Sincere Calvinists believed that divine grace vouchsafed only to the elect the power of perceiving absolute truth. The elect, chosen at God's arbitrary pleasure, might just as probably be found among the laity as the unregenerate might be found among the clergy. And any mistake anywhere in the system was no trivial matter; it literally meant hell-fire. The deepest fact in the personal life of oldest New England, then, on the part of clergy and laity alike, was this intensely earnest, reciprocally tyrannical, lifelong search for absolute truth.

Toward the period of the American Revolution the mercantile prosperity of Boston had tended to develop in the capital city of New England the social class familiar to us in the portraits of Copley; and their manners were becoming superficially like those of their contemporary England. The

Boston gentry of the third quarter of the eighteenth century, were a wealthier class, and in closer contact with the old world than any had been before their time. In various aspects, then, it is probable that the society which Copley painted was beginning to lose some characteristic native traits. If these were momentarily disappearing from the surface of fashionable New England life, however, they remained a little beneath it in all their pristine force. The literary history of the Revolution shows that the arguments of the Tories may be distinguished from those of the Revolutionists by a pretty sharp line. The temper of that class which the Revolution overthrew was marked by strong attachment to established forms of law. The temper of that revolutionary party which ultimately triumphed was marked, despite respectful recognition of legal precedent, by a more instinctive liking for absolute right. In this revolutionary attachment to absolute right, there is something more analogous to the unquestioning faith in absolute truth which marked the ancestral Calvinists than we can discern in that respect for law and order which had become the dominant sentiment of the Tories. However debatable the suggestion may be, then, the work of the Revolution in New England sometimes looks like the reassertion of the old native type in a society which for a little while had seemed to be yielding precedence to persons of somewhat more extensive sympathy.

An accidental fact familiar to people who know Boston will illustrate this. Copley painted the Boston gentry of his time. Forty or fifty years later the gentry then controlling the destinies of New England were painted by Gilbert Stuart. Many old Boston families still preserve Copley portraits as heirlooms; many, too, similarly preserve portraits by Stuart; and a familiar passage in the first section of Holmes's "Autocrat of the Breakfast Table" describes as among the essential possessions of a man of family in Boston portraits by both of these masters. Whoever knows modern Boston, however, will be apt to feel that, according to this test, such men of family are few. You do not often find Copleys and Stuarts in the same dining-room. When you do, one or the other have generally got there either by purchase or by intermarriage. The Copleys and the Stuarts usually bear different names; they rarely represent direct ancestral lines. A little inquiry will generally reveal another fact about them. As likely as not the Stuart portraits represent people whose fortunes still persist; in general, the Copleys are pathetic survivals of fortunes which went down in the general economic crash of revolutionary times. For at least in New England the American Revolution not only shook to its foundations the structure of fashionable society, but it so disturbed business that hardly anybody was able to pay his debts. The men whom Copley painted were mostly ruined by the Revolution; the men whom Stuart painted were those who, as the country subsided into peace, were able to establish fortunes which have lasted.

This new generation of New England aristocracy, however, many of whose leaders were born in the country and came to Boston in search of fortune, was in many ways sounder and more characteristically native than the generation which it supplanted. To speak of it as if it were a commonplace lower class which had emerged from a great political convulsion, would be totally to misunderstand the situation. In the first place, the men of whom it was composed would have been recognised anywhere as remarkably able; in the second place, if generally descended from families for the moment less conspicuous than those whom Copley had painted a generation earlier, they were generally people who had inherited the sturdiest traditions of New England manhood. Many of them could trace descent from the " quality " of a century or so before; and at least until after the Revolution, even the lower classes of native New England had never so far departed from the general native type as to resemble a European populace or mob. So the New England gentlemen who came to their best when Stuart was painting were mostly people who retained, in rather more purity than the provincial aristocracy which for a while had been more fortunate, the vigorous traits of the original native character. Coming to prominence and fortune, too, with the growth of our new national life, they combined with the vigour of their untired blood a fine flush of independence.

At the same time the society of which they found themselves leaders was one in which fixed traditions had prevailed; and whatever the patriotism of these gentlemen, they were far from radical in social temper. Finding themselves in the position which before the Revolution had been maintained by the people whom Copley painted, they instinctively copied many of the best external characteristics of the elder aristocracy. A petty but significant indication of this tendency may be found in their general habit of assuming coats of arms. Yankee heraldry has never been punctilious. Long before the Revolution people who found themselves prosperous were apt to adopt armorial bearings, often far from grammatical, which are still reverently preserved on silver, tombstones and embroidered hatchments. Till well into the nineteenth century, this innocent vanity remained a general trait of prosperous New Englanders. Just as the new and stronger gentry imitated such innocent foibles of their forerunners, too, they imitated their manners. The chief difference between the two classes seems to have been a distinct improvement in minor morals. The extreme propriety which has marked the surface of Boston life since 1800 seems far less evident in the records of society there before the Revolution. The rise of the gentry whom Stuart painted, in short, meant a maintenance of all the better traits of the elder time, together with a distinct improvement in vigour among the ruling classes of New England, and with a somewhat more rigorous code of social conduct. The traditions which come from this period may be a bit priggish; they are not a bit weak. And the rise of this generation to power marked in New England the beginning of a new era.

Materially this new era declared itself in several obvious ways. The first was a development of foreign commerce, particularly with the East Indies. This brought our native sailors and merchants into personal contact with every part of the world where they could make trade pay. The consequent enlargement of the mental horizon of New England was almost incalculable. Incidentally this foreign trade helped develop that race of seamen which so asserted the naval power of the United States in the otherwise ignominious war of 1812. The embargo which preceded that war, and which brought into being the first poem of Bryant, considerably diverted the more energetic spirits of New England from foreign commerce. Before long there ensued that development of manufactures, particularly on the Merrimac River, which remains so conspicuous a source of New England wealth. And at just about the time when these manufactures were finally established, railways at last brought Boston into constant and swift communication with all parts of the New England country, — with Salem and Newburyport, with Fitchburg, with Worcester, with Providence, and with various parts of the old Plymouth colony.

For almost two hundred years New England, with its intensely serious temper, its rigid social traditions, and its instinctive belief in absolute truth, had been not only an isolated part of the world, but had itself consisted of small isolated communities. Now at a moment when, at least relatively, its material prosperity was not only greater than ever before, but probably greater than it will ever be again, the whole region was suddenly flashed into unity. It was during this period that Boston produced the most remarkable literary expression which has yet declared itself in America. To say that this resulted from social and economic causes is too much; what can surely be asserted is that the highest development of intellectual life in New England coincided with its greatest material prosperity. From the time when Benjamin Franklin left Boston, where Cotton Mather was still preaching, until the days when Unitarianism broke out there, while cotton mills sprung up on the Merrimac, Boston even in America was hardly of the first importance. At this moment it has probably ceased to be so. But during the first three quarters of the nineteenth century its economic importance was pronounced; and intellectually it was superior to any other city which America has yet known.

What happened there economically and politically, is not our immediate business. What does concern us is the intellectual outburst; and this, as we shall see, took, on the whole, a form which may best be described as renascent. In all sorts of intellectual life a new spirit declared itself; but this new spirit was more like that which aroused old Italy to a fresh sense of civilised antiquity than like a spontaneous manifestation of native thought or feeling. In a few years New England developed a considerable political literature, of which the height was reached in formal oratory; it developed a new kind of scholarship, of which the height was reached in admirable works of history; in religion it developed Unitarianism; in philosophy, Transcendentalism; in general conduct, a tendency toward reform which deeply affected our national history; and meantime it developed the most mature school of pure letters which has yet appeared in this country. To these various phases of the New England Renaissance we may now devote ourselves in turn.

II

THE NEW ENGLAND ORATORS

IN the seventeenth century, the literary expression of New England had been chiefly theological. In the eighteenth century this expression, at least in the region of Boston, became chiefly political and was on the whole less important than the political writing produced to the southward. In each case the dominant phase of New England expression had been decidedly serious, and had been concerned with one of the ideals most deeply associated with our ancestral language. These ideals we have broadly called those of the Bible and of the Common Law ; the former incessantly reminds us that we must do right, the latter that we must maintain our rights. And they have in common another trait than either their deep association with the temper of English-speaking races or their pervasive seriousness ; both are generally and most characteristically set forth by means of public speaking.

From the very beginning, then, the appetite for public discourse in New England had been keen. In the seventeenth century a minister who preached or prayed well was sure of admiration and popularity ; in the eighteenth century a similar popularity was the certain reward of a lawyer, too, who displayed oratorical power. Some early records of Yankee appetite for oral discourse are surprising : Sewall somewhere records, for example, that having begun to pray at a devotional meeting, where he lost sight of his hour-glass, he continued an unbroken petition to the Lord for something like two hours, nor did he remark on the part of his hearers any distracting manifestation of fatigue. For two hundred years, Sunday

services in Boston were crowded; and so until well into the
nineteenth century were the regular Thursday lectures, given
by various ministers, who often discussed theological subjects,
but frequently fell to treating public matters from a more or
less theological point of view. Meanwhile, there were few
frivolous amusements. Theatres were held in such abhorrence
that even so lately as 1850 the Boston Museum, whose stock
company at that time admirably preserved the old traditions of
the English stage, advertised its auditorium as a lecture-room
and its performances of standard comedies and farces as
lectures. Although church-going was a duty, then, and even
going to the Thursday lectures was represented as something
of the kind, there can be little doubt that Boston people felt
genuine interest in what their preachers and lecturers said to
them; and until long after 1800 native Yankees had a traditional liking, which they honestly believed unaffected, for
hearing people talk from platforms or pulpits.

When the Revolution came, accordingly, the surest means
of attaining eminence in New England was public speaking.
James Otis, always a man rather of speech than of action,
began the career which made his name national by his spoken
argument against Writs of Assistance. The heroic memory of
Joseph Warren is almost as closely associated with his oration
at the Old South Church concerning the so-called Boston
Massacre as with his death at Bunker Hill. Samuel Adams,
too, is remembered as eloquent; and John Adams, the founder
of that family line which to this day preserves its distinction,
was a skilful public speaker. There is something widely
characteristic, indeed, in the speech which Webster's eulogy
of 1826 attributed to this first New England President of the
United States. The famous "Sink or swim, live or die,
survive or perish," closely imitates the harangues and speeches
of classical historians. In each case the speeches may possibly have been based on some tradition of what was actually
said; in each case, obeying the conventional fashion of his

time, the writer — Thucydides, Livy, or Webster — puts into the mouth of a hero eloquent words which are really his own.   In each case these words not only characterise the personages who are feigned to have uttered them, but as elaborately artificial pieces of rhetoric they throw light as well both on the men who composed them, and on the public for which they were composed.   In more than one way, then, the speech which Webster's superb fiction of 1826 attributed to the John Adams of half a century before illustrates the New England oratory of which Adams was one of the first exponents and Webster himself the greatest.

For between the time of Adams's early maturity and Webster's prime there was a flood of public speaking in New England, more and more punctilious and finished in form. The name of an eminent Federalist, for one thing, who died in 1808 at the age of fifty has been so excellently remembered that a Chief Justice of Massachusetts, in a eulogy on a fellow-judge who died little more than twenty years ago, declared with no intention of anti-climax that " his English was purified by constant reading of the greatest models, — the English Bible, Shakspere, Addison, and Fisher Ames."   And were oratory pure literature, and not rather related to the functions of the pulpit or the bar, one might well give a whole volume to the American oratory of the century which followed the Revolution.   In a study like ours, however, we have time only for a glance at it ; and this hasty glance shows clearly that its most eminent exponent in New England was Daniel Webster.

Webster's public life is a matter of familiar history.   Born in 1782, the son of a New Hampshire farmer, he graduated at the little country college of Dartmouth.   He began his legal career in his native State; but Portsmouth, the chief city of New Hampshire, was already declining in importance, and before 1820 Webster removed to Boston.   At that time the material prosperity of New England was well under way.

Webster's active life in Massachusetts coincided with the full development of those manufacturing industries on which the older Boston fortunes are still generally based. At the head of these industries and of other similar activities was that class of native Massachusetts gentlemen whom Stuart painted. Before long this developed politically into the old Whig party, in which was long concentrated the political energy of the educated and socially eminent people who for a good while controlled Massachusetts politics. Of this party Webster soon became the recognised leader, acquiring such power as no other political leader of New England has known before or since.

Not the least remarkable phase of this extraordinary dominance lies in the fact that Webster was foreign in temperament to the social class of which he thus became the acknowledged chief. The Massachusetts Whigs were Boston gentlemen who embodied the general traits at which we have glanced. Webster was the son of a New Hampshire countryman; and despite the formal dignity of his manners, his character, from their point of view, left something to be desired. Undoubtedly a man of commanding ability, he was with equal certainty a good fellow, robust in personal habits, and not very careful of his minor morals; you could generally trust him to win a case, and not to pay a bill. Yet for half a lifetime he justly maintained personal leadership amid the most severely moral and commercially punctilious aristocracy of America. In view of this fact the means by which he attained eminence becomes significant.

For, in the first place, as an advocate at the bar, in the second place, as a representative of public sentiment on memorable festal occasions, and finally as the most influential of American Senators, Webster's means of asserting himself remained the same. He had an unsurpassed power of getting up before great bodies of his fellow-citizens and talking to them in a way which should hold their attention, influence their convictions, and guide their conduct. It is worth our while, then, to glance at two or three passages from his speeches.

There is no more familiar example of his occasional oratory than his Apostrophe to the survivors of the battle of Bunker Hill, which occurs in an oration delivered in 1825, when the cornerstone of the Bunker Hill Monument was laid :

"Venerable men! you have come down to us from a former generation. Heaven has bounteously lengthened out your lives, that you might behold this joyous day. You are now where you stood fifty years ago, this very hour, with your brothers and your neighbours, shoulder to shoulder, in the strife for your country. Behold, how altered! The same heavens are indeed over your heads; the same ocean rolls at your feet; but all else how changed! You hear now no roar of hostile cannon, you see no mixed volumes of smoke and flame arising from burning Charlestown. The ground strewed with the dead and the dying; the impetuous charge; the steady and successful repulse; the loud call to repeated assault; the summoning of all that is manly to repeated resistance; a thousand bosoms freely and fearlessly bared in an instant to whatever of terror there may be in war or death; — all these you have witnessed, but you witness them no more. All is peace. The heights of yonder metropolis, its towers and roofs, which you then saw filled with wives and children and countrymen in distress and terror, and looking with unutterable emotions for the issue of the combat, have presented you to-day with the sight of its whole happy population, come out to welcome and to greet you with a universal jubilee. Yonder proud ships, by a felicity of position appropriately lying at the foot of this mount, and seeming fondly to cling around it, are not means of annoyance to you, but your country's own means of distinction and defence. All is peace ; and God has granted you this sight of your country's happiness, ere you slumber in the grave. He has allowed you to behold and to partake the reward of your patriotic toils ; and he has allowed us, your sons and countrymen, to meet you here, and in the name of the present generation, in the name of your country, in the name of liberty, to thank you ! "

However impressive you may find such work as this, you can hardly avoid feeling it to be elaborately artificial ; and yet its artificiality has a ring of genuineness. It comes very near bombast, but it is not quite bombastic. It does not caricature itself.

Similar traits you may find in Webster's legal arguments, such as his description of the murder of Joseph White of Salem : —

"The deed was executed with a degree of self-possession and steadiness equal to the wickedness with which it was planned. The circumstances now clearly in evidence spread out the whole scene before us. Deep sleep had fallen on the destined victim, and on all beneath his roof. A healthful old man, to whom sleep was sweet, the first sound slumbers of the night held him in their soft but strong embrace. The assassin enters, through the window already prepared, into an unoccupied apartment. With noiseless foot he paces the lonely hall, half-lighted by the moon; he winds up the ascent of the stairs, and reaches the door of the chamber. Of this, he moves the lock, by soft and continued pressure, till it turns on its hinges without noise; and he enters, and beholds his victim before him. The room is uncommonly open to the admission of light. The face of the innocent sleeper is turned from the murderer, and the beams of the moon, resting on the gray locks of his aged temple, show him where to strike. The fatal blow is given! and the victim passes without a struggle or a motion, from the repose of sleep to the repose of death! It is the assassin's purpose to make sure work; and he plies the dagger, though it is obvious that life has been destroyed by the blow of the bludgeon. He even raises the aged arm, that he may not fail in his aim at the heart, and replaces it again over the wounds of the poniard! To finish the picture, he explores the wrist for the pulse! He feels for it, and ascertains that it beats no longer! It is accomplished. The deed is done. He retreats, retraces his steps to the window, passes out through it as he came in, and escapes. He has done the murder. No eye has seen him, no ear has heard him. The secret is his own, and he is safe!"

It would be hard to find a more vivid description of appallingly tragic fact; and the speech of which this formed a part carried a Salem jury against the evidence to a morally just verdict. As one looks at it, however, after an interval of seventy years, one feels along with its consummate skill, an artificiality of both conception and phrase, nowadays as foreign to us as a totally foreign language. The words "bludgeon" and "poniard," for instance, just as palpably as the slip into the historical present tense, instantly betray elaborate, though spontaneous, artifice.

Just such artificiality and power combine in the famous climax of Webster's reply to Hayne, delivered in that same 1830 : —

"I have not allowed myself, sir, to look beyond the Union, to see what might be hidden in the dark recess behind. I have not coolly weighed the chances of preserving liberty when the bonds that unite us together shall be broken. asunder. I have not accustomed myself to hang over the precipice of disunion, to see whether, with my short sight, I can fathom the depth of the abyss below; nor could I regard him as a safe counsellor in the affairs of this government, whose thoughts should be mainly bent on considering, not how the Union may be best preserved, but how tolerable might be the condition of the people when it should be broken up and destroyed. While the Union lasts, we have high, exciting, gratifying prospects spread out before us, for us and our children. Beyond that I seek not to penetrate the veil. God grant that in my day, at least, the curtain may not rise! God grant that on my vision never may be opened what lies behind! When my eyes shall be turned to behold for the last time the sun in heaven, may I not see him shining on the broken and dishonoured fragments of a once glorious Union; on States dissevered, discordant, belligerent; on a land rent with civil feuds, or drenched, it may be, in fraternal blood! Let their last feeble and lingering glance rather behold the gorgeous ensign of the republic, now known and honoured throughout the earth, still full high advanced, its arms and trophies streaming in their original lustre, not a stripe erased or polluted, nor a single star obscured, bearing for its motto, no such miserable interrogatory as 'what is all this worth?' nor those other words of delusion and folly, 'Liberty first and Union afterwards;' but everywhere, spread all over in characters of living light, blazing on all its ample folds, as they float over the sea and over the land, and in every wind under the whole heavens, that other sentiment, dear to every true American heart, — Liberty *and* Union, now and forever, one and inseparable!"

It was such oratory as this, in Congress, in the courts, and at all sorts of public meetings alike, which for more than thirty years sustained Webster's commanding influence. To call it artificial is perhaps a mistake. The man spoke and wrote in a way which to him, as well as to the public of his time, seemed the only fit one for matters of such dignity as those with which he had to deal; and he wrote and spoke with a fervid power which any one can recognize. All the same, his style is certainly more analogous to Dr. Johnson's published prose than to those idiomatic utterances recorded by Boswell which have made Johnson immortal. If Webster's power is beyond dispute, so is its essentially histrionic character. There used to be a saying that no human being was ever really so great as Daniel Webster always looked; he had, in fact, that temperamental tendency to pose which you generally find in actors, and often in preachers. And this he enforced, in a manner which was thoroughly acceptable to the America of his time, by an extremely elaborate rhetoric based partly on the parliamentary traditions of eighteenth century England, and partly, like those traditions themselves, on the classical oratory of Rome and Greece.

Such highly developed oratory as Webster's is a kind of thing which never grows into existence alone. Like Shakspere before him, he was only the most eminent member of a school which has left many other memories, in their own day of almost equal distinction; and the fact that he retained so many traces of his far from eminent New Hampshire origin makes him somewhat less typical of the Boston orators of his time than were some natives of Massachusetts.

Of these none was more distinguished than Edward Everett. Born in 1794, the son of a minister, but not sprung from a family which had enjoyed high social consideration before the Revolution, he took his degree at Harvard in 1811, and two years later he became for a while minister of the Brattle Street Church in Boston. A year or so later, having been appointed professor of Greek at Harvard, he went abroad, to prepare himself for his academic duties, and was among the earliest of American scholars to study at a German university. The effect which he produced on his return from Europe has been vividly described by Emerson : —

"There was an influence on the young people from the genius of Everett which was almost comparable to that of Pericles in Athens.

He had an inspiration which did not go beyond his head, but which made him the master of elegance. If any of my readers were at that period in Boston or Cambridge, they will easily remember his radiant beauty of person, of a classic style, his heavy large eye, marble lids, which gave the impression of mass which the slightness of his form needed ; sculptured lips ; a voice of such rich tones, such precise and perfect utterance, that, although slightly nasal, it was the most mellow and beautiful and correct of all the instruments of the time. The word that he spoke, in the manner in which he spoke it, became current and classical in New England. He had a great talent for collecting facts, and for bringing those he had to bear with ingenious felicity on the topic of the moment. Let him rise to speak on what occasion soever, a fact had always just transpired which composed, with some other fact well known to the audience, the most pregnant and happy coincidence. . . . In the lecture-room, he abstained from all ornament, and pleased himself with the play of detailing erudition in a style of perfect simplicity. In the pulpit (for he was then a clergyman) he made amends to himself and his auditor for the self-denial of the professor's chair, and, with an infantine simplicity still, of manner, he gave the reins to his florid, quaint, and affluent fancy.

"Then was exhibited all the richness of a rhetoric which we have never seen rivalled in this country. Wonderful how memorable were words made which were only pleasing pictures, and covered no new or valid thoughts. He abounded in sentences, in wit, in satire, in splendid allusion, in quotation impossible to forget, in daring imagery, in parable and even in a sort of defying experiment of his own wit and skill in giving an oracular weight to Hebrew or Rabbinical words : . . . feats which no man could better accomplish, such was his self-command and the security of his manner. All his speech was music, and with such variety and invention that the ear was never tired. This was a triumph of rhetoric. It was not the intellectual or the moral principles which he had to teach. It was not thoughts. But his power lay in the magic of form ; it was in the graces of manner ; in a new perception of Grecian beauty, to which he had opened our eyes. In every public discourse there was nothing left for the indulgence of his hearer, no marks of late hours and anxious, unfinished study, but the goddess of grace had breathed on the work a last fragrancy and glitter."

If this sketch of Emerson's gives the impression that Everett was a mere rhetorician, as distinguished from a man of power, the facts of his career should suffice instantly to correct it. Among other phases of his later activity, he was

an editor of the " North American Review ; " for ten years he
was a member of Congress ; for four years he was governor
of Massachusetts ; for four more he was Minister to England ; he succeeded Webster as Secretary of State ; he was
president of Harvard College ; he was senator from Massachusetts ; and in 1860 he was nominated for the vice-presidency
of the United States by the party which bravely tried to avert
secession. In person he embodied that dignified grace which
marked the Whig gentry of Massachusetts ; and if his distinction of feeling and his formality of manner prevented him at
once from popularity and from unrestrained fervour of utterance,
no man of his time has been remembered with more admiration
or respect. What makes Emerson's sketch noteworthy, then,
is not so much its critical acuteness as the precision with which
it reminds us that a career so brilliant and useful as Everett's
was based on consummate mastery of rhetoric.

Everett's published works consist of four volumes, entitled
" Orations and Speeches," beginning with an address before
the Phi Beta Kappa Society of Harvard College on " The
Circumstances Favourable to the Progress of Literature in
America," delivered in 1824 ; and closing with a brief address
at Faneuil Hall in aid of a " Subscription to Relieve the Suffering People of Savannah," delivered on the 9th of January,
1865, less than a week before his death. Throughout these
four volumes, comprising the utterances of more than forty
years, every paragraph seems a studied, masterly work of
art. Everett's natural feeling was warm and spontaneous ;
but he had acquired and he unswervingly maintained that
incessant self-control which his generation held among the
highest ideals of conduct. So whatever he publicly uttered,
and still more whatever he suffered himself to print, was deliberately considered to the minutest detail.

His familiar description of the voyage of the Mayflower,
from his oration at Plymouth in 1824, will show his oratory in
its earliest stage : —

" Methinks I see it now, that one solitary, adventurous vessel, the Mayflower of a forlorn hope, freighted with the prospects of a future state, and bound across the unknown sea. I behold it pursuing, with a thousand misgivings, the uncertain, the tedious voyage. Suns rise and set, and weeks and months pass, and winter surprises them on the deep, but brings them not the sight of the wished-for shore. I see them now, scantily provided with provisions, crowded almost to suffocation in their ill-stored prison, delayed by calms, pursuing a circuitous route, and now, driven in fury before the raging tempest, in their scarcely seaworthy vessel. The awful voice of the storm howls through the rigging. The labouring masts seem straining from their base ; the dismal sound of the pumps is heard ; the ship leaps, as it were, madly from billow to billow ; the ocean breaks, and settles with ingulfing floods over the floating deck, and beats with deadening weight against the staggered vessel. I see them, escaped from these perils, pursuing their all but desperate undertaking, and landed at last, after a five months' passage, on the ice-clad rocks of Plymouth, weak and exhausted from the voyage, poorly armed, scantily provisioned, depending on the charity of their ship-master for a draught of beer on board, drinking nothing but water on shore, without shelter, without means, surrounded by hostile tribes. Shut now the volume of history, and tell me on any human probability, what shall be the fate of this handful of adventurers. Tell me, man of military science, in how many months were they all swept off by the thirty savage tribes enumerated within the boundaries of New England ? Tell me, politician, how long did this shadow of a colony, on which your conventions and treaties had not smiled, languish on this distant coast ? Students of history, compare for me the baffled projects, the deserted settlements, the abandoned adventures of other times, and find the parallel of this. Was it the winter's storm, beating upon the houseless heads of women and children ? was it hard labour and spare meals ? was it disease ? was it the tomahawk ? was it the deep malady of a blighted hope, a ruined enterprise, and a broken heart, aching in its last moments at the recollection of the loved and left, beyond the sea ? — was it some or all of these united that hurried this forsaken company to their melancholy fate ? And is it possible that neither of these causes, that not all combined, were able to blast this bud of hope? Is it possible that from a beginning so feeble, so frail, so worthy, not so much of admiration as of pity, there have gone forth a progress so steady, a growth so wonderful, a reality so important, a promise yet to be fulfilled so glorious ? "

The close of his address at the inauguration of the Union Club in Boston, delivered on the 9th of April, 1863, in the midst of the Civil War, typifies his eloquence at the end : —

"The cause in which we are engaged is the cause of the Constitution and the Law, of civilisation and freedom, of man and of God. Let us engage in it with a steadiness and a fortitude, a courage and a zeal, a patience and a resolution, a hope and a cheer, worthy of the fathers from whom we are descended, of the country we defend, and of the privileges we inherit. There is a call and a duty, a work and a place, for all ; — for man and for woman, for rich and for poor, for old and for young, for the stout-hearted and strong-handed, for all who enjoy and all who deserve to enjoy the priceless blessings at stake. Let the venerable forms of the Pilgrim Fathers, the majestic images of our Revolutionary sires, and of the sages that gave us this glorious Union ; let the anxious expectations of the Friends of Liberty abroad, awakened at last to the true cause and the great issues of this contest ; let the hardships and perils of our brethren in the field and the fresh-made graves of the dear ones who have fallen ; let every memory of the past and every hope of the future, every thought and every feeling, that can nerve the arm, or fire the heart, or elevate and purify the soul of a patriot, — rouse and guide and cheer and inspire us to do, and, if need be, to die, for our Country ! "

Between these two extracts there is certainly a contrast ; but it is rather such a contrast as exists between the history of the very different times in which they were delivered than a temperamental one. The earlier, of course, is more conventional, more elaborate and more florid ; the latter, spoken at a moment of gravest national danger, at a moment too when the speaker had attained his full maturity, is more compact, more fervid, more stirring. But both alike reveal the consummate skill of a deliberate master of the art of oratory.

The eloquence and the rhetorical skill of Webster and of Everett were the more admired in their own day for the reason that they were exercised in behalf of those political principles which then commanded the support of all conservative people in Massachusetts. So too was the eloquence of many other men, each of whom may fairly be held a master of the art of which Everett and Webster were the most eminent exponents. Even so cursory a study as ours may not neglect the name of Rufus Choate, like Webster a graduate of Dartmouth, like Everett a lifelong reader of the classics, and for years not only eminent in public life, but acknowledged to be the most powerful advocate at the New England bar. A little later than the prime of these men there arose in Boston another generation of orators, differing from their predecessors both in principle and to some degree in method, who used their great powers for purposes which impressed conservative people as dangerously demagogic. Of these the most eminent were Wendell Phillips, Theodore Parker, and Charles Sumner. On all three we shall touch later. But we may hardly again have occasion to mention an eminent citizen of the elder type who survived until 1894, and preserved to the end the traditions of that great school of formal oratory of which he was the last survivor, — Mr. Robert Charles Winthrop.

With Mr. Winthrop, one may say, the oratory of New England expired. And now, as one considers its century and more of history, one discerns more and more clearly why the period in which it reached its height may best be understood when we call it a period of Renaissance. Almost from the time of the Revolution, isolated New England, like the rest of America, was awakening to a new sense of national consciousness; so the society of New England, traditionally one which venerated its leaders, looked to the men whom circumstances brought prominently forward for indubitable assertion of dignity in our national character. The professional circumstances which brought men forward were generally those of the pulpit or the bar; clergymen and lawyers accordingly found that they could no longer maintain their eminence by merely treading in the footsteps of their predecessors. Trained in our old Yankee colleges at a time when such education meant a little mathematics and a tolerable reading knowledge of the classics, these men, who felt themselves called upon admirably to express our new nationality, turned instinctively to that mode of expression which in crude form had long been characteristic of their country. In their impulsive desire to give this a new vitality, they instinctively began to emulate first the formal oratory of England, which had reached its acme in the preceding century; and then, perhaps more consciously, they strove to saturate themselves with the spirit of those immemorial masterpieces of oratory which help to immortalise the literatures of Rome and of Greece.

On general principles, the world might have expected America to produce public utterances of a crudely passionate kind, marked rather by difference from what had gone before than by respect for traditional models. Instead, without a touch of affectation, our orators, obeying the genuine impulse of their nature, exerted their most strenuous energy in surprisingly successful efforts to emulate the achievements of an extremely elaborate art which had attained final excellence in the days of Cicero and Demosthenes. The oratorical models of Greece and of Rome they imitated in just such spirit as that in which the masterpieces of antique plastic art were imitated by fifteenth-century Italy. Apart from its political significance, as embodying principles which controlled the American history of their time, their work is significant in our study as proving how spontaneously the awakening national consciousness of New England strove to prove our country civilised by conscientious obedience to eldest civilised tradition.

III

THE NEW ENGLAND SCHOLARS AND HISTORIANS

SUCH high development of mental activity as was indicated by the renascent oratory of New England is never solitary. As Emerson's memories of Everett implied, something similar appeared at the same period in the professional scholarship of the region. From the beginning, the centre of learning there had been Harvard College, founded to perpetuate a learned ministry. This it did throughout its seventeenth-century career; and in the eighteenth century it also had the distinction of educating many lawyers and statesmen who became eminent at the time of the Revolution. Thomas Hutchinson was a Harvard man, and so were almost all the leading Boston Tories, of whom he is the best remembered. So, too, were James Otis, and Joseph Warren, and the Adamses, and almost every Bostonian who attained distinction on the revolutionary side. Up to the beginning of the nineteenth century, however, Harvard College remained little more than a boys' school. It received pupils very young; it gave them a fair training in Latin and Greek, a little mathematics, and a touch of theology if they so inclined; and then it sent them forth to the careers of mature life. It contented itself, in brief, with somewhat languidly preserving the tradition of academic training planted in the days of Charles I.; and this it held, in rather mediæval spirit, to be chiefly valuable as the handmaiden of theology, and later of law too. One principal function of a true university — that of acquiring and publishing fresh knowledge — it had not attempted.

At the close of the eighteenth century, indeed, learning at Harvard was probably inferior to that which had existed there a century before. In 1800, Latin seems to have been far less familiar to either teachers or students than it was to those who taught and studied under the presidency of Increase Mather. Until well into the nineteenth century, too, Harvard appeared less and less vital. In the surrounding air, however, a new and fresh spirit of learning declared itself, and the leaders of this, as well as the followers, were generally either Harvard men or men who in mature life were closely allied with our oldest college. The celebrated Count Rumford, for one, a Yankee country boy, began his regular study of science by attending the lectures of Professor John Winthrop of Harvard, before the Revolution; and in spite of his permanent departure from his native country, he retained a keen interest in New England. In 1780 he had something to do with the founding in Boston of the American Academy of Arts and Sciences, which, with the exception of Franklin's Philosophical Society in Philadelphia, is the oldest learned society in America. For more than a century the American Academy has maintained, in its proceedings and its publications, a standard of learning recognised as excellent all over the world. Nor was it long alone in Boston. In 1791, the Massachusetts Historical Society was founded for the purpose of collecting, preserving, and publishing historical matter, chiefly relating to its ancestral Commonwealth. Like the American Academy, this society still flourishes, and during its century of existence it has published a considerable amount of material, admirably set forth and often of more than local importance.

In the early years of the nineteenth century, too, certain young gentlemen of Boston, mostly graduates of Harvard and chiefly members of the learned professions, formed themselves into an Anthology Club, with the intention of conducting a literary and scholarly review. Their Anthology did not last long; but their Club developed on the one hand into the Boston Athenæum, which in ninety years has grown into a remarkably well selected library of some two hundred thousand volumes; and in 1815, on the other hand, into that periodical which long remained the serious vehicle of scholarly New England thought, — the "North American Review." This was modelled on the great British Reviews, — the "Edinburgh" and the "Quarterly;" and under the guidance of such men as William Tudor, Edward Tyrrell Channing, Jared Sparks, James Russell Lowell, Charles Eliot Norton, and the late Dr. Andrew Preston Peabody, it maintained its dignity for more than fifty years. The present "North American Review," which has passed by purchase into different control, is, however admirable, entirely changed in character.

Though the American Academy, the Massachusetts Historical Society, the Boston Athenæum, and the old "North American Review" may hardly be taken as comprehensive of the new learning which was springing into life among Boston men bred at Harvard, they are typical of it. In no aspect are they more so than in the fact that none of them was indigenous; all alike were successful efforts to imitate in our independent New England such learned institutions as were among the most salient evidences of civilisation in Europe. What they stand for — the real motive which was in the air — was an awakening of American consciousness to the fact that serious contemporary standards existed in other countries than our own; and that our claim to respect as a civilised community could no longer be maintained by the mere preservation of a respectable classical school for boys. Our first outbreak of the spirit of learning, indeed, was even more imitative than the contemporary literature which sprang up in New York, or than the oratory which in the same years so elaborately developed itself in Massachusetts.

It was not until a little later that the scholarly impulses of New England produced either persons or works of literary distinction; but the form which the characteristic literature of this scholarship was to take had already been indicated both by the early literary activities of this part of the country and by the nature of our most distinguished learned society. From the earliest period of Massachusetts, as we have seen, there was, along with theological writing, a considerable body of publications which may be roughly classified as historical. The " Magnalia " of Cotton Mather, for instance, the most typical literary production of seventeenth-century America, was almost as historical in impulse as it was theological. Earlier still, the most permanent literary monument of the Plymouth colony was Bradford's manuscript " History ; " and such other manuscripts as Winthrop's " History " and Sewall's " Diary " show how deeply rooted in the colony of Massachusetts too was a lasting fondness for historical record. Other than local history, indeed, seems to have interested the elder Yankees chiefly as it bore on the origins and development of New England. A comical example of this fact is to be found in the " Chronological History of New England in the Form of Annals," published in 1736, by the Reverend Thomas Prince, minister of the Old South Church. Prince had unrivalled opportunities for collecting and preserving the facts of our first century; but, having thought proper to begin his work by " an introduction, containing a brief *Epitome* of the most remarkable *Transactions and Events* ABROAD, from the CREATION," he had the misfortune to die before he had brought the chronology of New England itself to a later period than 1630. A more philosophical work than Prince's was that " History of Massachusetts " by Thomas Hutchinson, which may perhaps be called the most respectable American book before the Revolution. From the foundation of the colony, in short, New England men had always felt strong interest in local affairs and traditions ; and this had resulted in a general habit of collecting and sometimes of publishing accounts of what had happened in their native regions.

The temper in question is still familiar to any one who knows with what ardour native Yankees abandon themselves to the delights of genealogical research. Throughout the nineteenth century it has borne fruit in those innumerable town histories which make the local records of New England so minutely accessible to all who have patience to plod through innumerable volumes of trivial detail. It may fairly be regarded as the basis in New England character of the most considerable scholarly expression which New England developed during its period of Renaissance. For during the nineteenth century there appeared in Boston a group of historians whose work became widely and justly celebrated.

The first of these who occurs to one, although he made a deeper impression on the intellectual life of Boston than almost anybody else, is hardly remembered as of high literary importance. This was George Ticknor, who was born in 1791, the only son of a prosperous but not eminent man of business. He was sent to Dartmouth College, and after graduation prepared himself for the practice of law; but finding this not congenial, and having in prospect fortune enough to maintain himself respectably without a profession, he determined to devote himself to pure scholarship. In 1815 he accordingly went abroad with letters of introduction which combined with his exceptional social qualities to give him during the next four years access to the most distinguished and interesting society in almost every European country. A portion of his stay abroad, which he devoted to serious study, he passed at the University of Göttingen, where Edward Everett came in the same year, 1815. Together these were the first of that distinguished and continuous line of American scholars who have supplemented their native education by enthusiastic devotion to German learning. In 1819, having returned to America, Ticknor became the first Smith Professor of the French and Spanish languages and Belles Lettres at Harvard College; Everett at the same time began his lectures there as professor of Greek. Together they stood for a new principle in our old college, — that instructors ought not only to assure themselves that students have learned, but actually to teach. Everett relinquished his professorship in 1824, betaking himself to that more public career which is better remembered. Ticknor, the first Harvard professor of modern languages, retained his chair until 1835; and during this time he strenuously attempted to enlarge the office of Harvard from that of a respectable high school to that of a true university. At that period, however, hardly any other New England scholars had had personal experience of foreign learning; and time was not ripe for the changes which Ticknor so ardently advocated. For a while his efforts bade fair to succeed; reaction followed; but it is hardly too much to say that the germs of those modern phases of learning which have distinguished Harvard College during the last thirty years, are discernible in the plans which George Ticknor cherished thirty years before.

Besides this service to professional learning, Ticknor, in later life, had more than any one else to do with the establishment of that great engine of popular education which for some time distinguished Boston from other American cities, — the Public Library. Ticknor's private library was in its day among the largest and best selected on this side of the Atlantic; and his enthusiasm in the cause of learning induced him to lend his books freely to any respectable persons who satisfied him that they really wanted to use them. His book-plate, inscribed simply with his name and the words *Suum Cuique*, pleasantly records this admirable generosity, which is said to have resulted in no considerable loss. This experience, persisting through the renascent period of New England, convinced him that if he could bring the American public into free contact with good literature, the general taste for good reading would increase, and the general intelligence and consequent civilisation would improve, in accordance with the aspirations of human nature toward what is best. The idea of a great public library, then, grew in his mind; and in

1852 he was an eager leader in the movement which established in Boston the first and best public circulating library of America.

As the first learned professor of modern languages in an American university, as the first exponent in our university life of continental scholarship, as the earliest of Americans to attempt the development of an American college into a modern university, and finally as the chief founder of the chief public library in the United States, Ticknor's claims upon popular memory are remarkable. What is more, those who knew him well felt for him a strong personal attachment; and it is probable that no scholar or man of letters was ever more generous in aiding and encouraging whomever he found eager in learning or letters. At least in his later years, however, Ticknor's manners did not impress the public as engaging. His dignity seemed forbidding; his tongue was certainly sharp; to people who did not attract him his address was hardly sympathetic; and his social habits, confirmed by almost lifelong intimacy with good European society, were a shade too exclusive for the growingly democratic taste about him. Yet it is hard to overestimate the difference which Ticknor's personal presence made in the intellectual history of New England, or the diffusion of knowledge which sprang from his generous impulse.

If Ticknor's chief labours, however, took other than literary form, Ticknor would probably have regarded as his principal claim to recognition the "History of Spanish Literature," which he published in 1849. From the time of his first journey abroad he had been attracted to Spanish matters; his professorship at Harvard, too, was partly devoted by its very terms to Spanish literature; and incidentally he collected, and bequeathed to the Public Library of Boston, a Spanish library, said to be the most complete outside of Spain itself. It was not until thirty years after he began the work of the Smith professorship that he published his history. Fifty years later, this deeply scholarly book, which involved untiring investigation of the best German type, remains authoritative; and it was perhaps the first American book to establish throughout the learned world the position of any American scholar. On the other hand, it is not interesting. Ticknor's mind was rather acquisitive and retentive than creative. His work is that of a thoroughly trained scholar; of a man, too, so sincerely devoted to literature that, as we have seen, his services to literary culture in America can hardly be overestimated; of a man, furthermore, whose letters and journals show him, though deficient in humour, to have had at command an agreeable and fluent every-day style. When all is said, however, the " History of Spanish Literature," taken by itself, is heavily respectable reading. A more winning example of Ticknor's literary power is the life of his friend and contemporary, Prescott, which he wrote partly at the instance of the Massachusetts Historical Society, shortly after Prescott's death. Ticknor himself died at the age of eighty in 1871.

About the time when Ticknor began his teaching in the Smith professorship at Harvard, a subsequently famous declaration of the Unitarian faith was made in the sermon preached at Baltimore by William Ellery Channing, on the occasion of the ordination to the Unitarian ministry of a man no longer in his first youth, Jared Sparks. Sparks's ministerial career was not very long. In 1824 he became an editor of the " North American Review," and for the rest of his life he remained in New England. From 1839 to 1849 he was professor of history at Harvard; from 1849 to 1853 he was President of the College; and after his resignation he continued resident in Cambridge until his death, in 1866.

Sparks left behind him no original writings which have survived; but his special services to historical study in New England were almost as great as were those of Ticknor to the study of modern languages and to the modern spirit in learning. As early as 1829 he began to issue an elaborate

collection of the diplomatic correspondence of the American
Revolution. Between 1834 and 1840 he collected and issued
the first authoritative editions of the writings of Washington
and of Franklin; and although his editorial principles were
not in all respects such as have been sanctioned by later
scholarship, he was scrupulously exact in statements of fact
and untiring in methodical accumulation of material. In
1834 appeared the first volume of his " Library of American
Biography," the publication of which continued until 1847.
In each volume are the lives of three or four eminent Americans, generally written by enthusiastic young scholars, but all
subjected to the editorial supervision of Sparks, who thus
brought into being a still valuable biographical dictionary.

Such work as this clearly evinces wide and enthusiastic
interest in the study and writing of history. Though not
educated in Germany, Sparks, with his untiring energy in
the accumulation and arrangement of material, and his unusual power of making other people work systematically,
was very like a sound German scholar. He really established
a large historical factory; with skilled help, he collected all
the raw material he could find; and he turned out something like a finished article in lengths to suit, — somewhat
as his commercial contemporaries spun excellent cotton. In
a mechanical way his work was admirable; he really advanced New England scholarship; and he may be said to
have founded that school of earnest historical study which to
this day remains so energetic and distinguished at the college
of which he was a faithful professor and president.

If neither Ticknor nor Sparks contributed to permanent
literature, the names of both are closely connected with that
of the first man in New England who wrote history in a spirit
as literary as that of Gibbon or Macaulay. This is the personal friend whose biography by Ticknor is the most sympathetic work which Ticknor has left us, — William Hickling
Prescott. In the first volume of Sparks's " Library of Amer-

ican Biography," published in 1834, is Prescott's "Life of Charles Brockden Brown," written in the somewhat florid style then fashionable. At the time when this was published, Prescott was known as a gentleman of scholarly temper and comfortable fortune, approaching the age of forty, whose life had probably been ruined by an accident at college. The students of his day had been boisterous in table manners; and on one occasion somebody thoughtlessly threw a piece of bread across the dining-room, striking Prescott in the eye. This resulted in something so near permanent blindness that he could never read again, and that he could write only with the aid of a machine composed of parallel wires by which he painfully guided his pencil.

In spite of these obstacles he quietly set to work on his history of "Ferdinand and Isabella." As the book approached completion, he was beset with doubts of its merit. Unable to use his eyes, he had been compelled to collect his material through the aid of readers, and then to compose it in his head before proceeding to the process of dictation; and he was so far from satisfied with the result of his labours that he hesitated about publication. An anecdote which Ticknor relates of this moment is characteristic of the man and of his time. " He consulted his father, as he always did when he doubted in relation to matters of consequence. His father not only advised the publication, but told him that ' the man who writes a book which he is afraid to publish is a coward.' " So in 1837 " Ferdinand and Isabella " was published; and at last New England had produced a permanent historian. The " Conquest of Mexico " followed in 1843, the " Conquest of Peru " in 1847, and Prescott was still engaged on his " Life of Philip II." when, in 1859, apoplexy overtook him at the age of sixty-three.

Since Prescott's time, the tendency has been more and more to regard history as a matter rather of science than of literature; the fashion of style, too, has greatly changed from that which prevailed when New England found the model of rhetorical excellence in its formal oratory. Prescott's work, then, is often mentioned as rather romantic than scholarly. In this view there is some justice. The scholarship of his day had not collected anything like the material now at the disposal of students; and Prescott's infirmity of sight could not help limiting the range of his investigation. His style, too, always clear and readable, and often vivid, is somewhat florid and generally coloured by what seems a conviction that historical writers should maintain the dignity of history. For all this, his works so admirably combine substantial truth with literary spirit that they are more useful than many which are respected as more authoritative. What he tells us is the result of thoughtful study; and he tells it in a manner so clear, and for all its formality so agreeable, that when you have read one of his chapters you remember without effort what it is about. With a spirit as modern as George Ticknor's, and with much of the systematic scholarship of Jared Sparks, Prescott combined unusual literary power.

For our purposes, however, the most notable phase of his work is to be found in the subjects to which he turned. At first his aspirations to historical writing took a general form. At last, after hesitation whether to write of antiquity, of Italy, or of what not, he was most attracted by the same romantic Spain which a few years before had captivated Irving. Sitting blind in his New England of the early Renaissance, whose outward aspect was so staidly decorous, he found his imagination most stirred by those phases of modern history which were most splendidly unlike his ancestral inexperience. He chose first that climax of Spanish history when in the same year, 1492, native Spaniards triumphantly closed their eight hundred years of conflict against the Moorish invaders, and the voyage of Columbus opened to Spain those new empires of which for a while our own New England had seemed likely to be a part. Then he found deeply stirring the fatal conflict between Spanish invaders and the civilisations of prehistoric America. Finally, having written of Spanish power at its zenith, he began to record the tale of its stormy sunset in the cloudy reign of Philip II. So the impulse of this first of our literary historians seems very like that of Irving. Irving's books on Spain, however, are rather historical romances than scholarly histories. Instead of being a serious narrative, for example, duly referred to authority, Irving's " Conquest of Granada " takes the form of a make-believe chronicle similar to that in which Mark Twain lately told the story of Joan of Arc. Prescott, a little later, treated Irving's subjects in the spirit of a scholarly historian. In Irving and Prescott alike, however, the inexperienced American imagination, starved at home of all traces of antique splendour, found itself most strongly stimulated by the most brilliant pageant of the romantic European past.

There were New England historians, to be sure, who wrote about our own country. The most eminent of these was George Bancroft, born in 1800, who graduated at Harvard, and like Ticknor and Everett was a student in Germany. Afterwards he was for a while a tutor at Harvard, and later a master of the celebrated Round Hill school in Western Massachusetts. Not long afterwards he became a public man ; he was collector of the port of Boston, he was Secretary of the Navy under President Polk, and subsequently he was Minister to both England and Germany. His political principles, however, so differed from those prevalent among the better classes of his early days in Boston, that he left New England at about the age of forty and afterwards resided chiefly in Washington. In 1834, the year in which Prescott's " Life of Brockden Brown " was published, appeared, too, the first volume of Bancroft's " History of the United States," a work on which he was steadily engaged for fifty-one years, and which he left unfinished. The dominant politics of New England had been Federalist ; Bancroft's history sympathised with the Democratic party. In consequence, sharp fault was found with him, and he was never on cordial terms with the other New England historians; but he persevered in writing history all his life, and for all the diffuse floridity of his style, he is still a respectable authority. A little later, Mr. Richard Hildreth, a somewhat younger man, wrote a "History of the United States" from the Federalist point of view; and Dr. John Gorham Palfrey was for years engaged on his minutely lifeless "History of New England." In these, however, and in the other historians who were writing of our own country there was less imaginative vigour and far less literary power than in Prescott or in the two younger New England historians whose works are indubitably literature.

The first of these younger men was John Lothrop Motley, born in 1814. He graduated at Harvard; he studied for a while in Germany, where he began in youth a lifelong friendship with his fellow-student Prince Bismarck; and toward the end of his life he lived mostly in Europe. At one time he was Minister to Austria, and later to England. He died in England in 1877. As early as 1839 he wrote a novel which deserved its unusual lack of success. A little later he anonymously wrote for the "North American Review" an article on Peter the Great which attracted much favourable attention; but it was not until 1856, when he was already past forty years old, that he published his first permanent work, "The Rise of the Dutch Republic." This was followed, between 1861 and 1868, by his "History of the United Netherlands," and finally in 1874 by his "John of Barneveld."

Motley's historical work is obviously influenced by the vividly picturesque writings of Carlyle. It is clearly influenced, too, by intense sympathy with that liberal spirit which he believed to characterise the people of the Netherlands during their prolonged conflict with Spain. From these traits result several obvious faults. In trying to be vivid, he becomes artificial. In the matter of character, too, his Spaniards are apt to be intensely black, and his Netherlanders ripe for the heavenly rewards to which he sends them as serenely as romantic novelists provide for the earthly happiness of heroes and heroines. Yet, for all his sincerely partisan temper, Motley was so industrious in accumulating material, so untiring in his effort vividly to picture its external aspect, and so heartily in sympathy with his work, that he is almost always interesting. What most deeply stirred him was his belief in the abstract right of man to political liberty; and this he wished to celebrate with epic spirit. Belief and spirit alike were characteristically American; in the history of his own country there was abundant evidence of both. The assertion of liberty which finally stirred his imagination to the point of expression, however, was not that of his American forefathers, but the earlier, more brilliantly picturesque, and above all more remote one which had marked the history of a foreign race in Europe. Even so late as Motley's day, in short, the historical imagination of America still needed more ardent stimulant than could be distilled from the copious but juiceless material which had satisfied the acquisitive appetite of Jared Sparks.

The latest and most mature of our New England historians was more national. Francis Parkman, the son of a Unitarian minister, was born at Boston in 1823 and graduated at Harvard in 1844. By that time his health had already shown signs of infirmity; and this was so aggravated by imprudent physical exposure during a journey across the continent shortly after graduation that he was a lifelong invalid. The brief record of his ailments which he left as a scientific document to the Massachusetts Historical Society unwittingly reveals his astonishing courage. Threatened for a full half-century with ruinous malady of both brain and body, he persisted, by sheer force of will, with literary plans which he had formed almost in boyhood. His imagination was first kindled by the forests of our ancestral continent. These excited his interest in the native races of America; and this, in turn, obviously brought him to the frequent alliances between the French and the Indians during the first two centuries of our American history. His lifelong work, then, finally resulted in those volumes which record from beginning to end the struggles for the possession of North America between the French, with their Indian allies, and that English-speaking race whose final victory decided that our continent was to be a seminary of English Law.

In the end, then, Parkman's works prove to possess great philosophic interest. With full sympathy for both sides, with untiring industry in the accumulation of material, with good sense so judicial as to forbid him the vagaries of preconception, and with a literary sensitiveness which made his style — at first marked by the floridity fashionable in 1850 — finally a model of sound prose, he set forth the struggles which decided the political future of America. Moved to this task by an impulse rather romantic than scientific, to be sure, gifted with a singularly vivid imagination, too careful a scholar to risk undue generalisation, and throughout life so hampered by illness that he could very rarely permit himself prolonged mental effort, Parkman sometimes appears chiefly a writer of romantic narrative. As you grow familiar with his work, however, you feel it so true that you can infuse it with philosophy for yourself. It is hardly too much to say that his writings afford as sound a basis for historic philosophising as does great fiction for philosophising about human nature.

Parkman, who died in 1893, brings the story of renascent scholarship in New England almost to our own day. When the nineteenth century began, our scholarship was merely a traditional memory of classical learning, generally treated as the handmaiden either of professional theology or of professional law. When the spirit of a new life began to declare itself here, and people grew aware of contemporary foreign achievement, there came first a little group of men who studied in Europe and brought home the full spirit of that continental scholarship which during the present century has so dominated learning in America. As this spirit began to express itself in literary form, it united with our ancestral fondness for historic records to produce, just after the moment when formal oratory most flourished here, an eminent school of historical literature. Most of this history, however, deals with foreign subjects. The historians of New England were generally at their best when stirred by matters remote from any actual human experience enjoyed either by themselves or by such forefathers as they could personally have known even by tradition.

Considering the relation of this school of history to the historical literature of England, one is inevitably reminded that the greatest English history, Gibbon's " Decline and Fall of the Roman Empire," first appeared in the very year of our Declaration of Independence. In one aspect, of course, the temper of Gibbon is as far from romantic as possible. He is the first, and in certain aspects the greatest, of modern philosophical historians; and his style has all the formality of the century during which he wrote. In another aspect the relation of Gibbon's history to the England which bred him seems very like that of our New England histories to the country and the life which bred their writers. Gibbon and our own historians alike turned to a larger and more splendid field than was afforded by their national annals. Both alike were distinctly affected by an alert consciousness of what excellent work had been done in contemporary foreign countries. Both carefully expressed themselves with conscientious devotion to what they believed the highest literary canons. Both produced work which has lasted not only as history but as literature too. Gibbon wrote in the very year when America declared her independence of England; Prescott began his work in Boston nearly sixty years later. There is an aspect, then, in which our historical literature seems to lag behind that of the mother country much as Irving's prose — contemporary with the full outburst of nineteenth-century romanticism in England — lags behind the prose of Goldsmith.

The name of Gibbon suggests another fact about our American historians which is not quite so obvious or so certain, but which may help us in our effort to define their national character. Gibbon's power was incomparably greater than that of any American writer; but along with that power Gibbon had a trait which no one can fail to observe, — he relished indecency. Whoever shares this relish will find in the untranslated notes to many of his passages plenty of morsels which our present customs forbid us either to translate or to mention in general society. In our American historians there is nothing of the sort. Their writings may not much have enriched human imagination, but they have never befouled it. In the literature of every other country you will find lubricity; in that of America hardly any. Foreigners are apt to think this trait hypocritical; whoever knows the finer minds of New England will be disposed to believe it a matter not of conscientious determination but rather of instinctive preference.

Very cursory, all this; and there can be no doubt that the historians of New England, like the New England orators, might profitably be made the subject of minute and interesting separate study. Our own concern, however, is chiefly with pure letters. Before we can deal with them intelligently we must glance at still other aspects of renascent New England. We have glanced at its oratory, and at its scholarship. We must now turn to its religion and its philosophy.

IV

UNITARIANISM

MARKED as was the change in the oratory and the scholarship of New England during the first quarter of the nineteenth century, the change in the dominant religious views of a community which had always been dominated by religion was more marked still. From the beginning till after the Revolution, the creed of New England had been the Calvinism of the emigrant Puritans. In 1809, William Ellery Channing, then a minister twenty-nine years old, wrote of this old faith in the following terms: —

"Calvinism teaches, that, in consequence of Adam's sin in eating the forbidden fruit, God brings into life all his posterity with a nature wholly corrupt, so that they are utterly indisposed, disabled, and made opposite to all that is spiritually good, and wholly inclined to all evil, and that continually. It teaches, that all mankind, having fallen in Adam, are under God's wrath and curse, and so made liable to all miseries in this life, to death itself, and to the pains of hell forever. It teaches, that, from this ruined race, God, out of his mere good pleasure, has elected a certain number to be saved by Christ, not induced to this choice by any foresight of their faith or good works, but wholly by his free grace and love; and that, having thus predestinated them to eternal life, he renews and sanctifies them by his almighty and special agency, and brings them into a state of grace, from which they cannot fall and perish. It teaches, that the rest of mankind he is pleased to pass over, and to ordain them to dishonour and wrath for their sins, to the honour of his justice and power; in other words, he leaves the rest to the corruption in which they were born, withholds the grace which is necessary to their recovery, and condemns them to 'most grievous torments in soul and body without intermission in hell-fire for ever.' Such is Calvinism, as gathered from the most authentic records of the doctrine. Whoever will consult the famous Assembly's Catechisms and Confession, will see the peculiarities of the system in all their length and breadth of deformity. A man of plain sense, whose spirit has not been broken to this creed by education or terror, will think that it is not necessary for us to travel to heathen countries, to learn how mournfully the human mind may misrepresent the Deity."

"How mournfully the human mind may misrepresent the Deity!" You will be at pains to find nine words which shall more thoroughly express the change which the Renaissance brought to the leading religious spirits of Boston.

The resulting alteration in dogmatic theology has given to the new school of New England divines the name of Unitarians. According to the old creed, which held salvation from Adam's fall to be attainable only through God's grace, won by the mediation of Jesus Christ, the divine character of Christ was essential to redemption; without his superhuman aid all human beings were irrevocably doomed. But the moment you assumed human nature to contain adequate seeds of good, the necessity for a divine Redeemer disappeared, and redemption became only a matter of divine convenience. The second person of the Trinity having thus lost his mystic office, the third spread wing and vanished into the radiance of a new heaven. In this glorious region the New England Unitarians discerned singly and alone the one God, who had made man in his image. One almost perfect image they recognised in Jesus Christ; a great many inferior but still indubitable ones they found actually to populate the Commonwealth of Massachusetts.

Although this radical change in theology was what gave Unitarianism its name, the underlying feeling which gave it being had little concern with mystic dogmas. Whatever the philosophy of primitive Christianity, the philosophy of traditional Christianity had for centuries taught the depravity of human nature; this dogma the Puritans had brought to New England, where they had uncompromisingly preserved it. Now, whatever your philosophy, this dogma does account for such social phenomena as occur in densely populated lands where economic pressure is strong. In our own great cities you need a buoyant spirit and a hopefully unobservant eye to perceive much besides evil; and if you compare Boston or New York with London or Paris, you can hardly avoid discerning, beneath the European civilisation which is externally lovelier than ours, depths of foulness to which we have not yet sunk. The Europe of Calvin's time seems on the whole even more pervasively wicked; and more wicked still seems that decadent Roman Empire where Augustine formulated the dogmas which at last Channing so unfalteringly set aside. If you chance to believe in Hell, most people in crowded dense societies really seem bound thither; and those who have the strength morally to resist such environment seem by contrast totally different from the mass of humanity.

We need hardly remind ourselves, however, that up to the time of Channing the history of America, and particularly of New England, had been a history of national inexperience. When Cotton Mather wrote his " Magnalia " in the closing seventeenth century, his purpose was to prove that during the first seventy-five years of New England there had flourished and lived and died there so many regenerate human beings that a man of sense might almost statistically infer New England to be specially favoured by God. The governors of the region, and its preachers and teachers, not to speak of their many godly servants and followers, had revealed Christian graces to a degree which Mather's common-sense held to evidence an unprecedented outpouring of divine grace. In this contention there was an element of truth; compared with other races, the Yankee people, released for generations from the pressure of dense European life, found a considerable degree of goodness surprisingly practicable. This social fact resembled a familiar domestic one: an eldest child is apt to be angelic until some little brother gets big enough to interfere with him; and if by chance no little brother appears, the angelic traits will very likely persist until the child goes to school or otherwise comes in contact with external life. Up to the days of Channing himself, the Yankee race may be likened to a Puritan child gravely playing alone. However crude its traits, however simple, however unwinsome, they were hardly such as reasonable men, without the guidance of dogmatic teaching, would conclude to indicate irrevocable damnation.

So even by the time of Edwards, Calvinistic dogma and national inexperience were unwittingly at odds. Our glances at subsequent American letters must have shown how steadily the native human nature of America continued to express itself in forms which could not reasonably be held infernal. In New York, for example, the first third of the nineteenth century produced Brockden Brown and Irving and Cooper and Bryant; and, at a period distinctly later than that with which we are now concerned, the literature of which they were the leaders faded into no deeper decadence than the work of Poe, of Willis, and of the Knickerbocker School. Not eternally memorable, even the worst of these personages does not seem worthy of perdition as distinguished from neglect. Turning to certain phases of New England at about the same time, we saw in its public life the patriotic intensity of Webster and the classical personality of Everett, establishing a tradition of sustained dignity which passed only with Mr. Winthrop, who lies beneath the well-earned epitaph, " Eminent as a scholar, an orator, a statesman, and a philanthropist, — above all, a Christian." And when we came to the scholarship of New England, we found it finally ripening into the stainless pages of Ticknor, of Prescott, of Motley, and of Parkman.

In a society like this, Calvinistic dogma seems constantly further from truth, as taught by actual life. If everything which men do is essentially damnable, if they can be saved from eternal punishment only by the divine redemption which comes to the elect through Christ, the incarnate son of God, men ought continually to behave abominably. However true to experience in dense old worlds, such habitually abominable conduct was untrue to the national inexperience of America, and particularly of renascent New England. The social structure of this region had been pretty rigid from the beginning. Well into the nineteenth century the clergy maintained much of their pristine social lead; and this partly because of a trait which remained unaltered throughout the rise and the decline of Unitarianism. As a class, they were deeply earnest and sincerely truthful. Even in the eighteenth century, then, a considerable number of these ministers, particularly of the region about Boston, began insensibly to relax the full rigour of dogmatic Calvinism. There was no formal break, but in the utterances of Boston pulpits you were less and less apt to scent hell-fire.

When good Dr. Freeman, then, minister of King's Chapel, was compelled to revise the Anglican Prayer Book, and found himself conscientiously disposed so to alter the liturgy as obviously to modify the dogma of the Trinity, he may not have felt half so radical as time has proved him. After the interval of a century, his King's Chapel liturgy, still in use and sometimes held to mark the beginning of Boston Unitarianism, presents a startling contrast to most older forms of Christianity on this continent. Its insistence on the divine unity of God, and on the loving inspiration of God's word, undeniably implies a tendency to regard Christ only as an excellent earthly manifestation of God's creative power. He seems no longer a mystic being whose divine interposition is needed to preserve humanity from destruction. The question of his essential nature is rather neglected. Half-God and half-man, if you choose so to believe, he is not exactly God. Men need him not as a redeemer, but as an example.

The King's Chapel liturgy was published in 1785. About twenty years later, Harvard College succumbed to the temper which the liturgy embodies. The chief theological chair at Harvard is the Hollis Professorship of Divinity,— at present held by a scholar whose knowledge of Babylonian inscriptions is justly celebrated. Up to 1805 it had remained a stronghold of Calvinistic doctrine. In that year it was given to the Reverend Henry Ware, an avowed Unitarian, whose conceptions of human nature were introspectively confirmed by lifelong contemplation of the fact that " Ware was honest as all Wares be." The orthodox party at Harvard had opposed Ware with all their might; so when he was made Hollis Professor, the ancestral college of Puritan New England was finally handed over to Unitarianism. Until very recent years this remained its acknowledged faith. At last its liberalism became such as to make even Unitarian dogmas inconvenient; its avowed religion is now described as non-sectarian, and its chapel has long abandoned the use of the sacrament.

Defeated at Harvard, the orthodox party retreated to Andover, where they founded the Theological Seminary which until very lately forlornly defended old Calvinism in a region abandoned to its enemies. Nowadays the whole thing is fading into history, but at first the conflict was heart-breaking. There is a pathetic story of Professor Pearson, who, on the election of Ware, retired from Harvard to become one of the founders of Andover. In his last days the good man's speech was paralysed; and when toward the end of his life an old Harvard friend, who had not seen him for years, came to visit him, time had done its work. With mournful tears in his eyes the dumb old Calvinist took his friend's hand and stroked it, unable to speak his grief that their ways had parted for eternity. For on each side faith was fervent; and if the conquering Unitarians believed themselves to be destroying pernicious and ugly heresy, the Calvinists believed just as sincerely that in angelic guise the devil had possessed himself of New England. In their mood, there was a consequent depth of despair to which the Unitarians have hardly done full justice. To the Unitarian mind there has never been any valid reason why good men of other opinions than theirs should

not enjoy everlasting bliss; but the very essence of the
Calvinists' creed condemned to everlasting woe every human
being who rejected the divinely revealed truth of their grimly
uncompromising system.

To suppose, however, that the founders of Unitarianism
meant to be unchristian would be totally to misunderstand them.
They revered the Scriptures as profoundly as ever Calvinists
did. The difference was that they discerned in Scripture no
such teaching as the experience of old-world centuries had
crystallised into Calvinistic dogma. In the first place, they
found in the Bible no passages which necessarily involved the
dogma of the Trinity. There might be puzzling sentences;
but there were also clear, constant statements that there is one
God, who made man in His image. Very good, they held;
this assertion amounts to proof that men are the children of
God, and that incidentally they have inherited from God the
divine faculties of reason and of conscience. When in
the Bible, then, there are puzzling texts, or when in life
there are puzzling moments, our duty is to face them in a
conscientiously reasonable temper. If we are truly made in
the image of God, we shall thus reach true conclusions; and
meanwhile, to guide our way, God has made that most excellent of his creatures, Jesus Christ, and has authentically recorded his career in the Gospels of Matthew, Mark, Luke,
and John. Search these yourself; use the light of the Scriptures; remember the example of Christ; and all will be well.
If there be any such thing as damnation, it can result only
from lack of self-searching, from deliberate neglect of scriptural light, or from wilful disregard of Christ's example.

From this state of faith there naturally resulted in Unitarianism a degree of spiritual freedom which allowed each
minister to proclaim whatever truth presented itself to his
conscience. Unitarianism has never formulated a creed. It
has tacitly accepted, however, certain traditions which have
been classically set forth by its great apostle, William Ellery

Channing. He was born at Newport in 1780; he took his degree at Harvard in 1798; and from 1803 to 1840 he was minister at the Federal Street Church in Boston. He died in 1842.

In 1819, he preached at Baltimore, on the occasion of the ordination of Jared Sparks, his famous sermon on Unitarian Christianity. He took his text from 1 Thess. v. 21 : "Prove all things; hold fast that which is good." His first point is that "we regard the Scriptures as the records of God's successive revelations to mankind, and particularly of the last and most perfect revelation of his will by Jesus Christ." The Scriptures, he goes on to say, must be interpreted by the light of reason. So, applying reason to Scripture, he deduces in the first place the doctrine of God's unity, "that there is one God, and one only;" secondly, that "Jesus is one mind, one soul, one being, as truly one as we are, and equally distinct from the one God;" thirdly, that "God is morally perfect;" fourthly, that "Jesus was sent by the Father to effect a moral or spiritual deliverance of mankind; that is, to rescue men from sin and its consequences, and to bring them to a state of everlasting purity and happiness;" and, fifthly, that "all virtue has its foundation in the moral nature of man, that is, in conscience, or his sense of duty, and in the power of forming his temper and life according to conscience."

On this supreme authority of conscience Unitarianism tended to throw more and more emphasis. Toward the end of Channing's life he wrote some introductory remarks to a collected edition of his works from which the following paragraph is worth attention : —

"We must start in religion from our own souls. In these is the fountain of all divine truth. An outward revelation is only possible and intelligible, on the ground of conceptions and principles, previously furnished by the soul. Here is our primitive teacher and light. Let us not disparage it. There are, indeed, philosophical schools of the present day, who tell us that we are to start in all our speculations from the Absolute, the Infinite. But we rise to these conceptions from the contemplation of our own nature; and even if it were not so, of what avail would be the notion of an Absolute, Infinite existence, and Uncaused Unity, if stripped of all those intellectual and moral attributes, which we learn only from our own souls? What but a vague shadow, a sounding name, is the metaphysical Deity, the substance without modes, the being without properties, the naked unity, which performs such a part in some of our philosophical systems? The only God, whom our thoughts can rest on, and our hearts can cling to, and our consciences can recognise, is the God whose image dwells in our own souls. The grand ideas of Power, Reason, Wisdom, Love, Rectitude, Holiness, Blessedness, that is, of all God's attributes, come from within, from the action of our own spiritual nature. Many indeed think that they learn God from marks of design and skill in the outward world; but our ideas of design and skill, of a determining cause, of an end or purpose, are derived from consciousness, from our own souls. Thus the soul is the spring of our knowledge of God."

A more astonishing departure from all the traditions of ecclesiastical Christianity was never phrased. Human nature, Channing holds, is essentially good; man is made in the image of God, and all man need do is to follow the light which God has given him. The greatest source of that light, of course, is Christ. Whether Christ was literally the son of God or not makes no difference: he walked the earth; he was the most perfect of men; and we can follow him. He suffered little children to come unto him, and he will suffer us larger children to come likewise. He was human, and so are we. In earthly life he could avoid damnation, and all we need do — if indeed there be real danger of damnation at all — is to behave as nearly like him as we can. If the false teachings of a moribund heresy make all this reasonable truth seem questionable, look about you: do you find your friends damnable, or, on the whole, made in the image of God? Do they deserve, as in that sermon of Edwards's, to be held suspended by a spider-like thread over a fiery furnace into which they may justly be cast at any moment; or rather, for all their faults and errors, do they not merit eternal mercy?

So if all of us try to do our best, is there any reasonable cause for fearing that everything shall not ultimately go right? The old Unitarians looked about them and honestly found human nature reassuring.

What ultimately distinguishes early Unitarianism from the Calvinism which it so calmly dethroned, then, is this respect for what is good in human nature as contrasted with the Calvinistic insistence on what is bad. What is good needs encouragement; what is bad needs checking. What is good merits freedom; what is bad demands control. Obedience to authority, the Calvinists held, may reveal in you the tokens of salvation; spiritual freedom, the Unitarians maintained, must result in spiritual growth. For a dogmatic dread they substituted an illimitable hope. Evil and sin, sorrow and weakness, they did not deny; but trusting in the infinite goodness of God, they could not believe evil or sin, the sorrows or the weaknesses of humanity, to be more than passing shadows. Inspired with this newly hopeful spirit, they held their way through the New England whose better sort were content for half a century to follow them.

Channing has been dead for more than fifty years, and the religious movement of which he was the central figure is no longer in the ascendant. He himself protested against doctrinal stagnation: " Unitarianism," . . . he wrote in 1841, " began as a protest against the rejection of reason, — against mental slavery. It pledged itself to progress as its life's end; but it has gradually grown stationary, and now we have a Unitarian orthodoxy." The good man need not have troubled himself about that. Almost in his own time, on the one hand, the progress of personal freedom led to something like rejection of Christianity; on the other hand, it reacted into acceptance of the oldest Christian traditions. Typical examples of these tendencies may be found in the careers of Mr. George Ripley and his wife. Beginning in full sympathy, as ardent Unitarians, they so parted in faith that Mrs. Ripley died in communion with the Roman Catholic Church, while Mr. Ripley, who long survived her, became a devout free-thinker.

Our present concern, however, is not with that decay of New England Unitarianism so inevitably involved in the individualism of its teaching. Here we are concerned rather with its pristine growth and vigour. In the article on " Unitarianism in Boston," contributed by the late Dr. Andrew Preston Peabody to the third volume of Winsor's " Memorial History of Boston," there is a list of the Unitarian ministers of the town from the beginning to about 1875. Whoever knows anything of the personalities for which these names stand will be struck with one fact : even more certainly than the elder worthies whom Cotton Mather recorded in his " Magnalia," these are a company of such sweet, pure, noble spirits as must arouse in men who dwell with them a deep respect for human nature. The last commanding spiritual teacher of New England chanced to be of another faith ; but what made Phillips Brooks such a power in Boston was the same kind of personality which half a century before him had generally distinguished the Unitarian clergy. Whoever knew the great bishop personally can hardly have failed to observe the trait which was at once his strongest and his weakest : his instinctive nature was so good that he never quite realised the badness and the uncleanness which beset the lives of common men with temptation. In him, just as in the fathers of Unitarianism, the national inexperience of America permitted almost unrestrained the development of a moral purity which to those who possess it makes the grim philosophy of damnation seem an ill-conceived nursery tale.

The Unitarianism of New England, of course, was not unique either theologically or philosophically. In its isolated home, however, it chanced to develop one feature which distinguishes its early career from similar phases of religious history elsewhere. The astonishing personal purity and moral beauty of its leaders combined with their engaging theology to effect the rapid social conquest of the whole region about Boston. We have seen how King's Chapel and Harvard College passed into Unitarian hands. The same was true of nearly all the old Puritan churches. The First Church of Boston, John Cotton's, became Unitarian; so did the Second Church, which throughout their lives the Mathers had held as such a stronghold of orthodoxy; so, with less violence to its history, did the Brattle Street; the only Boston church of consequence which held out was the Old South, which adhered to its pristine dogmas until 1899. The ancestral church of Cambridge broke in two; and the section of its parishioners who deposed Abiel Holmes for faithfulness to his old creed captured both the meeting-house and the communion plate. Something similar occurred at Plymouth, where at the entrance of the oldest burying-ground of New England may now be seen two edifices, each of which claims direct descent from the earliest of all New England churches. One has maintained orthodoxy; but the more impressive is that which followed the fashion and became Unitarian.

This general conquest of ecclesiastical strongholds by the Unitarians deeply affected the whole structure of Massachusetts society. Elsewhere in America, perhaps, and surely in England, Unitarianism has generally presented itself as dissenting dissent, and has consequently been exposed to the kind of social disfavour which aggressive radicalism is apt anywhere to involve. In the isolated capital of isolated New England, on the other hand, where two centuries had established such a rigid social system, the capture of the old churches meant the capture, too, of almost every social stronghold. In addition to its inherent charm, the pristine Unitarianism of Massachusetts was strengthened by all the force of fashion in a community where somewhat eccentric fashion has always had great weight. Whoever clung to the older faith did so at his social peril.

This fact is nowhere more evident than in the history of New England letters. Almost everybody who attained literary distinction in New England during the nineteenth century was either a Unitarian or closely associated with Unitarian influences. The single man of letters whom Boston orthodoxy produced was poor Willis; and he found the social atmosphere of New England too stifling for the convivial son of an orthodox deacon. At least in letters, which throughout the literary dominance of New England preserved there the same kind of social distinction that marked Mr. Bryant's career in New York, creative energy declared itself chiefly among those who had been taught to believe themselves created in the image of the Creator.

19

TRANSCENDENTALISM

THOUGH we have followed the oratory, the scholarship, and the Unitarianism of New England almost to the present time, there has been reason for considering them before the other phases of Renaissance in that isolated region where the nineteenth century produced such a change. At various times we have touched on the fact that the period from 1798 to 1832 — marked in England by everything between the " Lyrical Ballads " and the death of Scott, and in America by all the New York literature from Brockden Brown to Bryant — really comprised an epoch in the literary history of both countries. It was during this period that the three phases of intellectual life which we have now considered fully declared themselves in New England; and in these years nothing else of equal importance developed there.

The very mention of the dates in question should remind us that throughout the English-speaking world the revolutionary spirit was in the air. It showed itself in the extreme individualism of literature in England, where the writers suddenly became almost as unlike one another as those of the preceding century had been similar; it showed itself there in that constitutional revolution which finally resulted in the Reform Bill; and in native American letters it showed itself in the somewhat imitative but soundly sweet writings of Brockden Brown, Irving, Cooper, and Bryant. The contrast between these and the contemporary writings of England may already have suggested a marked difference in the societies to which, as we can now see, the revolutionary spirit came at the same time.

The essence of this spirit is its fervid faith in the excellence of human nature; let men be freed from all needless control, it holds, and they may be trusted to work out their admirable salvation. In the old world, where the force of custom had been gathering for immemorial centuries, the speech and behaviour of enfranchised humanity was apt to take extravagant form. In America, on the other hand, where the one thing which had been most lacking was the semblance of polite civilisation, the very impulse which in Europe showed itself destructive appeared in a guise which at first makes it hard to recognise.

One need not ponder long, however, to feel, even in this staid new America, a note as fresh as was the most extravagant revolutionary expression in Europe. Our elaborately rhetorical oratory, to be sure, and our decorous scholarship, seem on the surface far from revolutionary; and so does the gently insignificant literature which was contemporary with them a bit further south. Yet all alike were as different from anything which America had uttered before as was the poetry of Wordsworth or of Shelley from what had previously been known in England. When we came to the Unitarianism of New England, the revolutionary spirit showed itself more plainly. The creed of Channing was of a kind which, except for the unusual chance of immediate social dominance, might almost at once have revealed its disintegrant character. Happening, as it did, however, to possess itself of the ecclesiastical system established by generations of ancestral orthodoxy, it produced at first no more obvious superficial change than a refreshing amelioration of the prospects visible from the good old Boston pulpits.

The enfranchised human nature of New England, too, at first expressed itself in no more appalling forms than the oratory of Webster or of Everett; than the Anthology Club, the Boston Athenæum, and the " North American Review ; " than the saintly personality and the ethereal speculations of

Channing. Under such revolutionary influences as these the new generation of Boston grew up, which was to find expression a few years later.

In all such considerations as this there is danger of taking consecutive phases of development too literally. To say that Unitarianism caused the subsequent manifestation of free thought in New England would be too much; but no one can doubt that the world-wide revolutionary spirit, of which the first New England manifestation was the religious revolution effected by Unitarianism, impelled the following generation to that outbreak of intellectual and spiritual anarchy which is generally called Transcendentalism.

This queerly intangible Transcendentalism can best be understood, indeed, by recurring to the text of Channing's celebrated sermon on Unitarian Christianity. " Prove all things," asserted the cheerful theologian; " hold fast that which is good." Prove all things; do not accept tradition; scrutinise whatever presents itself to you. If evil, though defended by the Bible itself, cast it aside; if good, even though the Bible utterly neglect it, cherish it as a gift of God. To this principle Channing adhered all his life; but Channing's life was essentially clerical; it was that of a conscientious and disinterested religious teacher, whose great personal authority was strengthened by rare purity of nature. Educated in something like the old school of theology, he generally consecrated his devout boldness of thought to religious matters.

In the generation which grew up under the influence of which Channing is the most distinguished type, the revolutionary spirit declared itself more broadly. The traditional education of New England had been confined to theology, to classics and mathematics, and to the Common Law. So far as it had indulged itself in speculative philosophy, it had treated this as ancillary, mostly to theology and sometimes to jurisprudence. Meanwhile it had paid little attention to the modern literature even of England, and none at all to that of other languages than English. Obviously there were many things in this world which intelligent young Yankees might advantageously prove, with a view to discovering whether they were worth holding fast. To say that they did so in obedience to Channing's specific teachings would be mistaken ; but certainly in obedience to the same motive which induced his choice of that Thessalonian text, the more active and vigorous young minds of New England attacked, wherever they could find them, the records of human wisdom. They wished to make up their own minds as to what they believed about the eternities, and to do so with no more deference to any authority than that authority seemed rationally to deserve.

The name commonly given to the unsystematised results at which they arrived — widely differing with every individual — is apt. However they differed, these impulsive and untrained philosophical thinkers of renascent New England were idealists. With the aid of reading as wide as their resources would allow, they endeavoured to give themselves an account of what the universe really means. They became aware that our senses perceive only the phenomena of life, and that behind these phenomena, beyond the range of human senses, lurk things not phenomenal. The evolutionary philosophy which has followed theirs holds a similar conception ; it divides all things into two groups, — the phenomenal or knowable, concerning which our knowledge can be tested by observation or experiment, and the unknowable, concerning which no observation or experiment can prove anything. With scientific hardness of head evolutionary philosophy consequently confines its energies to phenomena. With unscientific enthusiasm for freedom the first enfranchised thinkers of New England troubled themselves little about phenomena, and devoted their energies to thinking and talking about that great group of undemonstrable truths which must always transcend human experience. In so doing, we can see now, they followed an instinct innate in their race. They were descended from two

centuries of Puritanism; and though the Puritans exerted
their philosophic thought within dogmatically fixed limits,
they were intense idealists, too.   Their whole temperamental
energy was concentrated in efforts definitely to perceive absolute truths quite beyond the range of any earthly senses.   The
real distinction between the Puritan idealists and the Transcendental idealists of the nineteenth century proves little more
than that these discarded all dogmatic limit.

A typical example of the state of things which ensued
lately transpired in the talk of a Bostonian, educated more
than fifty years ago under Transcendental influences, but long
since become an earnest Christian.   Some discussion of meta-
physics arising, he gravely said that of course no one doubted
human nature to be quadruple, — consisting of mind, body,
soul, and spirit.   The distinction between mind and body is
generally familiar, and that which separates the soul from
these is nowise strange to any one familiar with the Transcendental period; but what the difference may be between soul
and spirit only a Transcendentalist could ever have told you.
Yet this dogmatic assertion of old Transcendentalism had survived as unquestioned truth in a mind which for years had been
devoutly obedient to orthodox Christianity.   Idealists, like
this, making dogmatic assertions about unknowable things,
pretty much all the Transcendentalists were.

A second agreement among them one can generally assert :
almost all believed in innate ideas.   Such a belief, of course,
is inherent in the doctrine of conscience so vigorously maintained by Channing.   Metaphysically the matter is endlessly
disputable, belonging to the region where proof is out of the
question.   Do men come into the world with blank minds on
which images are impressed by the accidents of our earthly
experience ? or are they born with certain ideas, definitely and
unchangeably true ? The question has been discussed and perhaps will be discussed by many schools of philosophy.   Transcendentalism did not trouble itself with much formal discussion.

It assumed innate ideas; it found no reason for questioning the assumption; and the innate ideas which it most insisted on concerned not so much body and mind as soul and spirit. Just as the normal body is born with a sense of touch or of sight, the Transcendentalists held, the normal soul and spirit are born with a sense of right and wrong. So, less certainly but very probably, the normal mind is born with a sense of truth and falsehood. Very good; when a question is presented, all you need do is to inquire of yourself whether it is true. Answer yourself earnestly, and the question is settled. This is particularly true when the question concerns right and wrong. Human nature is good; you are made right, — mind, body, soul, spirit, and all. Obey yourself, and you need have no fear. All things worth serious interest transcend human experience; but a trustworthy clew to them is to be found in the unfathomable excellence of human minds, souls, and spirits.

Though very possibly no single Transcendentalist would have accepted so baldly stated a creed, some such system may be conceived as the Platonic ideal toward which Transcendentalists generally tended. You can understand them best by comparing one and all with such a generalised type, which no one precisely represented. With a temper which, however it began, soon developed into this hopefully impalpable philosophy, the more ardent youths who grew up in Boston when its theology was dominated by Unitarianism, and when its scholarship was at last so enlarged as to include the whole range of human learning, faced whatever human records they could find, to prove and to hold fast those which were good.

The influences thus brought to bear on New England were almost innumerable, but among them two or three were specially evident. The most important was probably German thought, at a time when German philosophy was most metaphysical and German literature most romantic. This, indeed, had had great influence on contemporary England. No two men of letters in the nineteenth century affected English thought more evidently than Coleridge and Carlyle; and both were saturated with German philosophy. To New England these influences swiftly spread. In 1800, it has been said, hardly a German book could be found in Boston. Before Channing died, in 1842, you could find in Boston few educated people who could not talk with glib delight about German philosophy, German literature, and German music. Another thing which appears very strongly in Transcendental writings is the influence of French eclectic philosophy. At one time the names of Jouffroy and Cousin were as familiar to Yankee ears as were those of Locke or Descartes or Kant. Perhaps more heartily still this whole school of enthusiastic seekers for truth welcomed that wide range of modern literature, English and foreign alike, which was at last thrown open by contemporary scholars so distinct from them in temper as the Smith Professors, — Ticknor and Longfellow and Lowell.

For this almost riotous delight in pure literature there was a reason now long past. The Puritans generally had conscientious objections to fine art. So only at the moment to which we are now come could the instinct of native New England for fine art conscientiously be satisfied. Now, the fine arts, however else they may be classified, may pretty certainly be divided into two groups: those of which the masterpieces may be indefinitely reproduced and those of which each masterpiece must inevitably remain unique. Architecture, for example, must remain permanently settled on the foundations laid for each building; a great painting can exist only in the one place where it is actually hung, and a great statue in that where it actually stands. During the last twenty or thirty years, to be sure, the astonishing development of photography has to some degree extended the range of plastic arts. Until long after the Transcendental period, however, processes of reproduction were at once so costly and so uncertain that architecture, painting, and sculpture could be appreciatively studied and enjoyed only by people who could travel to where masterpieces exist. With music the case was decidedly different. Musical scores can be carried anywhere; so in general can musical instruments; and provided that you brought to New England proper scores, proper instruments, and tolerably trained musicians, you could have in New England pretty good music. When it came to poetry, things were better still. All you had to do was to import the books in which the masterpieces of poetry were printed; then every educated man could read the masterpieces for himself.

Nowadays music and literature are as familiar in Boston as anywhere in the world; and along with this familiarity has come, as always comes, a definite standard of taste, which combines with awe-stricken respect for established reputations to make everyday people feel more at ease in the presence of works which need not be taken seriously. Seventy years ago the Renaissance of New England was in no aspect more typically renascent than in the unfeigned eagerness with which its love of novelty delighted in the excellences of those newly found fine arts, poetry and music. The masterpieces of music gave people some such unfeigned delight as is now found only in popular tunes. The masterpieces of poetry similarly delighted them as genuinely and as spontaneously as nowadays people are delighted by sensational novels, or plays from the French. Scholarly criticism had not yet murdered spontaneous appreciation. The Transcendental youth of New England delighted in excellent modern literature and excellent modern music as unaffectedly as fifteenth-century Italians delighted in the freshly discovered manuscripts of classic Greek.

At the same time these Transcendentalists were native Yankees; and true native Yankees always yearn for absolute truth. A characteristic result followed; they really delighted in literature with all the fervour of a race which had been æsthetically starved for five or six generations; with equal fervour they believed their interest in literature to be largely conditioned by the fact that literature can teach us how we ought to behave.

In the second number of the " Dial " is a paper, attributed to Emerson, which oddly illustrates this.   He speaks of doubts which may linger concerning the excellence of the age in which he has the good fortune to flourish; and goes on thus : —

" How can the age be a bad one which gives me Plato and Paul and Plutarch, Saint Augustine, Spinoza, Chapman, Beaumont and Fletcher, Donne, and Sir Thomas Browne, beside its own riches? "

Whether Emerson wrote this passage or not, his collected works teem with similar evidence of his guileless confusion of values, a trait strongly characteristic of our earlier Renaissance.   His father and his grandfather, and those who had gone before, had known their Bibles, their Latin classics, and perhaps a little Greek, had had fairly distinct notions of the Common Law, and had regarded Beaumont and Fletcher, if they had ever heard of them, as sinfully obscene playwrights. Emerson, turning to Beaumont and Fletcher, found what is truly there, — many examples of noble and beautiful Elizabethan aphorism.   He might equally have found what his ancestral tradition emphasised, endless depths of corruption; but these did not attract his attention.   The inner light told him that the beauties were virtues and the basenesses faults. He chose to regard the beauty as essential, the baseness as accidental; and in his admiration for the superb phrasing of decadent Elizabethan dramatists he threw them into the same category with Plato and Augustine, in a temper much like that which has made dogmatic theology group the Song of Solomon with the Epistles of the apostle Paul.

By 1832 a considerable group of Transcendentalists had arisen in Boston, agreeing in little else than the eager scope of their interest and investigations, and their desire to attain absolute truth by other means than that of previously accepted authority. In a certain aspect, as we have seen, their impulse closely resembled that of the Unitarians half a generation before. It may be distinguished from Unitarianism, however, by its unrestrained ardour. In this the Transcendentalists unwittingly reverted to the old native type. With the Unitarians they held, though not literally, that man is made in God's image. Very well: God, morally perfect, has only to look within Himself and know what is true and right; let us, made in His image, do likewise. Truth and Right are absolute things; we shall find them within ourselves, and from their deepest essential nature they cannot mislead us. The Puritans, of course, had strenuously denied any such dogma as this; the light which God vouchsafed to them was vouchsafed through no secret faculties of their forlornly lost human nature, but only in scriptural phrases, which must be duly interpreted by orthodox parsons. During the heyday of the Puritans, however, there had flourished a kind of spiritual thinkers as like them in temperament as they were different in doctrine, and therefore held the most dangerous of heretics. These were the Quakers, like Woolman, who measured truth by that inner light which they believed that the grace of God vouchsafes to every human being. The Transcendentalists were too far from orthodox to trouble themselves about a Christian God, but they believed in the inner light as enthusiastically as ever Quakers did, and they followed it almost as ardently.

The intensity of their emotional nature not only distinguished them from contemporary Unitarians, but carried them to greater lengths than even their Puritan ancestors. When Unitarians got beyond the range of human senses, they phrased the unknowable almost as conventionally as the Puritans themselves, talking of God, of Heaven, of Hell; and so did the Quakers. The Transcendentalists, with all the enfranchised ardour of revolutionary temper, talked rather about Nature and the Over-Soul; and instead of yielding enthusiastic assent to the divinely implanted authority of conscience, they found that the ideas innate in the human soul and spirit gave warrant enough for unquestioning belief in the unfathomable truths which they so boldly proclaimed.

In one way or another this Transcendental movement affected almost all the ardent natures of New England from 1825 to 1840. In that year it found final expression in the "Dial," a quarterly periodical which flourished until 1844. Its first editor was among the most characteristic figures of Transcendentalism. This was a woman, regarded in her own time as the prophetess of the new movement, and prevented by a comparatively early death from struggling through days when the movement had spent its force.

Sarah Margaret Fuller, daughter of an eccentric but very assertive citizen of Cambridge, was born in 1810. Educated by her father according to his own ideas, she was much over-stimulated in youth, and grew into something which impressed people who disliked her as intellectual monstrosity. She was early a teacher and a writer. She contracted with Emerson a Platonically intimate friendship, of which the records enliven the humours of this period. And among her most characteristic proceedings was a series of conversations to which for a year or two she invited people to subscribe. The subscribers were duly admitted to her small drawing-room, where she proceeded to talk about all manner of literary and intellectual things, until you could hardly tell whether she were more like an unsexed version of Plato's Socrates or a Yankee Lyceum lecturer. In 1840 she became editor of the "Dial." In 1842 she relinquished the editorship to Emerson, and removed to New York. Horace Greeley, whose sympathy with New England reformers was always encouraging, had invited her to become the literary critic of the New York "Tribune."

Two years later she went abroad. Up to this time the records of her life indicate deficiency of passion. In the little time which followed, her passion so asserted itself that, had she survived, her later work might have been surprisingly different from what she actually left us. She strayed to Italy, where in the revolutionary times of 1847 she married a gentleman named Ossoli, an Italian patriot some years younger than she. The marriage was kept secret, amid the stormy hopes and fears of reviving Italy, until her approach to confinement compelled her to admit it. She was in Rome during the siege of 1848, and two years later started for America with her husband, virtually an exile, and her child. The ship on which they were journeying was wrecked off Fire Island; all three were lost.

An obviously extravagant legend about her indicates at once something of how Transcendentalists presented themselves to other people and perhaps a little of their real temper. As we may remember, one of the poems which Poe approvingly remarked among those of the New York Literati was written by a certain Mrs. Osgood about Fanny Ellsler. This same Fanny Ellsler danced in Boston; and there is said to be in the " Dial " a grave argument that in spite of her personal errors it was morally permissible to see and admire her performances as an artist. The story runs that, in obedience to this moral right and æsthetic duty, Emerson and Margaret Fuller went together to see the most accomplished ballet-dancer of the '40's. Neither of them had ever seen a ballet before; neither knew quite what to expect. The dance began; both sat serenely silent; at last Emerson spoke. " Margaret," he said, "this is poetry." " No, Waldo," replied Margaret, " it is not poetry, it is religion."

This Margaret Fuller was the first editor of the " Dial." Its precise purpose is hard to state; it may best be grouped with that little company of evanescent periodicals, which now and then endeavour to afford everybody a full opportunity

to say anything. The deepest agreement of Transcendentalism was in the conviction that the individual has a natural
right to believe for himself and freely to express his belief.
In a community so dominated by tradition as New England,
meanwhile, a community of which the most characteristic
periodical up to this time had been the " North American Review," freedom of speech in print, though not theoretically
denied, was hardly practicable. With a mission little more
limited than this ideal of freedom, the " Dial " started.

The cover of the first number was distinguished by a single
advertisement, — that of Mr. Jacob Abbott's Rollo books, then
publishing by the same printer. This happy accident can
hardly fail to suggest the reflection that Rollo was the body
of which Transcendentalism was the soul. Whoever wishes
to know the external aspect of the period now in question
will waste none of the moments which he may devote to Mr.
Abbott's luminous pages. Nor will time be wasted which
those whose curiosity is less centred on phenomena may find
themselves able to give to the " Dial " itself. For though
the " Dial " was impractical, never circulated much, and
within four years came to a hopeless financial end, its pages
are at once more interesting and more sensible than tradition
has represented them. Of the writers, to be sure, few have
proved immortal. Bronson Alcott and Theodore Parker
seem fading with Margaret Fuller into mere memories ;
and George Ripley has become more nebulous still.
But Thoreau was of the company ; and so was Emerson, who
bids fair to survive the rest much as Shakspere has survived
the other Elizabethan dramatists.

This is perhaps what now makes the " Dial " most significant. No eminent literary figure can grow into existence
without a remarkable environment ; and as the pages of the
" Dial " gradually reveal what the environment of Emerson's
most active years was, it proves on the whole more vigorous
than you would have been apt to expect. Its vigour, however,

appears more plainly in the earlier volumes of the " Dial "
than in the later. Up to the time when the periodical was
founded, the general temper for which it stands had been
gathering force. Merely as literature, then, the first two
or three numbers are surprisingly good. As you turn the
pages of the later numbers you are sensible of disintegration.
The thought tends to grow more vague; the kinds of reform
which interest people grow more various and wilder; and,
above all, the tendency, so fatal to periodical literature, of
running to inordinate length, becomes more and more evident. You begin to feel as if each writer would have liked
to write the whole thing himself. The " Dial " begins with
an auroral glow, which soon fades into a rather bewildering
mist. From beginning to end, however, it is fresh in feeling, wide in scope, earnest in its search for truth, and less
eccentric than you would have thought possible. For all its
ultimate failure, it leaves a final impression not only of auroral
hopefulness, but of moral sanity.

Tradition has remembered about it chiefly such oddities as
the " Orphic Sayings " of Bronson Alcott, — " awful sayings,"
they have since been called, in days when the adjective " awful"
had attained its cant meaning. There is room for grave doubt
whether Alcott ever knew what some of them meant; certainly
no one else ever knew, and for many years no one has wanted
to know. Tradition has remembered, too, Emerson's tendency in the later numbers to lay before the world the inspired
truths of other scriptures than the Christian, — Chinese, Indian, whatever else. At the same time tradition has forgotten
the more solid and contemporary stuff that appeared there. In
the second number, for example, among other things, Mr.
George Ripley has much to say about that Unitarian orthodoxy against which Channing himself was protesting; and
in the course of his article Ripley uses concerning his awakened New England the words " new life," in just the sense
in which we have found the word " Renaissance " so truly

to express the spirit of the moment. A little later a writer believed to be Margaret Fuller expounds that Christianity is a prison; not long afterwards Theodore Parker, remembered as the most radical of the divines who still called themselves Unitarian, stoutly insists on the inexpressible merit of Christ as an example. In subsequent numbers of the first year there are articles on abolition, — a movement which logically enlisted the sympathies of almost all who were affected by the Transcendental movement; and Theodore Parker, radical from beginning to end, has some thoughts on labour by no means welcome to his conservative contemporaries. In the later volumes theoretical socialism comes more and more to the front, and there is a good deal about the community at Brook Farm in which a considerable number of Transcendentalists found material expression for their enthusiasm. Along with such articles as these there is much poetry, on the whole worth reading. Little of it is excellent; the best of course is Emerson's, mostly reprinted again and again. If not great, however, the poetry of the " Dial " is genuine, — a sincere effort on the part of increasingly cultivated people earnestly and beautifully to phrase emotions which in their freshly enfranchised New England they truly felt.

Though the " Dial " had little positive cohesion, its writers and all the Transcendentalists, of whom we may take them as representative, were almost at one as ardent opponents of lifeless traditions. Generally idealists, and believers in innate ideas, they were stirred to emotional fervour by their detestation of any stiffening orthodoxy, even though that orthodoxy were so far from dogmatic as Yankee Unitarianism. And naturally passing from things of the mind and the soul to things of that very palpable part of human nature, the body, they found themselves generally eager to alter the affairs of this world for the better. If any one word could certainly arouse their sympathetic enthusiasm, it was the word " reform."

Whoever at any moment contemplates life is bound to find many displeasing things. He is bound to find at the same time a perceptible infusion of merit and virtue. Thus contemplating the mazed and confusing panorama of existence, some people shrink from any effort radically to alter the condition of human affairs; for bad as things are, alteration may by chance involve more destruction of good than suppression of evil. To reformers, on the other hand, the darker aspect of actual affairs seems the more conspicuous They are always for putting down the evil, trusting that the good shall survive by its inherent strength ; and when reform takes up arms, we have revolutions. Transcendentalists never thought of resorting to arms ; but they did eagerly inspect life, and finding there many unsatisfactory things, they eagerly welcomed any effort to make things better, without much question as to how practicable that effort was, or as to what it might incidentally destroy. A glance at the contents of the " Dial " will accordingly show that the periodical fervently advocated two distinct reforms. The more specific, which reached its highest development later, was the abolition of slavery, a measure important enough in the intellectual history of New England to deserve separate discussion. The more general, which developed, flourished, and failed decidedly before the antislavery movement became a political force, was that effort to reform the structure of society which found expression in the community of Brook Farm near Boston.

In 1841, a number of people, — all in sympathy with the Transcendentalists, and most of them writers for the " Dial," — among the more conspicuous of whom were Mr. George Ripley, Mr. Charles Anderson Dana, and Mr. John Sullivan Dwight, bought a farm ten or twelve miles from Boston. Here they proposed to found an ideal community, where everybody should work to support the establishment and where there should be plenty of leisure for scholarly and edifying pleasure. Incidentally there was to be a school, where children from their earliest years were to give their infantile help in the work of the community. The experiment began. At least during its earlier years, Brook Farm attracted considerable notice, and the sympathetic attention of many people afterward more eminent than its actual members. Hawthorne came thither for a while, and his " Blithedale Romance " is an idealised picture of the establishment. Emerson, though never an actual member, was there off and on, always with shrewd, kindly interest. Thither, too, occasionally came Margaret Fuller, in whom some have discovered the original of Hawthorne's Zenobia. But if Margaret Fuller really suggested Zenobia, Zenobia is probably Hawthorne's most wonderful creation. For Zenobia is profoundly feminine ; and whatever else poor Margaret Fuller seems, at least until after her passionate marriage, she seems so lost in Transcendental abstraction that nothing short of genius could connect with her the idea of sex.

Brook Farm, of course, was only a Yankee expression of the world-old impulse to get rid of evil by establishing life on principles different from those of economic law. From earliest times, theoretical writers have proposed various forms of communistic existence as a solution of the problems presented by the sin and suffering of human beings in any dense population. The writer whose principles most definitely affected Brook Farm in its later development was Fourier, a French philosopher, who sketched out a rather elaborate ideal society. The basis of his system was that people should separate themselves into phalanxes of no considerable numbers, and that each phalanx should be mutually helpful and self-supporting. This conception so commended itself to the Brook Farmers that, at an expense decidedly beyond their means, they actually built a phalanstery, or communal residence, as nearly as might be on the lines which Fourier suggested.

What marked the peculiarly Yankee character of the Brook Farmers, was their calm disregard of a vital point in

Fourier's system. There can be no doubt that a considerable part of human unhappiness is caused by the loves of men and women. This phase of unhappiness some theorists would avoid by lifelong celibacy. Fourier less austerely avoided it by introducing into his phalansteric system a decent variety of free love, whereby adult men and women should be permitted to live together as long as they found it mutually agreeable, and to separate without inconvenient formalities whenever mutually so inclined, thus perpetuating an ideal race in obedience to unimpeded affinities of nature. When the Brook Farmers arrived at this phase of Fourier's applied philosophy, they simply ignored it. Cynical contemporaries rather looked for a development of free love in a community whose principles so clearly involved this form of freedom as well as those which they openly advocated. Nothing of the kind appeared. However absurd, however eccentric and irritating, Brook Farm may have seemed to people of strong sense, it passed from beginning to end without scandal. People who were married lived there as respectable married people should; unmarried people lived there with all that unaffected purity of personal life which is so generally characteristic of the better classes throughout America. The same native trait which appears in the absence of lubricity from American writings appears again in the fact that at Brook Farm, freely given over to theoretical socialism and to the teachings of Fourier, men and women lived sweet, clean lives. You might have watched them throughout the seven years of their communal existence, you might have listened to every word which they uttered about the teachings of their revered French apostle; but unless you had turned to Fourier's own writings, you would never have found reason to suspect that among his teachings was the doctrine of free love.

Brook Farm inevitably went to pieces. Its members were not skilled enough in agriculture to make farming pay; they found manual labour too exhausting to permit much activity of mind in the considerable leisure which their system afforded them; they discovered no new truths; and incidentally they discerned with more and more certainty that when you get together even so small a company of human beings as are comprised in one of Fourier's phalanxes, you cannot avoid uncomfortable incompatibility of temper. In 1847 their new phalanstery, which had cost ten thousand dollars and had almost exhausted their funds, was burned down; it was not insured, and before long the whole community had to break up.

The " Dial " had come to its innocent end three years before. Transcendentalism proved unable long to express itself in any coherent form. Yet many of those who were connected with it never relapsed into commonplace. Emerson's career we shall consider in a little detail, and Hawthorne's, too, when the time comes. Margaret Fuller hardly survived the period of which she was so conspicuous an ornament; when Brook Farm faded away, she was already in Italy. She had gone thither by way of New York, whither she had been invited by Mr. Horace Greeley's sympathy with all sorts of New England reform. Greeley also had something to do with the settlement in New York of two eminent Brook Farmers. One was Mr. George Ripley, perhaps the chief spirit of the community. He began life as a Unitarian minister, and with the possible exception of Theodore Parker was the most cultivated Boston divine of his day. He found even the Unitarian ministry too narrow in its orthodoxy. When Brook Farm proved impracticable, he became the literary critic of the New York " Tribune," with which he retained his connection to the end of a long and honourable life. His wife, who began in ardent sympathy with him, became a devout Roman Catholic. Mr. Ripley himself developed into a completely free-thinking and agreeably accomplished man of the world. Mr. Charles Dana, too, was for a while connected with the " Tribune." After a varied career, he finally became editor of the New York " Sun," which in his day enjoyed the reputation of being at once the most unprincipled and the most readable newspaper in America. Mr. George William Curtis became associated with the periodicals published by the Harpers, maintaining more of the purely ideal quality of his early days. Mr. Dwight returned to Boston, where, as editor of the " Journal of Music," he did rather more than any one else to make the city what it is now acknowledged to be, — a vital centre of musical art. And so in various ways Brook Farm faded into a memory, but one which always remained dear to those who knew the dreamy old days as they flitted through the sunshine. For though in one sense the movement came to nothing, it was an earnest, sincere, beautiful effort to make human life better by practising the principles of ideal truth. Brook Farm was typical of all Transcendentalism. It had a bright beginning, a rather bewildering adolescence, and a confused, misty end; but it left no one the worse for its influence.

This New England Transcendentalism developed most vigorously in those years when the intellectual life of New York was embodied in the Knickerbocker school of writers. By contrasting these two neighbouring phases of thought we can see how unalterably New England kept the trace of its Puritan origin, eagerly aspiring to knowledge of absolute truth. The literature of the Knickerbocker school was never more than a literature of pleasure. Even the lesser literature of Transcendentalism, not to speak of its permanent phases, constantly and earnestly aspired to be a literature of both knowledge and power, seeking in the eternities for new ranges of truth which should broaden, sweeten, strengthen, and purify mankind.

In brief, just as Unitarianism represents the temporary orthodoxy of renascent New England, Transcendentalism represents its vagrant spiritual philosophy. Mr. Cabot, in his biography of Emerson, calls the movement an outburst of Romanticism; by "Romanticism" he means something very like what we have called the revolutionary spirit, — a phase of that world movement which had shown itself in Europe more than a generation before. On Continental Europe this had expressed itself in the excesses of the French Revolution. In England it had expressed itself in that outburst of romantic poetry which made the first third of the nineteenth century a distinct epoch in English letters. The human nature of New England meanwhile asserted its independence of tradition in the vagaries of an ideal philosophy, and in a fervid assertion of the right of individuals to seek truth each for himself. This enfranchised Yankee human nature may perhaps seem vague, untutored, far from wise; but whatever its errors, and whatever the limits of its good sense, one fact about Transcendentalism must be evident even to those who are most sensible of its humourous aspect. Throughout it was aspiring; and its aspiration had a touch of almost unearthly sweetness and purity. The old dogmas of the Puritans had taught that uncontrolled human nature must instantly reveal itself as damnable. To any honest mind the human nature of nineteenth-century New England, in the first enfranchisement of Transcendentalism, must seem as far from damnable as if damnation had never darkened the dreams of humanity.

VI

As time passes, it grows more and more clear that by far the most eminent figure among the Transcendentalists, if not indeed in all the literary history of America, was Ralph Waldo Emerson. Born at Boston in 1803, and descended from a long line of ministers, he was as truly a New England Brahmin as was Cotton Mather, a century and a half before. His father was minister of the First Church of Boston, already Unitarian, but still maintaining unbroken the organisation which had been founded by John Cotton at the settlement of the town. The elder Emerson died early. His sons were brought up in poverty; but they belonged on both sides to that hereditary clerical class whose distinction was still independent of so material an accident as fortune. In 1821 Waldo Emerson graduated from Harvard College, where, as his " Notes on Life and Letters in New England " record, the teaching of Edward Everett was filling the air with renascent enthusiasm. After graduation Emerson supported himself for a few years by school-teaching, studying meanwhile his hereditary profession of divinity. In 1829 he was made colleague to the Reverend Henry Ware, Jr., pastor of the Second Church in Boston. This was the church which had remained for above sixty years in charge of the Mathers. His ministerial career, then, began in lineal succession to Cotton Mather's own. Mr. Ware, infirm in health, soon resigned; and before Emerson was thirty years old, he had become the regular minister of the Second Church.

On the 9th of September, 1832, he preached there the sermon which brought his pastoral career to a close. The subject was the Lord's Supper, and his text was : " The kingdom of God is not meat and drink, but righteousness and peace and joy in the Holy Ghost. Rom. xiv. 17." — " In the history of the Church," he begins, " no subject has been more fruitful of controversy than the Lord's Supper. There never has been any unanimity in the understanding of its nature, nor any uniformity in the mode of celebrating it." He goes on with a long paragraph stating various divergencies of custom in sacramental observance, and then proceeds : —

" I allude to these facts only to show that, so far from the supper being a tradition in which men are fully agreed, there has always been the widest room for difference of opinions upon this particular. Having recently given particular attention to this subject, I was led to the conclusion that Jesus did not intend to establish an institution for perpetual observance when he ate the Passover with his disciples; and, further, to the opinion, that it is not expedient to celebrate it the way we do."

The body of the sermon is devoted to a cool statement of his reasons for this conclusion and opinion ; and at the end comes the decision at which he had arrived : —

" Influenced by these considerations, I have proposed to the brethren of the Church to drop the use of the elements and the claim of authority in the administration of this ordinance, and have suggested a mode in which a meeting for the same purpose might be held, free of objection.

" My brethren have considered my views with patience and candour, and have recommended, unanimously, an adherence to the present form. I have therefore been compelled to consider whether it becomes me to administer it. I am clearly of the opinion I ought not. This discourse has already been so far extended that I can only say that the reason of my determination is shortly this : — It is my desire, in the office of a Christian minister, to do nothing which I cannot do with my whole heart. Having said this, I have said all. I have no hostility to this institution; I am only stating my want of sympathy with it. Neither should I ever have obtruded this opinion upon other people, had I not been called by my office to administer it. That is the end of my opposition, that I am not interested in it. I am content that it stand to the end of the world, if it please men and please Heaven, and I shall rejoice in all the good it produces."

"I am content that it should stand to the end of the world," but "I am not interested in it," — that is the view expressed of the holiest mystery of Christianity by a man who stood for three years in the pulpit of Cotton Mather. It is doubtful whether the whole literature of heresy contains two phrases which to any mind still affected by traditional Christian faith must seem more saturated with serene insolence.

Serenely insolent, at least to orthodox Christians, Emerson remained all his life. This life was far from eventful. After giving up his pastorate he supported himself as a lecturer, occasionally preaching. He went abroad for a year, beginning that friendship with Carlyle which resulted in their life-long correspondence. In 1836 appeared his first book, "Nature," beautiful, serene, obscure, stimulating, permeated with the idealism which was the basis of his philosophy. In 1837 he gave, before the Phi Beta Kappa Society of Harvard College, his celebrated address on "The American Scholar," of which the closing paragraph is among the most articulate assertions of his individualism : —

"If the single man plant himself indomitably on his instincts, and there abide, the huge world will come round to him. Patience, — patience; with the shades of all the good and great for company; and for solace the perspective of your own infinite life; and for work the study and communication of principles, the making those instincts prevalent, the conversion of the world. Is it not the chief disgrace in the world not to be an unit; — not to be reckoned one character; — not to yield that peculiar fruit which each man was created to bear, but to be reckoned in the gross, in the hundred, or the thousand, of the party, the section, to which we belong; and our opinion predicted geographically, as the north or the south? Not so, brothers and friends, — please God, ours shall not be so. We will walk on our own feet; we will work with our own hands ; we will speak our own minds. The study of letters shall no longer be a name for pity, for doubt, and for sensual indulgence. The dread of man and the love of man shall be a wall of defence and a wreath of joy around all. A nation of men will for the first time exist, because each believes himself inspired by the Divine Soul which also inspires all men."

In the following year, his address before the Divinity School at Cambridge carried his gospel of individualism to a point which staggered even that heretical seminary. Full of theoretical liberalism, its authorities had deliberately invited to their baccalaureate pulpit a self-disfrocked divine, who had discarded the Lord's Supper because he happened not to find it interesting. What he said frightened Harvard theology itself back toward at least Unitarian orthodoxy. Here are two bits of his unfettered exhortation : —

" Let me admonish you, first of all, to go alone; to refuse the good models, even those which are sacred in the imagination of men, and dare to love God without mediator or veil. . . . Thank God for these good men, but say, ' I also am a man.' Imitation cannot go above its model. The imitator dooms himself to hopeless mediocrity. The inventor did it because it was natural to him, and so in him it has a charm. In the imitator something else is natural, and he bereaves himself of his own beauty, to come short of another man's.

" Yourself a new-born bard of the Holy Ghost, cast behind you all conformity, and acquaint men at first hand with the Deity.

. . . .

" I look for the hour when that supreme Beauty which ravished the souls of those eastern men, and chiefly of those Hebrews, and through their lips spoke oracles to all time, shall speak in the West also. The Hebrew and Greek Scriptures contain immortal sentences, that have been bread of life to millions. But they have no epical integrity; are fragmentary; are not shown in their order to the intellect. I look for the new Teacher that shall follow so far those shining laws that he shall see them come full circle; shall see their rounding complete grace; shall see the world to be the mirror of the soul; shall see the identity of the law of gravitation with purity of heart; and shall show that the Ought, that Duty, is one thing with Science, with Beauty, and with Joy."

In such spirit as these earlier works show, he went on lecturing and writing all his life, incidentally, it is said, displaying practical good sense. Although he never made a fortune, he managed to lay by more money than most of his literary contemporaries and to provide for a comfortable old age. He lived until 1882. Plenty of Boston people not yet past middle age still remember his figure, which so beautifully embodied the gracious dignity, the unpretentious scope, and the unassuming distinction of those who led the New England Renaissance.

Emerson's work is so individual that you can probably get no true impression of it without reading deeply for yourself. To many this may be irksome. Like all powerful individualities, his can hardly leave a reader indifferent; you will be either attracted or repelled, and if repelled, the repulsion will very likely make the reading demand a strenuous act of will. But any student of American letters must force himself to the task; for Emerson, thinking, talking, writing, lecturing from that Concord where he lived during the greater part of his life, produced, in less than half a century, work which as time goes on and as the things which other men were making begin to fade, seems more and more sure of survival. America produced him; and whether you like him or not, he is bound to live.

As one grows familiar with his work, its most characteristic trait begins to seem one which in a certain sense is not individual at all, but rather is common to all phases of lasting literature.

Classical immortality, of course, is demonstrable only by the lapse of cumulating ages. One thing, however, seems sure: in all acknowledged classics, — in the great works of antique literature, sacred and profane alike, and, to go no further, in the great poetry of Dante or of Shakspere, — there proves to reside a vitality which as the centuries pass shows itself less and less conditioned by the human circumstances of the writers. No literary expression was ever quite free from historical environment. Homer — one poet or many — belongs to the heroic age of Greece; Virgil, or Horace, to Augustan Rome; Dante to the Italy of Guelphs and Ghibellines; Shakspere to Elizabethan England. But take at

random any page from any of these, and you will find something so broadly, pervasively, lastingly human, that generation
after generation will read it on with no sense of the changing epochs which have passed since the man who spoke this
word and the men for whom it was spoken have rested in
immortal slumber.   In the work of Emerson, whatever its
final value, there is something of this note.   Every other
writer at whom we have glanced, and almost every other
at whom we shall glance hereafter, demands for understanding that we revive our sympathy with the fading or faded
conditions which surrounded his conscious life.   At best these
other works, vitally contemporaneous in their own days, grow
more and more old-fashioned.   Emerson, on the other hand,
from beginning to end, seems constantly modern, with a con-
temporaneousness almost as perennial as that of Scripture
itself.   Though his work may lack something of true greatness, it surely seems alive with such unconditioned freedom
of temper as makes great literature so inevitably lasting.

Take, for example, the first page at which a volume of his
" Essays " chances to open, — that where the verse is printed
with which he prefaced his essay on " Spiritual Laws " : —

> " The living Heaven thy prayers respect,
>   House at once and architect,
>   Quarrying man's rejected hours,
>   Builds there with eternal towers ;
>   Sole and self-commanded works,
>   Fears not undermining days,
>   Grows by decays,
>   And, by famous might that lurks
>   In reaction and recoil,
>   Makes flame to freeze and ice to boil ;
>   Forging, through swart arms of Offence,
>   The silver seat of Innocence."

What this means we may admit ourselves unable to understand ; but with all due vexation or humility, we can hardly
help feeling that here is not a word or even a lurking mood

which might not have emerged from eldest human time, or might not as well emerge from the most remote human future our imagination can conceive. In essence throughout, Emerson's work bids fair to disregard the passing of time; its spirit seems little more conditioned by the circumstances of nineteenth-century Concord or Boston than Homer's was by the old Ægean breezes.

In form, on the other hand, Emerson's work seems almost as certainly local. Broadly speaking, it falls into two classes, — essays and poems. The essays are generally composed of materials which he collected for purposes of lecturing. His astonishing lack of method is familiar; he would constantly make note of any idea which occurred to him; and when he wished to give a lecture, he would huddle together as many of these notes as should fill the assigned time, trusting with all the calm assurance of his unfaltering individualism that the truth inherent in the separate memoranda would give them all together the unity implied in the fact of their common sincerity. But though this bewildering lack of system for a moment disguise the true character of his essays, the fact that these essays were so often delivered as lectures should remind us of what they really are. The Yankee lecturers, of whom Emerson was the most eminent, were only half-secularised preachers, — men who stood up and talked to ancestrally attentive audiences. And these eager hearers were disposed at once to respect the authority of their teachers, to be on the look-out for error, and to go home with a sense of edification. Emerson's essays, in short, prove to be an obvious development from the endless sermons with which for generations his ancestors had regaled the New England fathers. In much the same way, Emerson's poems, for all their erratic oddity of form, prove on consideration to possess many qualities of temper for which an orthodox mind would have sought expression in hymns. They are designed not so much to set forth human emotion or to give æsthetic delight as to stimulate moral or spiritual ardour.   For all his individualism, Emerson could not help being a good old inbred Yankee preacher.

The orthodox clergy of New England, however, came, as truly as Paul himself, to preach Christ crucified.   To say that preaching so various as Emerson's excludes anything, would be presumptuous.   But certainly the impression produced by more than one examination of Emerson's writings goes far to warrant the assertion that the one thing which he ignored was the crucifixion.   Christ as a philosopher he respected and reverenced ; but Christ the Redeemer, who takes upon Himself the sins of the world, interested him no more than the Lord's Supper.   So far as Christ was a prophet, a speaker of beautiful and noble truth, a living example of stainless life, Emerson could reverently bow before him; but when it came to considering Christ as more divine than other good men, this same Emerson found the act as far from reasonable as asserting one day's sunshine superior to that of another. The Christian Scriptures he thought on the whole nobler than even the Greek, and still more so than those more remote ones with which he overloaded some later numbers of the " Dial." All alike, however, great and small, interested him merely as guides, neither more nor less authoritative than such other guides as experience or the inner light.   Each and all he valued only so far as they might help mankind toward perception of the truth which he felt it his business to preach.   His business, he felt it, rather than his duty.   That fact of "interest," for lack of which he discarded the most sacred of all Christian traditions, really went to the depths of his nature. What interested him he was prepared to set forth so long as the interest lasted ; what did not interest him he was equally prepared serenely to neglect, no matter what anybody else thought about it.   He had, however, the native grace never to relax his interest in what he conceived to be the deepest of all truths ; namely, that beyond human ken there lie unfathomable, unseen, inexhaustible depths of reality.   Into these depths he was constantly seeking to pry as deeply as his human limitations would allow; and what he saw there he was constantly and eagerly interested to reveal. A Yankee preacher of unfettered idealism, one may call him; better still, its seer, its prophet.

Idealism, of course, is ancestrally familiar to any race of Puritan origin. That life is a fleeting manifestation of unfathomable realities which lie beyond it, that all we see and all we do and all we know are merely symbols of things unseen, unactable, unknowable, had been preached to New England from the beginning. But Emerson's idealism soared far above that of the Christian fathers. Their effort was constantly to reduce unseen eternities to a system as rigid as that which addressed their human senses; and this effort has so far succeeded that to-day those who call God by His name thereby almost clothe Him in flesh and blood, in Jove-like beard and flowing robes, turning Him once more, even though immortally, into a fresh symbol of the infinite divine self which essentially transcends all limitation. To Emerson, on the other hand, the name of God, like the life of Christ, grouped itself with the little facts of every-day existence as simply one more phenomenal symbol of unspeakable, unfathomable, transcendental truth. There is for ever something beyond; you may call it God, you may call it Nature, you may call it Over-Soul; each name becomes a fresh limitation, a mere symbolic bit of this human language of ours. The essential thing is not what you call the everlasting eternities; it is that you shall never cease, simply and reverently, with constantly living interest, to recognise and to adore them.

Now, in contrast with this infinite eternity of divine truth, no man, not even Christ himself, is free from the almost equally infinite limitations of earthly life. The essence of truth is that it comprehends and comprises all things, phenomena and ideals alike; and we men, great or small, ourselves on any eternal scale little more wonderful than are the leaves of grass which spring and wither in the field, can perceive at any moment only one aspect of this truth. Look at the moon ; when it is full you shall see it as a silvery disk in the heavens ; again it is shrunk to a sickle; and yet again you shall see no moon at all. By and by you learn a little of the secret law which reveals the same satellite first in one of its protean forms and then in another throughout the changing months of our fleeting human years. Gaze next into the infinities, whereof the system is so unspeakably further from simplicity than the motions of any moon or planets. At one moment you shall see them in one aspect, at the next in another, and so on till life and eternity shall merge. Nay, you shall have less true knowledge of them than if for a little while one should revisit the glimpses of the moon, and, seeing only a curved line dimly gleaming in sunset skies, should return to the shades with news that there is no moon left but a sinking new one.

Would you strive to reconcile one with another the glories of eternity ? strive, with your petty human powers, to prove them consistent things ? —

" Why should you keep your head over your shoulder ? Why drag about this corpse of your memory, lest you contradict somewhat you have stated in this or that public place ? Suppose you should contradict yourself : what then ? . . . A foolish consistency is the hobgoblin of little minds, adored by little statesmen and philosophers and divines. With consistency a great soul has simply nothing to do. He may as well concern himself with the shadow on the wall. Speak what you think now in hard words and to-morrow speak what tomorrow thinks in hard words again, though it contradict everything you have said to-day. . . . Pythagoras was misunderstood, and Socrates, and Jesus, and Luther, and Copernicus, and Galileo, and Newton, and every pure and wise spirit that ever took flesh. To be great is to be misunderstood."

In Emerson's calm impatience of philosophic system there is a fresh touch of that unhesitating assurance with which he brushed aside the most sacred of Christian institutions, when

for a moment it threatened to limit him. " See," he seems
to bid you, " and report what you see as truly as language will
let you. Then concern yourself no more as to what men
shall say of your seeing or of your saying." For even though
what you perceive be a gleam of absolute truth, the moment
you strive to focus its radiance in the little terms of human
language, you must limit the diffusive energy which makes it
radiant. So even though your gleams be in themselves consistent one with another, your poor little vehicle of words,
conventional and faint symbols with which mankind has
learned to blunder, must perforce dim each gleam by a limitation itself irreconcilable with truth. Language at best was
made to phrase what the cant of our passingly fashionable
philosophy has called the knowable, and what interested
Emerson surged infinitely throughout the unknowable realms.

Take that famous passage from his essay in " Society and
Solitude," on " Civilisation " : —

" ' It was a great instruction,' said a saint in Cromwell's war, ' that
the best courages are but beams of the Almighty.' Hitch your
wagon to a star. Let us not fag in paltry works which serve our pot
and bag alone. Let us not lie and steal. No god will help. We
shall find all their teams going the other way, — Charles's Wain,
Great Bear, Orion, Leo, Hercules; every god will leave us. Work
rather for those interests which the divinities honor and promote, —
justice, love, freedom, knowledge, utility."

In one sense this seems hodge-podge; in another, for all
its lack of lyric melody, it seems an almost lyric utterance
of something which all men may know and which no man
may define. " Hitch your waggon to a star " has flashed into
the idiom of our speech; but if you try to translate it into
visual terms you must find it a mad metaphor. The waggon is
no real rattling vehicle of the Yankee country, squalid in its
dingy blue; nor is the star any such as ever twinkled through
the clear New England nights. No chain ever forged could
reach far on the way from a Concord barn to Orion. Yet

behind the homely, incomplete symbol there is a thought, an emotion, flashing swifter than ever ray of starry light, and so binding together the smallest things and the greatest which lie within our human ken that for an instant we may feel them both alike in magnitude, each alike mere symbols of illimitable truth beyond, and both together significant only because for an instant we have snatched them together, almost at random, from immeasurable eternity.

For phenomena, after all, are only symbols of the eternities, and words at their best are trivial, fleeting, conventional symbols of little nobler than these mere phenomena themselves : —

"Good as is discourse, silence is better, and shames it. The length of the discourse indicates the distance of thought betwixt the speaker and the hearer. If they were at a perfect understanding in any part, no words would be necessary thereon. If at one in all parts, no words would be suffered."

So in a way of his own Emerson disdained words. This peculiarity appears perhaps most clearly when he is avowedly dealing with matters of fact. In 1856 he published a book named " English Traits," in which he recorded the impressions made on him by two visits to England, some fifteen years apart. His subject here is what he had observed as a traveller ; his treatment of it falls into unsystematic notes, each phrased in terms of unqualified assertion. As you read, you find few statements which do not seem full of shrewd, suggestive truth : —

"Man in England," he says, for example, " submits to be a product of political economy. On a bleak moor a mill is built, a banking house is opened, and men come in as water in a sluiceway, and towns and cities rise. Man is made as a Birmingham button. The doubling of the population dates from Watt's steam-engine. A landlord who owns a province, says, ' The tenantry are unprofitable; let me have sheep.' He unroofs the houses and ships the population to America."

Again, a little later we read : —

" There is an English hero superior to the French, the German, the Italian, or the Greek. When he is brought to the strife with fate, he sacrifices a richer material possession and on more purely metaphysical grounds. He is there with his own consent, face to face with fortune, which he defies. On deliberate choice and from grounds of character, he has elected his part to live and die for, and dies with grandeur."

Each of these statements seems true, and they are not really incompatible ; but each needs the other to qualify the impression of universality which Emerson somehow conveys with every sentence. Qualification he rarely stoops to. All he says is true, all incomplete, all suggestive, all traceable to the actual facts of that complex England which gave rise to all. And just as Emerson writes about England, with its wealth and its manufactures, its aristocracy and its cockneys, its " Times " and its trade and its Stonehenge, so he writes elsewhere of God, of the eternities, of Concord farmers, of the Over-Soul, of whatever else passes before his untiring earthly vision.

A dangerous feat, this. Any one may attempt it, but most of us would surely fail, uttering mere jargon wherein others could discern little beyond our several limitations. As we contemplate Emerson, then, our own several infirmities slowly reveal to us more and more clearly how true a seer he was. With more strenuous vision than is granted to common men, he really perceived in the eternities those living facts and lasting thoughts which, with all the careless serenity of his intellectual insolence, he rarely troubled himself intelligibly to phrase.

Sometimes these perceptions fairly fell within the range of language ; and of language at such moments Emerson had wonderful mastery. Open his essays at random. On one page you shall find phrases like this : —

" By the same fire, vital, consecrating, celestial, which burns until it shall dissolve all things into the waves and surges of an ocean of light, we see and know each other."

On another, which deals with Friendship, comes this fragment of an imaginary letter : —

" I am not very wise; my moods are quite attainable, and I respect thy genius; it is to me as yet unfathomed; yet dare I not presume in thee a perfect intelligence of me, and so thou art to me a delicious torment."

And there are hundreds of such felicitous passages. Often, however, as in that little verse which preludes the essay on " Spiritual Laws," Emerson was face to face with perceptions for which language was never framed; and then comes his half-inspired jargon. Yet, through it all, you grow more and more to feel that with true creative energy he was always striving to make verbal images of what to him were true perceptions; and more deeply still you grow aware that in his eager contemplation of truth he suffered astonishingly little of himself to intervene between perception and expression. So long as what he said seemed for the moment true, he cared for little else.

Again, one grows to feel more and more in Emerson a trait surprising in any man so saturated with ideal philosophy. As the story of Brook Farm indicated, the Transcendental movement generally expressed itself in ways which, whatever their purity, beauty, or sincerity, had not the grace of common sense. In the slang of our day, the Transcendentalists were cranks. With Emerson the case was different; in the daily conduct of his private life, as well as in the articulate utterances which pervade even his most eccentric writings, you will always find him, despite the vagaries of his ideal philosophy, a shrewd, sensible Yankee, full of a quiet, repressed, but ever present sense of humour which prevented him from overestimating himself, and compelled him when dealing with phenomena to recognise their relative practical value. He was aware of the Over-Soul, in whose presence Orion is no better than a team which should plod before a Concord haycart. He was equally aware that a dollar is a dollar, and a cent a cent, and that dollars and cents are convenient things to have in pocket. When you think of him as a lecturer or as a writer of books, then, you find all the old contradiction in a new form. You go to him as a prophet; you find a kindly gentleman with a good-natured smile lurking in the corners of his lips, who seems to tell you: " Dear me, I am no more of a prophet than you are. We are all prophets. If you like, I will look into the eternities with great pleasure, and tell you what I see there; but at the end of the business I shall present you with a little bill. If you will pay it, I shall receipt it, and dine a trifle better in consequence."

He was the prophet of Transcendentalism, if you like; but, after all, his general manner and temper were less prophetic than those of conventional parsons who thunder forth divine authority. He was farther still from the authoritative prophets of antiquity. He did not passionately seek God and phrase his discoveries in the sacred mysteries of dogma. He was rather a canny, honest Yankee gentleman, who mingled with his countrymen, and taught them as well as he could; who felt a kindly humour when other people agreed with him, and troubled himself little when they disagreed; who hitched his waggon to star after star, but never really confused the stars with the waggon.

And so descending to Concord earth, we find in him a trait very characteristic of the period when he happened to live, and one at which he himself would have been the first good-humouredly to smile. He was born just when the Renaissance of New England was at hand, when at last the old tripod of theology, classics, and law was seen not to be the only basis of the human intellect, when all philosophy and letters were finally opening to New England knowledge. With all his contemporaries he revelled in this new world of human record and expression. To the very end he never lost his consequent, exuberantly boyish trick of dragging in allusions to all sorts of personages and matters which he knew only by name. Take that sentence at which we glanced from his essay on Self-Reliance : " Pythagoras was misunderstood, and Socrates, and Jesus, and Luther, and Copernicus, and Galileo, and Newton." These great names he mentions with all the easy assurance of intimacy; he could hardly speak more familiarly of seven Concord farmers idling in a row on some sunny bench. Turn to him anywhere, and in any dozen pages you will find allusions as complacent as these, and about as accidental, to the bewilderingly various names at which his encyclopedia chanced to open. He had, in short, all the juvenile pedantry of renascent New England at a moment when Yankees had begun to know the whole range of literature by name, and when they did not yet distinguish between such knowledge and the unpretentious mastery of scholarship.

It is now nearly twenty years since Emerson's life gently faded away, and it is a full sixty since his eager preaching or prophecy of individualistic idealism stirred renascent New England to its depths. We have been trying to guess what Emerson may mean in permanent literature. To understand what he means historically, we must remind ourselves again of the conditions which surrounded his maturity. When he came to the pulpit of the Second Church of Boston, the tyranny of custom, at least in theoretical matters, was little crushed. Heretical though Unitarianism was, it remained in outward form a dominant religion. Statesmanship and scholarship, too, were equally fixed and rigid ; and so, to a degree hardly conceivable to-day, was the structure of society. Even to-day untrammelled freedom of thought, unrestrained assertion of individual belief, sometimes demands grave self-sacrifice. In Emerson's day it demanded heroic spirit.

To say that Emerson's lifelong heroism won us what moral and intellectual freedom we now possess would be to confuse the man with the movement of which he is the great exemplar. As the years pass, however, we begin to understand that no other American writings record that movement half so vitally as his. As our individual freedom becomes more and more surely established, we may delight in Emerson more or less. According as our individuality responds or not to the idealism which touched him, we may find him repellent or sympathetic; and although it may hardly be asserted, it may fairly be surmised, that even in Emerson's most memorable utterances the future may find no considerable truth not better phrased by others. For in his effort to express truth, just as in his whole knowledge of life, he was limited by the national inexperience which throughout his time still protected New England. Yet whether or no, in generations to come, Emerson shall prove to have made lasting contributions to human wisdom, one thing which will remain true of him should commend him to the regard of all his countrymen who love spiritual freedom. We may not care for the things he said, we may not find sympathetic the temper in which he uttered them, but we cannot deny that when, for two hundred years, intellectual tyranny had kept the native American mind cramped within the limits of tradition, Emerson fearlessly stood forth as the chief representative of that movement which asserted the right of every individual to think, to feel, to speak, to act for himself, confident that so far as each acts in sincerity good shall ensue.

Whoever believes in individualism, then, must always respect in Emerson a living prophet; and, just as surely, those who find prospect of salvation only in obedience to authority must lament the defection from their ranks of a spirit which, whatever its errors, even they must admit to have been brave, honest, serene, and essentially pure with all that purity which is the deepest grace of ancestral New England.

VII

CONCORD, Massachusetts, until Emerson's time celebrated as the place where the embattled farmers made their stand against the British regulars in 1775, is now even better known as the Yankee village where for half a century Emerson lived, and gathered about him a little group of the intellectually and spiritually enlightened. Until very lately, indeed, something of this atmosphere lingered in Concord air. Among the humours of New England for some fifteen years has been a Concord School of Philosophy, where of a summer fantastic people have collected to hear and to give lectures. And everybody has been happy, and no human being is known to have been harmed. When the Concord School of Philosophy began its blameless existence, however, what makes Concord memorable was no longer there: Emerson had passed away. Whatever Concord retained, it had lost that saving grace of sound good sense which is among Emerson's most certain claims to distinction.

This trait of his appears most clearly when we compare him with one or two of his fellow-townsmen. Of the men who flourished in Emerson's Concord, to be sure, the most eminent was Hawthorne, whose work belongs not to philosophy, but to pure letters, and whom we shall consider later. He would hardly have expected a place among the prophets of the eternities. At least two other men would have been disposed to call themselves philosophers, and, with artless lack of humour, to expect immortality in company with Emerson and Plato, and the rest. These were Amos Bronson Alcott and Henry David Thoreau.

Alcott was the elder, and older even than Emerson. Born in 1799, the son of an every-day Connecticut farmer, he began life as a peddler, in which character he sometimes strayed a good way southward. A thoroughly honest man of unusually active mind, his chief emotional trait appears to have been a self-esteem which he never found reason to abate. In the midst of peddling, then, he felt himself divinely commissioned to reform mankind. He soon decided that his reform ought to begin with education. As early as 1823, having succeeded in educating himself in a manner which he found satisfactory, he opened a school at his native town, Wolcott, Connecticut. Five years later he removed to Boston, where he announced that if people would send him their children, he would educate them as children had never been educated before.

At that time, in 1828, the spirit of reform was so fresh in the air of New England as to affect many heads which ought to have been too strong for just that intoxication. Among Mr. Alcott's pupils at different times were children and grandchildren of eminently conservative Bostonians. Dissatisfied with the mechanical lifelessness of the regular schools, they eagerly accepted Mr. Alcott's novel theories. His method of teaching, as reported by himself in a volume or two of conversations with his pupils, appears to have been Socratic. In the midst of his disciples, Mr. Alcott posed as a purified and beautified Greek philosopher, whose interlocutors were Boston children, ranging between the ages of three and ten. He would ask them questions about the soul and the eternities, and occasionally about matters of scientific and other fact. He would try to set their infant minds constructively working; and incidentally he would always be on the watch for any accents of perfected praise which might by chance issue from the mouths of these Yankee babes and sucklings. Apart from abstract wisdom, indeed, and its incidental humour, the most obvious trait which distinguishes Mr. Alcott from Plato's Socrates was his honest disposition to learn, if so might be, from the lips which he was persuading to babble. Very non-sensical, no doubt, this must seem nowadays; but there is an aspect in which it is touchingly characteristic of our renascent New England, which hoped that freedom from shackling tradition might open an illimitably excellent future.

Mr. Alcott's pristine innocence of good sense appeared most pleasantly in his notions of discipline. He had remarked that when people misbehave, the suffering which ensues is apt to fall on others than the sinners. If I hit you, for example, it is you who get a black eye. Now, if human nature is naturally good, men must instinctively shrink from consciously injuring others; the strongest deterrent force from misconduct, it follows, must arise from the normal philanthropy of human beings. In order to impress this wisdom on children four or five years old, Mr. Alcott hit on an ingenious device. Some children, he noticed, were disposed to be worse than others. When these bad ones were naughty, he reasoned, they should be made to feel that others suffered, and that the better the others were, the greater were their sufferings. Accordingly, when a bad child made a noise, he would regularly shake a good one in the offender's presence. It is said, furthermore, that he did not shrink from extreme conclusions. Discerning in his relation to his pupils an analogy to that which exists between a benevolent Creator and mankind, and holding that when man misbehaves, God is troubled, he is believed on occasions of unusual gravity unflinchingly to have inflicted corporal punishment on himself, in the presence of his assembled pupils.

Extreme as this example of Transcendental doctrine applied to life may seem, it is very characteristic of Bronson Alcott, who all his life maintained the gospel of Transcendental individualism. Before many years his school came to an end. Mr. Alcott developed into a professional philosopher, lecturing, writing, and failing to support his family in decent comfort. When the " Dial " was started, he contributed to it his " Orphic Sayings." The fountain of these was inexhaustible; and even Margaret Fuller had practical sense enough to inform him with regret that she could not afford to fill the " Dial " with matter, however valuable, from a single contributor.   His reply was characteristic ; he loftily regretted that the " Dial " was no longer an organ of free speech.   In 1842 he visited England, where certain people of a radical turn received him with a seriousness which he found gratifying.   Returning to America, he endeavoured to establish at Harvard, Massachusetts, a community called Fruitlands, something like the contemporary Brook Farm, but free from the errors which he detected in the more famous community, founded under other auspices than his own.   Before long Fruitlands naturally collapsed.   For most of his ensuing life, which lasted until 1888, he lived in Concord, supporting himself, so far as he at all contributed to his support, by writing and lecturing in a manner which satisfied his self-esteem and very slightly appealed to the public.   Toward the end of his life he was the chief founder of the Concord School of Philosophy, and he had a senile relapse into something like orthodox Christianity.

There is an aspect, no doubt, in which such a life seems the acme of perverse selfishness ; but this is far from the whole story.   The man's weakness, as well as his strength, lay in a self-esteem so inordinate that it crowded out of his possibilities any approach either to good sense or to the saving grace of humour.   On the other hand, he was honest, he was sincere, he was devoted to idealism, and he attached to his perceptions, opinions, and utterances an importance which those who found him sympathetic were occasionally inclined to share. When his religious views were affected by that touch of senile orthodoxy, sundry good people seemed disposed to think that there might be unusual rejoicing in Heaven.   Most likely he thought so himself.   His diary, which consisted largely of philosophical speculations, he labelled " Scriptures " for each year. He seems to have held these utterances in as high respect as ever churchman felt for Scripture of old.   He saw no reason why his inspiration should not be as sacred as Isaiah's or Jeremiah's or Paul's. Of his published writings none was remembered, unless by his immediate friends, a year after he died. In life the man was a friend of Emerson's, holding in the town of Concord a position which he probably believed as eminent as Emerson's own. In death he is the extreme type of what Yankee idealism could come to when unhampered by humour or common-sense.

If Alcott is rapidly being forgotten, the case is different with Thoreau. For whatever the quality of Thoreau's philosophy, the man was in his own way a literary artist of unusual merit. He was born in 1817, of a Connecticut family, not long emigrated from France. On his mother's side he had Yankee blood, but not of the socially distinguished kind. What little record remains of his kin would seem to show that, like many New England folks of the farming class, they had a kind of doggedly self-assertive temper which inclined them to habits of personal isolation. Thoreau graduated at Harvard College in 1837. While a student he gained some little distinction as a writer of English; his themes, as undergraduate compositions are still called at Harvard, though commonplace in substance, are sensitively good in technical form. After graduation, he lived mostly at Concord. Though not of pure Yankee descent, he had true Yankee versatility; he was a tolerable farmer, a good surveyor, and a skilful maker of lead-pencils. In one way or another, then, he was able by the work of comparatively few weeks in the year to provide the simple necessities of his vegetarian life. So he early determined to work no more than was needful for self-support, and to spend the rest of his time in high thinking.

In the general course which his thinking and conduct took, one feels a trace of his French origin. Human beings, the French philosophy of the eighteenth century had strenuously held, are born good; evil, then, must obviously spring from the distorting influences of society. Accepted by the earlier Transcendentalists, this line of thought had led to such experimental communities as Brook Farm and the still more fleeting Fruitlands. Thoreau was Frenchman enough to reason out individualism to its logical extreme. The reform of society must be accomplished, if at all, by the reform of the individuals who compose it. Communities, after all, are only microcosmic societies, wherein must lurk all the germs of social evil. Let individuals look to themselves, then; under no other circumstances can human nature unobstructedly develop its inherent excellence. So for twenty-five years Thoreau, living at Concord, steadily tried to keep himself free from complications with other people. Incidentally he had the good sense not to marry; and as nobody was dependent on him for support, his method of life could do no harm.

His best-known experiment was his residence for about two years in the woods near Concord, where he built himself a little cabin, supported himself by cultivating land enough to provide for his immediate wants, and devoted his considerable leisure to philosophic thought. The fruit of this experiment was his well-known book, "Walden;" published in 1854, it remains a vital bit of literature for any one who loves to read about Nature.

Of course Thoreau was eccentric, but his eccentricity was not misanthropic. Inclined by temperament and philosophy alike to this life of protestant solitude, he seems to have regarded his course as an experimental example. He was not disposed to quarrel with people who disagreed with him. All he asked was to be let alone. If his life turned out well, others would ultimately imitate him; if it turned out ill, nobody else would be the worse. Though his philosophising often seems unpractically individual, then, it never exhales such unwholesomeness as underlay Alcott's self-esteem. What is more, there can be no question that his speculations have appealed to some very sensible minds. All the same, if he had confined himself to ruminating on the eternities and human nature, with which his sympathy was at best limited, his position in literary history would hardly be important. What gave him lasting power was his unusually sympathetic observation of Nature. A natural vein of indolence, to be sure, prevented him from observing either precociously or systematically; but when, as was more and more the case, he found himself alone with woods and fields and waters, he had true delight in the little sights which met his eyes, in the little sounds which came to his ears, in all the constant, inconspicuous beauties which the prosaic toilsomeness of Yankee life had hitherto failed to perceive.

Nature, as every one knows, had been a favourite theme of that romantic revival in England whose leader was Wordsworth. In one aspect, then, Thoreau's writing often seems little more than an American evidence of a temper which had declared itself in the old world a generation before. Nothing, however, can alter the fact that the Nature he delighted in was characteristically American. First of all men, Thoreau brought that revolutionary temper which recoils from the artificialities of civilisation face to face with the rugged fields, the pine woods and the apple orchards, the lonely ponds and the crystalline skies of eastern New England. His travels occasionally ranged so far as the Merrimac River, Cape Cod, or even beyond Maine into Canada; but pleasant as the books are in which he recorded these wanderings, as exceptional as were Cotton Mather's infrequent excursions through the bear-haunted wilds to Andover, we could spare them far better than "Walden," or than the journals in which for years he set down his daily observations in the single town of Concord. Thoreau's individuality is often so assertive as to repel a sympathy which it happens not instantly to attract; but that sympathy must be unwholesomely sluggish which would willingly resist the appeal of his communion with Nature. If your lot be ever cast in some remote region of our simple country, he can do you, when you will, a rare service, stimulating your eye to see, and your ear to hear, in all the little commonplaces about you, those endlessly changing details which make life everywhere so unfathomably, immeasurably wondrous. For Nature is truly a miracle; and he who will regard her lovingly shall never lack that inspiration which miracles breathe into the spirit of mankind.

Nor is Thoreau's vitality in literature a matter only of his observation. Open his works almost anywhere, — there are ten volumes of them now, — and even in the philosophic passages you will find loving precision of touch. He was no immortal maker of phrases. Amid bewildering obscurities, Emerson now and again flashed out utterances which may last as long as our language. Thoreau had no such power; but he did possess in higher degree than Emerson himself the power of making sentences and paragraphs artistically beautiful. Read him aloud, and you will find in his work a trait like that which we remarked in the cadences of Brockden Brown and of Poe; the emphasis of your voice is bound to fall where meaning demands. An effect like this is attainable only through delicate sensitiveness to rhythm. So when you come to Thoreau's pictures of Nature you have an almost inexhaustible series of verbal sketches in which every touch has the grace of precision. On a large scale, to be sure, his composition falls to pieces; he never troubled himself about a systematically made book, or even a systematic chapter. In mere choice of words, too, he is generally so simple as to seem almost commonplace. But his sentences and paragraphs are often models of art so fine as to seem artless. Take, for example, this well-known passage from " Walden " : —

" Early in May, the oaks, hickories, maples, and other trees, just putting out amidst the pine woods around the pond, imparted a brightness like sunshine to the landscape, especially in cloudy days, as if the sun were breaking through mists and shining faintly on the hillsides here and there. On the third or fourth of May I saw a loon in the pond, and during the first week of the month I heard the whippoorwill, the brown thrasher, the veery, the wood-pewee, the chewink, and other birds. I had heard the wood-thrush long before. The phebe had already come once more and looked in at my door and window, to see if my house were cavern-like enough for her, sustaining herself on humming wings with clinched talons, as if she held by the air, while she surveyed the premises. The sulphur-like pollen of the pitch-pine soon covered the pond and the stones and the rotten wood along the shore, so that you could have collected a barrelful. This is the 'sulphur showers' we hear of. Even in Calidas' drama of Sacontala, we read of 'rills dyed yellow with the golden dust of the lotus.' And so the seasons went rolling on into summer, as one rambles into higher and higher grass."

The more you read work like that, the more admirable you will find its artistic form.

With Thoreau's philosophising the case is different. Among Emerson's chief traits was the fact that when he scrutinised the eternities in search of ideal truth, his whole energy was devoted to the act of scrutiny. Vague, then, and bewildering as his phrases may often seem, we are sensible of a feeling that this Emerson is actually contemplating the immensities; and these are so unspeakably vaster than all mankind — not to speak of the single human being who for the moment is striving to point our eyes toward them — that our thoughts again and again concern themselves rather with the truths thus dimly seen than with anything concerning the seer. The glass through which Emerson contemplated the mysteries is achromatic. Now, Thoreau's philosophic speculations so surely appeal to powerful minds who find them sympathetic that we may well admit them to involve more than they instantly reveal to minds not disposed to sympathise. Even their admirers, however, must admit them to be coloured throughout by the unflagging self-consciousness involved in Thoreau's eccentric, harmless life. Perhaps, like Emerson, Thoreau had the true gift of vision; but surely he could never report his visions in terms which may suffer us to forget himself. The glass which he offers to our eyes is always tinctured with his own disturbing individuality. In spite, then, of the fact that Thoreau was a more conscientious artist than Emerson, this constant obtrusion of his personality ranges him in a lower rank, just as surely as his loving sense of nature ranges him far above the half-foolish egotism of Bronson Alcott. More and more the emergence of Emerson from his surroundings grows distinct. Like truly great men, whether he was truly great or not, he possessed the gift of such common-sense as saves men from the perversities of eccentricity.

We come now to a fact on which we must lightly touch. When we glanced at the first number of the " Dial " we remarked that the only advertisement on its cover was that of Mr. Jacob Abbott's " Rollo Books," which remain, with their unconscious humour and art, such admirable pictures of Yankee life about 1840. Twenty-eight years later, Louisa Alcott, the admirably devoted daughter of that minor prophet of Transcendentalism, published a book for girls, called " Little Women," which gives almost as artless a picture of Yankee life in the generation which followed Rollo's. A comparison between these two works is interesting. Comically limited and consciously self-content as the world of Rollo is, it has a refinement which amounts almost to distinction. Whatever you think of the Holiday family and their friends, who may be taken as types of the Yankee middle class just after Gilbert Stuart painted the prosperous gentlemen of Boston, they are not vulgar. The world of " Little Women " is a far more sophisticated world than that of Rollo, a bigger one, a rather braver one, and just as sweet and clean. But instead of unquestioning self-respect, its personages display that rude self-assertion which has generally tainted the lower middle class of English-speaking countries.

This contrast suggests a contrast between the personal careers of Alcott and of Thoreau and those of the New England men of letters whom we have hitherto mentioned. Whatever their superficial manners, Alcott and Thoreau alike remained in temper what they were born, — farmers' sons,

men of the people.   Emerson and Channing, on the other
hand, and the historians and the scholars and the public men
of New England, belonged either by birth or by early acquired
habit to the traditional aristocracy of their native region.   A
similar contrast we remarked in New York, where Irving
and Cooper and Bryant were succeeded by Poe and the
Knickerbocker School.   As the nineteenth century proceeded,
literature in America tended to fall into the hands of people
not less worthy, but perceptibly less distinguished than those
who had first illustrated it.

We have now followed the Renaissance of New England
from its beginning in the fresh vitality of public utterances
and scholarship, through the awakening optimism of the Unitarians, to the disintegrant vagaries of the Transcendentalists.
We have seen how, as this impulse proceeded to affect the
less distinguished social classes, it tended to assume forms
which might reasonably alarm people of sagely conservative
habit.   Reform in some respects is essentially destructive ;
and the enthusiasm of Yankee reformers early showed symptoms of concentration in a shape which ultimately became
very destructive indeed.   This, to which we must now turn,
and which enlisted at least the sympathies of almost every
Transcendentalist, — which was warmly advocated by Channing himself, which stirred Emerson to fervid utterances concerning actual facts, and which inspired some of the latest
and most ardent writings of Thoreau, — was the philanthropic
movement for the abolition of negro slavery, an institution
which still persisted throughout our Southern States.

VIII

THE ANTISLAVERY MOVEMENT

ENTHUSIASM for reform was obviously involved in the conception of human nature which underlay the world-wide revolutionary movement whose New England manifestation took the forms of Unitarianism and Transcendentalism. If human nature is essentially good, if evil is merely the consequence of what modern evolutionists might call artificial environment, it follows that relaxation of environment, releasing men from temporary bondage, must change things for the better. The heyday of Transcendentalism, then, had a humourous superficial aspect, which was admirably described in the opening passage of Lowell's essay on Thoreau, published in 1865 : —

"What contemporary, if he was in the fighting period of his life, (since Nature sets limits about her conscription for spiritual fields, as the State does in physical warfare,) will ever forget what was somewhat vaguely called the 'Transcendental Movement' of thirty years ago? Apparently set astir by Carlyle's essays on the 'Signs of the Times,' and on ' History,' the final and more immediate impulse seemed to be given by 'Sartor Resartus.' At least a republication in Boston of that wonderful Abraham à Sancta Clara sermon on Falstaff's text of the miserable forked radish gave the signal for a sudden mental and moral mutiny. *Ecce nunc tempus acceptabile !* was shouted on all hands with every variety of emphasis, and by voices of every conceivable pitch, representing the three sexes of men, women and Lady Mary Wortley Montagues. The nameless eagle of the tree Ygdrasil was about to sit at last, and wild-eyed enthusiasts rushed from all sides, each eager to thrust under the mystic bird that chalk egg from which the new and fairer Creation was to be hatched in due time. *Redeunt Saturnia regna,* — so much was certain, though in what shape, or by what methods, was still a matter of debate. Every possible form of intellectual and physical dyspepsia brought forth its gospel. Bran had its prophets, and the presartorial simplicity of Adam its martyrs, tailored impromptu from the tar-pot by incensed neighbours, and sent forth to illustrate the 'feathered Mercury,' as defined by Webster and Worcester. Plainness of speech was carried to a pitch that would have taken away the breath of George Fox; and even swearing had its evangelists, who answered a simple inquiry after their health with an elaborate ingenuity of imprecation that might have been honourably mentioned by Marlborough in general orders. Everybody had a mission (with a capital M) to attend to everybody else's business. No brain but had its private maggot, which must have found pitiably short commons sometimes. Not a few impecunious zealots abjured the use of money (unless earned by other people), professing to live on the internal revenues of the spirit. Some had an assurance of instant millennium so soon as hooks and eyes should be substituted for buttons. Communities were established where everything was to be common but common sense. Men renounced their old Gods, and hesitated only whether to bestow their furloughed allegiance on Thor or Budh. Conventions were held for every hitherto inconceivable purpose. The belated gift of tongues, as among the Fifth Monarchy men, spread like a contagion, rendering its victims incomprehensible to all Christian men; whether equally so to the most distant possible heathen or not was unexperimented, though many would have subscribed liberally that a fair trial might be made. It was the pentecost of Shinar. The day of utterances reproduced the day of rebuses and anagrams, and there was nothing so simple that uncial letters and the style of Diphilus the Labyrinth could not turn it into a riddle. Many foreign revolutionists out of work added to the general misunderstanding their contribution of broken English in every most ingenious form of fracture. All stood ready at a moment's notice to reform everything but themselves. The general motto was: —

> ' And we 'll *talk* with them, too,
> And take upon 's the mystery of things
> As if we were God's spies.' "

So long as reform remains in this stage, it can hardly impress people of common-sense as worse than ridiculous. When reform becomes militant, however, trouble heaves in sight; and the militant shape which New England reform took in the '40's clearly involved not only a social revolution, but an unprecedented attack on that general right of property which the Common Law had always defended.

Negro slavery, at one time common to all the English-speaking colonies, had died out in the Northern States. During the first quarter of the nineteenth century, meanwhile, the condition of industry in the South had tended to stimulate the institution in that region until it assumed unforeseen social and economic importance. Throughout colonial history there had been considerable theoretical objection to it, a line of American thought which may be adequately traced by consulting the index of Stedman and Hutchinson's "Library of American Literature." Samuel Sewall opposed slavery; so from the beginning did the Quakers; and even in the South itself there were plenty of people who saw its evils and hoped for its disappearance; but no thoroughly organised movement against it took place until the air of New England freshened with the spirit of its Renaissance.

Channing, who passed the years from 1798 to 1800 in Richmond, wrote from thence a letter which strikingly expresses the feeling excited by slavery in earnest Unitarians : —

"There is one object here which always depresses me. It is *slavery*. This alone would prevent me from ever settling in Virginia. Language cannot express my detestation of it. Master and slave! Nature never made such a distinction, or established such a relation. Man, when forced to substitute the will of another for his own, ceases to be a moral agent: his title to the name of man is extinguished, he becomes a mere machine in the hands of his oppressor. No empire is so valuable as the empire of one's self. No right is so inseparable from humanity, and so necessary to the improvement of our species, as the right of exerting the powers which nature has given us in the pursuit of any and of every good which we can obtain without doing injury to others. Should you desire it, I will give you some idea of the situation and character of the negroes in Virginia. It is a subject so degrading to humanity that I cannot dwell on it with pleasure. I should be obliged to show you every vice, heightened by every meanness and added to every misery. The influence of slavery on the whites is almost as fatal as on the blacks themselves."

To Channing, the conclusion here stated was unavoidable. If human beings are essentially good, they have a natural right to free development. No form of environment could more impede such development than lifelong slavery. When any honest. Unitarian was brought face to face with slavery, then, he was confronted with a dilemma. Either this thing was a monstrous denial of fundamental truth, or else the negroes were not human. Something like the latter view was certainly held by many good people. In the South, indeed, it became almost axiomatic. In Mark Twain's " Huckleberry Finn " there is an admirably compact expression of this temper. A boy, drawing the long bow, tells a simple-hearted and charitable woman that the boiler of a steamer has just exploded.

> " ' Good gracious ! ' she exclaims, ' anybody hurt ? '
> " ' No, 'm. Killed a nigger.'
> " ' Well, it 's lucky ; because sometimes people do get hurt.' "

With which sigh of relief the good creature goes on to relate some melancholy experiences of the boy's Uncle Silas.

It is hardly extreme to say, however, that this opinion is more consonant with New England temper to-day than it was seventy years ago. Modern ethnology seems to recognise a pretty marked distinction between human beings in the Stone Age and human beings as developed into the civilisation of the nineteenth century ; and though native Africans are not literally neolithic, they certainly linger far behind the social stage which has been reached by modern Europe or America. To philanthropic people in 1830, on the other hand, the distinction between Caucasians and Africans seemed literally a question of complexion. Men they believed to be incarnate souls ; and the colour which a soul happened to assume they held a mere accident.

Accordingly, a full nine years before the foundation of the " Dial," there was unflinchingly established in Boston a newspaper, which until the close of the Civil War remained the official organ of the New England antislavery men. This was the " Liberator," founded in 1831 by William Lloyd Garrison, then only twenty-six years old. Born of the poorer classes at Newburyport in 1805, by trade a printer, by temperament an uncompromising reformer, he was stirred from youth by a deep conviction that slavery must be uprooted. When he founded the " Liberator," he had already made himself conspicuous ; but the educated classes thought him insignificant. In 1833 he was a principal founder of the Antislavery Society in Philadelphia. From that time, the movement strengthened. Garrison died in 1879. For the last fifteen years of his life he was held, as he is held by tradition, a great national hero, a man who stood for positive right, who won his cause, who deserves unquestioning admiration, and whose opponents merit equally unquestioning contempt.

So complete a victory has rarely been the lot of any earthly reformer, and there are aspects in which Garrison deserves all the admiration accorded to his memory. Fanatical, of course, he was absolutely sincere in his fanaticism, absolutely devoted and absolutely brave. What is more, he is to be distinguished from most Americans who in his earlier days had attained eminence and influence by the fact that he never had the advantage or limit, as you will, of such educational training as should enable him to see more than one side of a question. The greatest strength of an honest, uneducated reformer lies in his unquestioning singleness of view. He really believes those who oppose him to be as wicked as he believes himself to be good. What moral strength is inherent in congenitally blind conviction is surely and honourably his.

But because Garrison was honest, brave, and strenuous, and because long before his life closed, the movement to which he unreservedly gave his energy proved triumphant, it does not follow that the men who opposed him were wicked. To understand the temper of the conservative people of New England we must stop for a moment, and see how slavery presented itself to them during the years of the antislavery struggle.

In the first place, the institution of slavery was honestly

regarded by many people as one phase of the more comprehensive institution which really lies at the basis of modern civilisation; namely, property. Property in any form involves deprivation. Property in land, for example, deprives many human beings of access to many portions of the earth, and still more of liberty to cultivate it and to enjoy the fruits of their labours. Property in corporations involves the payment of interest to those who possess capital, and this payment certainly impresses many worthy labouring men as wantonly subtracted from their earnings. So in our own day we have seen many honest attacks on property, not only in land, but in every form of corporations. Once for all, we may admit that there is some ground for these moral crusades. So far as property involves deprivation and incidentally results in grinding hardships, property involves evil. On the other hand, it always involves a great deal of good. Take, for example, not private persons whose incomes exceed their actual needs, but public institutions which are unquestioningly regarded as vitally important to the general welfare, such as universities or libraries. To do their service to learning and wisdom, these need incomes. They must possess investments which shall return a certain annual percentage; otherwise their work must stop. Very good: is the suffering and inequality involved in property, when property takes the form of land or shares, an evil so serious as to counterbalance the good done to civilisation by institutions of learning? Some admirable people, holding property essentially wrong, declare that it is; most men of hard sense, who may be taken as a type of the conservative classes, maintain the contrary.

The conviction that slavery, whatever its evils, was really a form of property, and that an attack on slavery therefore involved a general attack on the whole basis of civilisation, was one of the strongest convictions of conservative New England. In many minds which abhorred the evils of slavery, furthermore, this conviction was strengthened by an equally honest one that when you have made a bargain you should stick to it. The Constitution of the United States was presenting itself more and more in the light of an agreement between two incompatible sets of economic institutions, assuring to each the right freely to exist within its own limits. The fact that as a man of business you have given a note to some one whose personal morals you believe deplorable, is no reason why your note should not be paid. Among the conservative classes of New England, then, the antislavery movement seemed as threatening to the Union as to property itself. Whatever threatened Union or property, they conceived, clearly threatened civilisation, and on civilisation rests all that is best in human life or human society; for civilisation is the mother of ideals.

A third consideration, also, had great weight among thoughtful people. During the French Revolution the negroes of the French colonies in the West Indies had effected the triumphant insurrection which resulted in the still existing republics of San Domingo and Hayti; and in 1830 there were gentlemen in New England who personally remembered the horrors of that tragic time. The blacks had risen in overwhelming numbers; white males they had slaughtered; their wives and daughters, often women educated under the gentlest influences of France during the Old Régime, they had done to death more cruelly still. To cite a single instance, recorded by a Boston gentleman who escaped from San Domingo with his life: "The women, old and young, were collected together on the floor of a church about twelve or fifteen miles from the Cape, where many of them fortunately died under the brutality to which they were subjected." Something of the same kind, on a very small scale, has lately resulted in that deplorable lynching of Southern negroes which so puzzles unthinking Northern minds. To the conservative classes of old New England, in short, — to the men whom Gilbert Stuart had painted, and their sons, — the antislavery movement not only meant an attack on property, the institution on which civilisation is based; it not only proposed a violation of the Constitution, the compact on which our political security rests; but in all probability it threatened to abandon the white women of half a continent to the lust of brutal savages.

When at last, then, the antislavery movement began to gather disturbing force, this conservative opposition to it was as violent, as sincere, as deep, and in many aspects as admirable, as was the movement itself. But the fact that the conservative temper of New England was not, as some antislavery men asserted, wicked, in no way involves what conservative New England passionately proclaimed, — namely, wickedness on the part of the antislavery men themselves. The truth is that an irrepressible social conflict was at hand, and that both sides were as honourable as were both sides during the American Revolution, or during the Civil Wars of England. To the extreme antislavery men civilisation appeared a secondary consideration when human rights were concerned. Property? If property cannot protect itself, away with property! The Constitution? If the Constitution is a compact with Hell, let the Constitution fall! Liken it, if you will, to wedlock; there are phases of wedlock more sinful than any divorce. And as for the lust of the negro, why, the negro is human, and human nature is excellent! Enfranchise him, and God may be trusted to bring about the millennium. During the earlier phases of the antislavery movement it produced no pure literature; but it did excite the most characteristic utterances of at least three orators who are still remembered among public speakers.

The one of these who most clearly marks the relation of the antislavery movement to Unitarianism and Transcendentalism was the Reverend Theodore Parker. Born of country folk at Lexington, Massachusetts, in 1810, he graduated at Harvard in 1834, and in 1837 he became a Unitarian minister. In the history of Unitarianism, he has a prominent place; in the history of Transcendentalism, too, for his writings are

among the most vigorously specific in the "Dial," to which
he was a constant contributor; but his most solid strength lay
in his scholarship. There have been few men in New England whose learning has equalled his in range and in vitality.
The manner in which his ardent nature impelled him to express himself, however, was so far from what is generally
characteristic of scholars that in popular memory his scholarship has almost been forgotten. As a Unitarian minister,
Parker is remembered mostly for having carried individual
preaching to its most unflinching conclusions. So far as one
can judge, this preaching was actuated by unswerving devotion to what he believed true. The range of his scholarship
had made him familiar with thousands of facts which seemed
inconsistent with many forms of Christian tradition. These
he unhesitatingly preached with a fervid eloquence which even
in his own days, when New England oratory was at its height,
commanded unusual attention. His teaching consequently
carried Unitarianism so far from orthodox Christianity, in days
when the Higher Criticism was still to come, that he did more
than any other man to frighten less daring spirits into the
Episcopal communion, which now maintains alliance with
the ancestral church of England. As a Transcendentalist,
Parker's enthusiastic and active temperament made him far
more reformer than philosopher. He was content to let others
pry into the secrets of the ideal eternities. What chiefly interested him were the lines of conduct which men ought to
follow in view of the new floods of light; and among these
lines of conduct none seemed to him so important as that
which should lead straightest to the abolition of slavery. He
never lived to see his passionate purpose accomplished. Intense activity broke down his health; he died and was buried
at Florence, whither he had gone for recuperation, in the
spring of 1860.

Among his virtues and graces was not that of sympathy
with opponents; and when it came to public utterances on

the subject of abolition he indulged himself in a freedom of personal vituperation which, after the lapse of half a century, seems extreme. For this might be pleaded the excuse that Theodore Parker, like Garrison, sprang from that lower class of New England which never intimately understood its social superiors. A self-made man, however admirable, can rarely quite outgrow all the limitations of his origin. No such excuse may be pleaded for the two other antislavery orators who are best remembered,—Wendell Phillips and Charles Sumner. Born in the same year, 1811, both of these survived to hear the emancipation proclamation of 1863. Sumner remained an eminent member of the United States Senate until his death in 1874. Phillips survived ten years longer, but for the last twenty years of his life he did little else than exhibit the somewhat senile vagaries of a character whose leading passion seems to have become an ardour for disagreement with mankind.

Phillips was born of the oldest New England gentry. Kinsmen of his had founded the academies of Exeter and Andover, and his father had been the first Mayor of the city of Boston at a time when political power there still resided in the hands of a few leading families. He graduated at Harvard College in 1831, and in 1834 he was admitted to the bar. A man of extremely active and combative temperament, he sincerely wished to practise his profession; but his position during the next two or three years was one frequent with young gentlemen of position and fortune. People who had legal business either gave it to established members of the bar, or else preferred young men who had the luck to need fees for their support. There can be little doubt that Phillips's failure to obtain practice did something to arouse that sentiment of opposition to his social equals which characterised his later life. A college classmate used to tell a story of him in 1837. For three years he had been a briefless barrister, and his classmate, meeting him in the street, asked him good-humouredly whether he had yet found any clients. Phillips's eyes flashed angrily : " No," he said ; " and if they don't come soon, I shall take up a cause."

It was not long after the time of this probably apocryphal anecdote that a meeting was held in Faneuil Hall, where among other speakers the Attorney-General of Massachusetts defended the action of a western mob which in a frenzy of resentment had taken the life of Lovejoy, a very outspoken Abolitionist who had invaded their part of the country. Phillips was in the audience ; he interrupted the speaker, made his way to the platform, and then and there delivered an antislavery outburst which carried the audience by storm. So, having publicly declared war against society, by passionately inciting a public meeting to disregard the authority of that governing class to which he himself hereditarily belonged, he embarked on a lifelong demagogic career.

There can be little question that he believed himself to believe in the antislavery cause which, with full knowledge of the social sacrifice involved, he chose to advocate when less than thirty years old. Nor can there be any doubt that the course of political agitation which he thus deliberately began, in the midst of a society dominated by traditional conservatism, demanded rare courage, physical and moral alike. For not only was he exposed to danger of personal violence from those considerable portions of the lower classes who were at first disposed to disagree with him, but he knew that the price he must pay for lifelong demagogism was to be regarded as an unprincipled fanatic by the people whom he would naturally have found most sympathetic. Throughout, too, his oratory was highly finished. A man of distinguished personal appearance, with all the grace and formal restraint of hereditary breeding, he had mastered, to a rare degree, the subtle art of first winning the sympathy of audiences, and then leading them, for the moment unresisting, to points where, on waking from his spell, they were astonished to find themselves. Many people, particularly of the less educated sort, ended by yielding themselves to his power. Of the better sort, more grew to feel that at heart this power was only the consummate adroitness of a man so impatient of rivalry as recklessly to indulge his inordinate passion for momentary dominance. His speeches were true speeches. In print, lacking the magic of his delivery, they are like the words of songs which for lyric excellence need the melodies to which they have once been wedded. Whoever heard him speak remembers his performance with admiration. As the years pass, however, this admiration often proves qualified by suspicion that, with the light which was his, he might have refrained from those denunciations of established order which, to conservative thinking, still do mischief.

Like Phillips, the other Bostonian orator whose name is associated with the antislavery movement sacrificed his social career to his principles. He did this, however, rather less deliberately; and throughout his life displayed a density of perception concerning his personal relation with the people whom in public utterances he violently denounced. Charles Sumner was born of a respectable family at Boston in 1811; he graduated at Harvard, became a lawyer, and before the age of thirty had spent three years in Europe, where he made permanent friendships. A man of fine and cultivated tastes, he appears at his best in the records of his lifelong intimacy with the poet Longfellow. Like Phillips's, his career began as one which might have been expected to carry on the old traditions of the cultivated classes of New England; but he early found himself stirred by his fervent belief in the moral wrong of slavery. Sumner's sincere devotion to principle seems beyond question. The violence with which he permitted himself to abuse those who did not share his opinions, on the other hand, is still difficult to reconcile with the fact that, unlike Phillips, he felt personally aggrieved when they struck him off their visiting lists.

This license of speech brought on Sumner the assault which

all her work, this rambling story of life near Boston about the beginning of the nineteenth century is careless in detail and very uneven. As you consider it, however, you grow to feel that above almost any other accessible book "Old Town Folks" sets forth the circumstances and the temper of the native Yankee people. What is more, the carefully deliberate passages — the opening chapters, for example — are written in a manner which approaches excellence. In brief, Mrs. Stowe differed from most American novelists in possessing a spark of genius. Had this genius pervaded her work, she might have been a figure of lasting literary importance.

Even as it was, she had power enough to make "Uncle Tom's Cabin" the most potent literary force of the anti-slavery days. She differed from most Abolitionists in having observed on the spot all the tragic evils of slavery. Until the publication of "Uncle Tom's Cabin," slavery had on the whole presented itself to the North as a deplorable abstraction. Wherever the book went, — and it went so far that to this day dramatised versions of it are said to be popular in the country, — it awakened this abstraction into life, much as powerful preaching sometimes awakens a dormant sentiment of religion. Of course, "Uncle Tom's Cabin" is partisan, but it is honestly so; and if, as occasionally seems the case, the negro characters are so white at heart that there is a certain fitness in their dramatic representation by people with temporarily blackened faces, there can be no doubt that Mrs. Stowe believed her negroes as true to life as later, and rightly, she believed the Yankees of "Old Town Folks." Whatever you may think of "Uncle Tom's Cabin," you can never truly feel it to have been instigated by a demagogic purpose. It was written by one who, like the men who maintained anti-slavery principles amid every social obloquy and could never have foreseen their final popularity, was profoundly convinced that her cause was supremely true.

"Uncle Tom's Cabin" was published in 1852. To its

unprecedented popularity may be perhaps traced the final turn of the public tide. After ten years the conflict between the slave States and the free reached the inevitable point of civil war. The 1st of January, 1863, saw that final proclamation of emancipation which, by confiscating, as virtually contraband property, all slaves in the States which were then in arms against the Federal government, practically achieved the end for which the antislavery men had unfalteringly striven.

Into political history we cannot enter. For obvious reasons there has arisen during the last twenty-five years an antislavery legend, which has cast into an obloquy as deep as ever Abolitionists suffered the memory of every opposition to these men, whose chief heroism lay in their unflinching devotion to unpopular principle. In so far as this legend has led the growing generation of American youth to assume that because you happen to think a given form of property wrong, you have a natural right to confiscate it forthwith, the antislavery movement has perhaps tended to weaken the security of American institutions. At least in Massachusetts, too, the prevalence of this movement seems permanently to have lowered the personal dignity of public life, by substituting for the traditional rule of the conservative gentry the obvious dominance of the less educated classes. These shadows on the picture have been so generally neglected that we have perhaps allowed ourselves to dwell on them unduly. As fact begins to fade into history, it is sometimes the critical aspects of it which the world proves apt for a while to forget.

No doubt the evil of slavery was real; no doubt the spirit in which the antislavery movement attacked it was conscientious, brave, in many aspects heroic; but neither can there be doubt that the antislavery leaders of New England were of different origin from the Southerners whom they denounced, and that they mostly knew only by report the things which they abhorred. In the history of the South, for one thing, social and intellectual development had proceeded more slowly than in the North. The social and intellectual development of America has never proceeded so fast as that of England. The England of King William III. was far more different from the England of Queen Elizabeth than was the Boston of Joseph Dudley from that of John Winthrop. In the same way there was far more likeness between the Southern States of President Buchanan's time and the Southern States of General Washington's than between the New England of 1860 and the New England of 1789. Up to the time of the Civil War, indeed, the South still lingered in the eighteenth century; and at least in New England the force of what we have called its Renaissance was bringing men nearer to the contemporary nineteenth century of Europe than anything American between 1650 and 1800 had ever been to any Europe contemporary with itself.

Yet in the fact that the impulses of the New England reformers to set the world right finally concentrated themselves on the affairs of other people, and not on their own, there proves to be a trait which reveals how little the temper of New England has ever strayed from the temper of the mother country. For no peculiarity has been more characteristic of the native English than a passion to reform other people than themselves, trusting meantime that God will help those who forcibly help somebody else.

IX

JOHN GREENLEAF WHITTIER

AMONG the antislavery leaders of Massachusetts was one who, with the passing of time, seems more and more distinguished as a man of letters. John Greenleaf Whittier, born at Haverhill, Massachusetts, in 1807, came of sound country stock, remarkable only because for several generations the family had been Quakers. The first New England manifestations of Quakerism, in the seventeenth century, had taken an extravagantly fanatical form, which resulted in tragedies still familiar to tradition. As the Friends of New England had settled down into peaceful observance of their own principles, however, letting alone the affairs of others, they had become an inconspicuous, inoffensive body, neglected by the surrounding orthodoxy. Theologically, they believed in God, Jesus Christ, and the Bible. The interpreter of the divine word they found not in any established church nor in any officially sanctified order of ministers, but in the still, small voice given to mankind by the Heavenly Father.

"To all human beings, they held, God has given an inner light, to all He speaks with a still small voice. Follow the light, obey the voice, and all will be well. Evil-doers are they who neglect the light and the voice. Now the light and the voice are God's, so to all who will attend they must ultimately show the same truth. If the voice call us to correct others, then, or the light shine upon manifest evil, it is God's will that we smite error, if so may be by revealing truth. If those who err be Friends, our duty bids us expostulate with them; and if they be obdurate, to present them for discipline, which may result in their exclusion from our Religious Society. The still small voice, it seems, really warns everybody that certain lines of conduct are essentially wrong, — among which are the drinking of spirits, the frequenting of taverns, indulgence in gaming, the use of oaths, and the enslavement of any human being."

In this faith there is clearly involved a conclusion at odds with Calvinism. To Quakers, inasmuch as every man possesses within himself the power of seeing the inner light and of hearing the still, small voice of God, all men are essentially equal. When the antislavery movement began, then, Whittier, a lifelong adherent of this traditional faith, found himself in a relation to militant philanthropy very different from that of ancestral Calvinists. These, lately emancipated by the new life of Unitarianism and Transcendentalism, came to the reform with all the hotness of head which marks converts. Whittier, on the other hand, had inherited the principles to which the men with whom he allied himself had been converted; and so, although a lifelong and earnest reformer, he is the least irritating of reformers to those who chance not to agree with him.

Again, sprung from a class which made his childhood literally that of a barefoot boy, and growing up in days when the New England country was still pure in the possession of an unmixed race whose capacity for self-government has never been surpassed, Whittier naturally and gently, without a tinge of invidiousness, could base not only on religious theory, but also on personal inexperience, his fervent faith in the equality of mankind. In the fact that throughout his connection with the antislavery movement he unswervingly advocated the use of strictly constitutional means to bring about reform, there is again something deeply characteristic. From the beginning some abolitionists were for resort to force; but Whittier always believed that their end might be attained by the ballot. For, after all, an election is an opportunity given every mature man in the community, to declare by his vote what ought to be done and who ought to do it. Very good; if, as Whittier's faith taught him, God speaks to every human being who will listen, the voice of the people, provided they listen to the voice within them, is literally the voice of God. When a popular election goes wrong, it is only because the people have been deaf to the divine whisper of truth.

Whittier's youth was passed in the Yankee country. His education never went beyond country schools and two terms at the Haverhill Academy; but he had a natural love for literature. When he was nineteen years old, a poem of his was printed in the Newburyport "Free Press," then edited by William Lloyd Garrison. At twenty-one he was already a professional writer for country newspapers. At twenty-three he was editor of the "Haverhill Gazette." A year later he was made editor of a paper in Hartford, Connecticut; but his health, never robust, troubled him, and he returned to Massachusetts. In 1831 he published his first volume, a little book of verses called "New England Legends;" and during the same year, that in which Garrison established the "Liberator" at Boston, he became actively and ardently interested in the movement against slavery. Until 1840 this kept him constantly busy; in that year he resigned his charge of the "Pennsylvania Freeman," — a journal devoted to the cause of abolition in Philadelphia. He removed to Amesbury, Massachusetts, where he lived thenceforth. From 1826 until the end, no year went by without his publishing poems. His temperament was shy, and his later life uneventful. He died just across the border of New Hampshire in 1892.

Though Whittier was precocious, and his literary career extended over more than sixty-five years, he was not prolific. He never wrote much at a time, and he never wrote anything long. In the seven volumes of his collected works there are very few which might not have been produced at a single sitting. Again, his work throughout these sixty-five years was far from varied in character; like Bryant, he rarely excelled himself and rarely fell below. The limited circumstances of his life combined with lack of humour to make his writings superficially commonplace. What gives them merit are occasional passages where simplicity emerges from commonplace into dignity and sometimes into passion. For half a century, Bryant remained correct and delicately sentimental; for longer still Whittier remained simple, sincere, and fervent.

His masterpiece, if the word be not excessive, is "Snow-Bound," written when he was about fifty-seven years old. At that time, when most of his immediate family were dead, he tenderly recalled his memories of childhood. The vivid simplicity of his descriptions every one must feel; his picture of a winter evening at his old home, for example, almost appeals to the eye : —

> "Shut in from all the world without,
> We sat the clean-winged hearth about,
> Content to let the north-wind roar
> In baffled rage at pane and door,
> While the red logs before us beat
> The frost line back with tropic heat;
> And ever, when a louder blast
> Shook beam and rafter as it passed,
> The merrier up its roaring draught
> The great throat of the chimney laughed;
> The house-dog on his paws outspread
> Lay to the fire his drowsy head,
> The cat's dark silhouette on the wall
> A couchant tiger's seemed to fall ;
> And, for the winter fireside meet,
> Between the andirons' straggling feet,
> The mug of cider simmered slow,
> The apples sputtered in a row,
> And close at hand the basket stood
> With nuts from brown October's wood."

Nor is the merit of "Snow-Bound" merely descriptive. Throughout it you will find phrases which, except for mere lyric music, have a simple felicity almost final. Take the couplet, for example, in which he speaks of his aunt, no longer young, who never married : —

> "All unprofaned she held apart
> The virgin fancies of the heart."

Or take the lines in which he remembers a sister, dead early in life : —

> " And while in life's late afternoon,
> Where cool and long the shadows grow,
> I walk to meet *the night that soon*
> *Shall shape and shadow overflow,*
> I cannot feel that thou art far."

Throughout " Snow-Bound " you may discover lines as excellent as these.

Quite apart from its artistic merit, " Snow-Bound " is an important document for one who would understand the native Yankee country. " Flemish pictures of old days," Whittier calls the poem ; and in one sense the term is happy. He lovingly sets forth a very simple form of existence, with a minute detail something like that of the Flemish painters. Typical Flemish pictures, however, representing a European peasantry whose life is consciously that of an inferior class, abound in touches which indicate profound coarseness of temper. No Flemish life could have been humbler, none more simple, than the life which " Snow-Bound " pictures ; but this life of self-respecting dignity is utterly free from the grossness which usually depraves the lower ranks of any old, complex society. One begins to see how the national inexperience of New England was bound to teach earnest Yankees those lessons of human equality which Whittier never for a moment doubted.

Such vividness as distinguishes the descriptive passages of " Snow-Bound " transpires throughout Whittier's descriptive verse. Here, for example, are some lines which take one to the very heart of our drowsy New England summers : —

> " Along the roadside, like the flowers of gold
> The tawny Incas for their gardens wrought,
> Heavy with sunshine droops the golden-rod,
> And the red pennons of the cardinal flowers
> Hang motionless upon their upright staves.
> The sky is hot and hazy, and the wind,
> Wing-weary with its long flight from the south,
> Unfelt ; yet, closely scanned, yon maple leaf
> With faintest motion, as one stirs in dreams,

Confesses it. The locust by the wall
Stabs the noon-silence with his sharp alarm.
A single hay-cart down the dusty road
Creaks slowly, with its driver fast asleep
On the load's top. Against the neighbouring hill,
Huddled along the stone-wall's shady side,
The sheep show white, as if a snow-drift still
Defied the dog-star. Through the open door
A drowsy smell of flowers — gray heliotrope,
And white sweet clover, and shy mignonette —
Comes faintly in, and silent chorus lend
To the prevailing symphony of peace."

And here are more lines, which always come to mind when
one looks across the salt-marshes of Hampton : —

" Just then the ocean seemed
To lift a half-faced moon in sight ;
And shoreward o'er the waters gleamed,
From crest to crest, a line of light.

. . . .

" Silently for a space each eye
Upon that sudden glory turned ;
Cool from the land the breeze blew by,
The tent-ropes flapped, the long beach churned
Its waves to foam ; on either hand
Stretched, far as sight, the hills of sand ;
With bays of marsh, and capes of bush and tree,
The woods' black shore line loomed beyond the meadowy sea."

Superficially commonplace, if you will, passages like these,
as they grow familiar, prove more and more admirable in
their simple truth. Of course they lack lyric beauty. Whittier's metrical range was very narrow, and his rhymes were
often abominable. But whenever he dealt with the country
he knew so well, he had an instinctive perception of those
obvious facts which are really most characteristic, and within
which are surely included its unobtrusive beauty and its slowly
winning charm. With this excellent simplicity of perception
he combined excellent simplicity of heart and phrase.

In general, of course, the most popular literature is narrative. So Whittier's Yankee ballads often seem his most obvious works, — " Skipper Ireson's Ride," for example, or that artlessly sentimental " Maud Muller," where a New England judge is made to play the part of a knight-errant of romance. Like his admirable poetry of Nature, these are simple and sincere. In sentiment, too, the first is fervid. Both in conception and in phrase, however, these, with all the rest we may let them stand for, are so commonplace that one finds critical admiration out of the question. They belong to that school of verse which perennially flourishes and withers in the poetical columns of country newspapers.

Whittier's true claim to remembrance will rest on no such popularity as this, even though that popularity chance to be more than momentary. In the first place, his simple pictures of New England Nature are often excellent. In the second place, the fervour of his lifelong faith in the cause of human freedom sometimes breathed undying fire into the verses which he made concerning the conflict with slavery. Throughout them his faults appear. In 1836 Congress passed a bill excluding from the United States Post Office all Abolitionist publications; against this bill Whittier wrote a passionate " Summons to the North," which among other verses contains the following : —

> " Torture the pages of the Holy Bible,
>   To sanction crime, and robbery, and blood?
> And in oppression's hateful service libel
>   Both man and God?"

Worse rhymes than he thus comprised in four lines, you shall search the language for in vain ; but in that same poem are stanzas like these : —

> " Methinks from all her wild, green mountains ;
>   From valleys where her slumbering fathers lie
> From her blue rivers and her welling fountains,
>   And clear cold sky ;

" From her rough coast and isles, which hungry Ocean
　　Gnaws with his surges ; from the fisher's skiff,
　With white sail swaying to the billows' motion
　　Round rock and cliff ;

" From the free fireside of her unbought farmer ;
　　From her free labourer at his loom and wheel ;
　From the brown smith-shop, where, beneath the hammer,
　　Rings the red steel ;

" From each and all, if God hath not forsaken
　　Our land, and left us to an evil choice,
　Loud as the summer thunderbolt shall waken
　　A People's voice."

Seven years later, when the Fugitive Slave Law was enforced in Boston, he wrote that passionate address, " Massachusetts to Virginia," of which the following passage is an example ; —

" From Norfolk's ancient villages, from Plymouth's rocky bound
　To where Nantucket feels the arms of ocean close her round ;

" From rich and rural Worcester, where through the calm repose
　Of cultured vales and fringing woods the gentle Nashua flows,
　To where Wachuset's wintry blasts the mountain larches stir,
　Swelled up to Heaven the thrilling cry of ' God save Latimer ! '

" And sandy Barnstable rose up, wet with the salt sea spray ;
　And Bristol sent her answering shout down Narragansett Bay !
　Along the broad Connecticut old Hampden felt the thrill,
　And the cheer of Hampshire's woodmen swept down from Holyoke
　　Hill.

" The voice of Massachusetts !　Of her free sons and daughters,
　Deep calling unto deep aloud, the sound of many waters !
　Against the burden of that voice what tyrant power shall stand ?
　No fetters in the Bay State !　No slave upon her land ! "

War, of course, was utterly abhorrent to his Quaker principles ; but when inevitable war came, he greeted it in such spirit as this : —

" We see not, know not ; all our way
Is night — with Thee alone is day :
From out the torrent's troubled drift,
Above the storm our prayers we lift,
Thy will be done !

" Strike, Thou the Master, we Thy keys,
The anthem of the destinies !
The minor of Thy loftier strain,
Our hearts shall breathe the old refrain,
Thy will be done ! "

And when in 1865 the amendment to the Constitution,
abolishing slavery, was at last adopted, he wrote perhaps his
noblest poem, " Laus Deo," of which these three stanzas may
show the quality : —

" It is done !
Clang of bell and roar of gun
Send the tidings up and down.
How the belfries rock and reel !
How the great guns, peal on peal,
Fling the joy from town to town !
.   .   .   .   .   .

" Did we dare,
In our agony of prayer,
Ask for more than He has done ?
When was ever His right hand
Over any time or land
Stretched as now beneath the sun ?
.   .   .   .   .   .

" Ring and swing,
Bells of joy !   On morning's wing
Send the song of praise abroad !
With a sound of broken chains
Tell the nations that He reigns
Who alone is Lord and God ! "

At heart Whittier was no more stirred than were the other
antislavery leaders, nor was he gifted with such literary power
as sometimes revealed itself in the speeches of Parker or of
Phillips, or as enlivened Mrs. Stowe's novel with its gleams
of creative genius.   But Whittier surpassed all the rest in the

impregnable simplicity of his inborn temper, derived from his Quaker ancestry and nurtured by the guilelessness of his personal life.

Another trait he possessed, and a trait rare in temperaments eager for reform. This is magnanimity. It appears nowhere more clearly than in almost the only departure from chronological order in the final collection of his works, which he himself arranged. Until 1850, Webster, whose devotion to the ideal of Union had compelled him to oppose every aggression of the South, had been held by the antislavery men an heroic leader. His Seventh of March Speech, which supported a Fugitive Slave Bill, brought down on him a storm of antislavery indignation never expressed more fervently than in a poem by Whittier, still generally included in popular collections of American lyrics. He called this poem " Ichabod ; " and here are some of its verses : —

> " So fallen ! so lost ! the light withdrawn
>   Which once he wore !
> The glory from his grey hairs gone
>   Forevermore !
> .   .   .   .   .   .
> " Let not the land once proud of him
>   Insult him now,
> Nor brand with deeper shame the dim,
>   Dishonoured brow.
>
> " But let its humbled sons instead,
>   From sea to lake,
> A long lament, as for the dead,
>   In sadness make.
> .   .   .   .   .   .
> " Then pay the reverence of old days
>   To his dead fame ;
> Walk backwards, with averted gaze,
>   And hide the shame ! "

In 1850 no man condemned Webster more fiercely than Whittier. No more sincere poem than " Ichabod " was ever written. But two years after " Ichabod " saw the light,

Webster was dead; and it was nine years more before the Civil War came; and Whittier survived the Civil War for nearly a generation. In 1880, reflecting on the past, he wrote about Webster again. This poem he called the "Lost Occasion," and in his collected works he put it directly after the "Ichabod" which he had so fervently written thirty years before. The "Lost Occasion" has generally been neglected by the makers of American anthologies, so "Ichabod" is traditionally supposed to express Whittier's final feeling about Daniel Webster. In this case tradition is unjust to both men. The single deviation from chronology in Whittier's collected works shows that the poet desired his final sentiment concerning our greatest statesman to be phrased in no lines of fervid denunciation, but rather in such words as these : —

> "Thou shouldst have lived to feel below
>   Thy feet Disunion's fierce upthrow;
>   The late-sprung mine that underlaid
>   Thy sad concessions vainly made.
>   Thou shouldst have seen from Sumter's wall
>   The star flag of the Union fall,
>   And armed rebellion pressing on
>   The broken lines of Washington.
>
> "No stronger voice than thine had then
>   Called out the utmost might of men,
>   To make the Union's charter free
>   And strengthen law by liberty.
>   .   .   .   .   .   .
> "Wise men and strong we did not lack;
>   But still, with memory turning back,
>   In the dark hours we thought of thee,
>   And thy lone grave beside the sea.
>   .   .   .   .   .   .
> "But, where thy native mountains bare
>   Their foreheads to diviner air,
>   Fit emblem of enduring fame,
>   One lofty summit keeps thy name.
>   For thee the cosmic forces did
>   The rearing of that pyramid,

The prescient ages shaping with
Fire, flood, and frost thy monolith.
Sunrise and sunset lay thereon
With hands of light their benison,
The stars of midnight pause to set
Their jewels in its coronet.
And evermore that mountain mass
Seems climbing from the shadowy pass
To light, as if to manifest
Thy nobler self, thy life at best!"

Throughout the records of antislavery you may find passionate indignation and self-devoted sincerity; but you shall search those records far and wide before you shall find a mate for this magnanimous utterance. As time passes, Whittier seems more and more the man among the antislavery leaders of New England whose spirit came nearest to greatness.

So, as the years pass, he tends to emerge from the group of mere reformers, and to range himself too with the true men of letters. To them — to the literature of renascent New England, as distinguished from its politics, its scholarship, its religion, its philosophy, or its reform — we are now to turn. And we have come to this literature almost insensibly, in considering the work of one who, beginning life as a passionate reformer, may remain for posterity a living poet.

24

X

In the autumn of 1857 there appeared in Boston the first number of the periodical, still in existence, which more than anything else represents the literature of the New England Renaissance. In the early years of the century, the characteristic publication of literary Boston was the "North American Review." In the 40's the "Dial," limited as was its circulation, was equally characteristic of contemporary literary energy. From 1857 until the renascent literature of New England came to an end, its vehicle was the "Atlantic Monthly."

This youngest and last of the native periodicals of Boston may be distinguished from its predecessors in various ways. Obviously, for one thing, while the primary function of the "North American Review" was scholarly, and that of the "Dial" philosophic, that of the "Atlantic" was literary. In the second place, the "North American Review" was started by young men who at the moment had no vehicle for expression, and who thought they had a good deal to say. The "Dial" was similarly started by a group of enthusiasts comparatively little known in letters. The "Atlantic," on the other hand, did little more than establish a regular means of publication for men whose reputation was already established. After the dignified fashion of half a century ago, the articles in its earlier numbers were not signed. Whoever takes the trouble to ascertain their writers, however, will be surprised to find how few of them had not attained distinction before 1857. In more senses than one, the earlier periodicals began youthfully; and the "Atlantic" was always mature.

To understand the mature literature which at last thus concentrated, we have spent what may have seemed excessive time on its environment. Yet without a constant sense of the influences which were alive in the New England air, the literature which finally arose there can hardly be understood. It was all based on the traditions of a rigid old society, Puritan in origin and immemorially fixed in structure. To this, at the beginning of the nineteenth century, came that impulse of new life which expressed itself in such varied ways, — in the classically rounded periods of our most finished oratory; in the scholarship which ripened into our lasting works of history; in the hopeful dreams of the Unitarians, passing insensibly into the nebulous philosophy of the Transcendentalists, and finally into first fantastic and soon militant reform. Each of these phases of our Renaissance gave us names which are still worth memory: Webster, Everett, and Choate; Ticknor, Prescott, Motley, and Parkman; Emerson, Margaret Fuller, and Thoreau; Theodore Parker, Phillips, and Sumner; Mrs. Stowe, and Whittier. Thus grouped together, we can see these people to have been so dissimilar, and sometimes so antagonistic, that human friendship between them, or even mutual understanding, was hardly possible. At the same time, as we look at them together, we must see that all possessed in common a trait which marks them as of the old New England race. Each and all were strenuously earnest; and though the earnestness of some confined itself to matters of this world, — to history, to politics, or to reform, — while that of others was centred, like that of the Puritan fathers, more on the unseen eternities, not one of them was ever free from a constant ideal of principle, of duty. Nor was the idealism of these men always confined to matters of conduct. In Emerson, more certainly than in the fathers themselves, one feels the ceaseless effort of New

England to grasp, to understand, to formulate the realities which must forever lie beyond human ken. The New Englanders of our Renaissance were no longer Puritans; they had discarded the grim dogmas of Calvinism; but so far as Puritanism was a lifelong effort to recognise and to follow ideals which can never be apprehended by unaided human senses, they were still Puritan at heart.

Herein lies the trait which most clearly distinguishes New England from those neighbouring Middle States where the letters of America sprang into life a few years earlier. In both, the impulse to expression which appeared so early in the nineteenth century may be held only an American phase of the world-wide tendency to revolution which during the century effected so many changes in Europe. To both, too, this impulse came in a guise which may make the term " Renaissance " seem applicable equally to both. In New York, however, the impulse tended immediately to the production of an imitative literature which had done its best work by 1832; in New England, meanwhile, that same year, which is so convenient a landmark, was marked chiefly by Emerson's sermon on the Lord's Supper. Oratory was at its best; scholarship was swiftly developing; Unitarianism had completely dominated Boston; Transcendentalism was just beginning its course of wild, disintegrant luxuriance; and not only destructive reform but pure letters too were still to come. The humours of any period often show its characteristics most plainly. There is an aspect in which the name of Scriptures, by which Bronson Alcott chose to call his philosophic diaries, seems comically applicable to all the earlier writing of the New England where he calmly displayed his innocence of commonsense. When a new impulse came to the children of the Puritans, their first instinctive effort was to formulate a new law and gospel.

This new law and gospel was concerned with a spirit hitherto strange to the region, the spirit to which the cant of later days has given the name of Culture.   Ancestral New England knew the Bible, the Common Law, the formal traditions of the older classical education, and little else. With the Renaissance there came at last to New England an eager knowledge of all the other phases of human thought and expression which enrich the records of modern civilisation.   The temper in which this new learning was received there is nowhere better typified than by the title and the contents of a book which preserves some lectures given by Emerson in 1844, — the year when the " Dial " faded out of existence.   " Representative Men " is the name of it, — a name which suggests those countless volumes of contemporary biography wherein successful men of business are frequently invited to insert their lives and portraits at an expense so slight as to be within reach of any respectable citizen of every considerable village.   Emerson's " Representative Men " were of different stripe from these.   The personages whom he chose to group under his every-day title were Plato, the Philosopher; Swedenborg, the Mystic; Montaigne, the Sceptic; Shakspere, the Poet; Napoleon, the Man of the World; and Goethe, the Writer.   To Emerson, in short, and to the New England of which in his peculiar phrase he was a representative man, the whole range of literature was suddenly opened.   Two centuries of national inexperience had deprived the region not only of critical power, but for the moment of all suspicion that this was lacking.   With the fresh enthusiasm of discovery New England faced this newly found company of the good and great, feeling chiefly that even like ourselves these were men.   To any who hold fervent faith in the excellence of human nature the fact of common humanity must seem the chief of all.   Plato was a man, and Swedenborg, and the rest.   We are men, too.   Let us meet our elder brethren, face to face, asking what they may have to tell us. We shall be glad to hear, and doubtless they will gladly be heard.   The mood is like that of good old Father Taylor, the sailor-preacher of Boston Methodism. By some odd chance, he once got into the presence of Gregory XVI., and he is said, in describing the incident, to have ended, in all gravity, with the words, "So the Pope blessed me, and I blessed the Pope."

Fifty years and more have done their work since those aspiring old times. From contemporary New England the fact of greatness obscures the humanity of all classic letters, ancient or modern. In the full flush of our Renaissance, on the other hand, there was left in us something like the artless unconsciousness of healthy children. No wonder, then, we were a little slow to make pure letters for ourselves. It is not that we lacked them, of course. The names we have already considered belong not only to the history of those various phases of Renaissance with which we have chosen to consider them, but to that of letters, too. Hardly any of these men, however, was primarily a maker of literature. All deserve distinction in literary history chiefly because they did with loving care the writing which they held their earthly business.

Naturally, then, the literature of New England was comparatively slow in reaching maturity. It is more than an accident of date that the years when the "Knickerbocker Magazine" began to fade out of New York, and with it the whole elder school of which it marked the blameless decline, saw in Boston the establishment of the first periodical whose function was chiefly literary. The innocent old literature of pleasure which began with the novels of Brockden Brown was truly exhausted. The literature of New England, meanwhile, which had been ripening as its elder was falling into decay, had only just reached the point where it demanded a regular vehicle of expression. This vehicle came, to be sure, only when the strength of the New England Renaissance was beginning to fail. None of the New England men of letters, however, had begun to feel the infirmities of age, when one and all found a common meeting-ground in the pages of the " Atlantic Monthly."

The " Atlantic " is thus associated with almost every name eminent in our later New England letters; but most closely of all, perhaps, with that of a man whose presence in Boston, from 1834 until his death in 1881, had incalculable influence on local literary life. This was James Thomas Fields, for many years publisher of the " Atlantic," and from 1862 to 1870 its editor.

Fields was a self-made man, born in 1816 at Portsmouth, New Hampshire, and educated only in the common schools there. When a mere boy he began active life as a clerk in a Boston book store. Like many intelligent Yankees he had business ability; at twenty-two he was already partner in a publishing house; and he remained an active publisher in Boston for thirty-five years, retiring with a comfortable fortune. What makes Fields memorable, however, are not his practical gifts, nor yet the fact that in a modest way he was himself a man of letters. His most familiar poem implies his limits. This " Ballad of the Tempest " tells the story of a storm at sea. Things go very wrong until

> " ' We are lost,' the captain shouted,
> As he staggered down the stairs.
> But his little daughter whispered,
> As she took his icy hand,
> ' Is n't God upon the ocean,
> Just the same as on the land ? ' "

And the next morning they come safe to harbour. All of which, though very pretty and moral, expresses a course of marine conduct quite inconceivable when you reflect that the author was brought up in a still busy Yankee seaport. So far as Fields was a poet or merely a man of business, he might be dismissed as unimportant.

And yet it is doubtful whether any one had greater or better influence on the literature of New England. From boyhood Fields devotedly loved letters; and his literary enthusiasm combined with great personal amiability and with sympathetic kindness of nature to make him, before he reached middle life, the intimate personal friend of every man of letters in New England, and of many such men in the old world too. The result of this is evident to any one who will glance at the trade-lists of the firm of which he was for years the head. Here, to go no further, you will find all the works of Emerson, Thoreau, Whittier, Longfellow, Lowell, Holmes, and Hawthorne. There are plenty of other honourable American names there, too, as well as those of eminent foreign writers. For one thing, Fields was the first to collect and to set forth in systematic form the work of Thomas De Quincey, until Fields's time lost in numberless periodicals. As a sincere lover of letters, then, and a publisher of unusual tact and skill, Fields, during the years between 1840 and 1870, afforded to the literary men of New England a rare opportunity. One and all had constantly near by a skilful publisher, who was at the same time a wise counsellor, a warm personal friend, and an ardent admirer. The stimulus to literary production afforded by such a patron of letters can hardly be estimated.

Though Fields was not the originator of the "Atlantic Monthly," he was for years its publisher and for some time its editor. He was not the originator, either, of a little society of which he was an early and enthusiastic member. This was the Saturday Club, which grew spontaneously into existence sometime about 1857, assembling at occasional dinners the principal literary personages of the day. Emerson was a member; so were Motley, Holmes, Longfellow, Agassiz, and many more. The club, which survives, is too private for detailed mention. As New England literature has faded, too, the club, though still distinguished in membership, is no longer a centre of literary creation. Very lately, however, a man familiar with the social history of Boston declared that in their own day the standard writers of New England were more concerned as to what the Saturday Club might think of their productions than they ever deigned to be about the public.

Such facts, of course, are indefinite. How far the opinion of the Saturday Club really affected the literature of its palmiest days may still be debatable; and so, indeed, may the question of how far the personality of Fields, at once an enthusiastic member of the club, the most successful of New England publishers, and the editor of the " Atlantic," was vitally stimulating. Surely, though, as one begins to see in perspective a period which is passing into history, the importance of these influences seems rather to grow than to lessen. At least, it was when these were at their strongest that much of the best New England literature was made and came to light. Some of its makers we have already considered. Four, however, more unreservedly devoted to letters than the rest, remain for us. These are Longfellow, Lowell, Holmes, and Hawthorne.

XI

AMONG the men of letters who in mature life gathered about the "Atlantic Monthly" the most popular was Henry Wadsworth Longfellow. He was born in 1807 at Portland, Maine, where his father was a lawyer. At the beginning of the nineteenth century the profession of the bar involved in New England a personal eminence similar to that which in colonial times had been held there by the clergy. Though a lawyer might not be rich, he was locally conspicuous, much as rich men have been since the Civil War; and, furthermore, his professional position usually implied what mere wealth has never yet implied among native Yankees, — that in private life he enjoyed a certain social distinction. A little earlier than Longfellow's time, the son of a lawyer would have found himself socially somewhat below the son of a divine; later the bar has had no more social distinction than other respectable callings. As the son of a lawyer in the palmiest days of the New England bar, then, Longfellow was fortunate in birth; and although his life was at times clouded by deep personal sorrows, its external circumstances seem throughout as fortunate as human ones can be.

In boyhood he showed delight in poetry; he early wrote verses, by no means remarkable, for the local papers of Portland. At fifteen he went to Bowdoin College, at Brunswick, Maine, where he took his degree in 1825. At that time there happened to be at Bowdoin more students who were subsequently distinguished than have ever been there since. Among them were J. S. C. Abbott, the historian, Franklin Pierce, who finally became President of the United States, and

Nathaniel Hawthorne.   These college years, too, were those when the spirit of Renaissance was freshest in New England air.   Channing's great sermon on Unitarianism had been preached in 1819; Emerson's sermon on the sacrament, which marks the beginning of transcendental disintegration, was not preached until 1832.   Longfellow's youth, in brief, came just when the religious and philosophic buoyancy of the New England Renaissance was surging; and this affected him all the more because in a region and at a college where old-fashioned orthodoxy still prevailed, he was from the beginning a Unitarian.   Surrounded by fellow-students of marked ability, he found himself in a somewhat militant position, as a champion amid Calvinistic traditions of a philosophy which held human nature essentially good.

At that very moment, another phase of Renaissance was strongly asserting itself not far away.   Harvard College had awakened to the existence of a wider range of culture than was comprised in the ancestral traditions of the ancient classics. In 1816, the Smith professorship of the French and Spanish languages was founded there.   In 1817, George Ticknor, fresh from his then rare European experience, became the first Smith professor.   He filled the chair until 1835; and in those sixteen years he may be said to have established the serious study of modern languages in America.   When his teaching began, an educated American was expected to be familiar with no later masters of literature than the Romans. It is to the influences which Ticknor first embodied that we owe the traditional familiarity of educated Americans with such names as Dante, Cervantes, Montaigne, Molière, and Goethe.   Nothing marks the spirit of our Renaissance more profoundly than this epoch-making recognition of the dignity and value of everything which is truly literature.

When Longfellow graduated from Bowdoin at the age of nineteen, Ticknor's teaching, then in its seventh year, had made such general impression that the authorities of Bowdoin began to desire something similar there. The intention of Longfellow's father had been that his son should study for the bar; and the boy, who had hardly ever been out of Maine, had no more obvious qualification for a professorship of modern languages than the fact that he had been a good scholar in an old-fashioned classical college. His enthusiastic love for literature, however, was soon recognised as what the godly would call a vocation; in 1826 he went abroad under an agreement to prepare himself, by a three years' study of modern languages, for a Bowdoin professorship which should resemble Ticknor's at Harvard. Like some old pilgrim to Christian Rome, he set forth, wonderingly ignorant of the truths which he thus proposed apostolically to proclaim. In 1829 he came home with a reading knowledge of Spanish, Italian, French, and German, and began to teach at Bowdoin. In this work he persisted for six years. In 1835, Ticknor grew tired of his professorship, and chancing to possess fortune decided to give up teaching. The question of his successor having presented itself, Ticknor discerned no man in America better qualified to follow him than Longfellow. He recommended Longfellow to the Corporation of Harvard; and Longfellow, who up to that time had had little personal relation with Cambridge, accepted the Smith professorship. To prepare himself for this wider field of work, he went abroad for a year more. In 1836 he began his teaching at Harvard, which continued for eighteen years.

Longfellow's temper, like Ticknor's, proved increasingly impatient of distracting academic routine. As must always be the case with men of literary ambition, he felt more and more how gravely the drudgery of teaching must interfere with work which time may well prove more lasting and significant. His constant, enthusiastic wish was to be a poet. In 1854, then, he resigned the professorship in turn. The next year it was given to James Russell Lowell, who held it, at least in title, until his death in 1891.

Since then the Smith professorship has remained vacant. When it may again be filled is uncertain; but one thing seems sure. For seventy-five years it had only three tenants, — George Ticknor, Henry Wadsworth Longfellow, and James Russell Lowell. When Ticknor began his work modern literature was virtually unknown to America; when Lowell died, modern literature was as familiar to this whole continent as ever were the classics. Meanwhile almost all the literature which our continent has yet produced, and certainly all the memorable literature of New England, had come into existence. In the literary history of New England no three names are more honourable than those of the three Smith professors. Nor is it invidious to add that there is no living man of letters in America who could be invited to the Smith professorship with any hope of increasing or even of maintaining its established personal distinction.

Up to 1854, Longfellow, although already popular as a poet, remained professionally a college professor of a new and radical subject; his business was to introduce into the mental and spiritual life of Harvard students that range of thought and feeling which since classical times has been gathering its records in Europe. Though he always loved his subject, he hated the use which his professional circumstances compelled him to make of it. The instinct which made him recoil from the drudgery of teaching was sound. He is remembered as a faithful teacher; but anybody can teach faithfully, and no faithfulness can make Yankee students very eager pupils. Longfellow's true mission was not to struggle with unwilling hearers; it was rather to set forth in words which should find their way to the eager readers of a continent the spirit as distinguished from the letter of the literatures with which as a professor he conscientiously dealt so long.

From 1854 to the end, Longfellow lived as a professional author in that fine old Cambridge house which before his time was conspicuous as the deserted mansion of some Tories exiled by the Revolution, and which is now consecrated as the home of the most widely popular and beloved American poet. Long before he died, in 1882, his reputation as a man of letters had so far transcended any other aspect of his work that people had almost forgotten how he had once been a college teacher.

For this forgetfulness there is plenty of reason. Though throughout Longfellow's professorship he had felt its duties seriously to prevent literary labour, he had produced during his incumbency much of his most familiar verse. His " Voices of the Night " appeared in 1839, his " Evangeline " in 1847, and his " Golden Legend " in 1851. Already, then, before he laid his professorship down, there were hundreds who knew him as a poet for every one who knew him as a college teacher. In point of fact, too, the work which he did during the twenty-seven years of his purely literary life hardly extended, although it certainly maintained, the reputation as a poet which he had already established during his twenty-five years of teaching. To understand his real character as a poet, however, we must constantly keep in mind that other profession of teacher which he so faithfully practised for a full third of his life.

The subjects which Longfellow taught now have a familiar place in every respectable institution of the higher learning from the Atlantic to the Pacific. In his time, they resembled some new discovered continent, where whole realms of country are still unvisited by man. To Longfellow, accordingly, the true business of his professorship seemed like that of an enthusiastic explorer. The languages which he learned so eagerly never seemed to him deserving of lifelong study for themselves ; they were merely vehicles of expression which carried him into new and wonderful worlds of beautiful old humanity. These vehicles were to be cared for so far as they are efficient ; they were to be loved so far as in beautiful form they convey to us thoughts intrinsically beautiful and noble ; but they were at best vehicles whose use was to lead him into inexhaustible regions of humanity, unknown except by vague tradition to his countrymen who had gone before him.

In his love for literature thus considered, Longfellow never wavered. What vexed him throughout the years of his teaching was not the matter with which he dealt; it was rather that he shrank from imparting literature to unwilling pupils, that he longed to saturate himself with it and to express unfettered the sentiments which it unfailingly stirred within him. These sentiments, which he uttered in a manner so welcome to all America, seemed to him as spontaneous as ever inspiration seemed to poets who have heard the true whisper of the Muse. Yet one who now studies his work can hardly help feeling that even though he never suspected the fact, his temper as a man of letters was almost as academic as was the profession to which he reluctantly devoted year after year of his maturity.

The task of universities is to deal not so much with actual life as with the records of it. From eldest time human beings have left traces of what their earthly experience has meant. In efforts to preserve, to understand, to elucidate these traces of the vanished past and vanished men, scholars exhaust energy enough for any human lifetimes. They are bound, then, to drift away from actuality. Their lives are employed, and importantly, in gleaning from books material which shall engender the scholarship and the books of the future. Now, Longfellow's temper, even as a teacher, was that of a man of letters; he felt constantly stirred to what he believed original expression, and he was never content unless he was phrasing as well as he could the emotions which arose within him amid all the drudgery of work. But if in this aspect Longfellow was a genuine man of letters, he was all the while an academic scholar; for the influence which stirred him most was not what he experienced, but rather what he read. From beginning to end he was inspired chiefly, if not wholly, by noble and beautiful records of facts long since dead and gone.

Though this limitation marks Longfellow apart from those great poets who have immortally expressed the meaning of actual life, it had at once the grace of sincerity, and the added grace of that natural gift which was perhaps Longfellow's most salient. His taste was unerring. Wherever he met the beauties of literature he delighted in them with inexhaustible zest; and in his instinctive feelings about literature there was something very like the guileless confidence in human nature which inspired the Unitarians and the Transcendentalists. For a little while the national inexperience of New England had so freed it from the vileness of dense humanity that in religion, in philosophy, in morals, the most earnest minds could honestly believe uppermost in mankind those traits which are best. In the literatures which Longfellow loved we can to-day see endless depths of baseness; and to-day we know these literatures so well that we can hardly neglect such shadows. To Longfellow, on the other hand, these whole regions of æsthetic delight were so fresh that he could delight in their beauties, which he perceived with such instant tact, and could honestly be blind to everything not beautiful or noble. His mood resembled that of some simple American boy who with all the innocence of our native youth is suddenly brought face to face with the splendours of European civilisation. Such a boy overwhelmingly feels the beauties which survive from an illimitable past. The evil and the turmoil of the days which produced the sculpture of Greece, or the painting of Italy, or the architecture of Gothic Europe, are dead and gone. To discover them nowadays demands the scrutiny of a scientific scholarship for which an untutored American boy is still immature. Intoxicated with delight in the beauty which old humanity has wrought, he is not even aware that about him grovels a social corruption baser than his native inexperience has ever dreamed on. From dreams like these there must generally be awakening, nor can there be much more tragic awakening than that which comes to such a boy when he begins to perceive all the evil so inextricably intermingled with the beauty which once he thought so pure. But Longfellow had the rare happiness to be a lifelong dreamer. He lived at a moment of such national youth that throughout his seventy-five years he never knew the maturity which disenchants our later time.

The impression which he made on his first readers has never been better phrased than by Mr. Stedman : —

" A new generation may be at a loss to conceive the effect of Longfellow's work when it first began to appear. I may convey something of this by what is at once a memory and an illustration. Take the case of a child whose Sunday outlook was restricted, in a decaying Puritan village, to a wooden meeting-house of the old Congregational type. The interior — plain, colourless, rigid with dull white pews and dismal galleries — increased the spiritual starvation of a young nature unconsciously longing for colour and variety. Many a child like this one, on a first holiday visit to the town, seeing the vine-grown walls, the roofs and arches, of a graceful Gothic church, has felt a sense of something rich and strange; and many, now no longer children, can remember that the impression upon entrance was such as the stateliest cathedral could not renew. The columns and tinted walls, the ceiling of oak and blue, the windows of gules and azure and gold, — the service, moreover, with its chant and organ-roll,— all this enraptured and possessed them. To the one relief hitherto afforded them, that of nature's picturesqueness, — which even Calvinism endured without compunction, — was added a new joy, a glimpse of the beauty and sanctity of human art. A similar delight awaited the first readers of Longfellow's prose and verse. Here was a painter and a romancer indeed, who had journeyed far and returned with gifts for all at home, and who promised often and again to

'sing a more wonderful song
Or tell a more marvellous tale.' "

The hold which Longfellow thus took on enthusiastic American youth he soon took on the whole reading public of our country. His popularity is evident in our general familiarity with the creatures of his fancy. The village blacksmith, the youth who bears 'mid snow and ice a banner with the strange device Excelsior, the skipper wrecked on the reef of Norman's Woe, Evangeline, Hiawatha, Miles Standish, John Alden, Priscilla the Puritan maiden, and even Paul Revere, — figures and names which but for Longfellow would hardly have been known, — he has made us apt to group with Bible patriarchs or the world-old heroes of antiquity. Such popularity almost implies a weakness. Profundity of substance, or excellence of form, rarely touches the masses; and Longfellow's very popularity resulted long ago in a reaction against him among the fastidious. This never affected the serenity of his temper; and, indeed, amid the sincere adulation which was constantly brought to his feet during his last years at Cambridge, he may very possibly not have remarked that his admirers were apt to be less and less educated. Even in early days, however, when his popularity had only just transpired, the admiration which his work excited was clouded by occasional dissent. Margaret Fuller, for example, conscientiously devoted to the extravagance of Transcendental philosophy, found Longfellow shallow, and said so. Poe, as far from academic a personage as if he had been incontestably a great one, utterly misunderstood the academic character of Longfellow's mind, and accused him of plagiarism. And there was more such criticism.

For this there was ground. Longfellow never wrote anything more deeply sincere than the " Psalm of Life," which remains perhaps the most widely popular of his lyrics. " I kept it," he said, " some time in manuscript, unwilling to show it to any one, it being a voice from my inmost heart, at a time when I was rallying from depression." From the day, more than fifty years ago, when it first saw light in the " Knickerbocker Magazine," it has spoken, as it will speak for generations more, to the hearts of simple-minded men. Its deepest merit, however, lies in a gentle simplicity which unsympathetic moods must be at pains to distinguish from complace. Even of its most familiar stanza,

> "Life is real!   Life is earnest!
>   And the grave is not its goal;
>   Dust thou art, to dust returnest,
>   Was not spoken of the soul,"

one may well question whether the deeper trait is utter simplicity or reminiscent triteness.   And the whole poem is full not only of outworn metaphor, but of superficial literary allusion : "Art is long, and Time is fleeting," for example ; the " footprints on the sands of time," which so queerly mix up the beach of Robinson Crusoe with the unimpressionable contents of hour-glasses ; and, still more, the closing line,

> "Learn to labour and to wait,"

which so elusively misses the solemnity of that graver line,

> " They also serve who only stand and wait," —

the mournful close of Milton's great sonnet on his Blindness. Yet when all is said, a sense of the sweet sincerity which makes these commonplaces more dear than richer wisdom comes surging back.

Again, Longfellow, a lifelong friend of Charles Sumner, always sympathised with the antislavery movement ; and in 1842 he published some poems in its behalf.   Here are a few verses from one of them : —

> " Beside the ungathered rice he lay,
>   His sickle in his hand ;
>   His breast was bare, his matted hair
>   Was buried in the sand.
>   Again, in the mist and shadow of sleep,
>   He saw his native land.

> "Wide through the landscape of his dreams
>   The lordly Niger flowed ;
>   Beneath the palm-trees on the plain
>   Once more a king he strode ;
>   And heard the tinkling caravans
>   Descend the mountain road.

" He saw once more his dark-eyed queen
      Among her children stand ;
  They clasped his neck, they kissed his cheeks,
      They held him by the hand ! —
  A tear burst from the sleeper's lids
      And fell into the sand.

" The forests, with their myriad tongues,
      Shouted of liberty ;
  And the Blast of the Desert cried aloud,
      With a voice so wild and free,
  That he started in his sleep and smiled
      At their tempestuous glee.

" He did not feel the driver's whip,
      Nor the burning heat of day ;
  For death had illumined the Land of Sleep,
      And his lifeless body lay
  A worn-out fetter, that the soul
      Had broken and thrown away."

This, of course, came ten years before " Uncle Tom's Cabin," for which fact all allowance must be made ; but duly making it, one may fairly doubt whether in all antislavery literature there is a more humorous example of the way in which philanthropic dreamers often constructed negroes by the simple process of daubing their own faces with burnt cork. Compare with this a few phrases from a poem of Whittier's, written at about the same time, and based on the fact that an auctioneer recommended a female slave as a good Christian : —

" A Christian ! going, gone !
  Who bids for God's own image ? for His grace,
  Which that poor victim of the market-place
      Hath in her suffering won ?

" My God ! can such things be ?
  Hast Thou not said that whatsoe'er is done
  Unto Thy weakest and Thy humblest one
      Is even done to Thee ?

      .   .   .   .   .

" Oh, from the fields of cane,
  From the low rice-swamp, from the trader's cell ;
  From the black slave-ship's foul and loathsome hell,
      And coffle's weary chain ;

> " Hoarse, horrible, and strong,
> Rises to Heaven that agonising cry,
> Filling the arches of the hollow sky,
>   How long, O God, how long ? "

One poem is as honest as the other ; but by the side of Whittier's passion, one feels more strongly than ever the academic deliberation of Longfellow's emotion.

This trait, evident throughout his work, is nowhere more palpable than in that familiar " Tale of a Wayside Inn " which has made Paul Revere a national hero. In the middle of this ballad, Longfellow describes Revere, waiting beyond the Charles River for a signal which was to be shown from the steeple of a Boston church : —

> " Meanwhile, impatient to mount and ride,
> Booted and spurred, with a heavy stride
> On the opposite shore walked Paul Revere.
> Now he patted his horse's side,
> Now gazed at the landscape far and near,
> Then, impetuous, stamped the earth,
> And turned and tightened his saddle girth ;
> But mostly he watched with eager search
> The belfry tower of Old North Church,
> As it rose above the graves on the hill,
> Lonely and spectral and sombre and still.
> And lo ! as he looks, on the belfry's height
> A glimmer, and then a gleam of light !
> He springs to the saddle, the bridle he turns,
> But lingers and gazes, till full on his sight
> A second lamp in the belfry burns ! "

At a distance of some two miles from the belfry in question, Revere first sees, as would naturally be the case, a gleam of light from it ; but immediately afterwards he detects there, at this same distance, a second *lamp*. No single word could more unconsciously confess how Longfellow failed to visualise the situation. Compare with this any bit of excellent descriptive verse, such, for example, as the approach of the boats in the " Lady of the Lake," and you will feel the difference between creative work and work which is fundamentally academic.

But this is more than enough of Longfellow's faults and limitations. He has passed from us too lately to permit us to dwell upon the singular serenity and beauty of his personal life and character. No one can read its records or remember anything of its facts without feeling the rare quality of a nature which throughout a lifetime could persist unspoiled by prosperity and unbroken by poignant personal sorrows. To be sure, he was never passionate; neither in his life nor in his verse does he ever seem to have been swept away by feeling. On the other hand, as we have seen, his taste was unerring, and his sentiment gently sympathetic. His real office was to open the flood-gates of that modern literature in whose flashing beauty he delighted, and whose murky depths he never quite suspected. And if the verse in which he set forth his delight be hardly of the kind which enriches world-literature, its lucidity of phrase and its delicacy of rhythm combine to give it a sentimental beauty which must long endear it to those who love simplicity of heart.

Thereby, after all, Longfellow comes very near a world-old definition of literary greatness, which has sometimes been held the virtue of those who think the thoughts of the wise and who speak the language of the simple. It may be that he knew few wise thoughts which were all his own; but he so truly loved the wisdom and the beauty of those elder literatures which he was the first of Americans fully to recognise, that he absorbed in a way of his own the wisdom which the good and the great of the past had gleaned from experience. At first, to be sure, it may seem that those considerable parts of his work which deal with our native country are of another stripe. More and more, however, one grows to feel that, despite the subjects, these are not indigenous in sentiment. Rather, for the first time, they illuminate our American past with a glow of conventional romance. So by and by we find that our gently academic poet has just been thinking about New England in such moods as he loved in countless old-world poets who early and late recorded the historic romance of Europe. Yet Longfellow does not seem to have been consciously imitative. He sincerely believed that he was making spontaneous American poetry. Whatever his lack of passion or imagination, he was never false to himself. Whether he ever understood his mission it is hard to say; but what that mission was is clear; and so is the truth that he was a faithful missionary. Never relaxing his effort to express in beautiful language meanings which he truly believed beautiful, he revealed to the untutored new world the romantic beauty of the old.

Very lately, to be sure, an American man of letters, who has the happiness personally to remember our elder days, has said that great injustice is now done Bryant, by neglecting the influence of his translations from the Spanish. To many, it is said, these afforded a first, fascinating glimpse into the world of romance. Historically, then, Bryant may perhaps be held to have pointed out the way which Longfellow so faithfully followed. Certainly, however, Bryant's translations are no longer generally familiar; and Longfellow's still speak, as they spoke from the beginning, to the hearts of the people. Leader or follower, Longfellow worthily remains the most popular poet of his country.

In 1880 he wrote for " Ultima Thule," the last volume which he published, a final poem, entitled " The Poet and his Songs " : —

> " As the birds come in Spring,
>   We know not from where ;
> As the stars come at evening
>   From depths of the air ;

> " As the rain comes from the cloud
>   And the brook from the ground ;
> As suddenly, low or loud,
>   Out of silence a sound ;

> " As the grape comes to the vine,
>   The fruit to the tree;
> As the wind comes to the pine,
>   And the tide to the sea;
>
> " As come the white sails of ships
>   O'er the ocean's verge;
> As comes the smile to the lips,
>   The foam to the surge ;
>
> " So come to the Poet his songs,
>   All hitherward blown
> From the misty realm, that belongs
>   To the vast unknown.
>
> " His, and not his, are the lays
>   He sings ; and their fame
> Is his, and not his ; and the praise
>   And the pride of a name.
>
> " For voices pursue him by day
>   And haunt him by night,
> And he listens and needs must obey,
>   When the Angel says : ' Write ! ' "

Few men ever phrased more sweetly what seemed to them the deepest facts of their artistic lives. In the gentleness of this phrasing, as well as in the triteness of this imagery, there is something which tells at once of Longfellow's limitations and of his power. Thinking the thoughts of the wise, without suspicion that the wisdom was not always quite his own; speaking the language of the simple, with no consciousness of the commonplaces which lurk so near simplicity, — he believed till the end that to him the Angel had said " Write ! " To him this injunction seemed as divine as any that Muse ever spoke to singer of pristine Greece, or that the inspiration of the Holy Spirit ever breathed into the heart of Hebrew prophet. The man would be bold who should reflectively say to-day that this pure, true life and work, lived and done by the most popular poet of our Renaissance, is not, after all, as admirable as many which our later moods of criticism have been apt to think greater.

XII

In 1854 Longfellow resigned the Smith professorship at Harvard College. The next year James Russell Lowell was appointed his successor. Up to this time Lowell's career, though more limited than Longfellow's, had been similar. Sprung from a family already distinguished, which throughout the nineteenth century has displayed high quality both in private and in civic life, he was born at Cambridge in 1819, the son of a Unitarian minister, whose church was in Boston. He grew up in Cambridge. In 1838 he took his degree at Harvard; he studied law; but he found this profession distasteful, and his true interest was in letters. For fifteen years before his appointment to the Smith professorship, then, he had been professionally a literary man. From this time on, for a full twenty-two years, his ostensible profession became what Longfellow's had been from 1836 to 1854, and Ticknor's from 1817 to 1835, — the teaching of modern languages and literature to Harvard undergraduates.

The different tasks to which the successive Smith professors addressed themselves might once have seemed a question of different personalities; to-day, however, they seem rather a question of developing American culture. When Ticknor's work began, the names of Dante and Cervantes were hardly more familiar in America than that of the Japanese painter Hokusai is to-day. Ticknor's business, then, was to introduce to New England a fresh range of learning; and accordingly his most characteristic publication was the comprehensive, accurately unimaginative "History of Spanish Literature." When, after twenty years, Longfellow succeeded him, America knew modern literature by name, but, except perhaps for Bryant's translations, hardly more. Could anything have alleviated the drudgery of teaching, then, for a temperament always yearning to create, it would have been such a task as thus became Longfellow's. In brief, this was to make pupils enjoy excursions into that limitless world of modern literature which for America was still newly discovered. In 1855, when Lowell came to his work, the conditions had altered again. The main facts of modern literature had become almost classically familiar; and the influences which had expressed themselves in the various phases of New England Renaissance had greatly stimulated excellent general reading. To the generation with which Lowell came to his maturity, then, the great modern masters — Spenser and Shakspere, Dante and Cervantes and Goethe — were as freshly delightful as the old Greeks had been to the culture of fifteenth-century Italy. They were not yet stale. But scholarship cannot stagnate; modern literature had been discovered, it had been enthusiastically explored, and now came the task of understanding it. So as a college teacher, and as a critical writer too, Lowell's professional task proved interpretative.

The way in which he addressed himself to this task, and the ends he accomplished, were humorously illustrated not long ago when two Harvard men chanced to meet, who had been pupils of Lowell twenty-five years before. One happened to have in his hand a copy of the " Song of Roland." His friend, glancing at it, was reminded of the old times and said rather enthusiastically : " How Lowell used to give us the spirit of that ! " — " Yes," replied the other, who is an eminent philologist, " and that was *all* he gave us." In which emphatic little adjective is implied the phase which the study of modern literature has now assumed. This range of human expression has been discovered, it has been enjoyed, an attempt has been made to understand its spirit, and now, if

we are to keep pace with scholarship, we must pitilessly ana-
lyse its every detail.

Yet, though Lowell was not a severe modern scholar, he by
no means neglected severe learning. A pupil who inquired
about the minute works which were already beginning to interpose themselves between modern literature and human
beings, was apt to find that Lowell had glanced through them
and knew something of their merits. His sentiments about
them, however, resembled Emerson's about the Lord's Supper;
on the whole they did not interest him; and he always held that
until you were interested in literature, you could not understand it. The task he set himself as a teacher, then, was to
excite in his pupils intelligent interest in the texts with which
he was dealing. This task he found as irksome as Ticknor or
Longfellow had found theirs. In Lowell's teaching days the
Renaissance of New England was beginning to fade; undergraduates were less and less apt to delight in poetry; and the
very traits which prevented Lowell from generally appealing to
the reading public prevented him too from generally appealing
to Harvard students. On pupils whom he really touched, all
the while, his influence was probably as strong as any exerted
by a Harvard teacher of his time. How conscientiously he
did his task will be clear to any Harvard man whose memory
runs back five and twenty years.

In 1875 Longfellow and Lowell were both living in Cambridge; and though Longfellow was growing old, both men
seemed still in their prime. To Harvard students, then, both
names were generally familiar. Longfellow they knew to be
the most popular poet in America, so popular indeed that
clever undergraduates, despising Philistine favourites, inclined
to dismiss him as commonplace. Yet even these complacent
critics could not be insensible to the singular beauty and dignity
of Longfellow's presence, then daily familiar in Cambridge
streets; and some of them were dimly aware that in a remote
past this Olympian old man of letters had for a while been a

Harvard professor.   With Lowell the case was almost precisely the reverse.   His figure was less often visible; hundreds of men went through college without knowing him
by sight, but almost everybody knew that he was regularly
teaching French and Italian and Spanish.   They knew too
that this not very popular college teacher had literary reputation.   They had heard of the " Vision of Sir Launfal "
and the " Biglow Papers."   These, however, belonged to a
past as remote as Longfellow's professorship; and what
Lowell had written since, they did not trouble themselves to
inquire.   To them Longfellow was a poet who had once been
a professor; Lowell was a professor who had once written
poetry.   The eminence which finally made him a national
worthy came from the social accomplishment with which
from 1877 to 1885 he filled the office of United States minister, first to Spain and later to England.

This fact that Lowell's eminence came late in life is characteristic.   Throughout his career, as man of letters and as
teacher alike, he had been at once helped and hindered by
peculiarities of temperament conquerable only by the full experience of a slow maturity.   Born and brought up in Cambridge, when Cambridge was still a Middlesex village, he was
familiar with the now vanished country folk of old New England.   From youth he was passionately fond of general reading, in days when this led no Yankee away from sound
literature.   Though impatient of minute scholarship, too, he
possessed one of the most important traits of a minute scholar :
by nature he was aware of detail in every impression,
and careful of it in every expression.   What truly interested
him, to be sure, in life and in books alike, were the traits
which make books and life most broadly human ; nor did any
one ever feel more deeply that, for all its paradoxical incongruities, humanity is finally a unit.   In his effort to understand humanity, however, he was incessantly hampered by his
constitutional sense of detail.   The data of life, for one thing,

come to us in two distinct ways : the past is at rest in books; the present is throbbing all about us. To understand either we must keep the other in mind ; we must illustrate books by experience, and to correct the errors of experience we must retreat and observe them from regions to which only books can take us. Again, there are aspects in which both books and life seem profoundly serious; yet there are other aspects in which even the most serious phases of both seem whimsically absurd. And truly to understand the complex unity of humanity you must somehow fuse all these, — life and books, sublimity and humour, light and twilight and shadow.

The fact that Lowell was constantly sensitive to incompatible impressions was not his only temperamental obstacle. The well-known circumstance that he was amateurishly unable satisfactorily to revise his writing indicates how completely he was possessed by each of his various moods, which often chased one another in bewildering confusion, yet again left him for prolonged intervals in what seemed to him states of hopeless stagnation. Throughout all this uncertainty, however, one can feel in his literary temper two constant, antagonistic phases. His purity of taste was quite equal to Longfellow's; particularly as he grew older, he eagerly delighted in those phases of literature which are excellent. Yet all the while he was incessantly impelled to whimsical extravagance of thought, feeling, and utterance. Whoever knew him as a teacher, then, must often have found him disconcerting. At one moment his comment on the text would be full of sympathetic insight ; at the next, as likely as not, he would make an atrocious pun ; and he would take a boyishly perverse delight in watching the effect on his pupils of his spontaneous incongruities. The trait appears in his fondness for cramming his published essays with obscure allusions to unheard of oddities in the byways of literature and history. If one took these seriously, they would be abominably pedantic ; who under the sun, for example, was Abraham à Sancta Clara whom Lowell dragged into that opening passage of his essay on Thoreau ?   In fact, however, this mannerism was only a rather juvenile prank.   Life puzzled Lowell, and in revenge Lowell amused himself by puzzling the people he talked to or wrote for.   It is no wonder that this paradoxical conflict between purity of taste and mischievous extravagance of temper retarded his maturity until he had grown to the ripeness of nearly sixty years.

His impulsively volatile temperament, again, involved somewhat unusual sensitiveness to the influences which from time to time surrounded him.   Early in life he married a woman remarkable alike for charms and for gifts, who was enthusiastically devoted to the reforms then in the air.   It was partly due to her influence, apparently, that Lowell for a while proved so hot-headed a reformer.   After her premature death this phase of his temper became less evident.   It was revived, of course, by the passionate days of Civil War, when he upheld extreme Northern sentiments with all his might; and the depth of his experience finally resulted in that " Commemoration Ode " at Harvard which chiefly entitles him to consideration as a serious poet.   Yet this ode itself, though said to have been quickly written and little revised, is marked rather by exceptionally sustained seriousness of feeling than by anything which seems simply, sensuously passionate.   One of the traits for which you must search Lowell's volumes long is lyrical spontaneity.   An extravagant contemporary critic once declared in conversation that he had no more afflatus than a tortoise.   In this extravagance there is a touch of truth, but only a touch.   The real Lowell was a man of deep, but constantly various and whimsically incongruous, emotional nature, whose impulse to expression was constantly hampered by all manner of importunate external impressions.

For all this, the chances are that, like Longfellow, Lowell would have been apt to consider himself most seriously as a poet; and work classed among his poems most clearly expresses his individuality. His first volume of verse appeared in 1841, three years after his graduation, and in 1844 and 1848 he published other such volumes. In these there is nothing particularly characteristic. Honest, careful, sincere enough, the work seems; but except for the eminence finally attained by its author little of it would attract attention to-day. This kind of thing reached its acme in the " Vision of Sir Launfal," published in 1848. The familiar stanza from the prelude to Part I. is typical of the whole : —

> " And what is so rare as a day in June?
>   Then, if ever come perfect days;
> Then Heaven tries earth if it be in tune,
>   And over it softly her warm ear lays;
> Whether we look or whether we listen,
>   We hear life murmur, or see it glisten;
> Every clod feels a stir of might,
>   An instinct within it that reaches and towers,
> And groping blindly above it for light,
>   Climbs to a soul in grass and flowers;
> The flush of life may well be seen
>   Thrilling back over hills and valleys;
> The cowslip startles in meadows green,
>   The buttercup catches the sun in its chalice,
> And there's never a leaf or a blade too mean
>   To be some happy creature's palace;
> The little bird sits at his door in the sun,
>   Atilt like a blossom among the leaves,
> And lets his illumined being o'errun
>   With the deluge of summer that it receives;
> His mate feels the eggs beneath her wings.
>   And the heart in her dumb breast flutters and sings;
> He sings to the wide world, and she to her nest, —
>   In the nice ear of Nature which song is the best?"

Here is a man who has read a great deal of poetry, and who is thus impelled to write. Somewhat in the mood of Wordsworth — to whom three stanzas before he has alluded — he tries to express the impression made upon him by nature. He succeeds only in making nature seem a pretty phase of literature. It is all very serious, no doubt, and sweet in purpose; but it is never spontaneously lyric.

The "Vision of Sir Launfal" was published in 1848. In that same year came two other publications which show a very different Lowell; one is the "Fable for Critics," the other the first collection of the "Biglow Papers," which had begun to appear in the Boston "Courier" two years earlier. In a study like ours, the "Fable for Critics," of which we have already had a taste or two, is a useful document. Ten years out of college and already a professional writer, alertly alive to the contemporary condition of American letters, Lowell at last permitted himself to write about them, under a thin disguise of anonymity, with unrestricted freedom. The result is queer. It now seems wonderful that any human being could ever have had patience to read the poem through. The fable, so far as there is any, proves as commonplace as the "Vision of Sir Launfal;" and, besides, it is bewilderingly lost in such amateurishly extravagant whimsicality and pedantry as hampered Lowell all his life. At the same time, his portraits of contemporary American writers, in many cases made long before their best work was done, are marked not only by a serious critical spirit, but by acute Yankee good sense, and by surprising felicity of idiomatic phrase. The people he touches on are flung together pell-mell, amid allusions which would have taxed the ingenuity of Burton, and rhymes which would have put Samuel Butler to the blush, and puns which half rekindle the Calvinistic embers of eternal punishment. Over-minuteness never more tediously defeated its probable intention of amusing. Yet, to go no further, you can rarely find more suggestive criticism anywhere than what the "Fable for Critics" says of Emerson, Theodore Parker, Bryant, Whittier, Hawthorne, Cooper, Poe, Longfellow, Willis, Irving, or Holmes. It is good criticism, too, sincerely stating the impression made on a singularly alert contemporary mind by writers who have now acquired

what they did not then surely possess, a fair prospect of permanence; and the very fantastic oddity of its style, which makes
prolonged sessions with it so tiresome, has a touch not only of
native Yankee temper but of incontestable individuality. At
last permitting himself the full license of extravagant, paradoxical form, Lowell revealed all his amateurish faults; but he
revealed too all those peculiar contradictory qualities which made
the true Lowell a dozen men at once. Nobody else could
have written quite this thing, and it was worth writing.

More worth writing still, and equally characteristic, were
the " Biglow Papers," which were collected at about the same
time. They were written during the troubles of the Mexican
War. The slave States had plunged the country into that
armed aggression, which excited as never before the full fervour of the antislavery feeling in the North. Just at this time
the influence of Lowell's wife made his antislavery convictions strongest. No technical form could seem much less
literary than that in which he chose to express his passionate
sentiments. Using the dialect of his native Yankee country,
and emphasising its oddities of pronunciation by every extravagance of misspelling, he produced a series of verses which have
an external aspect of ephemeral popularity. At first glance,
the laborious humour of Parson Wilbur's pedantry, and the
formally interminable phrases in which he imbeds it, seem
radically different from the lines on which they comment. As
you ponder on them, however, Wilbur's elaborately over-
studied prose and the dialect verse of Hosea Biglow and Bird-
o'-Freedom Sawin fall into the same category. Both prove so
deliberate, both so much matters of detail, that in the end your
impression may well be, that, taken all in all, each paper is
tediously ingenious. No one number of the " Biglow Papers "
is so long as the " Fable for Critics; " but none is much easier
to read through.

In the " Biglow Papers," at the same time, just as in the
"Fable for Critics," you feel constant flashes of Lowell's

rarest power; in brief, idiomatic phrase he could sum up matters on which you may ponder with constantly fresh delight and suggestion. Take a familiar stanza from the first paper of all : —

> " Ez fer war, I call it murder, —
>   There you hev it plain and flat;
> I don't want to go no furder
>   Than my Testyment fer that;
> God hez sed so plump an' fairly,
>   It 's ez long ez it is broad,
> An' you 've gut to git up airly
>   Ef you want to take in God."

Nothing could seem much more paradoxical. Here you have a scholarly man of letters deliberately assuming the character of an ignorant Yankee countryman; he first emphasises this bit of private theatricals by the most obvious comic devices, and then, all of a sudden, with the passionate earnestness of a serious nature stirred to its depths, he utters solemn words concerning God Himself. To bring a phrase like those last two lines within the range of decency, requires a power for which genius is hardly an excessive name. Yet Lowell, spontaneously true to his paradoxical whimsical self, has made what looks like comic verse, and is phrased in a caricature of Yankee dialect, a memorable statement of tremendous truth.

In another familiar stanza from the first of the " Biglow Papers," you feel the man of letters more palpably : —

> " Massachusetts, God forgive her,
>   She 's akneelin' with the rest,
> She, thet ough' to ha' clung for ever
>   In her grand old eagle-nest ;
> She, thet ough' to stand so fearless
>   While the wracks are round her hurled,
> Holdin' up a beacon peerless
>   To the oppressed of all the world ! "

But you feel, too, a note to which Boston hearts will vibrate so long as Boston hearts are beating.

What Lowell did in this first " Biglow Paper," he did in all such verse which he ever wrote. It was more than fifteen years later, in 1862, that he produced " Mason and Slidell, a Yankee Idyll," the monstrous rhyme of which title exempifies his least pardonable vagaries. In this, the Bunker Hill Monument and Concord Bridge have a long colloquy, at the close of which the bridge bursts into the following apostrophe : —

> " I feel my sperit swellin' with a cry
>   Thet seems to say, ' Break forth an' prophesy ! '
> O strange New World, thet yit wast never young,
> Whose youth from thee by gripin' need was wrung,
> Brown foundlin' o' the woods, whose baby-bed
> Was prowled roun' by the Injun's cracklin' tread,
> An' who grew'st strong thru shifts an' wants an' pain
> Nussed by stern men with empires in their brains,
> Who saw in vision their young Ishmel strain
> With each hard hand a vassal ocean's mane,
> Thou, skilled by Freedom an' by gret events
> To pitch new States ez Old-World men pitch tents,
> Thou, taught by Fate to know Jehovah's plan
> Thet man's devices can't unmake a man,
> An' whose free latch-string never was drawed in
> Against the poorest child of Adam's kin, —
> The grave 's not dug where traitor hands shall lay
> In fearful haste thy murdered corse away !
> I see — "

And then he breaks off in nonsense, and winds up with his stanzas on Jonathan and John, wherein you may find that extraordinary comment on a weakness of our English brethren, of which the phrasing is as final as anything which Lowell's fantastic pen ever put on paper : —

> "The South says, ' *Poor folks down !* ' John,
>   An' 'All men up ! ' say we, —
> 'White, yaller, black, an' brown, John :
>   Now which is your idee ? '
>   Ole Uncle S. sez he, ' I guess,
>   John preaches wal,' sez he ;
> ' But, sermon thru, an' come to *du,*
>   Why, there 's the old J. B.
>   A crowdin' you an' me ! ' "

The man was really at his best when he let himself be most fantastic, and this because of that whimsical instability of temper, which he rarely managed quite to control. Beneath his wildest vagaries you will often feel as deep earnestness. But he lacked the power generally to sustain either mood quite long enough to express it with complete effect. The merit of his verses generally lies in admirable single phrases, single lines, or at most single stanzas. These flashing felicities never have quite the power which should fuse a whole poem into congruous unity. Like Lowell's personality, his most characteristic verse seems a bewildering collection of disjointed fragments, each admirable because of its sincere humanity.

The quality which so pervades Lowell's poetry equally pervades his prose writings. Open these wherever you will, even in the portions which deal with public affairs, and still more in those considerable portions which criticise literature, and you will anywhere find this same fantastic, boyishly pedantic range of allusion. You will find, too, all sorts of unexpected turns of phrase, often rushing into actual puns; again you will find elaborate rhetorical structure, stimulated by those great draughts of old English prose which Lowell could quaff with gusto all his life. " Literary " you feel this man again and again ; but by and by you begin to feel that, after all, this literature proceeds from an intensely human being with a peculiarly Yankee nature. Somewhere about him there is always lurking a deep seriousness strangely at odds with his obvious mannerisms, his occasional errors of taste, and his fantastic oddities of literary behaviour.

During Lowell's professorship at Harvard he was for some years editor of the " Atlantic Monthly," and later had a share in editing the " North American Review." At this period most of his prose was published. His later writing, produced after his diplomatic career began, was mostly occasional ; but all along it tended slowly to ripen. Towards the end it gained at least in simplicity and dignity ; and this dignity was not assumed, but developed. With his slowly attained maturity and with that experience of full European life which came during his diplomatic experience, — earlier he had known Europe only as a traveller, — he gained something which at last gave his utterances, along with their old earnestness and humanity, a touch of self-respecting humility. Nothing shows him more at his best than the short speech on "Our Literature" which he made in response to a toast at a banquet given in New York to commemorate the one hundredth anniversary of Washington's inauguration. The simple hopefulness of the closing paragraph, where for once Lowell was not afraid to be commonplace, is a fit and admirable conclusion for the six volumes of his collected prose : —

"The literature of a people should be the record of its joys and sorrows, its aspirations and its shortcomings, its wisdom and its folly, the confidant of its soul. We cannot say that our own as yet suffices us, but I believe that he who stands, a hundred years hence, where I am standing now, conscious that he speaks to the most powerful and prosperous community ever devised or developed by man, will speak of our literature with the assurance of one who beholds what we hope for and aspire after, become a reality and a possession for ever."

So if one asks where Lowell finally belongs in the history of our New England Renaissance, the answer begins to phrase itself. A born Yankee and a natural lover of letters, he instinctively turned at once to books and to life for the knowledge which should teach him what humanity has meant and what it has striven for. For all the oddities of temper which kept him from popularity, the man was always true to his intensely human self. In his nature there were constant struggles between pure taste and perverse extravagance. As a man of letters, then, he was most himself when he permitted himself forms of expression in which these struggles needed no concealment. But through it all there persists just such wholesome purity of feeling and purpose as we love to think characteristic of New England. Throughout, despite whimsical extravagance of phrase, you may finally discern a nature at once manly and human.

"Human," after all, is the word which most often recurs as one tries to phrase what Lowell means ; and "human" is an adjective which applies equally to two distinctly different nouns. In one sense the most truly human being is he who most strives to understand those records of the past to which we give the name of the humanities. In another sense the most deeply human being is he who strives most to understand the humanity about him. It was unceasing effort to fuse his understanding of the humanities with his understanding of humanity which made Lowell so often seem paradoxical. He was in constant doubt as to which of these influences signified the more ; and this doubt so hampered his power of expression that the merit of his writing lies mostly in disjointed phrases. At their best, however, these phrases are full of humanity and of the humanities alike. In distinction from the other Smith Professors, — from Ticknor, the scholar of our New England Renaissance, and from Longfellow, its academic poet, — Lowell defines himself more and more clearly as its earnest humanist.

XIII

WHEN the spirit of Renaissance had finally conquered Boston, and people who had clung to Calvinism there found themselves hopelessly out of fashion, the man whom they believed most conspicuously to embody those pomps and vanities of the wicked world for which account shall be demanded in a better, is said to have been Oliver Wendell Holmes. To the Calvinistic mind, indeed, his career was probably the most irritating in all New England record. He was born, in 1809, at Cambridge, where his father, a Connecticut man and a graduate of Yale, had for some years been the Orthodox minister of the First Church. Though Harvard College had already lapsed into Unitarian heresy, this had not yet achieved the social conquest of the region. During Dr. Holmes's boyhood and youth, however, the struggle grew fierce; and at about the time of his graduation, his father, whose devotion to the old creed never wavered, was formally deposed from the pulpit which, after nearly forty years of occupancy, he stoutly refused to open to Unitarian doctrine. The old man, than whom none was ever more faithfully courageous, was supported by a majority of the communicants of the Cambridge church. A majority of the parish, however, preferred the liberal side. This latter body retained the old church building, the slender endowment of the parish, and the communion-plate. Abiel Holmes, with his saving remnant of church-members, was forced to establish a new place of worship; and the question as to which of the two is the more direct descendant of the old Puritan society from which both

have sprung was long disputed by people who delight in such
dispute.   Now Dr. Holmes, in the matter of faithful courage,
was his father's counterpart.   So, in comparatively early life,
finding himself unable to accept the Calvinistic teachings of
his youth, he became what he remained all his life, — a sound
Unitarian.

This of itself might have been enough to arouse bitter dis-
approval among the Calvinists.   So, almost by itself, might have
been the pleasantly prosperous circumstances of his personal
life.   His maternal grandfather was a judge, and a Fellow of
Harvard College.   Holmes, then, hereditarily allied with both
pulpit and bar, was doubly what he used to call a New England Brahmin.   Like any good orthodox boy, he was sent to
school at Andover ; and thence, like any good Cambridge boy,
he was sent to Harvard too.   There he took his degree in
1829, — a year remembered in college tradition as that which
produced the most distinguished group of Bachelors of Arts in
Harvard history.   In obedience to the traditions of his mother's
family, he began the study of law ; but finding this not congenial, he soon turned to medicine.   In pursuance of this study
he went abroad for two or three years, finally receiving the
degree of Doctor of Medicine in 1836.   After a year or two
of practice, he became in 1839 Professor of Anatomy at Dartmouth College.   A year later he returned to Boston, where
he remained for the rest of his life; and from 1847 to 1882
he was Parkman Professor of Anatomy in the Harvard Medical School.

In the fact that a man of Dr. Holmes's temper and position
lived for fifty years in Boston as a Unitarian physician, there is
something characteristic of the city which he knew and loved
so well.   Not long ago there appeared in some English review
an article on the social position of American men of letters,
wherein the writer based on the facts that Dr. Holmes practised medicine and went to Unitarian meeting the conclusion
that Holmes was socially insignificant.   In England such an

inference would have been at least probable. There Unitarianism has often been held an almost blasphemous dissenting creed, abhorrent to seriously conservative temper; and only within the last few years has radicalism been socially tolerated in the mother country. In England, too, until very lately, the profession of medicine has been held in comparative social disesteem. In Boston, on the other hand, the isolated capital of isolated New England, which has stoutly developed and maintained traditions of its own, Unitarianism, in Dr. Holmes's time, enjoyed a social security similar to that of the Established Church across the water; and while the three learned professions were nominally of equal dignity, that of medicine had probably attracted, between 1800 and 1850, rather more men who combined breeding with culture than had either bar or pulpit. The very circumstances which made English prejudice assume Holmes to have been socially inconspicuous and temperamentally radical, then, were those which would soonest lead any one who knew the Boston of his time to assume him to have been precisely the reverse.

This extreme localism of professional character and social position is characteristic of Holmes's whole life. After 1840, when he finally settled in Boston, he rarely passed a consecutive month outside of Massachusetts. Among Boston lives the only other of eminence which was so uninterruptedly local is that of Cotton Mather. The intolerant Calvinistic minister typifies seventeenth-century Boston; the Unitarian physician typifies the Boston of the century just past. To both alike, Beacon Hill instinctively presented itself, in the phrase which Holmes has made so familiar, as the Hub of the Solar System.

Though throughout Holmes's fifty years of Boston residence he was a man of local eminence, his eminence was not quite of a professional kind. His practice, in which he took no excessive interest, gradually faded away; and long before he gave up his lectures on Anatomy, they were held old-fashioned. He neither neglected nor disliked his profession, but it did not absorb him; and as his life proceeded, he probably grew less and less patient of that overwhelming mass of newly discovered detail which modern physicians must constantly master. Another reason why his medical career became less and less important is that from the beginning he had a keen interest in literature, and was widely known as a poet. Now, a man eminent in a learned profession may certainly be eminent in letters too, but public opinion hates to have him so; and any youth who would succeed in law or medicine can hear no sounder advice than that which Dr. Holmes is said often to have given in his later years, — namely, that you should never let people suppose you seriously interested in anything but your regular work. In the very year when Holmes had returned from Europe to begin practice, he published a volume of poems; and at least three subsequent collections appeared before, with the beginning of the " Atlantic Monthly," he became known as a remarkable writer of prose. His writings, then, steadily distracted attention from his profession. Nor is this the whole story. Holmes's local eminence was perhaps chiefly due to his social gifts. Early in life he acquired the reputation of being the best talker ever heard in Boston; and this he maintained unbroken to the very end.

It has lately been observed of Boston society that the city is still so fixed in its traditions that everybody who becomes widely known there is assumed to possess distinct characteristics which it becomes his social business to maintain. In the beginning he chooses his part; then the unspoken force of local opinion compels him to play it straight through. Some such experience probably happened to Dr. Holmes. Years did their consequent work. In his later life his conversation and his wit alike, always spontaneous and often of a quality which would have been excellent anywhere, are said sometimes to have been overwhelming. His talk tended to monologue, and his wit to phrases so final that nobody could think of anything to say in return. There was humorous

and characteristic good-nature in that title, the " Autocrat of
the Breakfast Table," which he gave, so early as 1831, to a
couple of articles written for a now forgotten periodical called
the " New England Magazine." Fully twenty-five years
elapsed before he published anything else of the kind. Then,
when in 1857 he began those papers under the same title
which have become permanent in our literature, his opening
phrase is whimsically characteristic : " I was going to say,
when I was interrupted." Whereupon, after twenty-five
years of interruption, he proceeds with the autocratic utterances now familiar all over the world. The contagious
good-humour of this title, like the whimsicality of that little
reference to the lapse of a quarter of a century, indicates the
quality which made Holmes popular, despite his habit of
keeping the floor and of saying admirably unanswerable things.
His friends were heartily attached to him. They recognised
in him a social autocrat, but one to whom they were glad to
listen ; they fervently believed that nobody had ever been like
him, and that in all probability nobody ever would be.

Up to middle life Dr. Holmes's literary reputation was that
of a poet, whose work was chiefly social. Almost his first
publication, to be sure, " Old Ironsides," was " an impromptu
outburst of feeling," caused by a notice in a newspaper that the
old frigate " Constitution " was to be destroyed. His fervent
verses not only achieved their purpose of saving from destruction that historical craft, whose hulk still lies at the Charlestown Navy Yard, but have retained popularity. Few lines are
more familiar to American school-boys than the opening one :
" Ay, tear her tattered ensign down ! " Most of Holmes's
early verse, however, may be typified by the first stanza of
" My Aunt " : —

> " My aunt ! my dear unmarried aunt !
> Long years have o'er her flown ;
> Yet still she strains the aching clasp
> That binds her virgin zone ;

> I know it hurts her — though she looks
>   As cheerful as she can;
> Her waist is ampler than her life,
>   For life is but a span."

Such verse as this, with its light good-humour and its reckless pun, is of a sort which for want of a native English term we call *vers de société*.

Of social verse in every sense of the word Holmes early showed himself a master; and to the end his mastery never relaxed. At least during the nineteenth century it has been customary in the region of Boston to celebrate anniversaries and other formal occasions by regular orations and poems. A perpetual type of such functions may be found in the annual oration and poem delivered before the Phi Beta Kappa society of Harvard College. At formal dinners, too, it has been customary to vary the monotony of speeches by occasional essays in verse; and this custom has probably produced an amount of ephemeral metrical composition, sometimes avowed doggerel, sometimes aspiring to be poetry, more than equal in bulk to the entire lyric and dramatic poetry of Elizabethan England. Among the writers of this occasional verse socially demanded by his time, Holmes early acquired distinction; and as the work amid which it was produced has justly been forgotten, Holmes's occasional verse, which in both senses of the term forms the better part of his poetic utterance, has already acquired some such apparent isolation as one feels in the transcendental aphorisms of Emerson. The time is not far off, if indeed it be not on us already, when people will think of Holmes not as a man who did the common work of a school decidedly better than the rest, but rather as the only man who did it at all.

He wrote verses for almost every kind of occasion which demanded them. The occasions most frequent in their demands, however, were those which occur in the yearly life of Harvard College. Holmes was perhaps the most com-

pletely loyal Harvard man of his century. Both at the formal
ceremonies of the college, then, and at the more intimate
meetings of his college class, he was constantly called on for
poems which he never failed to give. So whoever wants to
understand the temper of Harvard cannot do better than saturate himself with those verses which Holmes has made part of
the college history. Many of these recall the older traditions
of Harvard, none more jauntily than the song he wrote for the
two hundredth anniversary of the college in 1836 : —

> "And when at length the College rose,
>   The sachem cocked his eye
>   At every tutor's meagre ribs
>   Whose coat-tails whistled by :
>   But when the Greek and Hebrew words
>   Came tumbling from his jaws,
>   The copper-coloured children all
>   Ran screaming to the squaws.

> "And who was on the Catalogue
>   When college was begun ?
>   Two nephews of the President,
>   And *the* Professor's son ;
>   (They turned a little Indian boy,
>   As brown as any bun ;)
>   Lord ! how the seniors knocked about
>   The freshman class of one ! "

More characteristic of his riper years was an inimitable combination of reckless fun and tender sentiment such as makes
peculiarly his own the first verses of his poem for the " Meeting of the Alumni " in 1857 : —

> " I thank you, Mr. President, you 've kindly broke the ice ;
>   Virtue should always be the first, — I 'm only Second Vice —
>   (A vice is something with a screw that 's made to hold its jaw
>   Till some old file has played away upon an ancient saw).

> " Sweet brothers by the Mother's side, the babes of days gone by,
>   All nurslings of her Juno breasts whose milk is never dry,
>   We come again, like half-grown boys, and gather at her beck
>   About her knees, and on her lap, and clinging round her neck.

" We find her at her stately door, and in her ancient chair,
    Dressed in the robes of red and green she always loved to wear.
Her eye has all its radiant youth, her cheek its morning flame ;
We drop our roses as we go, hers flourish still the same."

His class poems, again, tell of old-fashioned class feeling as
nothing else can.   Here is a random verse from one that he
made in 1867 : —

" So when upon the fated scroll
        The falling stars [1] have all descended,
And, blotted from the breathing roll,
        Our little page of life is ended,
We ask but one memorial line
        Traced on thy tablet, Gracious Mother :
' My children.   Boys of '29.
        In pace.   How they loved each other ! ' "

And Holmes could speak for the new Harvard as well as
for the old.   In 1886, when the college celebrated its two
hundred and fiftieth anniversary, Lowell delivered an oration
and Holmes a poem.   He was then an old man, addressed to a
task of solemn dignity, and his verse lacked the vivacity which
almost to that time had seemed perennial ; but passages of it
show him as sympathetic with the future as his older college
verses show him with the past.   Take, for example, the stirring
lines in which he sets forth the conflict of Harvard with the
ghost of Calvinism : —

" As once of old from Ida's lofty height
The flaming signal flashed across the night,
So Harvard's beacon sheds its unspent rays
Till every watch-tower shows its kindling blaze.
Caught from a spark and fanned by every gale,
A brighter radiance gilds the roofs of Yale ;
Amherst and Williams bid their flambeaus shine,
And Bowdoin answers through her groves of pine ;
O'er Princeton's sands the far reflections steal,
Where mighty Edwards stamped his iron heel ;

---

[1] In the Quinquennial Catalogue of Harvard, the names of the dead are
designated by asterisks.   When the catalogues were still phrased in Latin,
then, the Harvard dead were described by the quaintly barbarous term
Stelligeri.

> Nay on the hill [1] where old beliefs were bound
> Fast as if Styx had girt them nine times round,
> Bursts such a light that trembling souls inquire
> If the whole church of Calvin is on fire!
> Well may they ask, for what so brightly burns
> As a dry creed that nothing ever learns?
> Thus link by link is knit the flaming chain
> Lit by the torch of Harvard's hallowed plain."

In the form taken by this most serious of his occasional poems there is something characteristic. The verse groups itself in memory with that of another poem, not included in his collected works, which he read at a dinner given in honour of Lowell's seventieth birthday. Holmes was ten years older, and Mr. Sidney Bartlett, the acknowledged leader of the Boston bar, was ten years older still. So Holmes made some whimsical allusion to Lowell's youth and then to his own maturity; and finally spoke of Bartlett,

> "the lion of the law;
> All Court Street trembles when he leaves his den,
> Clad in the pomp of fourscore years and ten."

These lines were read on the 22d of February, 1889; yet if any student of English literature should be given that couplet by itself, he would probably guess it to be the work of some contemporary of Alexander Pope. The trait which appears here characterises Holmes's occasional verse throughout. So able a critic as Mr. Stedman, indeed, holds it to characterise all his poetry. In many aspects Holmes's temper was that of an earlier day than his. As Mr. Stedman happily observes, his verse is not a revival of eighteenth-century literature, but rather its last survival.

The more one considers Holmes's work in its entirety, the more significant one finds this criticism, which Mr. Stedman first uttered only of its versified phase. Revivals of the eighteenth century — "Henry Esmond," for example, or Mr. Dob-

----

[1] Andover Hill.

son's essays — have been common enough in these days when all fine art has been for a while eclectic. Modern artists are more apt to express themselves in the manner of some bygone age than in any spontaneously characteristic of their own time. Holmes, however, seems as far from artificial in manner as if he had flourished at a time which had an instinctively settled style of its own. That his manner proves so much in the spirit of the eighteenth century, then, indicates something characteristic not only of the man, but of the world about him. For full fifty years he rarely stirred from New England; no other writer lived under such completely local circumstances. His manner, then, so like that prevalent in the mother country a hundred years before, seems a fresh bit of evidence that, despite our superficial modernity, America has lagged behind that elder world with which it has not been at one for more than two hundred years.

The Boston where Holmes lived, however, and where for years he was so eminent a social figure, was the same Boston which was thrilling with all the fervid vagaries of our Renaissance. The old formal traditions had been broken; our native mind had been enfranchised; and people were searching the eternities for vistas of truth and beauty which had been obscured by the austere dogmas of Puritanism. Deeply conservative in external temper, loving social order, and distrusting vagaries of thought and of conduct alike, Holmes had small sympathy with the extravagances of Transcendentalism or of reform; but he could not have been truly contemporary with these movements without catching something of their spirit. So if in one aspect he was what Mr. Stedman has called him, a survivor of the eighteenth century, in another he was inevitably a Yankee of the Renaissance.

Like the men about him, he was seized with an impulse to search for truth and to report it. What chiefly distinguishes him from the rest is that they were most deeply stirred by the charm of romanticism. They were attracted by ideal phi-

losophy and mediæval poetry. In such history, too, as had
hitherto been neglected by New England, they found most
stimulating and satisfying those passages which appeal to
romantic emotion. In this they delighted with all the ardour
of a race which for two hundred years had been æsthetically
starved. America, however, had been poor in another range
of human experience. Throughout Europe, the eighteenth
century was a period of alert common sense, observing life
keenly, commenting on it with astonishing wit, but generally
behaving as if romantic emotion might be disregarded as
superstitious. When the Renaissance finally dawned on New
England, then, New England lacked not only the untrammelled
romanticism of a dozen old centuries, but also the eager
rationalism which had been the most characteristic trait of
eighteenth-century Europe.

This feature of the new learning Holmes found most congenial. In the form and spirit of his verse, as Mr. Stedman
says, there is something which makes him a survival of the
eighteenth century ; and though the form of his prose is freely
individual, its spirit seems as essentially that of the eighteenth
century as if every line of his essays and novels had been
thrown into heroic couplets.

The first instalment of his final "Autocrat of the Breakfast Table " — revived after that casual interruption of twenty-
five years — appeared in the first number of the " Atlantic
Monthly " in the autumn of 1857. Within the next thirty
years Holmes produced four volumes of such essays as the
" Autocrat," and three more or less formal novels. Throughout this prose work of his maturity and his age, — he was
nearly fifty years old when it began, — one feels the shrewd,
swift, volatile mind of a witty man of the world. One feels,
too, the temper of a trained though not very learned man of
science ; education and professional experience combined with
native good sense to make him understand the value of demonstrable fact. One feels almost as surely another trait,

too.   Holmes could not have been a Bostonian during those years of Renaissance when Boston was the intellectual centre of America, without keen interest in something like mysticism ; but beyond any other New England man of his time Holmes treats mystical vagaries as only fancies, — beautiful, perhaps, and stimulating, but inherently beyond the range of assertion as distinguished from speculation.   In one sense no Transcendentalist more constantly devoted himself to the task of proving all things and holding fast those which were good.   From beginning to end, however, Holmes knew that things can truly be proved only by observation and experiment.   So just as in our final view of the New England Renaissance Ticknor seems its most eminent scholar, Longfellow its most typical poet, and Lowell its deepest humanist, so Holmes seems its one uncompromising rationalist.

This aspect of him goes far to explain afresh why of all his contemporaries he was the most abhorrent to Calvinists.   The phase of mental activity which is least compatible with dogma is an ardent rational spirit ; and here the orthodox Calvinists of New England found the son of one of their most sturdy leaders, lapsed into Unitarianism, enjoying a career of social comfort and distinction forbidden them, and expressing himself in the temper which of all imaginable was most hostile to their dogmatic faith in the damnable wickedness of human nature. What was more, his personal life was such as to warrant the respect and kindliness with which his friends regarded him. But the devil showed plain traces in Holmes's way of talking lightly.   If this world is what the Calvinists hold it, for most of us only the antechamber of damnation, such frivolity of manner is among the most appalling evidences of depravity. Holmes's rationalism, then, advanced with all the gay ease of a fashion from which orthodoxy was debarred, might seem enough to account for orthodox detestation of him.

As you read his work, however, with this matter in view, you will find a deeper reason still.   Holmes's youth had been surrounded by the strictest Calvinism, at a moment when New England Calvinism had outlived its vitality and when the spiritual thought of his native region was at last taking its enfranchised Unitarian form. The whole horror of the old system, then, with its inhuman limitation of intellectual and spiritual freedom, had been within his personal experience at the period of life when impressions sink deepest. He early developed the liberal and kindly rationalism so admirably expressed in his personal and literary career. The horrors of the elder creed, however, were seared into his brain. In his later life, whether actually aware of them or not, he could never efface them from his subconsciousness. Long ago, when we were trying to understand Jonathan Edwards, we found ourselves contemplating that famous "One-Hoss Shay" of Holmes's, with which the impregnable logic of Calvinism somehow came to smash. Far from standing alone in his work, this well-known piece of verse seems rather to typify the greater part of it.

Take "Elsie Venner," for example, his first and most considerable novel. Although amateurish in detail, the book is vivid with New England life; but the gist of it is abhorrent to every tradition of the ancestral Calvinists. The fiction, which, to use one of Holmes's own terms, is medicated throughout, is designed to suggest that purely physical causes can so affect moral nature as to make gravely doubtful how far human beings ought to be held morally responsible. What is more, Holmes does not hesitate openly to expound this doctrine. A student of medicine, for example, puzzled by the case of ante-natal impression which forms the basis of the plot, writes about it to one of his professors. This incident gives the professor an opportunity to reply as follows : —

"Your question about inherited predispositions, as limiting the sphere of the will, and, consequently, of moral accountability, opens a very wide range of speculation. I can give you only a brief abstract of my own opinion of this delicate and difficult subject. Crime and sin, being the *preserves* of two great organised interests, have been guarded against all reforming poachers with as great jealousy as the Royal Forests. It is so easy to hang a troublesome fellow! It is so much simpler to consign a soul to perdition, or to say masses, for money, to save it, than to take the blame on ourselves for letting it grow up in neglect and run to ruin for want of humanising influences. . . .

"It is very singular that we recognise all the bodily defects that unfit a man for military service, and all the intellectual ones that limit his range of thought, but always talk at him as if all his moral powers were perfect. I suppose we must punish evildoers as we extirpate vermin ; but I don't know that we have any more right to judge them than we have to judge rats and mice, which are just as good as cats and weasels, though we think it necessary to treat them as criminals."

The passage from the " Professor at the Breakfast Table " in which Holmes savagely satirises both the dogmas and the discipline of Calvinistic orthodoxy is perhaps better known :

"If, before a medical practitioner would allow me to enjoy the full privileges of the healing art," it begins, "he expected me to affirm my belief in a considerable number of medical doctrines, drugs, and formulæ, I should think that he thereby implied my right to discuss the same, and my ability to do so, if I knew how to express myself in English.

"Suppose, for instance, the Medical Society should refuse to give us an opiate, or to set a broken limb, until we had signed our belief in a certain number of propositions, — of which we will say this is the first : —

" I. All men's teeth are naturally in a state of total decay, or caries ; and, therefore, no one can bite until every one of them is extracted and a new set is inserted according to the principles of dentistry adopted by this Society.

" I, for one, should want to discuss that before signing my name to it, and I should say this : — Why, no, that is n't true." —

And so on.

Nor were Holmes's attacks on the Calvinists only indirect. Some years ago the innumerable missionary and other godly societies which had sprung up in Boston were accustomed to hold their annual meetings at about the same time every spring. The feast of spiritual stimulant thus afforded by Anniversary Week attracted to town such flocks of blackbirds from the country pulpits that the face of the Common was annually darkened. To most people the sight of these visitants was mildly amusing. To Holmes they suggested rather such sentiments as he set forth in the " Moral Bully " : —

" Yon whey-faced brother, who delights to wear
A weedy flux of ill-conditioned hair,
Seems of the sort that in a crowded place
One elbows freely into smallest space;
A timid creature, lax of knee and hip,
Whom small disturbance whitens round the lip;
One of those harmless spectacled machines,
The Holy-Week of Protestants convenes ;

. . . .

Conspicuous, annual, in their threadbare suits,
And the laced high-lows which they call their boots,
Well mayst thou *shun* that dingy front severe,
But him, O stranger, him thou canst not *fear!*

" Be slow to judge, and slower to despise,
Man of broad shoulders and heroic size !

. . . .

In that lean phantom, whose extended glove
Points to the text of universal love,
Behold the master that can tame thee down
To crouch the vassal of his Sunday frown;
His velvet throat against thy corded wrist,
His loosened tongue against thy doubled fist !

" The MORAL BULLY, though he never swears,
Nor kicks intruders down his entry stairs,
Though meekness plants his backward-sloping hat,
And non-resistance ties his white cravat,
Though his black broadcloth glories to be seen
In the same plight with Shylock's gaberdine,
Hugs the same passion to his narrow breast,
That heaves the cuirass on the trooper's chest,
Hears the same hell-hounds yelling in his rear
That chase from port the maddened buccaneer,
Feels the same comfort while his acrid words,
Turn the sweet milk of kindness into curds,
Or with grim logic prove, beyond debate,
That all we love is worthiest our hate,
As the scarred ruffian of the pirate's deck,
When his long swivel rakes the staggering wreck ! "

Such were Holmes's comments on his contemporaries who followed in the footsteps of Jonathan Edwards. Of Edwards himself he wrote, if possible, more plainly still : —

" The practical effect of Edwards's teachings about the relations of God and man has bequeathed a lesson not to be forgotten. A revival in which the majority of converts fell away ; nervous disorders of all sorts, insanity, suicide, among the rewards of his eloquence ; Religion dressed up in fine phrases and made much of, while Morality, her Poor Relation, was getting hard treatment at the hands of the young persons who had grown up under the reign of terror of the Northampton pulpit ; alienation of the hearts of his people to such an extent as is rarely seen in the bitterest quarrels between pastor and flock, — if this was a successful ministry, what disasters would constitute a failure ? "

The truth is that Holmes was not only antagonistic to the temper of Calvinism in life and character ; he was also its most openly and bitterly persistent opponent. The more you read his prose, the more you feel his consciousness of the old creed cropping out in places where you least expect it. The traditional Unitarianism of New England was apt to neglect orthodoxy ; Holmes could not. The dogmas of Calvin lurked constantly in his mind ; and he never failed to attack them. This hideous system is untrue, he protests ; he will deny it ; he will oppose it in every possible way ; if so may be he will leave the world better for his work in the destruction of this most monstrous of its spiritual errors. So Holmes, who in his superficial life is remembered as the wittiest and happiest of New England social figures, and as the most finished as well as the most tenderly sentimental maker of our occasional verse, and who wrote so much even of his most serious work with the temper and the manner of a wit, proves to have another aspect. Among our men of letters this rationalist was the most sturdy, the most militant, the most pitiless enemy of a superstition whose tyranny over his childhood had left life-long scars. In the persistency with which this spectre of Calvinism rose before him there was something which he may well have fancied to be like the diabolic possessions so fervently believed in by the Puritan fathers. He might lay the spectre again and again, but every time he took up his pen it would arise inhuman as ever. That he never relaxed his fight shows rare courage. From beginning to end, then, Holmes was a survivor of the eighteenth century. Brave rationalistic attack on outworn superstitions is the bravest note of that past epoch.

If there be any one European figure whose position in world literature is analogous to that of Holmes in the literature of New England, it is Voltaire. The differences between Voltaire and Holmes, to be sure, are so much more marked than the analogies that any analogy may at first seem fantastic. For all his eminence, Voltaire was not born a gentleman and never had quite the traits of one ; in our little New England there was never a better gentleman than Holmes. Voltaire was a man of licentious life and pitiless temper, incensed and distracted by all the old-world corruptions which he spent his wits in stabbing to death ; Holmes's life had all the simple provincial decency and kindliness of his country. Voltaire's wit was the keenest and most sustained of modern Europe ; the wit of Holmes, after all, was only the most delightful which has amused nineteenth-century Boston. For all these differences, there is a true analogy between them : both alike, with superficial frivolity, bravely devoted themselves to lifelong war against what they believed to be delusions which terribly impeded the progress of human nature towards a better future. And each was so earnest that neither could help expressing himself in such manner as to his nature was true. Voltaire's wit, then, teems with blasphemy and licentiousness ; that of Holmes is pure of either. This does not mean that one man was essentially better or worse than the other ; it means rather that the worlds in which they lived and the superstitions which they combated were different.

Voltaire died in 1770; Holmes as a writer of prose hardly existed before 1857. The two are a full century apart, yet there is between them such likeness as almost seems intellectually contemporary. In the contrast between them, then, there is something which freshly throws familiar light on New England. The contrast between Holmes and Voltaire, if in one sense a contrast between the eighteenth century and the nineteenth, is in another sense a contrast between a foul old Europe and an America still pure in its national inexperience. Above all, it is a contrast which distinctly shows what freshness of nature and feeling still marked America in Holmes's time. Few man ever expressed themselves less guardedly than he ; yet so far as licentiousness or blasphemy is concerned every line of his printed works may be put unreservedly in the hands of any child. Even to our own time the history of American human nature implies our national inexperience. In the New England Renaissance, rationalism itself, and all the freedom of earnest satire, appears for once void of impurity.

XIV

NATHANIEL HAWTHORNE

In our study of the New England Renaissance we have glanced at Emerson, whom we may call its prophet; at Whittier, who so admirably phrased its aspirations for reform; at Longfellow, its academic poet; at Lowell, its humanist; and at Holmes, its rationalist. The period produced but one other literary figure of equal eminence with these, — Nathaniel Hawthorne, above and beyond the others an artist.

His origin was different from that of his contemporaries whom we have lately considered. Emerson and Longfellow and Lowell and Holmes were all born into the social class which at their time was dominant in New England; and Whittier sprang from sturdy country yeomen. Hawthorne came from a family eminent in early colonial days, but long lapsed into that sort of obscurity which modern cant would call social degeneracy. His father, a ship captain of the period when New England commerce was most vigorous, died in Guiana when Hawthorne was only four years old; and the boy, who had been born at Salem in 1804, grew up there in his mother's care, singularly solitary. His youthful experience was confined to Salem, then a more important town than now, but already showing symptoms of decline. He made at least one prolonged visit in search of health to the woods of Maine. To this day wild and then wilder still, these forests early made familiar to him the atmosphere of our ancestral wilderness. In 1821 he went to Bowdoin College. There he was a classmate of Longfellow, and of Franklin Pierce, afterwards President of the United States. His friendship with the latter was close and lifelong. In 1825, they took their degrees at Bowdoin.

For the ensuing fourteen years Hawthorne lived with his mother at Salem, so quietly that his existence was hardly known to the townsfolk of that gossipy little Yankee seaport. He spent much time indoors, constantly writing but neither successful nor generally recognised as an author. He took long solitary walks, and his personal appearance is said to have been romantic and picturesque. In 1839 he was appointed a clerk in the Boston Custom House; in 1841 the spoils system turned him out of office, and for a few months he was at Brook Farm. The next year he married, and from then until 1846 he lived at Concord, writing and by this time pleasantly recognised as a writer of short stories. From 1846 to 1849 he was Surveyor in the Custom House of Salem. During the ensuing four years, when he resided at various places in Massachusetts, he produced his three most characteristic long books, — the " Scarlet Letter," the " House of the Seven Gables," and the " Blithedale Romance," — as well as his two volumes of mythological stories for children, the " Wonderbook " and " Tanglewood Tales." In 1853, his friend, President Pierce, made him Consul at Liverpool. He remained abroad until 1860, passing some time during his later stay there in Italy. From this experience resulted the " Marble Faun." In 1860, he came home and returned to Concord, where he lived thenceforth. He died in the White Mountains, on the 18th of May, 1864.

Chronologically, then, Hawthorne's position in New England literature seems earlier than that of his contemporaries at whom we have glanced. He was only a year younger than Emerson, he was three years older than Longfellow and Whittier, five years older than Holmes, and fifteen years older than Lowell. He died thirty-six years ago; and Emerson and Longfellow survived until 1882, Lowell till 1891, Whittier till 1892, and Holmes till 1895. Though Hawthorne, however, was the first to die of this little company, he had been a fellow-writer with them during the thirty years when the full literary career of all had declared itself. In the time which followed Hawthorne's death, the survivors wrote and published copiously; but none produced anything which much altered the reputation he had achieved while Hawthorne was still alive. So far as character goes, in short, the literature of renascent New England was virtually complete in 1864.

Under such circumstances chronology becomes accidental. The order in which to consider contemporaries is a question simply of their relative character. We had good reason, then, for reserving Hawthorne till the last; for above all the rest, as we have already remarked, he was an artist. This term is so general that we may well linger on it for a moment. A little story of the Yankee country may help define our meaning. Not long ago a sportsman, who had started out in a dory along with a native fisherman, found himself becalmed at night off the New Hampshire coast. Observing that the fisherman, who had sat quiet for a little while, was staring at the North Star, he asked what he was thinking about. " I was thinkin'," drawled out the Yankee, " how fur off you 'd hev to be to get that south of you." Whereupon he shook himself and fell to his oars. That momentary experience, you see, had awakened in a Yankee countryman something like imaginative emotion. He spoke it out, and then forgot it; but just for a moment he had felt the impulse of artistic spirit, and had found relief in an expression imaginative enough to be memorable. Some such experience as this everybody knows sometimes, many people often; and occasionally there are born into the world natures so sensitive to impressions that they find almost every day overcharged with emotions from which they can find relief only in attempts at expression. Generally such expression is of only momentary value. Now and again, however, some human being proves endowed not only with sensitiveness to impulse but with mastery of expression as well. Such a man, whatever his art, is an artist; and such was Hawthorne.

It chances that fate has posthumously treated him with exceptional irony. The general solitude of his life was partly due to a fastidious reticence which made him shrink from personal revelation. This trait was not inherited by his children; so since his death we have had more publications from his note-books, and more records of his private life than is the case with anybody else in American literary history. Among these posthumous records none are more characteristic or valuable than the first which appeared. The " Passages from American Note Books," published in 1868, extend over many years, mostly before Hawthorne's sojourn abroad. For our purposes they are perhaps the most significant of all his work. They show him in various parts of the New England country, freshly impressed almost every day with some aspect of life which aroused in him concrete reaction. He actually published tales enough to establish more than one literary reputation. These note-books show how few fragments of his wealthy imaginative impulse he ever coined into finished literary form. They reveal, too, another characteristic fact. Though Hawthorne wrote hardly any formal verse, though his natural impulse to expression rarely if ever took metrical form, he was a genuine poet. His only vehicle of expression was language, and to him language meant not only words but rhythm too. Even in these memoranda, then, which he never expected to stray beyond his note-books, you feel the constant touch of one whose meaning is so subtle that its most careless expression must fall into delicately careful phrasing.

Such a temperament would inevitably have declared itself anywhere. Some critics, then, have lamented the accident which confined Hawthorne's experience for almost fifty years to isolated, æsthetically starved New England. In this opinion there is considerable justice. The extreme localism of Hawthorne's life, until his maturity was passing into age, may very likely have made world literature poorer. The " Marble Faun " is our only indication of what he might have done if his sensitive youth had been exposed to the unfathomably human influence of Europe. Yet, whatever our loss, we can hardly regret an accident so fortunate to the literature of New England.

This Hawthorne, whose artistic temperament would have been remarkable anywhere, chanced to be born in an old Yankee seaport, just at its zenith. It was soon to be stricken by the Embargo, and swiftly to be surpassed by a more prosperous neighbour. When he knew it best, it was like some iridescent old sea-shell, whose denizens are dead and gone, but whose hollows still faintly vibrate with the voices of the illimitable waters. From this passing, ancestral Salem he visited those woods of Maine which were still so primeval as to recall the shadowy forests whose mystery confronted the immigrant Puritans. Then he lived for a while in Boston, just when Transcendentalism was most in the air ; and he had a glimpse of Brook Farm ; and he passed more than one year in the Old Manse at Concord ; and finally he strayed among the hills of Berkshire. Until he finally set sail for England, however, he had never known any earthly region which had not traditionally been dominated by the spirit of the Puritans ; nor any which in his own time was not alive, so far as life was in it, with the spirit of the New England Renaissance.

In considering this period, we have hitherto dwelt only on its most obvious aspect. Like any revelation of new life, it seemed to open the prospect of an illimitably excellent future. Amid such buoyant hopes people think little of the past, tending indeed to regard it like some night of darkness to which at last the dawn has brought an end. They forget the infinite mysteries of the night, its terrors and its dreamy beauties, and the courage of those who throughout its tremulous course have watched and prayed. So when the dawn comes they forget that the birth of day is the death of night. Thus the men of our New England Renaissance forgot that their new, enfranchised life and literature meant the final passing of that elder New England so hopefully founded by the Puritan fathers. As our Renaissance has passed its swift zenith, and begun itself to recede into dimming memory, we can see more plainly than of old this tragic aspect of its earthly course. The world in which Hawthorne lived and wrote was not only a world where new ideals were springing into life; it was a world, too, where the old ideals were suffering their agony.

Of all our men of letters Hawthorne was most sensitive to this phase of the time when they flourished together. He was not, like Emerson, a prophet striving to glean truths from unexplored fields of eternity; he was not, like Whittier, a patient limner of simple nature, or a passionate advocate of moral reform; he was not, like Longfellow or Lowell, a loving student of world literature, moved by erudition to the expression of what meaning he had found in the records of a wonderful foreign past; he was not, like Holmes, a combatant who, with all the vivacity of lifelong wit and all the method of scientific training, rationally attacked the chimeras of his time; he was an artist, who lived for nearly fifty years only in his native country, daily stirred to attempt expression of what our Yankee life meant. Of all our men of letters he was the most indigenous; of all, the least imitative.

By hastily comparing his work, then, with some which was produced in England during the same years, we may perhaps define our notion of what the peculiar trait of American letters has been. His first collection of " Twice Told Tales " appeared in 1837; in England, where the Queen had just come to the throne, Dickens published " Oliver Twist," and Thackeray the " Yellowplush Papers." The second series of " Twice Told Tales " came in 1842, when Bulwer published " Zanoni," and Dickens his " American Notes," and Macaulay

his " Lays." In 1846, when Hawthorne published the
" Mosses from an Old Manse," Dickens published " Dombey
and Son." In 1850, the year of the " Scarlet Letter," came
Mrs. Browning's " Sonnets from the Portuguese," and Carlyle's " Latter Day Pamphlets," and Tennyson's " In Me-
moriam; " in 1851, along with the " House of the Seven
Gables," came " Casa Guidi Windows " and the " Stones of
Venice; " in 1852, with the " Blithedale Romance," came
Dickens's " Bleak House," and Charles Reade's " Peg Woff-
ington," and Thackeray's " Henry Esmond; " in 1853, along
with " Tanglewood Tales," came Kingsley's " Hypatia," Bulwer's " My Novel," and Miss Yonge's " Heir of Redclyffe; "
and in the year of the " Marble Faun," 1860, came the
" Woman in White," the " Mill on the Floss," the " Cloister
and the Hearth," and the last volume of " Modern Painters."
The list already grows tediously long for our purpose. Like
Irving and Poe, the two Americans who preceded him as literary artists, Hawthorne proves, the moment you compare him
with the contemporary writers of England, to be gifted or
hampered with a pervasive sense of form which one is half
disposed to call classic.

Yet that term " classic," applied even to Irving, and still more
to Poe or Hawthorne, must seem paradoxical if one has sym-
pathetically read them. Such terms as " romantic " and
" classic " of course are inexactly bewildering; but for general
purposes one would not go far wrong who should include under
the term " classic "that sort of human impulse which reached its
highest form in the fine arts of Greece, and under the term " romantic " that which most nearly approached realization in the
art and the literature of mediæval Europe. The essence of
classic art is perhaps that the artist realises the limits of his conception, and within those limits endeavours to make his expression completely beautiful. The essence of the romantic spirit
is that the artist, whatever his conception, is always aware of the
infinite mysteries which lie beyond it. Mr. Cabot, in his biog-

raphy of Emerson, described Transcendentalism as an outbreak of romanticism. The romantic spirit is almost always transcendental.

Now, even the stories of Irving are pervaded with one kind of romantic temper, — that which delights in the splendours of a vanished past, and in the mysteries of supernatural fancy. Something more deeply romantic underlies the inarticulate work of Brockden Brown, and still more the poems and the tales of Poe. Both Brown and Poe had a deep sense of what horror may lurk in the mysteries which always lie beyond human ken. Even Brown, however, and surely Poe conceived these melodramatically. Brown can sometimes thrill you; and Poe often; but when you wake again to normal placidity, you find in your nostrils some lingering trace of such fumes as fill theatres where red lights have been burning. In common with Irving and Poe, Hawthorne had an instinctive tendency to something like classic precision of form. In common with them he possessed, too, a constant sensitiveness to the mysteries of romantic sentiment; but the romanticism of Hawthorne differs from that of either Poe or Irving as distinctly as it differs from that of Brockden Brown. In Hawthorne's there is no trace of artificiality. Beyond human life he feels not only the fact of mystery; he feels the mysteries which are truly there.

In the mere fact of romantic temper, then, Hawthorne is broadly American, typically native to this new world which has been so starved of antiquity. In the fact that his romantic spirit is fundamentally true he proves individual, and more at one than our other artists with the deepest spirit of his peculiar country. The darkly passionate idealism of the Puritans had involved a tendency towards conceptions, which when they reached artistic form must be romantic. The phase of mystery on which the grim dogmas of these past generations incessantly dwelt lies in the world-old facts, which nothing shall ever much abate, of evil and sin and suffering. Now

Hawthorne had passed so far beyond Puritan dogma that in mature life he could rarely be persuaded to attend a religious service. His temper, indeed, when not concerned with the forms of artistic expression, was impatient of all formality. Just as truly, however, as his nature was that of a born artist, it could never shake off the temperamental earnestness of the Puritan. Throughout his work, then, he is most characteristic when in endlessly varied form he expresses that constant, haunting sense of ancestral sin in which his Puritan forefathers found endless warrant for their doctrines of depravity and of eternal retribution. With the Puritans, of course, this sense of sin was a conviction of fact; they believed in the Devil, whose essential wickedness, lurking within every human heart, is bound if we lack divine help to sweep us into deserved and lasting torment. Hawthorne, on the other hand, felt all this only as a matter of emotional experience. To him Puritanism was no longer a motive of life; in final ripeness it had become a motive of art. When any human impulse has thus ripened, we may generally conclude it historically a thing of the past.

Another aspect of this deep sense of sin and mystery shows us that it involves morbid development of conscience. Conscience in its artistic form Hawthorne displays throughout; and though artistic conscience be very different from moral, the two have in common an aspiration toward beauty. For all its perversities of outward form, the impulse of the moral conscience is really toward beauty of conduct; artistic conscience, often evident in works morally far from edifying, is a constant, strenuous impulse toward beauty of expression. In America this latter trait has generally seemed more frequent than in England; one feels it even in Brockden Brown, one feels it strongly in Irving and Poe, one feels it in the delicately sentimental lines of Bryant, and one feels it now and again through most of the expression of renascent New England. Whatever American writers have achieved, they have con-

28

stantly tried to do their best. Hawthorne, we have seen, surpassed his countrymen in the genuineness of his artistic impulse; he surpassed them, too, in the tormenting strenuousness of his artistic conscience. In his choice of words and, above all, in the delicacy of his very subtle rhythm, he seems never to have relaxed his effort to write as beautifully as he could. He displays the ancestral conscience of New England, then, in finally exquisite form.

Of course the man has limits. Comparing his work with the contemporary work of England, one is aware of its classically careful form, of its profoundly romantic sentiment, and of its admirable artistic conscience. One grows aware, at the same time, of its unmistakable rusticity; in turns of thought as well as of phrase one feels monotony, provincialism, a certain thinness. Throughout, one feels again that tendency to shrink from things of the flesh which to some foreign minds makes all American writing seem either emasculate or hypocritical. It is reported of Hawthorne, indeed, — who first saw Europe, we should remember, when he was nearly fifty years old, — that he could never reconcile his taste to the superbly unconscious nudities of masterly sculpture and painting. Here is an incalculable limit; and he has plenty more. One and all of these limits, however, prove, like his merits, to be deeply characteristic of the New England which surrounded his life.

It is hard to sum up the impression which such a writer makes. He was ideal, of course, in temper; he was introspective, with all the self-searching instinct of his ancestry; he was solitary; he was permeated with a sense of the mysteries of life and sin; and by pondering over them he tended to exaggerate them more and more. In a dozen aspects, then, he seems typically Puritan. His artistic conscience, however, as alert as that of any pagan, impelled him constantly to realise in his work those forms of beauty which should most beautifully embody the ideals of his incessantly creative imagination. Thus he grew to be of all our writers the least imitative, the most surely individual. The circumstances of his life combined with the sensitiveness of his nature to make his individuality indigenous. Beyond any one else, then, he expresses the deepest temper of that New England race which brought him forth, and which now, at least in the phases we have known, seems vanishing from the earth.

XV

THE DECLINE OF NEW ENGLAND

AMONG the numerous writers of the New England Renaissance on whom we have not touched there were doubtless some who wrote significantly. The unconscious selection of the public, however, has preferred those on whom we have consequently found it worth our while to dwell. What is more, little was thought or said in nineteenth-century New England, and above all little was written there which will not fall under one or another of the heads which we have considered. The earlier volumes of the "Atlantic," for example, taken with the "Dial" and the "North American Review," represent the literature of this period; and although among the contributors to each you may find persons whom we have neglected, you will be at pains to find in any of them traces of any general spirit in the air with which our study has not now made us reasonably familiar.

It is hard, too, quite to realise that we have been dealing not with the present but with the past. The days of the Renaissance are still so recent that plenty of Bostonians instinctively feel its most eminent figures to be our contemporaries. As we begin to ponder over the group of our lately vanished worthies, however, the most obvious fact about them grows to seem that they represent a kind of eminence which no longer distinguishes New England.

The social history of Boston, one begins to see, has been exceptional. Early in the reign of Charles II., Cotton Mather was born there. Living all his life in that remote colonial town, he managed, both as a man of science and as a busy theological writer, to win European recognition. Any American, it is said, who went abroad during Cotton Mather's lifetime, was apt to be asked whether he knew this one American whose name had strayed beyond the limits of his country. Cotton Mather died in 1728, forty-eight years before the Declaration of Independence; but he had been personally known to at least one distinguished signer of that document, Benjamin Franklin. Franklin, of course, lived little in Boston, and not at all after his early youth. During the middle half of the eighteenth century, then, one may perhaps say that Boston, although it contained men of unusual intelligence and power, contained few if any whose eminence was more than locally visible. By the time of the American Revolution, however, a leading citizen of Boston was John Adams, whose reputation as a public man ultimately become worldwide; and in the Boston of his day Adams's personality was not obviously exceptional. Though his attainment of the national presidency made him at last more conspicuous than any of his New England contemporaries, he was at home only one of an able and distinguished company. President Adams survived the Declaration of Independence by precisely half a century; he died on the 4th of July, 1826. At that time the Boston on which his eyes closed already contained many men not only of power, but of such eminence that at one time or another they attained far more than local recognition. John Quincy Adams, then President of the United States, was a diplomatist known throughout Europe. Daniel Webster and Edward Everett were members of Congress from Boston, George Ticknor was Smith Professor at Harvard, William Ellery Channing was in the very flood-tide of his career, and young Ralph Waldo Emerson was just being licensed to preach.

The name of Emerson carries us to another literary epoch. In 1879, Holmes, in his Memoir of John Lothrop Motley, wrote of that Saturday Club at which we have already glanced: —

" This Club, of which we were both members, and which is still flourishing, came into existence in a very quiet sort of way at about the same time as the 'Atlantic Monthly,' and although entirely unconnected with that magazine, included as members some of its chief contributors. Of those who might have been met at some of the monthly gatherings in its earlier days I may mention Emerson, Hawthorne, Lowell, Longfellow, Motley, Whipple, Whittier; Professors Agassiz and Peirce ; John S. Dwight; Governor Andrew, Richard H. Dana, Junior, Charles Sumner. It offered a wide gamut of intelligences, and the meetings were noteworthy occasions. If there was not a certain amount of ' mutual admiration ' among some of those I have mentioned it was a great pity, and implied a defect in the nature of men who were otherwise largely endowed. The vitality of this Club has depended in a great measure on its utter poverty in statutes and by-laws, its entire absence of formality, and its blessed freedom from speech-making."

In Mr. Morse's biography of Holmes there is a note referring to this Club, in which he mentions among its members a number of other gentlemen still living and these among the dead : Felton, once President of Harvard College ; Prescott; Tom Appleton ; J. M. Forbes ; Henry James, the elder ; William Hunt, the painter ; Charles Francis Adams ; Francis Parkman ; James Freeman Clarke ; Judge John Lowell ; Ebenezer Rockwood Hoar ; and Bishop Brooks. Including Holmes, this gives us twenty-six members of the Club, all typical Boston gentlemen of the Renaissance. Another member, we have already seen, was Fields. Twenty-seven names, then, we have mentioned in all, so carelessly collected that one so familiar as that of Fields was accidentally omitted. Among the six least widely known of the company, two had attained more than local reputation as men of letters. Edwin Percy Whipple was generally recognised as a professional literary critic ; and if Mr. Dana had lacked the claim to eminence which his admirable career at the bar deserved, and which was deserved as well by his high-minded devotion to the cause of antislavery at a time when such devotion demanded rare courage, he would still be remembered among our lesser literary figures as the writer of that excellent record of sea-life,

" Two Years Before the Mast." President Felton and Tom Appleton and John Lowell, on the other hand, left behind them little literary record ; whoever knew them, however, must remember them as men of such wit and breeding as would have been exceptional anywhere ; and any memory which embraces them will embrace too the figure of Mr. Forbes, a merchant of those elder days when mercantile Boston had something of the quality which tradition would confine to the old-world merchants who wore their swords.

This list, we must remember, is merely accidental, —the list of a few men who chanced to become fellow-members of a small, intimate Club. In the Boston where they lived they were not the only men of eminence. Webster was their fellow-citizen ; so was Everett ; so was Choate ; so were Theodore Parker and Wendell Phillips ; so was Mr. Winthrop. The list might extend indefinitely. Between 1840 and 1860, indeed, Boston was probably the spot in the English-speaking world where in proportion to the population a visitor was most apt familiarly to meet men whose reputation had extended as far as our language, amid fellow-citizens who seemed in all respects their equals.

In January, 1893, there suddenly died at Boston the late Bishop of Massachusetts, the youngest man whose name is included in Mr. Morse's list of the Saturday Club. Phillips Brooks, born in 1835, and graduated at Harvard at the age of twenty, was early known throughout the English-speaking world as among the few great preachers of his day. Cotton Mather had reached his full maturity in 1700 ; in 1875 Phillips Brooks was at the height of his powers ; and it is hardly too much to say that throughout those hundred and seventy-five years Boston had bred or had attracted to itself a succession of undeniably eminent men. To-day there has come a marked change. The city still possesses men of power, of breeding, of culture. Even a critic so little disposed to commendation as Mr. Godkin has lately mentioned

Boston as the one place in America where wealth and the knowledge of how to use it are apt to coincide. Just as surely, however, as the Boston of 1850 was surprisingly rich in men of wide distinction, so the Boston of 1900 seems comparatively poor.

Though this decline in the importance of Boston cannot yet be thoroughly accounted for, two or three facts about it are obvious. For one thing, as we have already seen, the intellectual Renaissance of New England coincided with its period of commercial prosperity; this began with foreign commerce, and soon passed into local manufactures and local railways. During the first half of the nineteenth century, then, Boston was apparently the most prosperous city in America. Throughout this period, however, the prosperity of Boston never crystallised in what nowadays would be considered large fortunes. Up to the time of the Civil War, indeed, a Bostonian worth a million dollars was still held extremely rich. The great West, meanwhile, was untamed prairie and wilderness.

The intellectual hegemony of Boston may roughly be said to have lasted until the Civil War. That great national convulsion affected the Northern States somewhat as an electric current affects temporarily isolated chemicals; it flashed the Union into new cohesion. The wildest imagination of 1860 could hardly have conceived such centralised national power as in 1900 has become commonplace to American thought. One price which every separate region must pay for such national union is a decline of local importance. New England has never lost its integrity, but since the Civil War New England has counted for less and less.

A few years after the Civil War the Pacific Railway was at last completed. Long before this, an extreme application of the policy of protection — a policy still strongly supported by the manufacturing interests of New England — had resulted in the disappearance of our foreign commerce. The opening of the

continental transportation lines naturally stimulated that already
great development of wheat-growing and the like which now
makes our western prairies perhaps the chief grain-producing
region of the world. Coal, and oil, too, and copper, and iron
began to sprout like weeds. The centre of economic importance in America inevitably shifted westward. Meantime
legislation had deprived New England of that mercantile
marine which might conceivably have maintained its importance in international trade.

Again, the immense development of Western wealth, during the past thirty or forty years, has resulted in private fortunes whose mere bulk is incredible. Though the fortunes
of wealthy New Englanders have undoubtedly increased, they
have increased in nothing like proportion with the fortunes of
the West. Such a state of economic fact could not
fail, at least for a while, to bring about a marked change in
American ideals. The immigrant clergy of New England
held such local power as involves personal eminence; such
power later passed into the hands of the bar; and during
our Renaissance, literature itself carried with it influence
enough to make great personal eminence its most stimulating
prize. To-day, for better or worse, power and eminence
throughout America have momentarily become questions
rather of material fortune.

External causes, then, would perhaps have brought to an
end the eminence of New England; but we can see now as
well that in the form which our Renaissance took there was
something which must have prevented it from lasting long.
As we look back on it now, its most characteristic phase
appears to have been that which began with Unitarianism,
passed into Transcendentalism, and broke out into militant
reform. All three of these movements, or, if you prefer, all
these three phases of one considerable movement, were based
on the fundamental conception that human beings are inherently good. This naturally involved the right of every individ-

ual to think and to act as he chose. Free exercise of this right for a while seemed to uphold the buoyant philosophy on which it was based. So long as human beings were controlled by the discipline of tradition, their vagaries were not so wild as to seem socially disintegrating; but before long, excessive individualism began evidently to involve the neglect and decay of standards.

The most typical example of the whole tendency is probably to be found in the history of Unitarianism. Fifty years ago this was certainly the dominant religious fact in Boston; and the Unitarian ministers of the city were men of such vigorous and distinguished personality, of such ethereal moral purity, too, as made them seem the fit spiritual leaders of a society remarkable for personal distinction. To-day this elder Unitarianism has tended either to recoil into the Episcopal Church, or else to dissipate itself in the reformatory vagaries of free-thinking pulpits. The tenants of these, frequently foreigners, have often been admirable persons whose origin and manners have perceptibly differed from those of their distinguished predecessors. More than one of the old Boston churches have meanwhile passed out of existence. The Brattle Street Church, which began its career of liberal Calvinism, under Benjamin Coleman, in the days of William and Mary, has totally disappeared; so has the Hollis Street Church, memorable as that of " the celebrated Mather Byles ; " so has the West Church, where the father of James Russell Lowell used to preach; so have more still. Nor is this wilting shrinkage merely a question of bricks and mortar. For a century and a half, until the dawn of Unitarianism, the pulpits of Boston were incessantly occupied by the most distinguished and powerful men of New England; to-day, after less than a hundred years of the work begun by Channing, the Boston pulpit, whatever the individual merits of its clergy, has locally become the least conspicuous and the least influential in America.

Along with this impressive change in New England has come another. Towards the end of his life, Bishop Brooks chanced to be privately talking of the difference between the Harvard College of his boyhood and the Harvard College to which, under the enfranchised system of non-sectarian religion which now prevails there, he was an official preacher. " In my time," he said, " Harvard students had poets; now they have n't." The truth is, one begins to see, that the old poets, whom the young Yankees used so enthusiastically to read, phrased one single old ideal, — that spirit of revolution whose aim is individual freedom. Intellectually and spiritually, that ideal has now come as near realisation as is ever the case on earth. Boston men, at present of mature years, have grown up in a generation whose individual freedom was ready to be used and enjoyed. Born under the influences for which the preceding generation had fought, then, this new generation has generally been content to cherish each his own individual ideal, which has usually been too individual to excite common enthusiasm.

An unremarked accident in merely literary history has meanwhile had perceptible effect on New England. The men who started the " North American Review," the later men who for a while expressed themselves in the " Dial," and later still the men whose work was finally concentrated in the " Atlantic Monthly " had one point in common, which they shared with the orators, the scholars, and the Unitarians who flourished along with them. Almost all these men either had been educated at Harvard College or else had early come under the influences of that oldest seat of American learning. How deeply coherent the Harvard spirit has always been may be felt by whoever will read that long series of occasional poems in which Dr. Holmes celebrated the history of the college and of the class of '29. Until Mr. Fields became editor of the " Atlantic Monthly," then, the chief vehicles of literary expression in New England were controlled by men in whom this Harvard tradition was inbred. Though not a college man, Mr. Fields was in close and intimate sympathy with the college men of his day. The gentlemen who succeeded him in control of the " Atlantic Monthly " are still living, are eminent in contemporary letters, and are worthily respected and admired by whoever knows them either personally or as authors. Neither of them, however, had chanced to have much to do with Harvard ; nor had either, during his days of editorship, instinctive sympathy with Harvard character. For years, then, the New England youth who came to Harvard with literary aspiration found themselves at odds with the conscientious and admirable men of letters who controlled the chief organ of New England literature. The " Atlantic Monthly " ceased to understand the constituency from which its older contributors had been drawn ; and Harvard College ceased perceptibly to affect the literature of New England.

The college itself was somewhat to blame. The spirit of individualism had more than done its work there. On the opening page of the " Autocrat of the Breakfast Table " Holmes launches into a characteristically whimsical and wise discussion of societies of mutual admiration : —

"What would our literature or art be without such associations? Who can tell what we owe to the Mutual Admiration Society of which Shakspere, and Ben Jonson, and Beaumont and Fletcher were members? Or to that where Johnson, and Goldsmith, and Burke, and Reynolds, and Beauclerk, and Boswell, most admiring among all admirers, met together? Was there any great harm in the fact that the Irvings and Pauldings wrote in company? or any unpardonable cabal in the literary union of Verplanck and Bryant and Sands, and as many more as they chose to associate with them?"

Whatever its disintegrant tendencies, the society of the Boston Renaissance was full of mutual admiration ; and the Saturday Club, in which the social side of Boston literature culminated, was a Mutual Admiration Society of the most stimulating kind. The extreme individualism of the later generation has made such mutual admiration seem incompatible with honest criticism. The younger men of Harvard have not only lacked common ideals; they have so far parted one from another that they have been honestly unable to perceive what virtues they may have possessed in common as distinguished from what faults an overdeveloped critical perception has revealed to each in the temper and the work of the others.

And so the Renaissance of New England has declined. At least for the moment literary New England is a thing of the past. What the future may bring, no man can say; but we are already far enough from the New England which was considerable in letters to ask what it has contributed to human expression.

Not much, we must answer, on any large scale; of the men we have scrutinised only two, Emerson and Hawthorne, will generally be held considerably to have enriched the literature of our language. And Emerson has vagaries which may well justify a doubt whether his work is among those few final records of human wisdom which are imperishable Scriptures. Beyond doubt, again, though Hawthorne's tales possess sincerity of motive and beauty of form, they reveal at best a phase of human nature whose limits are obvious. Mutual admiration has combined with such limits to make New England overestimate itself; and for want of anything better to brag about, all America has bragged about the letters of New England, until in reactionary moods one begins to smile at the brag. As we look back at the Renaissance now vanishing into the past, however, we find in it, if not positive magnitude of achievement, at least qualities which go far to warrant this national pride which we have loved to believe justified. For in every aspect its literature is sincere and pure and sweet.

The emigrants to New England were native Elizabethans, — stern and peculiar, but still temperamentally contemporary with Shakspere and the rest. In two centuries and a half, national experience forced English life and letters through many various phases, until at last the old country began to breed that fixed, conservative John Bull who has so lost Elizabethan spontaneity, versatility, and enthusiasm. In America, meantime, national inexperience kept the elder temper little changed until at the beginning of the nineteenth century it was aroused by the world-movement of revolution. Then, at last, our ancestral America, which had so unwittingly lingered behind the mother country, awoke. In the flush of its waking, it strove to express the meaning of life; and the meaning of its life was the story of what two hundred years of national inexperience had wrought for a race of Elizabethan Puritans. Its utterances may well prove lacking in scope, in greatness; the days to come may well prove them of little lasting potence; but nothing can obscure their beautiful purity of spirit.

For all its inexperience, New England life has been human. Its literal records are no more free than those of other regions and times from the greed and the lust, the trickery and the squalor, which everywhere defile earthly existence. What marks it apart is the childlike persistency of its ideals. Its nobler minds, who have left their records in its literature, retained something of the old spontaneity, the old versatility, the old enthusiasm of ancestral England. They retained, too, even more than they knew of that ardour for absolute truth which animated the grave fathers of the emigration. Their innocence of worldly wisdom led them to undue confidence in the excellence of human nature; the simplicity of their national past blinded them to the complexity of the days even now at hand, while the sod still lies light on their graves. We used to believe them heralds of the future; already we begin to perceive that they were rather chroniclers of times which shall be no more. Yet, after all, whatever comes, they possessed traits for which we may always give them unstinted reverence; for humanity must always find inspiring the record of bravely confident aspiration toward righteousness.

BOOK VI

THE REST OF THE STORY

BOOK VI

THE REST OF THE STORY

I

NEW YORK SINCE 1857

LONG as we have dwelt on the Renaissance of New England, we can hardly have forgotten that the first considerable American literary expression developed in the Middle States. Before New England emerged into literature, the work of Brockden Brown had been completed and the reputations of Irving and Cooper and Bryant established. Bryant, as we have seen, lived through the whole period which brought New England letters to their height and to their decline. He outlived Poe, he outlived Willis, and long before he died the Knickerbocker School had passed into a memory. Meanwhile those writers whose works had centred about the "Atlantic Monthly" had achieved their full reputation.

The "Atlantic Monthly," we remember, was started in 1857. That same year saw also the foundation of "Harper's Weekly," which still admirably persists in New York. At that time "Harper's Monthly Magazine" had been in existence for seven years; and the two New York newspapers which have maintained closest relation with literary matters, the "Evening Post" and the "Tribune," had long been thoroughly established. The other periodicals which now mark New York as the literary centre of the United States were not yet founded. In reverting to New York, then, we may conveniently revert to 1857.

Though the fact by which this year is commonly remembered in American history has left no mark on literature, we may conveniently remind ourselves that throughout America 1857 was marked by a memorable financial panic. The great expansion of the country during the preceding twelve or fifteen years had resulted in a general extension of credit and in a general overdevelopment of enterprises, particularly of railroads, which were bound to involve reaction. For a little while the material progress of the country came to a standstill. It was only when this material progress was renewed, partly under the stimulus of the Civil War, that the overwhelming superiority of New York as a centre of material prosperity made itself finally felt. Throughout the century, to be sure, the preponderance of New York had been declaring itself. In 1800 it had 60,000 inhabitants to only 24,000 in Boston. In 1830, when it had 200,000 inhabitants, Boston had only 61,000; and by 1857 the population of New York was at least three-quarters of a million, while that of Boston still proportionally lagged behind. From the time when the Erie Canal was opened, in fact, the geographical position of New York had already made that city by far the most considerable in America. Less than three hundred miles from Boston, it was and it remains geographically as central as Boston is isolated.

Until after the Civil War, however, the preponderating importance of New York had not proceeded so far as to deprive the place of a decided local character. Traces of this, indeed, it still retains; but most of its modern characteristics seem traceable to a political accident. Throughout the period during which its geographical position, at first slowly, then faster and faster, has declared its commercial superiority, New York has never been a political capital. In this respect its contrast with Boston is most marked. Though Boston has been the capital only of the small State of Massachusetts, this small State has always been the most important of isolated New England. Boston, then, its political capital, has enjoyed not only the commercial and economic supremacy of the region, but also such supremacy as comes from attracting and diffusing the most important influences of local public life. In this aspect Boston on a small scale resembles the great capitals of the world. New York, on the other hand, commercially and financially the most important spot in America, has never been much else. Almost from the beginning our national government has been centralised in Washington, — a city artificially created for political purposes at a point of small economic importance. The government of the State of New York, ever since New York was a State, has been situated at the comparatively insignificant town of Albany. The enormous growth of New York City, to be sure, has long given it great political weight. In current political slang there are few more picturesque phrases than that which describes some candidate for the Presidency of the United States as coming down to the Harlem River with a considerable majority, to be met at that traditional boundary of the metropolis by an overwhelming force of metropolitan voters. In point of fact, however, metropolitan New York has always had to seek legislation from a much smaller city more than a hundred miles away; and thither it has always had to take for decision every question carried to its court of highest appeal. Two natural results which have followed may be paralleled in various other American cities similarly placed, — Philadelphia, Chicago, St. Louis, or San Francisco. In the absence of far-reaching political activity, emphasis on merely local politics has been disproportionate; and meanwhile the city, which has prospered only from such preponderatingly material causes, has appeared excessively material in general character.

Throughout this century of material development, then, New York has lacked some of those advantages which make a true capital intellectually stimulating. Its extraordinary

growth has nevertheless brought into being there something
more like metropolitan life than has yet existed elsewhere in
America.   Any one whose memory of New York extends
back for thirty years can personally recall changes there which
prove by no means superficial.

The New York of the '60's was little changed from
that of 1857; you felt there traces of old local character
quite as marked as you would feel to-day in Boston or
Philadelphia.   How the New York of to-day might present
itself to a European, one can hardly say.   To any American
the change has become something more than the growth of
the old Dutch and English town into that endless extent of
towering commercial buildings, of palaces, and of slums,
which now begins to count its population by the million.
What the visitor from New England most feels in modern
New York is its metropolitan character.   In many aspects,
of course, the city remains American; in many others it
seems chiefly a great centre of world-life.   Nowhere before
on this continent have human beings and human energy so
concentrated; never before has life become so little local, so
broadly general.   With all its differences from the great cities
of the old world, you begin to feel that to-day it has more
in common with London and Paris, with Vienna and Berlin,
with old Rome and Babylon, and all the rest, than with
ancestral America.

Very material this development, of course; and from the
accident that New York is not a true capital, its materialism
has been more and more emphasised.   On such a scale as this
however, material development cannot help involving intellectual activity.   In world-centres life becomes more and more
strenuous.   The problems before individuals grow more complicated, the rewards larger.   The scale of everything in-
creases.   If you have things to sell, there you can find most
buyers; if you would buy things, there you can find most who
have things to sell.   So if as an artist you have things that

you would impart to other men, there you can surely find the greatest number of men to whom they may be imparted. If by chance what you do in such a place is worth doing, its effect will be wider and greater than anything done amid the smaller, less disturbing influences of isolation. While New York has been developing its material prosperity, then, it has also been developing higher life. From the moment when the Renaissance of New England began to decline, New York has more and more certainly been growing into the intellectual and artistic centre of America.

For many years our principal publishers have been centred there; so have the periodicals which are most generally read throughout the country. There is "Harper's Magazine," which dates from 1850; "Harper's Weekly," which dates from 1857; the "Century Magazine," founded as "Scribner's Monthly" in 1870, and translated to its present name in 1881; "Scribner's Magazine," founded in 1887; and more. Some twenty years ago the old "North American Review" was bought by New York people and its title transferred there to a periodical of less staid character than the conventional old quarterly so dear to New England tradition. In New York, too, there has been published since 1865 the only American weekly paper which seriously discusses public and literary affairs, "The Nation;" and there are comic weeklies as well, — "Puck" and "Life," and more. The list might go on endlessly; but for our purposes this is enough. The extent of literary activity involved in such production is incalculably greater than New England ever dreamed of.

All the same, this activity has been distinguished from the literary activity of renascent New England in two rather marked ways. The first is that, in spite of its magnitude, it is less conspicuous in New York than the old "North American Review" or even the "Dial," and still more than the earlier volumes of the "Atlantic Monthly" were in their contemporary Boston. As one looks back at Boston between 1800 and

1864, one inclines to feel that its intellectual life was rather more important than its material, and that even on the spot this intellectual importance was appreciated. In New York, however important our contemporary literary expression, material activity is more important still. The second way in which literary New York may be distinguished from our elder literary Boston results from the first; it was typified by an incident at a New York dinner-party eight or ten years ago. A Bostonian, in some small degree a man of letters, was invited to meet a company of literary New Yorkers. In the course of conversation one of the company happened casually to mention that he was in editorial charge of a well-known magazine. The visitor from New England laughingly confessed that he had no idea that his neighbour held so distinguished an office. This provincial ignorance so amused the company that they proceeded to ask their visitor to name the editors of the familiar periodicals on which we have already touched, — " Harper's Magazine," " Harper's Weekly," the " Century Magazine," " Scribner's Magazine," and the rest. The Bostonian, who knew all these publications perfectly well, had never known who conducted any of them. The only New York editorial fact about which he was certain was that Mr. Godkin had something to do with the " Nation." Though such ignorance was by no means to the credit of the Bostonian, it clearly indicates a truth concerning contemporary letters in New York. To a degree previously unprecedented in America, they have become impersonal. You know the names of publishers, you know the names of magazines, but in general you have misty notions of who is writing.

Yet New York has not lacked literary worthies. At various times, for example, while considering the literature of New England, we have had occasion to notice Horace Greeley, the founder of the " New York Tribune." Not precisely a man of letters, unless within the range of letters you include regular journalism, Greeley had marked influence on literature in New

York. A country boy from New Hampshire, a printer by trade, he arrived there, carrying all his worldly goods in a bundle, during the month of August, 1831. After various journalistic experiments, he established the " Tribune " just ten years later; from that time on he was more and more recognised as a remarkably individual journalist. He was a somewhat grotesque combination of simplicity and shrewdness, thoroughly honest and sincerely devoted to all manner of reform. Naturally, then, he warmly sympathised with many of the New England men at whom we have glanced. At one time or another he invited their co-operation with the " Tribune; " his influence brought to New York a number of memorable literary people. Charles Anderson Dana passed by way of the " Tribune " from Brook Farm to the " New York Sun ; " and George William Curtis wrote long for the " Tribune " before he finally became associated with the periodicals of the Harpers. For a year or two Margaret Fuller was in charge of the "Tribune's" literary criticism; she was followed by George Ripley, who continued the work all his life. Nor did the " Tribune " draw its literary strength only from New England. Henry Jarvis Raymond, founder of the New York " Times," was previously an assistant editor of the elder newspaper. The list of familiar names might extend indefinitely. However long or short, it would certainly include the name of Bayard Taylor, whose career fairly represents the condition of New York letters during the period now under consideration.

Bayard Taylor was a Pennsylvanian, born of Quaker parentage in 1825. He had only a common-school education, but he loved literature, and by the time he was sixteen years old he was publishing poems in local newspapers. At nineteen he had attracted the attention of Mr. Griswold, whose " Poets of America " and the like were once the chief American anthologies ; and, besides, he had been associated with Greeley in one of the journalistic ventures which preceded the successful " Tribune." So, in 1844, Taylor brought out a volume of poems; and in the same year he was commissioned by the " Tribune " to go abroad and write home letters of travel. He spent two years in strolling through Europe on foot. The records of this journey began those books of travel which he continued publishing for thirty years. Meanwhile he gave lectures, wrote for the " Tribune," brought out many volumes of poems and novels, and in 1871 published a translation of Goethe's " Faust " in the original metres. An elaborate life of Goethe, which he had planned, was fatally prevented. Appointed Minister to Germany by President Hayes, he died soon after his arrival at Berlin, in December, 1878.

Early in middle life Bayard Taylor had unquestionably attained such literary eminence as is involved in having one's name generally known. The limits of this eminence, however, appeared even while he was alive; if you asked people what he had written, the chances were that they could not tell. He was a traveller, of course, and they either artlessly admired the fact that he had visited almost every accessible country, or else recalled the unkind epigram that Bayard Taylor had travelled more and seen less than anybody else on earth. This ill-natured criticism had the sting of partial truth. Taylor's accounts of his journeyings are just about as instructive and amusing as those lectures illustrated by stereopticon views which have supplanted the earlier traditions of Yankee Lyceums. He was enthusiastic and untiring, but he was not a keen observer. Flourishing rather before the days of guide-books, he saw perceptibly less than he would have seen if in possession of a modern Baedeker, and he remarked nothing whatever to which Baedeker would not have called his starred attention. He preserved, however, an enthusiastic simplicity of unspoiled feeling which proved very sympathetic to the middle classes of America. So his books of travel stimulated sluggish, untrained imaginations, and at worst only bored people of more gifts or training.

These were his best-known writings. To him, however, they probably appeared little better than hackwork, — things

which he was compelled to manufacture for self-support.
His ambition was to make a great poem. In view of this
there is something pathetic in the list of forgotten titles which
he has left us : " Ximena," his first volume, was published in
1841 ; and after 1870, during the last six years of his busy
life, he produced the " Masque of the Gods," and " Lars," and
the " Prophet," and the " National Ode," and " Prince
Deukalion." Here is a passage from the opening scene of
that dreary drama, where an awakening shepherd hears a chorus
of nymphs interrupted by underground voices : —

" NYMPHS.
" We wait in the breezes,
We hide in the vapours,
And linger in echoes,
Awaiting recall.

" VOICES.
" The word is spoken, let the judgment fall!

" NYMPHS.
" The heart of the lover,
The strings of the psalter,
The shapes in the marble
Our passing deplore.

" VOICES.
" Truth comes, and vanity shall be no more !

" NYMPHS.
" Not wholly we vanish;
The souls of the children,
The faith of the poets
Shall seek us, and find.

" VOICES.
" Dead are the things the world has left behind.

" NYMPHS.
" Lost beauty shall haunt you
With tender remorses;
And out of its exile
The passion return.

" VOICES.
" The flame shall purify, the fire shall burn !

From boyhood Taylor had travelled, and had written, and had read poetry, and had tried to be a poet; and he certainly made something which looks poetic. As surely, however, as his verse never touched the popular heart, so his supreme literary effort never much appealed to those who seriously love poetry.

His most meritorious work, in fact, is his translation of " Faust." He put before himself the task of reproducing the original metres, and so far as possible the original rhymes of that extremely complex poem. The result in nowise resembles normal English; but he never undertook to turn " Faust " into an English poem; his object was rather to reproduce in English words the effect made upon his mind by prolonged, sympathetic, enthusiastic study of the German masterpiece. Whatever the positive value of his translation, he achieved one rare practical result. By simply comparing his work with Goethe's original, persons who know very little German can feel the power and beauty of Goethe's style, as well as of his meaning. If in years to come Taylor's memory survives, then, it will probably be for this achievement in which he made no attempt at originality. His career was honourable, but not brilliant, nor yet distinguished in the sense in which we found so our elder literature.

Another man who flourished in New York at about the same time, and lived there all his life, was Mr. Richard Grant White. After trying the pulpit, medicine, and the bar in turn, he settled down, before he was twenty-five years old, as a professional critic. His experience and training were mostly journalistic; for fourteen years he was connected with a New York paper called the " Courier and Inquirer." With little other equipment he attempted two kinds of work which for excellence require severe scholarship. He produced an edition of Shakspere; and he published two or three books on the English language. As editor and philologist, Mr. White was intelligent, clever, and eccentrically dogmatic. His quasi-scholarly writings are always interesting, and never quite authoritative. In the New York where he flourished, however, he enjoyed the reputation of a ripe scholar. He had a fondness meanwhile for anonymous writing; so for some time he was not recognised as the author of what now appears to be his most remarkable work. This was the "New Gospel of Peace," a satire made during the most critical period of the Civil War. In burlesque scriptural style, it attacked that school of Northern political thought, popularly called Copperhead, which denied the constitutional right of the Federal Government to maintain the Union by force. The satire, which still seems powerful, is said to have converted waverers. In all this there is something characteristic of the confused New York we now have in mind. A clever and versatile critical journalist, who sincerely and ardently assumed the authority of a professionally trained scholar, came nearest to success in an irreverent political satire. Mr. White died in 1885.

Another conspicuous figure in New York literature, equally different from Taylor and from White, was Dr. Josiah Gilbert Holland. He was born in 1819 in western Massachusetts. He took his medical degree at a small college in Pittsfield; he was a contributor to the "Knickerbocker Magazine;" he was for a time Superintendent of Public Schools in Missouri; and in 1849 he became editor of the "Springfield Republican" in Massachusetts. With this paper he retained his connection for seventeen years, at the end of which, partly through his shrewd agency, the "Springfield Republican" had become probably the most influential American newspaper published outside of New York. In 1870 he became editor of "Scribner's Monthly," which later took the name of the "Century," and of which he remained in charge until his death in 1888. Dr. Holland was not only a respectable and successful journalist, but a welcome lecturer on various social topics, and the writer of numerous books. Among these were a popular

"Life of Lincoln," published in 1865, and three or four novels which had considerable success. His most characteristic writings, however, were didactic essays, the most successful of which were the series entitled "Timothy Titcomb's Letters to Young People." Others were called "Lessons in Life," "Letters to the Joneses," and "Plain Talks on Familiar Subjects."

Here is a stray passage from this last : —

"I account the loss of a man's life and individuality, through the non-adaptation or the mal-adaptation of his powers to his pursuits, the greatest calamity, next to the loss of personal virtue, that he can suffer in this world. I believe that a full moiety of the trials and disappointments that darken a world which, I am sure, was intended to be measurably bright and happy, are traceable to this prolific source. Men are not in their places. Women are not in their places. John is doing badly the work that William would do well, and William is doing badly the work that John would do well; and both are disappointed and unhappy, and self-unmade. It is quite possible that John is doing Mary's work and Mary is doing John's work.

"'Of all sad words of tongue or pen,
  The saddest are these: "it might have been."'

"Now, I do not suppose that we shall ever get the world all right on this matter. I do not suppose that all men will find the places for which they were designed, or that, in many instances, Maud will marry the Judge; but an improvement can be made; and if an improvement ever shall be made, it will be through the inculcation of sounder views among the young."

The reverent way in which he quotes the very worst rhyme in which Whittier ever imbedded a commonplace, and then alludes to Maud Muller and her Judge as if they were equally immortal with the Bible, typifies that sort of commonplace which made Dr. Holland dear to less cultivated people. It is saved from indignity by its apparent unconsciousness of limitation. A similar quality pervaded his verse, some of which is preserved by Stedman and Hutchinson. His honesty, his kindness, and his sound moral sense endeared him to the general public, and in their own way did much to strengthen the homely principles of our level country. He sold thousands of volumes, he lived honourably, and he died respected.

Another writer, somewhat similar in general character, but less versatile, was the Reverend Edward Payson Roe, born in New York State in 1838, for a while a student at Williams College, a volunteer chaplain during the Civil War, and afterwards a Presbyterian minister at Highland Falls, New York. In 1872 he published a novel called " Barriers Burned Away " which proved so successful that he gave up the ministry, and settling down in a small town on the Hudson River produced a steady stream of novels until his death in 1888. Whitcomb's " Chronological Outlines of American Literature" record the titles of nineteen of them. They are said to have had extraordinary popular success. They did nobody any harm; and their general literary quality and power of doing good already seem inconsiderable.

There have been many other writers in New York meanwhile, but few of much eminence who are not still alive. Of one, who died not long ago, the promise seemed more than usual. Henry Cuyler Bunner, for years editor of " Puck," was so busy a journalist that only persistent effort allowed him time for any but his regular work. The verses and the stories which he has left us, then, are only a fragment of what might have been, had he had more leisure, or had he been spared beyond the early middle life when unhappily his career ended. Throughout this apparently ephemeral work, however, there is a touch so sympathetic, so sensitive, so winning, that there seems a peculiar fitness in his enduring monument. The chief literary prize at Columbia College, the chief seat of learning in his native city, is one lately founded in his memory.

Of all these writers, and of the scores more who wrote at the same time, and most of whom are writing to-day, the volumes of Stedman and Hutchinson will give some impres-

sion. In former times Griswold and Duyckinck made similar collections of literature in American. As we have seen,
both alike properly included many names for which Stedman
and Hutchinson have found no room. It is hard to resist
the conclusion that whoever shall make a new library of
American literature, thirty or forty years hence, will by the
same token find no place for many of our contemporaries momentarily preserved by our latest anthologists. As you turn
their pages, you can hardly avoid feeling that, however valuable these may be as history, they contain little which merits
permanence.

Depressing as this may at first seem to patriotic spirit, it
has another aspect. As we look back on the literary records
of New England, we can perceive in its local history a trait
like one which has marked those more fortunate regions of
the old world whose expression has proved lasting. Artistic
expression is apt to be the final fruit of a society about to
wither. For generations, or perhaps for centuries, traditions
grow until they reach a form which locally distinguishes the
spot which has developed them from any other in the world.
Then, at moments of change, there sometimes arises, in a race
about to pass from the living, a mysterious impulse to make
plastic or written records of what the past has meant. These
are what render even Greece and Italy and Elizabethan England more than mere names. So one gradually grows to feel
that only the passing of old New England made its literature
possible. The great material prosperity of New York, meanwhile, has attracted thither during the past forty years countless numbers of energetic people from all over the world, —
foreigners, New Englanders, Westerners, Southerners, and
whomever else. In this immigrant invasion the old New York
of Irving and Cooper and the rest has been swallowed up.
There is now hardly a city in the world where you are so
little apt to meet people whose families have lived there for
three successive generations. Our new metropolis, in fact, is

not only far from such a stage of decline as should mark the beginning of its passage from life to history, but it has not even formed the tangible traditions which may by and by define its spiritual character.

What its features may finally be, then, we may only guess. On the whole, one inclines to guess hopefully. Beneath its bewildering material activity there is a greater vitality, a greater alertness, and in some aspects a greater wholesomeness, of intelligence than one is apt to find elsewhere. It is not that the artists and the men of letters who live there have done work which even on our American scale may be called great. It is not that these men, or men who shall soon follow them, may be expected to make lasting monuments. It is rather that about them surges, with all its fluctuating good and evil, the irresistible tide of world-existence. The great wealth of New York and its colossal material power, of course, involve a social complexity, and at least a superficial corruption, greater than America has hitherto known ; and the men who live amid this bustling turmoil are habitually in contact with base things. Yet hundreds of them, sound at heart, think and speak with a buoyant courage which, even to a New Englander, seems almost youthfully to preserve that fresh simplicity of heart so characteristic of our ancestrally inexperienced America. You may shake your head at them, or smile, as much as you will ; they impart to you, despite yourself, a mood of inexplicably brighter hopefulness than their words, or the facts which those words set forth, seem to justify.

So, very generally, we may say that our Middle States, as they used to be called, are now dominated by New York. This town, whose domination for the moment is not only local but almost national, owes its predominance to that outburst of material force which throughout the victorious North followed the period of the Civil War. What may come of it no one can tell. Of the past and the present there is little to remark beyond what we have remarked already. There is, however, one exception. The Middle States, and to a great degree the city of New York itself, have produced just one eccentric literary figure, who has emerged into an isolation which is sometimes believed eminent. This is Walt Whitman.

II

WALT WHITMAN

WALT WHITMAN was older than one is apt to remember.
He was born on Long Island in 1819, and he died in 1892.
His life, then, was almost exactly contemporary with Lowell's.
No two lives could have been much more different in condition.
Lowell, the son of a minister, closely related to the best people
of New England, lived all his life amid the gentlest academic
and social influences in America. Whitman was the son of a
carpenter and builder on the outskirts of Brooklyn; the only
New England man of letters equally humble in origin was
Whittier.

The contrast between Whitman and Whittier, however, is
almost as marked as that between Whitman and Lowell.
Whittier, the child of Quaker farmers in the Yankee country,
grew up and lived almost all his life amid guileless influences.
Whitman, born of the artisan class in a region close to the
most considerable and corrupt centre of population on his
native continent, had a rather vagrant youth and manhood. At
times he was a printer, at times a school-master, at times
editor of stray country newspapers, and by and by he took up
his father's trade of carpenter and builder, erecting a number
of small houses in his unlovely native region. Meanwhile he
had rambled about the country and into Canada, in much the
temper of those wanderers whom we now call tramps; but
in general until past thirty years old, he was apt to be within
scent of the East River. The New York of which his erratic habits thus made the lower aspects so familiar to him
was passing, in the last days of the Knickerbocker School, into

its metropolitan existence. The first edition of Whitman's " Leaves of Grass " appeared in 1855, the year which produced the " Knickerbocker Gallery."

During the Civil War he served devotedly as an army nurse. After the war, until 1873, he held some small government clerkships at Washington. In 1873 a paralytic stroke brought his active life to an end ; for his last twenty years he lived an invalid at a little house in Camden, New Jersey.

Until 1855, when the first edition of " Leaves of Grass " appeared in a thin folio, some of which he set up with his own hands, Whitman had not declared himself as a man of letters. From that time to the end he was constantly publishing his eccentric poetry, which from time to time he collected in increasing bulk under the old title. He published, too, some stray volumes of prose, — " Democratic Vistas," and the like. Prose and poetry alike seem permeated with a conviction that he had a mission to express and to extend the spirit of democracy, which he believed characteristic of his country. To himself, then, he seemed the inspired prophet of an America which he asserted to be above all things else the land of the people ; few men have ever cherished a purpose more literally popular. His fate has been ironic. Though even in his lifetime he became conspicuous, it is doubtful whether any man of letters in his country ever appealed less to the masses. He was a prophet of democracy, if you like ; but the public to which his prophecy made its way was at once limited, fastidiously overcultivated, and apt to be of foreign birth.

Beyond question Whitman had remarkable individuality and power. Equally beyond question he was among the most eccentric individuals who ever put pen to paper. The natural result of this has been that his admirers have admired him intensely ; while whoever has found his work repellent has found it irritating. Particularly abroad, however, he has attracted much critical attention ; and many critics have been disposed to maintain that his amorphous prophecies of democracy are deeply characteristic of America. The United States, they point out, are professedly the most democratic country in the world; Whitman is professedly the most democratic of American writers; consequently he must be the most typical.

The abstract ideal of democracy has never been better summed up than in the well-known watchwords of republican France : Liberty, Equality, Fraternity. Disguised and distorted though these words may have been by a century of French Revolutionary excess, there is no denying that they stand for ideals essentially noble and inspiring. What is more, these ideals, which everywhere underlie the revolutionary spirit, have consciously influenced the nineteenth century on both sides of the Atlantic. In the progress of American democracy, however, one of these ideals has been more strenuously kept in mind than the other two. American democracy did not spring from abstract philosophising; it had its origin in the old conceptions of liberty and rights as maintained by the Common Law of England. Though no commonplace, then, has been more familiar to American ears than the glittering generality which maintains all men to be born equal, the practical enthusiasm of American democracy has been chiefly excited by the ideal of liberty. The theoretical democracy of Europe, on the other hand, has tended rather to emphasise the ideal of fraternity, which seems incidentally to include a sound thrashing for any brother who fails to feel fraternal; and still more this European democracy has tended increasingly to emphasise the dogma of human equality. Though this doubtless beautiful ideal eloquently appeals to many generous natures, it seems hardly to accord with the teachings either of natural law or of any recorded experience. Nothing, it maintains, ought really to be held intrinsically better than anything else. In plain words, the ideal of equality, carried to its extreme, asserts all superiority, all excellence, to be a phase of evil.

Now, Walt Whitman's gospel of democracy certainly included liberty and laid strong emphasis on fraternity. He liked to hail his fellow-citizens by the wild, queer name of "camerados," which, for some obscure reason of his own, he preferred to "comrades." The ideal which most appealed to him, however, was that of equality. Though he would hardly have assented to such orthodox terms, his creed seems to have been that, as God made everything, one thing is just as good as another. There are aspects in which such a proposition seems analogous to one which should maintain a bronze cent to be every whit as good as a gold eagle because both are issued by the same government from the same mint. At best, however, analogies are misleading arguments ; and people who share Whitman's ideal are apt to disregard as superstitious any argument, however impressive, which should threaten to modify their faith in equality. It is a superstition, they would maintain, that some ways of doing things are decent and some not; one way is really just as good as another. It is a superstition that kings, nobles, and gentlemen are in any aspect lovelier than the mob. It is a superstition that men of learning are intellectually better than the untutored. It is a superstition which would hold a man who can make a chair unable consequently to make a constitution. It is a superstition that virtuous women are inherently better than street-walkers. It is a superstition that law is better than anarchy. There are things, to be sure, which are not superstitions. Evil and baseness and ugliness are real facts, to be supremely denounced and hated ; and incidentally, we must admit, few arraignments of the vulgarity and materialism which have developed in the United States are more pitiless than those which appear in Whitman's "Democratic Vistas." The cause of these hurtful things, however, he is satisfied to find in the traces of our ancestral and superstitious devotion to outworn ideals of excellence. We can all find salvation in the new, life-saving ideal of equality. Let America accept this ideal, and these faults will vanish into that limbo of the past to which he would gladly consign all superstitions. Among these, he logically, though reluctantly, includes a great part of the poetry of Shakspere; for Shakspere, undoubtedly a poet, was a poet of inequality, who represented the people as a mob. For all his genius, then, Shakspere was an apostle of the devil, another lying prophet of the superstition of excellence.

Even though excellence be a wicked and tyrannical ideal, however, democratic prophecy does not forbid the whole world equally to improve. Equalisation need not mean the reducing of all that is admirable to the level of what is base. It may just as well mean the raising of much that is base towards the height of what is admirable. The superstition which has worked most sordid evil is that which denies human equality. Retract the denial, then; let human beings be equal, and the force which has most distorted mankind shall cease working. Then all alike may finally rise, side by side, into an equality superior to what has gone before. The prophets of equality are so stirred by dreams of the future that they half forget the horrors of present or past; and among prophets of equality Walt Whitman has the paradoxical merit of eminence.

Now, this dogma of equality clearly involves a trait which has not yet been generally characteristic of American thought or letters, — a complete confusion of values. In the early days of Renaissance in New England, to be sure, Emerson and the rest, dazzled by the splendours of that new world of art and literature which was at last thrown open, made small distinction between those aspects of it which are excellent and those which are only stimulating. At the same time they adhered as firmly as the Puritans themselves to the ideal of excellence; and among the things with which they were really familiar they pretty shrewdly distinguished those which were most valuable, either on earth or in heaven. With Walt Whitman, on the other hand, everything is confused.

Take, for example, a passage from his "Song of Myself," which contains some of his best-known phrases: —

" A child said *What is the grass?* fetching it to me with full hands;
　How could I answer the child? I do not know what it is any more
　　than he.

" I guess it must be the flag of my disposition, out of hopeful green
　　stuff woven.

" Or I guess it is the handkerchief of the Lord,
　A scented gift and remembrancer designedly dropt,
　Bearing the owner's name someway in the corners, that we may see
　　and remark, and say *Whose?*

" Or I guess the grass is itself a child, the produced babe of vegetation.

" Or I guess it is a uniform hieroglyphic,
　And it means, Sprouting alike in broad zones and narrow zones.
　Growing among black folds as among white,
　Kanuck, Tuckahoe, Congressman, Cuff, I give them the same, I
　　receive them the same.

" And now it seems to me the beautiful uncut hair of graves.

" Tenderly will I use you, curling grass,
　It may be you transpire from the breasts of young men,
　It may be if I had known them I would have loved them,
　It may be you are from old people, or from offspring taken soon out
　　of their mothers' laps,
　And here you are the mothers' laps.

" The grass is very dark to be from the white heads of old mothers,
　Darker than the colourless beards of old men,
　Dark to come from under the faint red roofs of mouths.

" O I perceive after all so many uttering tongues,
　And I perceive they do not come from the roofs of mouths for
　　nothing.

" I wish I could translate the hints about the dead young men and
　　women,
　And the hints about the old men and mothers, and the offspring
　　taken soon out of their laps.

" What do you think has become of the young and old men?
　And what do you think has become of the women and children?

" They are alive and well somewhere,
　The smallest sprout shows there is really no death,
　And if ever there was it had forward life, and does not wait at the
　　end to arrest it,
　And ceas'd the moment life appear'd.

> " All goes onward and outward, nothing collapses,
> And to die is different from what any one supposed, and luckier."

Here is perhaps his best-known phrase, " the beautiful uncut hair of graves." Here are other good phrases, like " the faint red roofs of mouths." Here, too, is undoubtedly tender feeling. Here, into the bargain, is such rubbish as " I guess it is the handkerchief of the Lord," — who incidentally uses perfumery, — and such jargon as " Kanuck, Tuckahoe, Congressman, Cuff." In an inextricable hodge-podge you find at once beautiful phrases and silly gabble, tender imagination and insolent commonplace, — pretty much everything, in short, but humour. In America this literary anarchy, this complete confusion of values, is especially eccentric; for America has generally displayed instinctive common-sense, and common-sense implies some notion of what things are worth. One begins to see why Whitman has been so much more eagerly welcomed abroad than at home. His conception of equality, utterly ignoring values, is not that of American democracy, but rather that of European. His democracy, in short, is the least native which has ever found voice in his country. The saving grace of American democracy has been a tacit recognition that excellence is admirable.

In temper, then, Walt Whitman seems less American than any other of our conspicuous writers. It does not follow that in some aspects he is not very American indeed. Almost as certainly as Hawthorne, though very differently, he had the true artistic temperament; life moved him to moods which could find relief only in expression. Such a temperament would have expressed itself anywhere; and Whitman's would probably have found the most congenial material for expression in those European regions which have been most disturbed by French Revolutionary excess. He chanced, however, to be born, and to attain the maturity which he awaited before he began to publish, in unmingled American surroundings. As obviously as Hawthorne's experience was confined to New England,

Whitman's was confined to that of the lower classes in those regions which were developing into modern New York.

Whoever remembers the growth of this region will remember what sometimes seemed the ugliest thing to the eye, the most overwhelmingly oppressive to any instinct of taste, the most sordidly hopeless atmosphere possible to human experience. Now, Whitman, we remember, came to his maturity within scent of the East River; and certainly the East River, separating New York and Brooklyn, was at that time the spot of spots where life seemed most material, most grindingly distant from ideal beauty. Yet the contemplation of this very East River evoked from Whitman the poem which sometimes seems his most nearly beautiful. Here is the last stanza of this " Crossing Brooklyn Ferry " : —

" Flow on, river! flow with the flood-tide, and ebb with the ebb-tide!
Frolic on, crested and scallop-edg'd waves!
Gorgeous clouds of the sunset! drench with your splendour me, or
the men and women generations after me!
Cross from shore to shore, countless crowds of passengers!
Stand up, tall masts of Mannahatta! stand up, beautiful hills of
Brooklyn!
Throb, baffled and curious brain! throw out questions and answers!
Suspend here and everywhere, eternal float of solution!
Gaze, loving and thirsting eyes, in the house or street or public
assembly!
Sound out, voices of young men! loudly and musically call me by
my nighest name!
Live, old life! play the part that looks back on the actor or actress!
Play the old rôle, the rôle that is great or small according as one
makes it!
Consider, you who peruse me, whether I may not in unknown ways
be looking upon you;
Be firm, rail over the river, to support those who lean idly, yet haste
with the hasting current;
Fly on, sea-birds! fly sideways, or wheel in large circles high in the
air;
Receive the summer sky, you water, and faithfully hold it till all the
downcast eyes have time to take it from you!
Diverge, fine spokes of light, from the shape of my head, or anyone's
head, in the sunlit water!

Come on, ships from the lower bay! pass up or down, white-sail'd
  schooners, sloops, lighters!
Flaunt away, flags of all nations! be duly lowered at sunset!
Burn high your fires, foundry chimneys! cast black shadows at
  nightfall! cast red and yellow light over the tops of the houses!
Appearances, now or henceforth, indicate what you are;
You necessary film, continue to envelope the soul,
About my body for me, and your body for you, be hung our divinest
  aromas,
Thrive cities, — bring your freight, bring your shows, ample and
  sufficient rivers,
Expand, being than which none else is perhaps more spiritual,
Keep your places, objects than which none else is more lasting.

" You have waited, you always wait, you dumb, beautiful ministers,
  We receive you with free sense at last, and are insatiate hence-
    forward,
Not you any more shall be able to foil us, or withhold yourselves
  from us,
We use you and do not cast you aside — we plant you permanently
  within us,
We fathom you not — we love you — there is perfection in you also,
You furnish your parts toward eternity,
Great or small you furnish your parts toward the soul."

The eight preceding stanzas are very like this, — confused,
inarticulate, and surging in a mad kind of rhythm which
sounds as if hexameters were trying to bubble through sewage.
For all these faults, Whitman has here accomplished a wonder.
Despite his eccentric insolence both of phrase and of temper
you feel that in a region where another eye would have seen
only unspeakable vileness, he has found impulses which prove
it, like every other region on earth, a fragment of the divine
eternities. The glories and beauties of the universe are really
perceptible everywhere; and into what seemed utterly sordid
Whitman has breathed ennobling imaginative fervour. Cultured and academic folk are disposed to shrink from what they
call base, to ignore it, to sneer at it; looking closer, Whitman
tells us that even amid base things you cannot wander so far
as to lose sight of the heavens, with all their fountains of
glorious emotion.

But what is this emotion? Just here Whitman seems to stop. With singular vividness, and with the unstinted sympathy of his fervent faith in equality, he tells what he sees. Though often his jargon is amorphously meaningless, his words are now and again so apt as to approach that inevitable union of thought and phrase which makes lasting poetry. When he has reported what he sees, however, utterly confusing its values, he has nothing more to say about it. At most he leaves you with a sense of new realities concerning which you must do your thinking for yourself.

Sometimes, of course, he was more articulate. The Civil War stirred him to his depths; and he drew of its byways such little pictures as " Ethiopia Saluting the Colours " : —

"Who are you dusky woman, so ancient, hardly human,
    With your wooly-white and turban'd head, and bare bony feet?
    Why rising by the roadside here, do you the colours greet?

" ('T is while our army lines Carolina's sands and pines,
    Forth from thy hovel door thou Ethiopia com'st to me,
    As under doughty Sherman I march toward the sea.)

" *Me master years a hundred since from my parents sunder'd,*
    A little child, they caught me as the savage beast is caught,
    Then hither me across the sea the cruel slaver brought.

" No further does she say, but lingering all the day,
    Her high-borne turban'd head she wags, and rolls her darkling eye
    And courtesies to the regiments, the guidons moving by.

" What is it fateful woman, so blear, hardly human?
    Why wag your head with turban bound, yellow, red and green?
    Are the things so strange and marvellous you see or have seen?"

In Lincoln he found his ideal hero; and his verse on Lincoln's death is probably his best : —

" O Captain! my Captain! our fearful trip is done,
    The ship has weathered every rack, the prize we sought is won,
    The port is near, the bells I hear, the people all exulting,
    While follow eyes the steady keel, the vessel grim and daring;

But O heart! heart! heart!
 O the bleeding drops of red,
  Where on the deck my Captain lies,
   Fallen cold and dead.

" O Captain! my Captain! rise up and hear the bells;
 Rise up — for you the flag is flung — for you the bugle trills,
For you bouquets and ribbon'd wreaths — for you the shores a-
  crowding,
For you they call, the swaying mass, their eager faces turning;
  Here Captain! dear father!
   This arm beneath your head!
    It is some dream that on the deck,
     You 've fallen cold and dead.

" My Captain does not answer, his lips are pale and still,
My father does not feel my arm, he has no pulse nor will,
The ship is anchored safe and sound, its voyage closed and done,
From fearful trip the victor ship comes in with object won;
  Exult O shores, and ring O bells!
   But I with mournful tread,
    Walk the deck my Captain lies,
     Fallen cold and dead."

Even in bits like this, however, which come so much
nearer form than is usual with Whitman, one feels his perverse rudeness of style. Such eccentricity of manner is bound
to affect different tempers in different ways. One kind of
reader, naturally eager for individuality and fresh glimpses of
truth, is disposed to identify oddity and originality. Another
kind of reader distrusts literary eccentricity as instinctively as
polite people distrust bad manners. In both of these instinctive reactions from such a method of address as Whitman's
there is an element of truth. Beyond doubt, eccentric masters of the fine arts give rise to perverse eccentricity in imita-
tors. Browning and Carlyle, to go no further, have bred in
brains feebler than their own much nonsensical spawn; and
so has Walt Whitman. But some artists of great power
prove naturally unable to express themselves properly. Their
trouble is like a muscular distortion which should compel
lameness, or a vocal malformation which should make utter-

ance hoarse or shrill. So there have been great men, and there will be more, whom fate compels either to express themselves uncouthly or else to stay dumb. Such a man, great or not, Whitman seems to have been. Such men, greater than he, were Carlyle and Browning. The critical temper which would hold them perverse, instead of unfortunate, is mistaken.

On the other hand, that different critical temper which would welcome their perversities as newly revealed evidences of genius is quite as mistaken in another way. If any general law may be inferred from the history of fine arts, it is that any persistent school of expression must be articulate. In any art, of course, vital expression must be spontaneous; academic training, dogmatic routine, has never originated much that is worth while. The nobler works of art, however, which have maintained themselves as permanent parts of the great structure of human expression, have form. Their lasting vitality comes partly from the fact that their makers have spontaneously obeyed natural laws which may be generalised into academic principles. The development of human expression seems like the growth of a tree. The same vital force which sends the trunk heavenward, puts forth branches, and from these in turn sends forth twigs and leaves; but the further they stray from the root, the weaker they prove. The trunk lives, and the greater branches; year by year, the lesser twigs and leaves wither. Now, eccentricity of manner, however unavoidable, is apt to indicate that art has strayed dangerously far from its vital origin. Oddity is no part of solid artistic development; however beautiful or impressive, it is rather an excrescent outgrowth, bound to prove abortive, and at the same time to sap life from a parent stock which without it might grow more loftily and strongly.

Walt Whitman's style is of this excrescent, abortive kind. Like Carlyle's or Browning's, it is something which nobody else can imitate with impunity; and so, like theirs, it is a style which in the history of literature suggests a familiar phase of

decline. That it was inevitable you will feel if you compare
" Ethiopia Saluting the Colours " or " My Captain " with the
unchecked perversities of Whitman's verse in general. The
" Song of Myself," or " Crossing Brooklyn Ferry," which we
may take as generally representative of his work, are so recklessly misshapen that you cannot tell whether their author was
able to write with amenity. When you find him, however, as
in those lesser pieces, attempting technical form, you at once
feel that his eccentricity is a misfortune, for which he is no
more to blame than a lame man for limping, or a deaf and
dumb for expressing emotion by inarticulate cries. The alter-
native would have been silence ; and Whitman was enough
of a man to make one glad that he never dreamed of it.

In this decadent eccentricity of Whitman's style there is
again something foreign to the spirit of this country. American men of letters have generally had deep artistic conscience.
This trait has resulted, for one thing, in making the short
story, an essentially organic form of composition, as characteristic of American literature as the straggling, inorganic three-
volume novel is of English. Now and again, to be sure,
American men of letters have chosen to express themselves
in quite another manner. They have tried to reproduce the
native dialects of the American people. This impulse has
resulted in at least one masterpiece, that amazing Odyssey of
the Mississippi to which Mark Twain gave the fantastic name
of " Huckleberry Finn." As we remarked of the " Biglow
Papers," however, this " dialect " literature of America often
proves on analysis more elaborately studied than orthodox
work by the same writers. Neither the " Biglow Papers "
nor " Huckleberry Finn " could have been produced without
an artistic conscience as strenuous as Irving's, or Poe's, or
Hawthorne's. The vagaries of Walt Whitman, on the other
hand, are as far from literary conscience as the animals which
he somewhere celebrates are from unhappiness or respectability. Whitman's style, then, is as little characteristic of

America as his temper is of traditional American democracy. One can see why the decadent taste of modern Europe has welcomed him so much more ardently than he has ever been welcomed at home; in temper and in style he was an exotic member of that sterile brotherhood which eagerly greeted him abroad. In America his oddities were more eccentric than they would have been anywhere else.

On the other hand, there is an aspect in which he seems not only native but even promising. During the years when his observation was keenest, and his temper most alert, he lived in the environment from which our future America seems most likely to spring. He was born and grew up, he worked and lived, where on either side of the East River the old American towns of New York and Brooklyn were developing into the metropolis which is still too young to possess ripe traditions. In full maturity he devoted himself to army nursing, — the least picturesque or glorious, and the most humanely heroic, service which he could have rendered his country during its agony of civil war. In that Civil War the elder America perished; the new America which then arose is not yet mature enough for artistic record. Whitman's earthly experience, then, came throughout in chaotic times, when our past had faded and our future had not yet sprung into being. Bewildering confusion, fused by the accident of his lifetime into the seeming unity of a momentary whole, was the only aspect of human existence which could be afforded him by the native country which he so truly loved. For want of other surroundings he was content to seek the meaning of life amid New York slums and dingy suburban country, in the crossing of Brooklyn Ferry, or in the hospitals which strove to alleviate the drums and tramplings of civil war. His lifelong eagerness to find in life the stuff of which poetry is made has brought him, after all, the reward he would most have cared for. In one aspect he is thoroughly American. The spirit of his work is that of world-old anarchy; its form has all the perverse oddity of world-old abortive decadence; but the substance of which his poems are made — their imagery as distinguished from their form or their spirit — comes wholly from our native country.

In this aspect, then, though probably in no other, he may, after all, throw light on the future of literature in America. As has been said before, "He is uncouth, inarticulate, whatever you please that is least orthodox; yet, after all, he can make you feel for the moment how even the ferry-boats plying from New York to Brooklyn are fragments of God's eternities. Those of us who love the past are far from sharing his confidence in the future. Surely, however, that is no reason for denying the miracle that he has wrought by idealising the East River. The man who has done this is the only one who points out the stuff of which perhaps the new American literature of the future may in time be made."

III

THE Middle States and New England, after certain literary achievements, seem now in a stage either of decline or at best of preparation for some literature of the future. The other parts of the country, at which we have now to glance, will not detain us long. However copious their production, it has not yet afforded us much of permanent value.

Professor Trent, formerly of the University of the South, and now of Columbia, promises a book concerning Southern literature which will be welcome to every American student. Meanwhile, the best authority on the subject is his admirable monograph on William Gilmore Simms, in the American Men of Letters Series. The impression produced by reading this work is confirmed by an interesting manuscript lately prepared by another Southern gentleman. In the winter of 1898, Mr. George Stockton Wills, a graduate both of the University of North Carolina and of Harvard, made an elaborate study of the literature produced in the South before the Civil War. A thoroughly trained student, he brought to light and clearly defined a number of literary figures whose very names have generally been forgotten. The more you consider these figures, however, the more inevitable seems the neglect into which they have fallen. They were simple, sincere, enthusiastic writers, mostly of verse; but their work, even compared only with the less important Northern work of their time, seems surprisingly imitative. Up to the Civil War, the South had produced hardly any writing which expressed more than a pleasant sense that standard models are excellent.

A ripe example of this may be found in Stedman and Hutchinson's "Library of American Literature." The most gifted and accomplished of Southern poets was Sidney Lanier; and among his more impressive poems Stedman and Hutchinson select one entitled "The Revenge of Hamish." Lanier, a native of Georgia, never strayed much farther from his birthplace than Baltimore; yet this "Revenge of Hamish" is a passionate account of how the cruelly abused retainer of a Highland chieftain murders his master's son after fiercely humiliating the father. In other words, the substance of this characteristic production of our most powerful Southern poet comes straight from the romantic mountains brought into literature by Walter Scott. Not a line of the poem suggests that it proceeds from our own Southern States. Unlike the "Revenge of Hamish," itself admirable, the imitative poetry of the South is generally commonplace and conventional.

For this comparative literary lifelessness there is obvious historical reason. The difference between the Southern climate and the Northern has often been dwelt on; so has the difference between the social systems of the two parts of the country. It has often been remarked, too, that the oligarchic system of the South developed powerful politicians. At the time of the Revolution, for example, our most eminent statesmen were from Virginia; and when the Civil War came, though the economic superiority of the North was bound to win, the political ability of the South seemed generally superior. One plain cause of these facts has not been much emphasised.

From the beginning, the North was politically free and essentially democratic; its social distinctions were nothing like so rigid as those which have generally diversified civilised society. There was no mob; the lower class of New England produced Whittier. In a decent Yankee village, to this day, you need not lock your doors at night; and when crime turns up in the North, as it does with increasing frequency, you can still trust the police to attend to it. In the South, at least from the moment when slavery established itself, a totally different state of affairs prevailed.   The African slaves, constantly increasing in number, seemed the most dangerous lower class which had ever faced an English-speaking government.   The agricultural conditions of Southern life meanwhile prevented population from gathering in considerable centres.   As slavery developed, the South accordingly grew to be a region where a comparatively small governing class, the greater part of whom lived separately on large country places, felt themselves compelled, by the risk of servile insurrection, to devote their political energies to the rigid maintenance of established order.   Whether slavery was really so dangerous as people thought may be debatable; there can be no question that people living in such circumstances could hardly help believing it so.   However human, native Africans are still savage; and although, long before the Civil War, the Southern slaves had shown such sensitiveness to comparatively civilised conditions as to have lost their superficial savagery, and indeed as still to warrant, in many hopeful minds, even the franchise which was ultimately granted them, the spectre of darkest Africa loomed behind them all.   Surrounded by an increasing servile population of unalterable aliens, then, in whose increase their fatal social system gave them irresistible interest, the ruling classes of our elder South dreaded political experiment to a degree almost incomprehensible in the North, where the social conditions permitted men of power to neglect politics for private business.   If any phase of the established Southern order were altered, no Southern mind dared guess what might happen; it might be such infernal horrors as had devastated San Domingo.   More and more, then, the ablest men of the South naturally tended to concentrate their energies on politics, and in politics to develop increasingly conservative temper.

The natural result was such as conservatism would produce anywhere. Up to the time of the Civil War a normal Southerner was far less changed from his emigrant ancestor than was any New England Yankee. Compared with what happened in Europe between 1620 and 1860 there was little alteration even in our Northern States; in the South the past lingered even more tenaciously. A Southern trait — familiar because it lends itself so pleasantly to burlesque — is a complacent opinion that Southerners descend from Cavaliers, and Yankees from the socially inferior Roundheads. Though this fact is more than debatable, the Southern belief in it indicates a truth; at least up to the Civil War the personal temper of the better classes in the South remained more like that of the better classes in seventeenth-century England than anything else in the modern world. Concrete examples of this may be found in two or three facts on which we have already touched. When Preston Brooks struck Charles Sumner in the United States Senate, for example, Brooks exhibited traits which neither England nor the Northern States had quite understood since Cromwell's Commonwealth. Again, the ablest legal presentation of the constitutional claims of the Southern Confederacy was the "War between the States," published before 1870 by Mr. Alexander Hamilton Stephens, of Georgia. Mr. Stephens was an accomplished lawyer, a statesman, and a gentleman. Until the moment of secession he endeavoured to preserve the Union on grounds of expediency; but he believed in State Rights, and he reluctantly but honestly gave himself to the Confederacy, of which he became Vice-President. After the war, he wrote this book, defending his course on constitutional grounds. His serious political argument was cast in the form of a dialogue, with three interlocutors, which proceeds through two large volumes. Now, in classical times dialogue was a familiar form of serious exposition. Plato wrote dialogues, and Cicero wrote them, and later Plutarch; and when the Renaissance revived classical tradition in Italy, people again took to arguing in dialogue form, because clas-

sical masters had so argued.   In England this mannerism was
in full feather when Dryden wrote about Dramatic Poesy and
Addison of Ancient Medals; by the middle of the eighteenth
century it had almost died out there.   More than a century
later it still seemed normal to the most accomplished statesman of Georgia.   As a rhetorician, Mr. Stephens lingered in a
stage nearly outgrown in England before Queen Anne yielded
the throne to the House of Brunswick.   A trivial symptom,
perhaps; but a true one.   In the development of national
character, even the North of America has lagged behind
England; and the South has lagged behind the North.
Long ago we saw how our first great civil war — the American Revolution — sprang almost inevitably from mutual mis-
understandings, involved in the different rates of development
of England and of her American colonies.   Something of the
same kind, we can see now, underlay the Civil War which
once threatened the future of the American Union.

Of course the South was never destitute of powerful or of
cultivated minds; and from the beginning there were Southern books.   A rather fantastic habit includes among these the
voyages of Captain John Smith and the Elizabethan translation of Ovid by George Sandys, a portion of which was made
on the banks of the James River; and there are various old
historical writings from the South.   The best of them seem
the posthumously published manuscripts of William Byrd of
Westover, a Virginian gentleman who lived from 1664 to
1744, who had considerable social experience in England, and
whose style is very like that of his contemporary Englishmen
of quality.   In the fact that Byrd's records of contemporary
history were written for his private pleasure by a great landed
proprietor, and that they saw the light only when he had been
nearly a century in his grave, there is something characteristic of the South.   Southern gentlemen of an intellectual turn
collected considerable libraries; but these libraries, chiefly of
serious standard literature, tended more and more to become

traditional repositories of culture. Southern taste commanded each generation to preserve its culture unaltered, much as political necessity compelled the South to keep unaltered its government and its society.

At the time of the Revolution, of course, the development of political intelligence in the South produced powerful political writing. In Professor Tyler's admirable "Literary History of the American Revolution" the Declaration of Independence, which came straight from the pen of the Virginian Jefferson, is treated as a literary masterpiece. So in certain aspects it is, — the masterpiece of a school in which Jefferson, though perhaps the principal figure, was no more solitary than Emerson was in New England Transcendentalism. As in the North, too, this political writing tended during the first half of the nineteenth century to develop into rhetorical oratory; and though among American orators Webster and Choate and Everett and their New England contemporaries seem the best, no special study of American oratory can neglect such men as Calhoun, Hayne, or Henry Clay. Oratory, however, is not pure letters, but rather a phase of public life; and our concern is chiefly with literature. A sufficient indication of the literary work of the South may be found in the chronological tables which form the appendix of Mr. Pancoast's excellent little "Introduction to American Literature."

The names which he gives after that of Jefferson are the following: George Washington, to whose "Farewell Address" he accords full literary recognition; William Wirt, a Virginia lawyer, for some years Attorney-General of the United States, to whose elaborately rhetorical "Life of Patrick Henry" he gives a place among standard American biographers; John Marshall, the most eminent Chief Justice of the Supreme Court of the United States, also a Virginian, whose place in literature according to Mr. Pancoast is earned by his celebrated "Life of Washington;" Edward Coate

Pinckney, a Maryland lawyer and professor, who died young in 1828, and who had published certain volumes of poetry which reveal a true lyric gift; Henry Clay, whose position in literature is due to his oratory; William Gilmore Simms; Edgar Allan Poe; Audubon, who, like Poe, seems Southern only by courtesy; John Pendleton Kennedy; Augustus B. Longstreet; Charles E. Gayarré; Francis Lieber, a German by birth, and for his last twenty years an eminent resident of New York; John Esten Cooke; Paul Hamilton Hayne; Henry Timrod; and Sidney Lanier. Mr. Pancoast mentions too the names of a few writers still happily living; and he remarks as notable Southern periodicals the " Southern Review," which was published at Charleston in 1828 and had a short life; the " Southern Literary Messenger," which was published in Richmond from 1835 to 1864; and the "Southern Quarterly Review," which was established at Charleston in 1848, remained for several years under the editorship of William Gilmore Simms, and came to an end in 1856.

Of these names the earlier clearly belong to the traditions of the eighteenth century. Several of the later are already almost forgotten. Kennedy, a Maryland man eminent in political life, was the author of a novel called " Horse-Shoe Robinson." Longstreet, a Georgia man born in 1790, a graduate of Yale, a lawyer, a judge, a Methodist minister, and the president of two or three colleges, contributed to various newspapers sketches of Southern. life, which in 1840 were collected into a volume called " Georgia Scenes." These, which had a considerable success, and have lately been reprinted, are pleasant prototypes of the local short stories which during the past fifteen or twenty years have so generally appeared in various parts of the country. Gayarré, a New Orleans lawyer born in 1805, survived until lately. His works on the history of his native State, published between 1847 and 1854, and culminating in a three-volume " History of Louisiana," published in 1866, are respectable and authoritative local histories. Late in life he produced one or two novels and comedies which have been kindly spoken of, but which were never widely read. Cooke of Virginia, a lawyer and a Confederate soldier, who was born in 1830 and died in 1866, devoted the chief activity of his mature years to literature, and early produced " The Virginia Comedians," which is still pleasantly mentioned. He wrote certain other romances connected with his native State before and after the Civil War. And so on. It is hardly too much to say that if these sporadic writers had not been Southerners, they would have been even more forgotten than they are, along with the Literati momentarily enshrined in 1846 by Edgar Allan Poe.

Poe himself, as we decided long ago, is Southern only by courtesy; he relates himself more closely to literary New York at the moment when its old traditions were passing into the Knickerbocker School. In Mr. Pancoast's list, then, there are only four Southern names which now seem of any literary importance; and of these only one stands for considerable work before the Civil War.

This is that of William Gilmore Simms, whose Life, by Professor Trent, remains, as we have seen, the most interesting and suggestive book concerning our Southern literature. Simms was born in 1806 at Charleston, South Carolina. Of this most typical Southern city Professor Trent gives an admirable sketch. If any one spot can be held completely characteristic of a region so extended as the elder South, that spot was Charleston,—a fact historically evident when we remember that from Charleston came the Nullification movement of 1832, and that thirty years later the bombardment of Fort Sumter by Charleston militia began our armed conflict. In Simms's youth the social hierarchy of Charleston was so rigid as to make Northern social distinctions seem the acme of human equality; and meantime the general conservatism of Southern temper was in Charleston at its most conservative. Simms was born there in a socially lower class. He had little education; as a boy he was apprenticed to an apothecary; later he began the study of law. In 1825 he made an excursion to the southwest to visit his father, who had removed thither, and who strongly urged him not to return to Charleston, where his social obscurity would almost certainly interfere with his ambition. Simms, however, who was in love with a Charleston girl, insisted on going home; at the age of twenty-one he married a lady of social position in no way superior to his own; and a year later he published a volume of commonplace poetry. From that time he was an extremely prolific writer. In a partial bibliography of his work Professor Trent mentions no less than eighty-seven volumes from his pen between 1827 and his death in 1870. His first wife died early; by 1836 he had so improved his condition that a second marriage happily allied him to the family of a considerable planter. From that time until the Civil War, though his personal sympathies never quite agreed with those of the traditional aristocracy, his social position was more and more secure.

The immense bulk of Simms's writings — for forty years he produced books at the rate of more than two volumes a year, and he did incalculable journalistic work, too — involved hasty and careless composition; and the romances, to which his popularity was chiefly due, are not only careless but obviously affected by both Cooper and Scott, not to speak of such minor influences as those of William Godwin and perhaps of Brockden Brown. In their day some of them were widely popular; at the present time even their names are almost forgotten. For all their careless haste, however, they indicate uncommon vigour of temperament, and amid the obvious conventions of their plots and characters they constantly reveal, like the earlier romances of Brockden Brown and of Cooper, a true sense of the background in which the scenes were laid.

Up to the time of the Civil War, beyond much question, Simms was by far the most considerable literary man whom

the Southern States produced.   In South Carolina he was long
recognised as the principal figure of a literary epoch contemporary with that which in New England produced Emerson
and Thoreau, and Whittier, and Longfellow, and Lowell, and
Holmes, and Hawthorne.   This collocation of names is
enough.   Our chief Southern man of letters before the Civil
War was at best one who did vigorous, careless work of the
sort which had produced more lasting monuments in the New
York of Fenimore Cooper.   Cooper's work, we have seen,
was virtually complete in 1832 ; and Simms's did not begin
until 1833.   In literature as in temper the South lagged
behind the North.

Simms lived through the Civil War.   An ardent, sincere
Secessionist, he suffered greatly for the cause to which he was
conscientiously devoted.   When the war broke out, however,
he was already fifty-five years old.   His work as a whole,
then, is not, like that of the other Southerners on whom we
shall touch, saturated with the spirit of the tragic years
which brought to its end the old civilisation of their native
region.   Solemn enough to the uninvaded North, the war
meant more than Northern imagination has yet realised to
those Southern States into whose heart its horrors were slowly,
surely carried.   Such a time was too intense for much expression ; it was a moment rather for heroic action ; and in
South and North alike it found armies of heroes.   Of these
there are few more stirring records than a simple ballad made
by Dr. Ticknor, of Georgia, concerning a Confederate private
soldier : —

" LITTLE GIFFEN.

" Out of the focal and foremost fire,
Out of the hospital walls as dire;
Smitten of grape-shot and gangrene,
(Eighteenth battle, and *he* sixteen !)
Spectre ! such as you seldom see,
Little Giffen, of Tennessee !

" ' Take him and welcome ! ' the surgeons said ;
Little the doctor can help the dead !
So we took him ; and brought him where
The balm was sweet in the summer air ;
And we laid him down on a wholesome bed —
Utter Lazarus, heel to head !

" And we watched the war with abated breath, —
Skeleton Boy against skeleton Death.
Months of torture, how many such ?
Weary weeks of the stick and crutch ;
And still a glint of the steel-blue eye
Told of a spirit that would n't die,

" And did n't. Nay, more, in death's despite
The crippled skeleton learned to write.
' Dear Mother,' at first, of course ; and then
' Dear Captain,' inquiring about the men.
Captain's answer : ' Of eighty-and-five,
Giffen and I are left alive.'

" Word of gloom from the war, one day ;
Johnston pressed at the front, they say.
Little Giffen was up and away ;
A tear — his first — as he bade good-bye,
Dimmed the glint of his steel-blue eye.
' I 'll write, if spared ! ' There was news of the fight ;
But none of Giffen. He did not write.

" I sometimes fancy that, were I king
Of the princely Knights of the Golden Ring,
With the song of the minstrel in mine ear,
And the tender legend that trembles here,
I 'd give the best on his bended knee,
The whitest soul of my chivalry,
For 'Little Giffen,' of Tennessee."

Dr. Ticknor, who survived till 1874, was not thought important enough for record in Mr. Pancoast's chronological tables. His poems were edited, however, by a friend who, though he never wrote anything so powerful as " Little Giffen " was deservedly recognised by Mr. Pancoast. This was Paul Hamilton Hayne, a member of that distinguished South Carolina family which produced the Senator whose speech on

Nullification in 1830 elicited Webster's famous reply. Paul Hayne was born in this very year when his uncle and Webster were debating in the Senate. He studied for the bar, but devoted himself chiefly to literature at a time when the literary activity of Charleston was dominated by Simms. When the Civil War came he entered the Southern army; he broke down his health in the service. The war left him, too, ruined in property; but he survived, working hard at letters in the Georgia country, until 1886.

Professor Trent's "Life of Simms" gives us many glimpses of Hayne, showing how eagerly he strove to maintain the literary dignity of the region which he passionately loved. A man of gentler origin than Simms, and distinctly better educated, his temper seems more in sympathy with the formal traditions of the South Carolina gentry. It shows too an academic sense of conventional standards. In this aspect Hayne had something in common with the New England poets. Certainly, compared with such verses as "Little Giffen," and with the best work of Timrod and of Sidney Lanier, his poetry seems deficient in individuality and passion; yet whoever will turn only to Stedman and Hutchinson must feel in Hayne a touch of genuineness almost unknown in the South until the fatal days of civil war.

It is characteristic of Hayne that he was held by his admirers, and probably liked to be held, an excellent maker of sonnets. The praise is excessive. Excellent sonnets are rare in the whole range of literature. The fact that Hayne loved to express himself in this studied and deliberate form, however, and that he managed it well enough to be remarked, means that he was at heart not only a man of deep emotional impulse, but an artist. The sonnet which Stedman and Hutchinson have chosen to represent him is not faultless; nor is lack of lyric smoothness its only fault. In substance, like so much American poetry, it is commonplace; in style it is rather reminiscent of many admirable models than strongly individual; but it has genuine fervour. Few American sonnets seem more sincere. "Fate or God?" he calls it; and here it is:

> " Beyond the record of all eldest things,
> Beyond the rule and regions of past time,
> From out Antiquity's hoary-headed rime,
> Looms the dread phantom of a King of kings :
> Round his vast brow the glittering circlet clings
> Of a thrice royal crown; beneath Him climb,
> O'er Atlantean limbs and breast sublime,
> The sombre splendours of mysterious wings ;
> Deep calms of measureless power, in awful state,
> Gird and uphold Him; a miraculous rod,
> To heal or smite, arms His infallible hands ;
> Known in all ages, worshipped in all lands,
> Doubt names this half-embodied mystery — Fate,
> While Faith, with lowliest reverence, whispers — God ! "

In 1873 Hayne edited the poems of his friend Henry Timrod. These have maintained such reputation that a new and enlarged edition has lately appeared. In the introduction to this collection one can feel throughout the provincial note of Southern literary temper. Its style is amiably florid to a degree which in the North would have always seemed a little ridiculous ; so, in spite of amiably modest temper, its superlative estimate of Timrod's merit makes his work at first glance seem less noteworthy than it really is. He had in him the stuff of which poetry is made, and the circumstances of his career made some of his expression of it admirable. Timrod was born in Charleston in 1829, the son of an artisan who was known as the Poet Mechanic. He was further than Simms, then, from belonging to the hereditary gentry of South Carolina ; but he had inherited love for literature. He studied for a while at the University of Georgia ; he then turned to the law ; and for some time before the Civil War he was private tutor in a gentleman's family. During the war he was a journalist. At the burning of Columbia during Sherman's march to the sea his property was totally destroyed ;

in 1867 his consequent poverty brought to an end a life which was never physically robust.

Among Timrod's poems, one, " The Cotton Boll," has emerged from the rest. It begins thus : —

> " While I recline
> At ease beneath
> This immemorial pine,
> Small sphere !
> (By dusky fingers brought this morning here
> And shown with boastful smiles),
> I turn thy cloven sheath,
> Through which the soft white fibres peer,
> That, with their gossamer bands,
> Unite, like love, the sea divided lands,
> And slowly, thread by thread,
> Draw forth the folded strands,
> Than which the trembling line,
> By whose frail help yon startled spider fled
> Down the tall spear-grass from his swinging bed,
> Is scarce more fine ;
> And as the tangled skein
> Unravels in my hands,
> Betwixt me and the noonday light
> A veil seems lifted, and for miles and miles
> The landscape broadens on my sight,
> As in the little boll, there lurked a spell
> Like that which in the ocean shell,
> With mystic sound
> Breaks down the narrow walls that hem us round,
> And turns some city lane
> Into the restless main,
> With all his capes and isles ! "

The eccentric irregularity of this laboured verse cannot disguise its lyric note; and the sense of Nature which it reveals is as fine, as true, and as simple as that which makes so nearly excellent Whittier's poems about New England landscapes. And so " The Cotton Boll" proceeds, turning into poetry what might seem a very commonplace motive, — namely, reflections on the various blessings brought to mankind by the chief staple of the South. The closing lines of the poem,

which touch on the Civil War, strike another note, and a
stirring : —

" As men who labour in that mine
   Of Cornwall, hollowed out beneath the bed
   Of ocean, when a storm rolls overhead,
Hear the dull booming of the world of brine
Above them, and a mighty muffled roar
Of winds and waters, yet toil calmly on,
And split the rock, and pile the massive ore,
Or carve a niche, or shape the archèd roof ;
So I, as calmly, weave my woof
Of song, chanting the days to come,
Unsilenced, though the quiet summer air
Stirs with the bruit of battles, and each dawn
Wakes from its starry silence to the hum
Of many gathering armies.   Still,
   In that we sometimes hear,
Upon the Northern winds, the voice of woe
Not wholly drowned in triumph, though I know
The end must crown us, and a few brief years
   Dry all our tears,
I may not sing too gladly.   To Thy will
Resigned, O Lord ! we cannot all forget
That there is much even Victory must regret.
   And, therefore, not too long
From the great burthen of our country's wrong
   Delay our just release !
   And, if it may be, save
These sacred fields of peace
From stain of patriot or of hostile blood !
Oh, help us, Lord ! to roll the crimson flood
Back on its course, and, while our banners wing
Northward, strike with us ! till the Goth shall cling
To his own blasted altar-stones, and crave
Mercy ; and we shall grant it, and dictate
   The lenient future of his fate
There, where some rotting ships and crumbling quays
Shall one day mark the Port which ruled the Western seas."

Our Civil War brought forth no lines more fervent, and
few whose fervour rises to such lyric height.   In the days of
conflict, North regarded South, and South North, as the incar-

nation of evil. Time, however, has begun its healing work; at last our country begins to understand itself better than ever before; and as our new patriotism strengthens, we cannot prize too highly such verses as Whittier's, honestly phrasing noble Northern sentiment, or as Timrod's, who with equal honesty phrased the noble sentiment of the South. A literature which in the same years could produce works so utterly antagonistic in superficial sentiment, and yet so harmonious in their common sincerity and loftiness of feeling, is a literature from which riches may come.

We can hardly have read even this short extract from Timrod, however, without feeling, along with his lyric quality, a lack of articulation which prevents his work from excellence. A similar trait appears in the work of the most memorable man of letters as yet produced by the South, — Sidney Lanier. Born at Macon, Georgia, in 1842, Lanier graduated from a Georgia college in 1860, and at the outbreak of the Civil War he enlisted as a Confederate volunteer. Towards the close of the war he was taken prisoner; the physical hardships of his military experience produced a weakness of the lungs from which he never recovered. After the war he was for a while a school-teacher, and for a while a lawyer in Alabama and Georgia. In 1873 he removed to Baltimore, where at first he supported himself by playing the flute in a symphony orchestra. Soon, however, he became known as a man of letters; and in 1879 he was made a lecturer on English literature at Johns Hopkins University. He survived this appointment two years, dying in 1881.

A true lyric artist, Lanier was a skilful musician, and he wrote genuine poetry. The circumstances of his life, however, were such as to preclude a very high degree of technical training, and, at least until after the war had broken his health, much systematic study. What he accomplished under these circumstances is astonishing. He was never popular, and probably never will be. His quality was too fine to appeal to the general public; his training was too imperfect to make his critical work or his theories of æsthetics seem important to technical scholars. He was compelled besides to write more than was good for him,—at least one novel, for example, and versions for boys of much old romance, concerning King Arthur, and the heroes of Froissart, and the Welsh tales of the " Mabinogion," and Percy's " Reliques." He wrote nothing more characteristic, however, than that " Science of English Verse " which comprises the substance of his first course of lectures at Johns Hopkins. To state his serious and earnest system of dogmatic poetics, would take too long. In brief, he believed the function of poetry to be far nearer to that of music than it has generally been held. The emotional effect of poetry he declared to arise literally from its sound quite as much as from its meaning; and the poetry which he wrote was decidedly affected by this deliberate, sincere, but somewhat cramping theory. Even in his earlier verse you feel this impediment. Here, for example, is a song which he is said to have made in 1866.

" Night and Day.

" The innocent, sweet Day is dead.
Dark Night hath slain her in her bed.
O, Moors are as fierce to kill as to wed !
— Put out the light, said he.

" A sweeter light than ever rayed
From star of heaven or eye of maid
Has vanished in the unknown shade.
— She 's dead, she 's dead, said he.

" Now, in a wild, sad after-mood
The tawny night sits still to brood
Upon the dawn-time when he wooed.
— I would she lived, said he.

" Star-memories of happier times,
Of loving deeds and lovers' rhymes,
Throng forth in silvery pantomines.
— Come back, O Day ! said he."

Though the allusions to "Othello" are far-fetched, and though the last verse evidently breaks down, the first three have an unmistakably lyric touch.

Lanier's lyric quality, as well as his self-imposed limitations, appear more clearly in a later work, which is becoming his most celebrated: "The Marshes of Glynn." Here his poetical impulse is expressed in a musical form which he might have called symphonic. He is no longer writing a song; he is working out a complicated motive, in a manner so entirely his own that the first thirty-six lines, as irregular in form as those of Timrod's "Cotton Boll," and more irregular in length, compose one intricate, incomprehensible sentence. The closing passage, easier to understand, possesses quite as much symphonic fervour. He has been gazing out over the marshes and trying to phrase the limitless emotion which arises as he contemplates a trackless plain where land and sea interfuse. Then the tide begins to rise, and he goes on thus:—

" Lo, out of his plenty the sea
  Pours fast: full soon the time of the flood-tide must be:
  Look how the grace of the sea doth go
  About and about through the intricate channels that flow
  Here and there, Everywhere,
  Till his waters have flooded the uttermost creeks and the low-lying
      lanes
  And the marsh is meshed with a million veins
  That like as with rosy and silvery essences flow
  In the rose-and-silver evening glow.
          Farewell, my lord Sun!
  The creeks overflow: a thousand rivulets run
  Twixt the roots of the sod; the blades of the marsh-grass stir;
  Passes a hurrying sound of wings that westward whir;
  Passes, and all is still; and the currents cease to run;
  And the sea and the marsh are one.

" How still the plains of the waters be!
  The tide is in his ecstasy.
  The tide is at his highest height:
      And it is night.

3²

" And now from the Vast of the Lord will the waters of sleep
    Roll in on the souls of men,
  But who will reveal to our waking ken
  The forms that swim and the shapes that creep
        Under the waters of sleep?
  And I would I could know what swimmeth below when the tide
    comes in
  On the length and the breadth of the marvellous marshes of Glynn."

Now this inarticulate verse is of a quality which can never be popular, and perhaps indeed is so eccentric that one should be prudent in choosing adjectives to praise it. The more you read the " Marshes of Glynn," however, and the more, indeed, you read any of Lanier's poetry, the more certain you feel that he was among the truest men of letters whom our country has produced. Genuine in impulse, fervid in temper, impressed but not overwhelmed by the sad and tragic conditions of his life, and sincerely moved to write in words which he constantly and ardently strove to make beautiful, he exhibits lyric power hardly to be found in any other American.

All this, however, seems hardly national. Some little time ago we touched on the fact that one of his most effective narrative poems, the " Revenge of Hamish," deals with an episode purely Scotch. His first novel, the " Tiger Lily," to be sure, which has survived only in name, dealt with an American subject. His books for boys, however, produced by an impulse something like Longfellow's, were meant to make the brave and romantic traditions of Europe familiar to American youth ; his " Science of English Verse," his " Lectures on the English Novel," and the volumes of posthumous essays which have appeared in later years, all dealt with general æsthetic subjects. Lanier's earthly career was wholly American, and almost wholly Southern ; the emotional temper with which he was filled must have been quickened by experience in our own country. The things with which he chose to deal, however, might have come to him anywhere. The very fact which keeps him permanently from popularity is perhaps this lack of local perception, as distinguished from a temper which could not help being of local origin. So if Lanier's work tells us anything about Southern literature, it only tells us, a little more surely than that of Dr. Ticknor, or of Hayne, or of Timrod, how the tragic convulsion of our Civil War waked in the South a kind of passion which America had hardly exhibited before.

Cursory as this glance at our Southern literature has been, it probably comprehends all that has been produced in the South by men no longer living. Reviewing it, we are compelled to say that our Southern regions have as yet produced little if any more significant literature than the North had produced before 1832. Since the Civil War the social and economic condition of the South has been too disturbed for anything like final expression. As yet, then, the South presents little to vary the general outlines of literature in America. The few Southern poets, however, who have phrased the emotion aroused by the Civil War which swept their earlier civilisation out of existence, reveal a lyric fervour hardly yet equalled in the North. As one thinks, then, of Dr. Ticknor, of Hayne, of Timrod, and of Lanier, one begins to wonder whether they may not perhaps forerun a spirit which shall give beauty and power to the American letters of the future.

IV

THE WEST

WHEN the father of Fenimore Cooper took his family to Central New York, a little more than a century ago, Central New York was still a Western wilderness. Amid the numerous conventions of Cooper's Leather-Stocking stories, then, there emerge many traces of actual experience which show what our Western country used to be. In this aspect, the conclusion of the Leather-Stocking stories is significant. The pioneer hero starts alone for a wilderness more Western still, pressed by the inconvenient growth of population in the regions where he has passed his mature life. The types of Western immigrants thus suggested are those most frequently kept in mind by tradition; and probably the most admirable Western settlers were on the one hand such people as the elder Cooper, who went to establish in a previously unbroken country new and grander fortunes, and, on the other hand, such personages as Fenimore Cooper idealised in his most popular hero. These latter, of whom perhaps the most familiar in traditional memory is Daniel Boone, were people adventurously impatient of conventions, who betook themselves with constantly fresh restlessness to places where, in virtue of solitude, they could live as independently as they chose. In this type, however, as the very popularity it achieved with European revolutionists would show, there was something more like reversion than development. Far enough from the ideal primitive man of the French Revolution, they tended in virtues and in vices alike rather back towards primitive manhood than forward towards maturer society. As we have already seen in various ways, national inexperience, which marks all American history until well into the present century, had tended to retard the variation of our native character from the original type of seventeenth-century England. Such complete relaxation of social experience as was involved in the temper and conduct of the pioneers tended to throw them back toward the kind of human nature which had vanished from the old world with the middle ages. Something of the kind, indeed, is apparent even in remote districts of New England. In many parts of the West, it was once frequent enough to be characteristic.

Another kind of Western settler has been less generally remarked. Among the New York Literati preserved from oblivion by Poe was Mrs. Kirkland, who happened about 1840 to pass three or four years in Michigan, then a sparsely settled Western region. Between 1839 and 1846, she published three books dealing with her Western experiences : " A New Home," " Forest Life," and " Western Clearings." In themselves little more than such good-humoured sketches as any clever, well-bred woman might write in correspondence, these books vividly show how the West once appeared to a cultivated Eastern observer. One fact which she treats as a matter of course is historically suggestive. When the country where the scene of her stories is laid began to get tamed, the more shiftless settlers were apt to avoid the increasing strenuousness of life by moving as much farther West as they could beg, borrow, or steal means to go. These personages typify an element of Western society which has been there from the beginning. That vast new region of ours has been partly settled, no doubt, by such admirable energy as is typified by the elder Cooper or Mrs. Kirkland herself. It has been partly settled, too, by the primitive, vigorous restlessness of the better sort of pioneers. Along with these admirably constructive types of character, however, there has mingled from the beginning a destructive type, which went West because it could not prosper at home, and which could not prosper at home because it was too shiftless to prosper anywhere.

Such a class as this, of course, is a recognised part of any colonising movement. Its influence on the general character of the West has been too little emphasised. In our older Northern States it is commonly supposed that at first the West was dominated by fine energy, and that the disturbing element now evident there came either from foreign immigration or from the incursion of Southern " poor whites." In fact, it seems more likely that those Western regions whose political and moral condition now leaves most to be desired are those where native Northern blood preponderates. If this be true, the shiftless immigrants of Mrs. Kirkland's day, evidently what we should now call social degenerates, have proved a more important factor in our history than tradition has remembered. For in our national politics the West has grown, from the nature of our Constitution, to exercise an influence almost as disproportionate to its numerical population as that exercised by the slaveholding South. As the Territories have been admitted States of the Union, each new State has been represented in the Senate equally with New York or Massachusetts, Pennsylvania or Virginia. Our national legislation, then, has had sometimes to adapt itself to the vagaries of these new commonwealths, whose inexperience was at the outset extreme, and whose wisdom — political and moral alike — often seems remote from recognised standards.

Our chief concern, however, is not with politics or even with society; it is rather with those aspects of feeling and temper which tend toward something which the West has not yet achieved, — namely, literary expression. Glimpses of these, as they appeared to foreign eyes, are to be found in the familiar old books of travel which formerly so incensed Americans against Mrs. Trollope; and a little later in those caricatures of " Martin Chuzzlewit " which so displeased American sensibilities that American readers are prone to forget how the same book caricatures the English too, in such figures as Mr. Pecksniff and Mrs. Sarah Gamp. A very different picture of the Middle West, a little later, is to be found in a book which in certain moods one is disposed for all its eccentricity to call the most admirable work of literary art as yet produced on this continent. This is that Odyssean story of the Mississippi to which Mark Twain gave the grotesque name of "Huckleberry Finn." The material from which he made this book he carelessly flung together a year or two before in a rambling series of reminiscences called "Life on the Mississippi." Mrs. Trollope, "Martin Chuzzlewit," "Life on the Mississippi," and "Huckleberry Finn" will combine to give a fair notion of Western life and character before the Civil War.

A picture of it, from a different point of view, may be found in a book of which the accuracy has been questioned. This is a loquacious "Life of Abraham Lincoln," by Mr. Herndon, at one time Lincoln's partner in the practice of law. Without power enough either to perceive or to set forth the traits which made Lincoln, whatever his faults, the most heroic American figure of the nineteenth century, Herndon, an every-day Western lawyer, was thoroughly familiar with the society amid which Lincoln grew up, and from which he ultimately emerged into national public life. Herndon, too, was so gossipy that he could not help writing vividly. As is generally known, Lincoln's family history resembled that of the shiftless immigrants sketched by Mrs. Kirkland. That so admirably powerful a character could spring from such humble origin is generally recognised among the hopeful facts of our national history. Herndon's book reveals a phase of the story hardly evident elsewhere. As you read the incidents of Lincoln's youth, whatever the authenticity of this anecdote or that, you can hardly avoid the impression that the social surroundings in which his life began were astonishingly like those of the Middle Ages. These people, of course, dressed in garments, and used words, and had traditions which imply various occurrences since early Plantagenet times. It is hardly excessive to say, however, that their general mental and moral condition was more like that attributed to the English peasantry in the days of Richard Cœur de Lion than like any native English existence much more recent. Amid the relaxed inexperience of Western life the lower sort of Americans had tended to revert towards a social state ancestrally extinct centuries before America was discovered. During Lincoln's career the West was rapidly settling; and as you read Herndon you have a curious sense that months and years are doing the work of generations and centuries. It is as if in 1809 Lincoln had been born under King Richard I.; and when the man was fifty years old, he was abreast of our own time. One thing which contributed to his amazing power was this exceptional social environment, of which Herndon's book gives so vivid a picture. Almost alone of eminent Americans, Lincoln had chanced to know the inexperience of our native country in almost all its phases.

In our Western regions this extraordinary confusion of the centuries is not yet past. The essay which Mr. Owen Wister has prefixed to his stories, "Red Men and White," points out that in the Far West there are still regions of which the civilisation is much less mature than that of Elizabethan England. Everybody knows that our national government has somehow to reconcile the purposes and interests of societies widely different in climatic conditions and historic origin. Even New England and New York differ in some respects; both alike differ from the older Southern colonies; and the Northwest differs from the Southwest, and Louisiana from everything else; and so do the regions of Spanish origin. Mr. Wister points out the less salient fact that varying phases of American inexperience have thrown certain parts of our country back into the Middle Ages, while others amid accumulating experience have advanced to fully modern conditions. The

problem of our national politics, then, is even more complicated than it has seemed; we must reconcile differences
which extend not only through widely divergent space, but
also through generations and centuries of social and historic
time.

From the causes at which we have glanced, two or three
familiar results have followed. A hundred years ago, the
greater part of our country was still a wilderness, and Central
New York itself a region where native Indians still lingered.
To-day, it is said, almost every available acre throughout the
United States is in private ownership; and regions which
within living memory were still unbroken prairie are the sites of
cities more populous than New York or Boston was fifty years
ago. From influences quite beyond human control, then, the
energies of our Western people have devoted themselves to
the conquest of Nature on a scale hitherto unattempted. No
wonder the most salient trait of our great confused West seems
enthusiasm for material prosperity as distinguished from spiritual
or intellectual ideals. Yet there are such things as Western
ideals, different from the older ideals of New England, but perhaps as admirable. Though these have not yet expressed themselves in literary form, they assumed, some few years ago, a
plastic form which must deeply have impressed any one who
saw it.

When, in 1893, the World's Fair was held at Chicago, one
might have expected colossal crudity of taste. The archi-
tects of the buildings, to be sure, were not always Western
men; but the controlling spirit which enabled the architect-
ural energy of America to concentrate itself in an imaginative effort hitherto unapproached came almost wholly from
Chicago. The structures which grew from this spirit and
energy became an imaginatively stimulating expression of
noble æsthetic temper. Whatever their imperfection of
detail, they were imperially beautiful. That transitory city,
too, which the energy of western America thus for a moment

created, had a transitory population drawn mostly from those regions which we still call Western. For the expense and difficulty of long journeys weighed more and more on people from a distance. As you watched this passing population day by day, you felt growing surprise and admiration at their simplicity of feeling, their eagerness to delight in excellence, and their cheerful observance of public order. For one thing, —a mere detail,—there is a general feeling among the ordinary people of America that the sale of intoxicating drink must necessarily lead to wide-spread drunkenness,—whence the prohibitory legislation so frequently vexatious to civilised travellers in the United States. At the Chicago Exhibition, intoxicating drinks were freely sold ; and the daily visitors numbered hundreds of thousands. They were people, too, of widely various social origin. Yet there was hardly more evidence of drunkenness than if the vice had never existed. The general manner of the crowd, too, though lacking the unconscious grace which one finds in gatherings of older nations, was good-humoured and polite. If the citizens from the four corners of the West who came to Chicago during those few weeks may be taken as typical of western America, the West is a region from which in time to come we may hope for broader and more superbly imaginative expression than any which America has hitherto known.

As yet, however, this great confused West has not developed any such unity of character as has marked our elder regions ; and happily most of the writers who pleasantly and worthily express certain aspects of Western life are still living. On the serious literature of the West, then, we cannot touch in detail. Its chief feature seems to be those short stories which set forth with accuracy, if not with lasting vitality, the local characteristics of California or of Kentucky, of Arkansas, of Arizona, or of wherever else. In Chicago, meantime, at this moment the most populous and characteristic Western city, there is considerable publication ; and this includes a fortnightly paper, the "Dial," which seems at present the most unbiassed, good-humoured, and sensible organ of American criticism. In general, however, Western literary expression is still confined to popular journalism.

Though American newspapers, particularly of that extremely unacademic kind popular in the West, can hardly be brought within any definition of literature, they form, for better or worse, the only habitual reading of most native Americans. Offensive though they generally be to taste, then, and often to civic morals as well, Western newspapers are significant in such considerations as ours. Their most obvious trait is sensationalism. So long as news is exciting, they care little whether it prove true. In a deliberate effort to please an untutored public, they do not hesitate to play on every passing prejudice of the moment; and, written for the most part by people of small education, often mere boys, their style in every phase but one is apt to be thoroughly vicious. Almost all, however, display one merit which atones for numberless errors; almost all are readable, to a degree which even educated minds find insidiously attractive.

As you grow familiar with American newspapers, it appears that besides their chief function of purveying news in a manner welcome to uneducated readers they undertake to provide such readers with fragmentary matter of which the substance comes nearer to literature. In recognised "departments," you will find many items of general information; many scraps of verse, too, some of which approaches poetry; and, above all, in most papers of much pretension you are apt to find regular contributions intended simply to make you laugh.

Mainly from this source, — the comic columns of American newspapers, — there has tended to develop a kind of native expression hardly recognised forty years ago and now popularly supposed to be our most characteristic. This is what is commonly called American humour.

Some vein of humour, of course, has existed in America

almost from the beginning. In the admirable analytic index
of Stedman and Hutchinson's " Library of American Literature," American humour is held to have existed as early as
1647, when Nathaniel Ward, minister of Ipswich, published
his " Simple Cobbler of Agawam," a work which contains
satirical sketches of character in the regular seventeenth-
century manner. There was plenty of conventional humour,
too, in the literature of the American Revolution. Hopkinson's " Battle of the Kegs," however, the most familiar example of this, needs only comparison with Cowper's nearly
contemporary " John Gilpin " to reveal that its chief American
trait is a somewhat unskilful touch. Franklin's humour was
somewhat more national ; that letter of his to a London newspaper, about 1760, proved the most hard-headed and versatile
of eighteenth-century Americans to have been capable of a
grave confusion of fact and nonsense which reminds one of
Mark Twain's. Among our acknowledged men of letters, in
later days, several have won recognition largely by means of
their humorous passages. Irving's " Knickerbocker," for
example, founded his reputation by just such confusion of literal
statement with extravagance as made Franklin's letter amusing fifty years before and Mark Twain's " Innocents Abroad "
fifty years later; in all three, you are constantly perplexed as
to what is so and what not. Something of the same kind
you find again in Lowell's " Fable for Critics " and his
" Biglow Papers." The humour of Parson Wilbur's interminable introductions, to be sure, seems mostly of the ponderous
old English type; but the verses themselves, amid all their
extravagance of dialect and puns, now and again state grave
truths in solemnly plain terms, and sometimes rise into noble
poetry. In the " Monument and the Bridge," the last of
Lowell's poems at which we happened to glance, these traits
are instantly apparent. Holmes, too, was so humorous in
temper that when, during his last visit to England, he had
the pleasure of seeing his portrait in " Vanity Fair," he

must have felt quiet amusement at the brief biography which accompanied it with the statement that so conservative a Boston gentleman was a typically American " funny fellow."

No criticism could have shown much less understanding of Holmes's real position in our letters. Like Lowell and Irving, and in many respects Franklin himself, Holmes was not only American in his humorous habit of shifting from seriousness to burlesque, and from burlesque back to seriousness, at moments when you least expected; but, like almost all American men of letters in his generation, he was a man of distinction. Whatever the strength or the weakness of the writers whom we have considered, their fun, like their seriousness and their commonplace, is of the sort which characterises gentlemen. Democratic though our country be, those actually recognised as our men of letters, even if, like Franklin or Whittier, of simple origin, have generally possessed in their ripeness a personal dignity, at once conscious and willingly acknowledged. In momentarily distinguished form, then, American humour first declared itself. The form which has been developing in Western newspapers has other traits.

The chief of these, which is inherent in the popularity of Western journalism, is hard to define, but palpable and vital. It amounts to a general assumption that everybody whom you address will entirely understand whatever you say. Such an assumption implies broad human feeling. We all know that men differ not only in temperament, but also in accordance with the conditions of their lives; and most of us are over-conscious of such differences. Now and again, however, you come across somebody who contagiously assumes that for all our differences every human being is really human, and so that everybody's emotions, sublime or ridiculous, may generally be excited in the same way. A familiar example of the temper now in mind pervaded a kind of entertainment frequent in America thirty or forty years ago, — the negro minstrel shows, now tending to vanish in performances like those of London music halls. In these shows a number of men would daub their faces with burnt cork, would dress themselves in preposterous burlesque of the florid taste still characteristic of negroes, and sitting in a row would sing songs and tell stories. The songs were sometimes sentimental, the stories almost always extravagantly comic; but underlying one and all was an assumption that everybody who heard what the performers said was familiar with everything they knew, — not only with local allusions and human nature, but also with the very names and personal oddities of the individuals they mentioned. To phrase the thing colloquially, the whole performance assumed that we were all in the crowd. You will find a touch of this temper in Falstaff, plenty of it in Sancho Panza; you will find it, too, in the conventional personages of the old European stage, — Policinello or Sganarelle; you will find it in the mountebanks who have plied their trade throughout human history. This temper is obviously akin to that broadly human feeling which underlies all great works of lasting art. The more we can assume that everybody is human, the more human our literary work will be.

Some such trait as this pervades the " funny " columns of American newspapers, particularly in the West; and it is mostly from these columns that American humour has emerged into what approach it has made to literary form. Generally, of course, this humour, like other recent phases of American expression, has come from men still living, and so is beyond our range; but at least three familiar humorous figures who are no longer with us typify the kind of literary impulse now in mind. The first was George Horatio Derby, an army officer, born of a good Massachusetts family in 1823, who spent a good deal of his life in the West, particularly in California. Here, under the name of John Phœnix, he took to writing whimsical letters for the newspapers, two volumes of which had been collected and published before his death in

1861. In their day, "Phœnixiana" and the "Squibob Papers," which grotesquely satirise life in California during the early days of American control there, were popular all over the country. To-day one feels their extravagance more than their fun; the whole thing seems overdone. John Phœnix, however, was undoubtedly among the earliest humourists of a school which has tended to produce better and better work.

About ten years after his time there came into notice a man whose name is still remembered both at home and in England. This was Charles Farrar Browne, born at Waterford, Maine, in 1834. At first a printer, then a newspaper man, he drifted to Ohio, where about 1858 he became a reporter on the Cleveland "Plain Dealer." For this he began to write, over the signature of Artemus Ward, humorous articles which carried both the "Plain Dealer" and his pseudonym all over the country. Just before the Civil War he took charge of a comic weekly newspaper in New York. The war brought this venture to an end; for the rest of his life he was a "funny" lecturer; he died in England on a lecturing tour in 1867. Like the humour of John Phœnix, that of Artemus Ward now seems tediously extravagant; but the essence of it lies in his inextricable confusion of fact and nonsense. He often assumes the character of a travelling showman, remotely resembling the late Mr. Barnum, in which character he has interviews not only with typical individuals of various classes, but with all sorts of notable persons, from Brigham Young to Queen Victoria. With all these he is on the most intimate terms; the fun lies chiefly in the grotesque incongruity between the persons concerned and what they say. Like Lowell in the "Biglow Papers," he emphasised his jests with mad misspelling and the like; but all his vagaries cannot conceal the sober confusion of fact and nonsense which groups his temper with that of Lowell and Irving and the other humourists of our standard literature. Essentially, however, as we have seen, Lowell and Irving and Holmes and the rest were

gentlemen and men of taste ; poor Artemus Ward was neither.
Personally he is said to have been so far from reputable that
even in his palmy days as a Cleveland reporter the better sort
of people in that Ohio city let him severely alone; and
throughout the volumes in which his newspaper articles were
from time to time collected, although you find no indecency,
you will find no vestige of taste.   The extreme extravagance
of Artemus Ward, however, peculiarly commended him to
many readers in England, who found his work so different
from what they were used to, that they welcomed him as
characteristically American.

In the history of American newspaper humour the grotesque
extravagance of Artemus Ward stands midway between that
of John Phœnix and that of the writers who are still at work.
The personal career of the man, no longer living, who may be
taken to represent this later stage of development resembled
that of Artemus Ward.   David Ross Locke was born in a
country village of New York in 1833.   Like Artemus Ward,
he was a printer, later a reporter, and later still, editor of a
local newspaper in Ohio.   At the beginning of the Civil
War he began to write political satires over the signature of
Petroleum V. Nasby.   The preposterousness of this pseudonym typifies the absurdity of his misspelt and otherwise
eccentric style.   His satire, however, which was widely circulated at a moment of national crisis, dealt with matters of
significance.   He had come intimately to know the border
regions between the North and the South.   He was a strong
Union man ; and with all the grotesque mannerisms of a newspaper humourist he satirised Southern character and those phases
of Northern character which sympathised with the constitutional contentions of the Confederacy.   Nasby's work, then,
had in its day political importance ; it really helped solidify
and strengthen Union sentiment.   In 1865, Mr. Locke became editor of the "Toledo Blade;" and he survived at
Toledo, Ohio, until 1888.   His work as a humourist, however,

belongs to the Civil War and to the disturbed ensuing administration of President Johnson, against whom some of his most pitiless satire was directed. The Nasby letters purport to come from a place called " Confederate X-Roads," and to be written by a good-for-nothing Southern politician with no redeeming trait except a Falstaffian presumption that everybody will agree with him. Addressing himself directly to the every-day readers of an Ohio newspaper, and popular throughout the Northern States, Nasby was at once a characteristic newspaper humourist and a satirist of considerable power. His work, then, has considerable interest for students of American political history.

Though, in general, American newspaper humour is not so significant, it has retained from Nasby's day the sort of contagious vitality found throughout his writings ; and in one or two cases of men still living it has emerged into something more notable. In one case, indeed, it has resulted in literary work so characteristically American, and so widely varied, that while happily the author in question is not yet a posthumous subject for such study as ours, it is impossible not to mention his name. If there be any contemporary work at once thoroughly American, and, for all its errors of taste, full of indications that the writer's power would have been exceptional anywhere, it is that of Mr. Clemens, more widely known as Mark Twain.

On the whole, however, we may say of our great confused West, that just as surely as New England has made its mark in the literary history of America, so as yet this West has not. Its general literary condition resembles that of the South, and of New York in the days which have followed the Knickerbocker School. Its varied, swiftly changing life has not yet ripened into an experience which can possibly find lasting expression.

33

V

THE PRESENT TIME

So at last we come to the question of what America is doing
in literature to-day. At this, of course, we must glance very
generally. Living men, we decided long ago, are not within
the scope of our study; we may properly inquire only what
literary symptoms we discern in our new nation, which almost
within our own time has tamed and settled the American continent from sea to sea.

Old New York, we saw, expressed itself in our first
school of renascent writing, which withered away with the
" Knickerbocker Magazine; " and modern New York seems
doing little more than contemplate the forces from which by
and by some newer and deeper literature may emerge. New
England ripened into renascent expression; but its Renaissance is now a thing of the past, and in many aspects the
New England of to-day seems otherwise past its prime. In
the older South, literature was never highly developed; and
the Civil War is hardly yet so remote as to allow the new
South to have declared its final character. The West, too,
has not yet reached maturity. The America of the future,
however, seems likely to be a country in which the forces which
have gathered separately may finally fuse into a centralised
nationality more conscious and more powerful than we have
yet known. It becomes interesting, then, to inquire what
literary symptoms, if any, are common to our whole country,
what kind of expression is now familiar throughout it.

The newspaper we have seen, for one thing, crude, sensational, and mostly addressed to the unthinking classes. It

emerges into literary quality, if at all, only in the form of a reckless humour whose history shows something like development. This humour is always extravagant, generally deficient in taste, and mostly ephemeral; but its underlying trait seems like that of the humour which has enlivened our standard literature. Our American temper has a shrewd sense of fact. Its instinctive conception of fun seems to lie in a preposterous confusion of hard fact with wild nonsense, complicated and freshly confused by a superficially grave manner. Its jumps from serious things to things which no human being could take seriously, and back again, are incalculably sudden. What looks like a vital trait in all this is the tendency among the " funny men " of our newspapers to deal with fact in growingly mature spirit. Artemus Ward came nearer life than John Phœnix, Nasby than Artemus Ward ; and, on the whole, the more recent of our newspaper humourists seem rather more firmly poised than Nasby. So far, this phase of American literature has produced nothing which can reasonably be expected to last. From this broadly popular origin, however, may perhaps come in future some lasting development. At least, if a man should appear in America with such gifts as now and again have made the humourists of other countries immortal, that man would find ready a vehicle of expression and a public which might help him to produce works of humour at once permanent and characteristically national.

Though newspapers are incalculably the most popular vehicles of modern American expression, there are other such vehicles generally familiar to our educated classes. The principal of these are the illustrated monthly magazines published in New York. These, which circulate by hundreds of thousands, and go from one end of the country to the other, provide the ordinary American citizen of to-day with his nearest approach to literature. A glance through any volume of any of them will show that the literary form which most luxuriantly flourishes in their pages is the short story. This development of short stories is partly a question of business. Short stories have usually been more profitable to writers and more convenient to editors than long novels; and at this moment poetry seems not to appeal to any considerable public taste. Partly, however, this prevalence of short stories seems nationally characteristic of American as distinguished from English men of letters. Of late, no doubt, England has produced one or two writers who do this kind of work extraordinarily well; there is no living American, for example, whose stories equal those of Mr. Kipling; but Mr. Kipling, a remarkable master of this difficult literary form, is a comparatively new phenomenon in English literature. From the days of Washington Irving, on the other hand, Americans have shown themselves able to write short stories rather better than anything else. The older short stories of America — Irving's and Poe's and even Hawthorne's — were generally romantic in both impulse and manner. Accordingly, however local their sentiment may have been, and however local in certain cases their descriptive passages, they were not precisely documents from which local conditions might be inferred. The short stories of modern Americans differ from these by being generally realistic in impulse and local in detail. We have stories of decaying New England, stories of the Middle West, stories of the Ohio region and Chicago stories, stories of the Southwest, stories of the Rocky Mountains and of California, of Virginia and of Georgia. In plot these generally seem conventionally insignificant. Their characters, too, have hardly reached such development as to become recognised national types. These characters, however, are often typical of the regions which have suggested them; and the description of these regions is frequently rendered in elaborate detail with workmanlike effectiveness. On the whole, like all the literature of the moment, in England and in America alike, these short stories lack distinction. The people who write them, one is apt to feel, are not Olympian in temper, but Bohemian. Our American Bohemia, however, is not quite like that of the old world; at least, it is free from the kind of recklessness which one so often associates with such regions; and the writing of our Bohemians preserves something of that artistic conscience which always makes the form of careful American work finer than that of prevalent work in the old country. In the short stories of American magazines, then, so familiar throughout the United States, we have a second type of popular literature not at present developed into masterly form, but ready to afford both a vehicle and a public to any writer of masterly power who may arise.

We have glanced at two of the forms which seem growing to literary ripeness in America, — the newspaper and the popular magazine. There is only one other form whose present popularity is anything like so considerable; this is the stage. So far, to be sure, the American theatre has produced no work which can claim serious consideration. During the last half-century, on the other hand, the American stage has developed all over the country a popularity and an organisation which seem favourable to serious expression in the future. At the beginning of this century there were very few theatres in the United States; in many places, indeed, the popular prejudice against the stage was as blind as that of the Puritans who closed the English theatres in 1642. To-day travelling dramatic companies patrol the continent. Every town has its theatre, and every theatre its audience. Until now, to be sure, the plays most popular in America have generally come straight from Europe, and the plays made here have been apt unintelligently to follow European models. Now and again, however, there have appeared signs that various types of American character could be represented on the stage with great popular effect; and the rapid growth of the American theatre has provided us with an increasing number of skilful actors. A large though thoughtless public of theatre-goers, a school of professional actors who can intelligently present a wide variety of character, and a tendency on the part of American theatrical men to produce, amid stupidly conventional surroundings, vivid studies from life, again represent conditions of promise. If a dramatist of commanding power should arise in this country, he might find ready more than a few of the conditions from which lasting dramatic literatures have flashed into existence.

At this moment newspaper humour, the short stories of the magazines, and the popular stage seem the sources from which a characteristic American literature is most likely to spring. The America of the future can probably be expressed only in some broadly popular form; and these three forms are the only ones which at present seem to promise broad popularity. At present, however, none of these forms, any more than the traditional forms which flourished earlier, are copiously fruitful. In America, as in England, and indeed as in all Europe, the last years of the nineteenth century have seemed artistically less important, less significant, less lasting, than those which lately preceded. The world is passing through experience too confused, too troubled, too uncertain, for ripe expression; and America seems more and more growing to be just another part of the world.

CONCLUSION

CONCLUSION

THE literary history of America is the story, under new conditions, of those ideals which a common language has compelled America, almost unawares, to share with England. Elusive though they be, ideals are the souls of the nations which cherish them, — the living spirits which waken nationality into being, and which often preserve its memory long after its life has ebbed away. Denied by the impatience which will not seek them where they smoulder beneath the cinders of cant, derided by the near-sighted wisdom which is content with the world-old commonplace of how practice must always swerve from precept, they mysteriously, resurgently persist.

The ideals which for three hundred years America and England have cherished, alike yet apart, are ideals of morality and of government, — of right and of rights. Whoever has lived his conscious life in the terms of our language, so saturated with the temper and the phrases both of the English Bible and of English Law, has perforce learned that, however he may stray, he cannot escape the duty which bids us do right and maintain our rights. General as these phrases must seem, — common at first glance to the serious moments of all men everywhere, — they have, for us of English-speaking race, a meaning peculiarly our own. Though Englishmen have prated enough and to spare, and though Americans have declaimed about human rights more nebulously still, the rights for which Englishmen and Americans alike have been eager to fight and to die are no prismatic fancies gleaming through clouds of conflicting logic and metaphor; they are that living body of customs and duties and privileges, which a process very like physical growth has made the vital condition of our national existence. Through immemorial experience, the rights which we most jealously cherish have proved themselves safely favourable at once to prosperity and to righteousness.

Threatened throughout history, both from without and from within, these rights can be preserved by nothing short of eternal vigilance. In this we have been faithful, until our deepest ideal of public duty, which marks Englishmen and Americans apart from others, and side by side, has long ago defined itself. The vitally growing rights bequeathed us by our fathers, we must protect, not only from invasion or aggression attempted by other races than ours, but also from the internal ravages both of reaction and of revolution. In loyalty to this conception of duty, the nobler minds of England and of America have always been at one.

Yet to careless eyes the two countries have long seemed parted by a chasm wider even than the turbulent and foggy Atlantic. Wide it has surely been, but never so vague as to interpose between them the shoreless gulf of sundered principle. The differences which have kept England and America so long distinct have arisen from no more fatal cause than unwitting and temporary conflicts of their common law. The origin of both countries, as we know them to-day, was the England of Queen Elizabeth, with all its spontaneity, all its enthusiasm, all its untired versatility. From this origin England has sped faster and further than America. Throughout two full centuries, then, America and England have faithfully, honestly quarrelled as to just what rights and liberties were truly sanctioned by the law which has remained common to both.

How their native tempers began to diverge we have already seen. During the seventeenth century, England proceeded from its spontaneous, enthusiastic Elizabethan versatility, through the convulsions of the Civil Wars, to

Cromwell's Commonwealth; and from the Commonwealth, through the baseness of the Restoration and the renewing health of the Glorious Revolution, to that state of parliamentary government which, in vitally altering form, still persists. English literature meanwhile proceeded from the age of Shakspere, through the age of Milton, to the age of Dryden. During this same seventeenth century, — the century of American immigration, — the course of American history was interrupted by no such convulsion as the wars and tumults which destroyed Elizabethan England. American character, then, which from the beginning possessed its still persistent power of absorbing immigration, preserved much of the spontaneity, the enthusiasm, and the versatility transported hither from the mother country when Virginia and New England were founded. So far as literature went, meantime, seventeenth-century America expressed itself only in occasional historical records, and in a deluge of Calvinistic theology. Though long since abated, these first outpourings of New England have left indelible traces. Partly to them, and still more to the devout source from which they welled, is due the instinctive devotion of America to such ideals of absolute right and truth as were inherent in the passionate idealism of the Puritans.

It was here that America most distinctly parted from the mother country. In England, the Puritan Commonwealth, with its nobly futile aspiration toward absolute right, so entwined itself about the life of Cromwell that when he died it fell. In America a similar commonwealth, already deeply rooted when Cromwell was still a sturdy country gentleman of St. Ives, flourished fruitful long after his relics had been cast out of Westminster Abbey. Generation by generation, the immemorial custom of America, wherein America has steadily discerned the features of its ancestral rights and liberties, grew insensibly to sanction more abstract ideals than ever long persisted in England.

Whoever will thus interpret the seventeenth century need be at little pains to understand the century which followed. The political events of this eighteenth century — the century of American independence — forced England into prolonged international isolation; and this, combined with reactionary desire for domestic order, bred in British character that insular conservatism still typified by the portly, repellent integrity of John Bull. English literature meanwhile proceeded from the Addisonian urbanity of Queen Anne's time, through the ponderous Johnsonian formality which satisfied the subjects of George II., to the masterly publicism of Burke and the contagious popularity of Burns.

Eighteenth-century America was politically free from the conditions which so highly developed the peculiar eccentricities of England. There is no wonder, then, that American character still retained the spontaneity, the enthusiasm, and the versatility of the elder days when it had shared these traits with the English. Nor is there any wonder that Americans went on traditionally cherishing the fervent idealism of the immigrant Puritans, wherein for a while the ancestral English ideals of right and of rights had fused. Unwittingly lingering in its pristine state, the native character of America became less and less like the character which historical forces were irresistibly moulding in the mother country. The traditional law of America — the immemorial rights, the customs and the liberties, of a newly conscious people eagerly responsive to the allurements of absolute truth — seemed on its surface less and less like the more dogged and rigid system which was becoming the traditional law of England. When disputes arose, the spirit of old Babel was reawakened. Despite their common language, neither of the kindred peoples, separated not only by the wastes of the ocean but also by the forgotten lapse of five generations, could rightly understand the other. Dispute waxed fruitlessly high. The inevitable result was the American Revolution.

The same causes which wrought this imperial disunion had tended to alter the literary character of America. American theology had already evaporated in metaphysical abstraction; its place, as the principal phase of American expression, had been taken by politics. Of this, no doubt, the animating ideal was not so much that of morality as that of law; the writings of eighteenth-century America have less concern with right than with rights. Yet America would not have been America unless these ancestral ideals had remained blended. A yearning for absolute truth, an unbroken faith in abstract ideals, is what makes distinctly national the political utterances of the American Revolution. The love of abstract right which pervades them sprang straight from that aspiration toward absolute truth which had animated the grim idealism of the Puritans.

So came the nineteenth century, — the century of American nationality, when, for all their community of language and of ideals, England and America have believed themselves mutually foreign. English history has proceeded from the extreme isolation which ended at Waterloo, through the constitutional revolution of the Reform Bill to the present reign. What the future may decide to have been the chief features of this Victorian epoch, it is still too soon to assert; yet, whatever else, the future can hardly fail to remember how, throughout these sixty and more years, England has continually developed in two seemingly divergent ways. At home, on the one hand, it has so tended toward democracy that already the political power of the English masses probably exceeds that of the American. In its world relations, on the other hand, England has become imperial to a degree undreamed of when Queen Victoria ascended the throne. Wherever the influence of England extends to-day, democracy and empire go hand in hand.

Throughout this nineteenth century, America has had the Western Hemisphere almost to itself. This it has dominated with increasing material power, believing all the while that it could keep free from entanglement with other regions of the earth. From this youthful dream it has at last been rudely awakened. In the dawning of a new century, it finds itself — like England, at once democratic and imperial — inevitably confronted with world conflict; either its ideals must prevail, or they must perish. After three centuries of separation, then, England and America are once more side by side. With them, in union, lies the hope of imperial democracy.

It is only during the nineteenth century — the century of American nationality — that America has brought forth literature. First appearing in the Middle States, this soon developed more seriously in New England, whose mental life, so active at first, had lain comparatively dormant for almost a hundred years. These two phases of American literary expression, the only ones which may as yet be regarded as complete, have been the chief subject of our study. On the impression which they have left with us must rest our estimate of what the literature produced in America has hitherto signified.

To define this impression, we may helpfully glance back at what the nineteenth century added to the literature of England. First came the poetry of Wordsworth and Coleridge and Shelley and Keats and Byron, — a poetry, for all its individual variety, aflame with the spirit of world-revolution. Then, just after Waterloo, came those bravely ideal retrospective romances which have immortalised the name of Scott. He died in 1832, the year of the Reform Bill. The later literature of England has expressed the meanings of life discerned and felt by men whose mature years have fallen within the democratic and imperial reign of Queen Victoria. This literature includes the great modern novelists, — Dickens and Thackeray and George Eliot, with their host of contemporaries and followers; it includes the poetry of Tennyson, and of the Brownings, and of more; it includes a wealth of serious prose, the work of Macaulay, of Carlyle, of Ruskin, of Newman, of Matthew Arnold, and of numberless others; it includes the studied and fastidious refinement of Stevenson; it still happily includes the scope and power of writers now living.

In the nineteenth century English literature began with a passionate outburst of aspiring romantic poetry; it passed into an era of retrospective romantic prose; it proceeded to a stage where, for all the merit of persistent poetry, the chief fact seems to have been fiction dealing mostly with contemporary life; its serious prose, all the while, tended more and more to dwell on the problems of the times; and these surely underlie the utterances of its latest masters. The more one considers what the century has added to English literature, the more one marvels at its riches. Yet all the while one grows aware of something which, if not a loss, is at least a change. Throughout the century, English letters have slowly lapsed away from the grace of personal distinction. The literature of nineteenth-century England, like its history, expresses an irresistible advance of democracy

Political democracy, no doubt, declared itself earlier and more outspokenly in America than in England. So far as literature is concerned, on the other hand, the first thirty years of the nineteenth century excited from America much less democratic utterances than came from the revolutionary poets of the mother country. If you doubt this, compare Brockden Brown with Wordsworth, Irving with Coleridge, Cooper with Shelley, Bryant with Byron. What that earlier literature of the Middle States chiefly certifies of American character is the trait which so far has most surely controlled the progress of the United States: whatever our vagaries of occasional speech, we Americans are at heart disposed, with good old English common-sense, to follow those lines of conduct which practice has proved safe and which prudence has pronounced admirable. The earlier literature of the Middle States has another trait which seems nationally characteristic: its sensitiveness of artistic conscience shows Americans generally to be more alive to artistic duty than Englishmen have often been. The first literary utterances of inexperienced America were marked by no wildness or vagary ; they showed, rather, an almost timid loyalty to the traditions of excellence.

A few years later came what so far seems the nearest approach of America to lasting literature, — the final utterances of New England during the years of its Renaissance, which, broadly speaking, were contemporary with the first half of the reign of Queen Victoria. The new life had begun, of course, somewhat earlier. It had first shown itself in the awakening of New England oratory and scholarship, and in the ardour which stirred Unitarianism to break the fetters of Calvinistic dogma. Scholarship bore fruit in the later works of the New England historians. Unitarianism tended, through Transcendentalism, to militant, disintegrating reform. Amid these freshening intellectual surroundings appeared some men whose names seem destined at least for a while to live in the records of literature. The chief of these were Emerson and Whittier and Longfellow and Lowell and Holmes and Hawthorne. If you will compare them with the writers who in their time were most eminent in England, — with Dickens, Thackeray, and George Eliot, with Tennyson and the Brownings, with Carlyle and Ruskin, with Newman and Matthew Arnold, — you can hardly help feeling a difference, palpable even though indistinct, undeniable even though hard to define.

One phase of this difference soon grows clear. Though the writers of renascent New England were generally better in prose than in poetry, — and thus resembled their English contemporaries, — their spirit was rather like that which had animated the fervent English poetry of a generation before. One and all of them, accepting the revolutionary doctrine that human nature is not evil but good, confidently hoped that illimitable development was at hand for a humanity finally freed from the shackles of outworn custom. In this faith and hope, the men of the New England Renaissance were sustained by a fact never true of any other civilised society than that from which they sprung. For more than two hundred years, national inexperience had protected American character from such distortion as the pressure of dense population always twists into human nature. With a justified enthusiasm, then, the literary leaders of New England, full of the earnest idealism inseparable from their Puritan ancestry, and finally escaped from the dogmas which had reviled humanity, fervently proclaimed democracy. And here, at first, their temper seems to linger a little behind that of the mother country. The undimmed confidence of their faith in human nature is like that which was beginning to fade from English literature before the death of Scott.

Yet these New England writers were no mere exotic survivors of the days when English Romanticism was fervid. They were all true Americans; and this they could not have been without an almost rustic limitation of worldly knowledge, without a shrewd sense of fact which should at once correct the errors of such ignorance and check the vagaries of their idealism, or without exacting artistic conscience. Their devotion to the ideals of right and of rights came straight from ancestral England. Their spontaneous aptitude for idealism, their enthusiastic love for abstractions and for absolute truth, they had derived, too, from the Elizabethan Puritans whose traits they had hereditarily preserved. What most surely marked them apart was the quality of their eager faith in democracy. To them this was no untested dream; it was rather a truth confirmed by the national inexperience of their still uncrowded country. Hence sprang the phase of their democratic temper which still seems most precious and most pregnant.

The spirit of European democracy has been dominated by blind devotion to an enforced equality. In many American utterances you may doubtless find thoughtless assertion of the same dogma. Yet if you will ponder on the course of

34

American history, and still more if you will learn intimately to know those more eminent American men of letters who remain the living teachers of our growing country, you must grow to feel that American democracy has a wiser temper, still its own.   The national ideal of America has never yet denied or even repressed the countless variety of human worth and power.   It has urged only that men should enjoy liberty within the range of law.   It has resisted both lingering and innovating tyranny; but all the while it has kept faithful to the principle that, so far as public safety may permit, each of us has an inalienable right to strive for excellence.   In the presence of approved excellence it has remained humble.

The history of such future as we can now discern must be that of a growing world-democracy.   The most threatening future danger, then, is often held to lurk in those dogged systems of authority which still strive to strangle humane aspiration.   No doubt these are dangerous, yet sometimes there must seem even deeper danger in that crescent phase of democracy itself which hates and condemns excellence.   If in the conflicts to come, democracy shall overpower excellence, or if excellence, seeking refuge in freshly imperious assertion of authority, shall prove democracy another futile dream, the ways before us are dark.   The more one dreads such darkness, the more gleams of counsel and help one may find in the simple, hopeful literature of inexperienced, renascent New England.   There, for a while, the warring ideals of democracy and of excellence were once reconciled, dwelling confidently together in some earthly semblance of peace.

AUTHORITIES AND REFERENCES

AUTHORITIES AND REFERENCES

THE following memoranda indicate, first, the chief general authorities on the whole matter in hand; secondly, the principal accessible authorities on the special topics discussed in the successive books and chapters; and thirdly, the most authoritative and available editions of the principal works mentioned in the text. For convenience, they are arranged under the following heads : I. General Authorities ; II. Special Authorities for each book and for each chapter.

Without pretending to be exhaustive, these memoranda should serve as guides to those who desire further to investigate the matter touched on. In general, they call attention to accessible bibliographies.

I. GENERAL AUTHORITIES

1. For English History, so far as it concerns us, any standard authority should serve; for example, the *Encyclopædia Britannica*.

2. For English Literature, in general, the best books seem —

STOPFORD BROOKE : *Primer of English Literature*, 1889.

HENRY CRAIK : *English Prose*, etc., 5 vols., 1893–96.

FREDERICK RYLAND : *Chronological Outlines of English Literature*, 1896.

THOMAS H. WARD : *English Poets*, 4 vols., 1896–1900.

3. For American History, the following works should serve as general guides : —

EDWARD CHANNING : *A Students' History of the United States*, New York, 1899.

EDWARD CHANNING and ALBERT BUSHNELL HART : *Guide to the Study of American History*, Boston, 1896.

JUSTIN WINSOR [editor] : *Narrative and Critical History of America*, 8 vols., Boston, 1886–89.

4. For literature in America, among numerous works, the following seem perhaps the most useful : —

a. Histories of Literature : —

J. NICHOL : *American Literature*, Edinburgh, 1882.

H. S. PANCOAST : *Introduction to American Literature*, New York, 1898.

C. F. RICHARDSON : *American Literature*, 2 vols., New York, 1887.

E. C. STEDMAN : *Poets of America*, Boston, 1885.

M. C. TYLER : *A History of American Literature during the Colonial Time*, 2 vols., New York, 1897.   [Vol. I., 1607–76 ; Vol. II., 1676–1765.]

M. C. TYLER : *The Literary History of the American Revolution*, 2 vols., New York, 1897.

BARRETT WENDELL : *Stelligeri*, etc., New York, 1893.

GREENOUGH WHITE : *Sketch of the Philosophy of American Literature*, Boston, 1891.

b. Collections of Extracts : —

G. R. CARPENTER : *American Prose*, New York, 1898.

E. A. and G. L. DUYCKINCK : *Cyclopædia of American Literature*, 2 vols., Philadelphia, 1875.

R. W. GRISWOLD : *The Poets and Poetry of America*, Philadelphia, 1842.

R. W. GRISWOLD : *Prose Writers of America*, Philadelphia, 1847.

R. W. GRISWOLD : *Female Poets of America*, Philadelphia, 1848.

E. C. STEDMAN : *An American Anthology*, Boston, 1900.

E. C. STEDMAN and ELLEN M. HUTCHINSON : *Library of American Literature*, 11 vols., New York, 1888–90.

c. Bibliography and Chronology : —

P. K. FOLEY : *American Authors 1795–1895*, etc., Boston, Privately Printed, 1897.

S. L. WHITCOMB : *Chronological Outlines of American Literature*, New York, 1894.

II. SPECIAL AUTHORITIES

INTRODUCTION

For a more complete statement of the theory of literary evolution, see B. WENDELL : *William Shakspere*, New York, 1894, pp. 401 ff.

BOOK I. THE SEVENTEENTH CENTURY

ENGLISH HISTORY FROM 1600 TO 1700
Book I. Chapter I.

See third paragraph of the bibliography at the end of JOHN FISKE's *Beginnings of New England*, Boston, 1889. The great books on this period are, of course, S. R. GARDINER's *History of England from the Accession of James I. to the Outbreak of the Civil War, 1603–1642*, 10 vols., London, 1883–84, and his *History of the Great Civil War, 1642–1649*, 3 vols., London, 1886–91. DAVID MASSON's *Life of John Milton: with the Political, Ecclesiastical, and Literary History of his Time* [1608–1674], 6 vols., London, 1859–80, is a work of great learning.

ENGLISH LITERATURE FROM 1600 TO 1700
Book I. Chapter II.

In addition to the general authorities may be mentioned GEORGE SAINTSBURY's *A History of Elizabethan Literature*, London, 1887, and A. W. WARD's *A History of English Dramatic Literature to the Death of Queen Anne*, 3 vols., London, 1899.

AMERICAN HISTORY FROM 1600 TO 1700
Book I. Chapter III.

Of the books mentioned in the text, the best editions are : —

WILLIAM BRADFORD : *History of Plymouth Plantation*, ed. Charles Deane, Boston, 1856. Reprinted from the Mass. Hist. Soc. *Collections*. There is also a serviceable edition of the text, with some interesting matter concerning the return of the Bradford MS., published by the Commonwealth of Massachusetts, Boston, 1898.

SAMUEL SEWALL's *Diary* (1674–1729), 3 vols., Boston, 1878–82. [Mass. Hist. Soc. *Collections*, 5th series, Vols. V.–VII.]

JOHN WINTHROP : *History of New England*, ed. James Savage, 2 vols., Boston, 1853. The best biography of Winthrop is the *Life and Letters of John Winthrop*, ed. Robert C. Winthrop, Boston, 1864 (copyrighted 1863).

LITERATURE IN AMERICA FROM 1600 TO 1700
Book I. Chapter IV.

For the literary history of America in the seventeenth century TYLER's first two volumes are almost sufficient. One may note also JOSIAH QUINCY's *History of Harvard University*, 2 vols., Cambridge, 1840, and J. L. SIBLEY's *Harvard Graduates*, 3 vols., Cambridge, 1873–85.

A literal reprint of the first edition of the *Bay Psalm Book* was made at Cambridge in 1862, under the direction of Dr. N. B.

Bay Psalm Book. Shurtleff. See TYLER: *History of American Literature during the Colonial Time*, etc., Vol. I. pp. 274–277; WINSOR: *Memorial History of Boston*, Vol. I. pp. 458–60; WILBERFORCE EAMES: *A List of Editions of the "Bay Psalm Book,"* etc., New York, 1885. STEDMAN AND HUTCHINSON's *Library*, Vol. I. pp. 211 ff., contains extracts.

The Works of Anne Bradstreet in Prose and Verse, edited by JOHN HARVARD ELLIS, were published at Charlestown in 1867. There is

Mrs. Bradstreet. also a handsome edition entitled *The Poems of Mrs. Anne Bradstreet* (1612–1672), with an introduction by Prof. C. E. NORTON [privately printed], 1897.

N. E. Primer. On the New England Primer, see PAUL LEICESTER FORD's *The New England Primer; History of its Origin and Development*, etc., New York, 1897.

Sandys. *Ovid's Metamorphosis englished* by G. S. [GEORGE SANDYS] appeared at London, in folio, 1626. [Br. Mus. Catalogue.]

On the works of John Smith see WINSOR's *America*, Vol. III.

Smith. Chap. V.; also the "Note on Smith's Publications," *ibid.*, pp. 211–212. The most accessible edition of Smith's writings is that by Arber in the "English Scholar's Library," Birmingham, 1884.

Of Wigglesworth there is nothing in print. Professor Tyler says (Vol. II. p. 34) : "The eighteen hundred copies of the first edition [of

Wigglesworth. the *Day of Doom*] were sold within a single year; which implies the purchase of a copy . . . by at least every thirty-fifth person then in New England, — an example of the commercial success of a book never afterward equalled in this country. Since that time, the book has been repeatedly published, at least once in England, and at least eight times in America — the last time being in 1867." This edition of 1867 was published at New York and contained a memoir by J. W. Dean. The chief biography of Wigglesworth, JOHN WARD DEAN's *Memoir of the Rev. Michael Wigglesworth, Author of the Day of Doom*, Albany, 1863, contains (pp. 140–151) a note on "Editions of Wigglesworth's Poems."

COTTON MATHER
Book I. Chapter V.

The life and works of Cotton Mather are adequately discussed in the Rev. ABIJAH PERKINS MARVIN's *The Life and Times of Cotton Mather*, Boston [1892], and in BARRETT WENDELL's *Cotton Mather, the Puritan Priest*, New York [1891]. Professor Wendell's book has a list of authorities on pages 309 and 310; SIBLEY's *Harvard Graduates*, Vol. III. pp. 42–158, has an elaborate Mather bibliography. The *Magnalia* has twice been reprinted in America : once in 1820 at Hartford, Conn., in 2 vols., 8vo, and again in the same form and at the same place in 1853. There is now no accessible edition.

BOOK II.   THE EIGHTEENTH CENTURY

ENGLISH HISTORY FROM 1700 TO 1800
Book II. Chapter I.

The great book on English history in the eighteenth century is W. E. H. LECKY's *A History of England in the Eighteenth Century*, 8 vols., 1878–90. LORD MAHON's *History of England from the Peace of Utrecht to the Peace of Versailles, 1713–1783*, 7 vols., 1853–54, is also valuable.

ENGLISH LITERATURE FROM 1700 TO 1800
Book II. Chapter II.

For the outlines of English literary history in the eighteenth century the following will serve tolerably well : ALEXANDRE BELJAME : *Le Public et les Hommes de Lettres en Angleterre au Dix-huitième Siècle (1660–1744)*, Paris, 1881 ; EDMUND GOSSE : *A History of Eigh-*

teenth Century Literature, London, 1889; Thomas S. Perry: *English Literature in the Eighteenth Century*, New York, 1883.

American History from 1700 to 1800
Book II. Chapter III.

For American history in the eighteenth century, the general authorities — Channing, Channing and Hart's *Guide*, and Winsor — will amply suffice. For religious matters, see G. L. Walker's *Some Aspects of the Religious History of New England, with Special Reference to Congregationalists*, Boston, 1897.

Literature in America from 1700 to 1776
Book II. Chapter IV.

On the literary history of America in the eighteenth century the standard authority is Professor Tyler, the second, third, and fourth volumes of whose work admirably cover the period from the beginning of the century through the year 1783.

John Woolman's *Journal*, with an introduction by John G. Whittier, was published at Boston in 1871. On Woolman's life and writings, see Tyler's *Literary History of the American Revolution*, Chap. XXXVII.

Of Thomas Hutchinson's *History of the Colony of Massachusets-Bay* (Vol. I. Boston, 1764; Vol. II. Boston, 1767; Vol. III. London, 1828), the first two volumes have been out of print **Hutchinson.** for over a century, the last edition having been published at Salem and Boston in 1795; the third volume is to be found only in the London edition of 1828. For biographical detail, see *The Diary and Letters of His Excellency Thomas Hutchinson, Esq.*, ed. P. O. Hutchinson, 2 vols., Boston, 1884–86. The late Charles Deane compiled a Hutchinson bibliography which was privately printed at Boston in 1857.

Jonathan Edwards
Book II. Chapter V.

Professor Allen writes: "The first edition of Edwards' works was published in Worcester, Mass., in 8 vols., 1809; afterwards republished in 4 vols. It is still in print, the plates being owned, it is said, by Carter Bros., New York. Dr. Dwight's edition was published in New York in 1829, in 10 vols., the first volume being occupied with the life. There is a London edition in 8 vols. by Williams, 1817 ; vols. 9 and 10 supplementary by Ogle, Edinburgh, 1847. Another London edition in 2 vols., bearing the imprint of Bohn, is still in print, and though cumbrous in form is in many respects excellent. It possesses the only portrait of Edwards which answers to one's idea of the man.'' The best biography of Edwards is Prof. A. V. G. ALLEN's *Jonathan Edwards*, Boston, 1889 ; it contains (pp. 391–393) a good bibliography. One should also note the essays on Edwards by Holmes (Works, Riverside ed., Vol. VIII. pp. 361–401) and by Leslie Stephen (*Hours in a Library*, 2d series, Chap. II., London, 1876).

BENJAMIN FRANKLIN
Book II. Chapter VI.

Of Franklin's works the best edition is that by JOHN BIGELOW, 10 vols., New York, 1887–88. Of Franklin's own *Life* the best edition is that by John Bigelow, in 3 vols., Philadelphia, 1875. The best biographies of Franklin seem those of Prof. JOHN BACH McMASTER, in the series of American Men of Letters, Boston, 1887, and of JOHN T. MORSE, Jr., in the American Statesmen series, Boston, 1889. PAUL LEICESTER FORD has compiled a *Franklin Bibliography*, Brooklyn, 1889.

THE AMERICAN REVOLUTION
Book II. Chapter VII.

On the literary aspect of the American Revolution, Professor TYLER's volumes are the best authority; for its history, JOHN FISKE's *American Revolution*, 2 vols., Boston, 1892, is entertaining and suggestive, while WINSOR's *Reader's Handbook of the American Revolution* (*1761–1783*), Boston, 1880, points the way to the authorities for study in detail. Dr. S. WEIR MITCHELL's *Hugh Wynne* is so accurate and vivid a fiction as to have the value of an authority.

The writings of JAMES OTIS have never been collected. For notes on his various speeches and articles, see WINSOR's *Reader's Handbook*, pp. 1–2, and his *America*, Vol. VI. pp. 68–70. Biographies of Otis have been written by William Tudor, Boston, 1823, and by Francis Bowen in SPARKS's *Library of American Biography*, 2d series, Vol. II., Boston, 1847.

Westchester Farmer. On the "Westchester Farmer," see WINSOR's *America,* Vol. VI. p. 104.

The Miscellaneous Essays and Occasional Writings of Francis Hopkinson, in 3 vols. were published at Philadelphia in 1792. **Hopkinson.** On Hopkinson's life and writings, see TYLER : *Literary History of the American Revolution,* Chap. XXX.

LITERATURE IN AMERICA FROM 1776 TO 1800
Book II. Chapter VIII.

On the general conditions of life in America between the close of the Revolution and the beginning of the nineteenth century, see HENRY ADAMS's *History of the United States,* 9 vols., New York, 1889–91.

On the Federalist group, the chief authorities are *The Federalist,* etc., ed. Paul Leicester Ford, New York, 1898 ; *The Works of* **Federalist.** *Alexander Hamilton,* ed. Henry Cabot Lodge, 9 vols., New York, 1885–86 ; Madison's *Papers,* . . . *being his Correspondence and Reports of Debates,* ed. Henry D. Gilpin, 3 vols., Washington, 1840, and his *Letters and Other Writings,* 4 vols., Philadelphia, 1865 ; *The Correspondence and Public Papers of John Jay,* ed. Henry P. Johnston, 4 vols., New York, 1890. For biographical detail, see HENRY CABOT LODGE's *Alexander Hamilton,* Boston, 1882 (American Statesmen series) ; WILLIAM C. RIVES's *History of the Life and Times of James Madison,* 3 vols., Boston, 1859–68 ; SYDNEY HOWARD GAY's *James Madison,* Boston, 1884 (American Statesmen series), and GEORGE PELLEW's *John Jay,* Boston, 1890 (American Statesmen series). Copious bibliographic detail will be found in WINSOR's *America,* Vol. VII. pp. 259–260, and in PAUL LEICESTER FORD's *Bibliotheca Hamiltoniana,* New York, printed for the author, 1886.

A sufficient notion of CRÈVECŒUR may be got from TYLER : *Literary History of the American Revolution,* Vol. II. pp. 347–358, and **Crèvecœur.** Stedman and Hutchinson's *Library,* Vol. III. pp. 138–146. Crèvecœur's *Letters from an American Farmer* were published at London in 1782 ; there is a French translation in two volumes, published at Paris in 1784.

Selections from the writings of the "Hartford Wits" are given in the third volume of Stedman and Hutchinson's *Library ;* while Pro-

fessor Tyler's *Literary History of the American Revolution* **Hartford Wits.**
discusses their work at some length. For an interesting
monograph on the Hartford Wits, see F. SHELDON: *The Pleiades of
Connecticut*, Atlantic Monthly, Vol. XV. p. 187 (Feb., 1865).

TIMOTHY DWIGHT's works are not in print. Original editions of
importance are: *The Triumph of Infidelity: A Poem. Printed in the
World*, 1788; *The Conquest of Canaan: A Poem, in
Eleven Books*, Hartford, 1785; *Greenfield Hill: A Poem,* **Dwight.**
in Seven Parts, New York, 1794; *Travels in New England and New
York (1796–1815)*, 4 vols., New Haven, 1821–22. For further
details, see Professor Tyler's excellent *Three Men of Letters* [Berkeley,
Dwight, Barlow], New York, 1895, pp. 184–185.

The Poetical Works of Jonathan Trumbull, LL.D., were published
at Hartford in 1820. Notable editions of *M'Fingal* are the first,
M'Fingal: a Modern Epic Poem, in Four Cantos, Hartford, 1782, 16mo; the sixth, London, 1793, with explana- **Trumbull.**
tory notes by Joel Barlow; and an edition with introduction and notes
by B. J. Lossing, New York, 1880.

Of JOEL BARLOW's writings no edition is in print. For
bibliography and other details, see TYLER's *Three Men of* **Barlow.**
Letters, pp. 131–183.

The writings of FRENEAU are no longer in print. Among early
editions should be noted *Miscellaneous Works of Mr. Philip Freneau,
Containing his Essays and Additional Poems*, Philadelphia,
1788; *Poems Written between the Years 1768 and 1794,* **Freneau.**
Monmouth, 1795; *Poems Written and Published during the Amer-
ican Revolutionary War . . . and Other Pieces not heretofore in
Print*, 2 vols., Philadelphia, 1809. On Campbell's borrowings from
Freneau, see TYLER: *Literary History of the American Revolution*,
Vol. I. pp. 177 ff.

BOOK III.   THE NINETEENTH CENTURY

ENGLISH HISTORY SINCE 1800
Book III. Chapter I.

For English history in the nineteenth century, the general reference will suffice.

English Literature since 1800
Book III. Chapter II.

The revolutionary temper of early nineteenth-century literature in England has nowhere been better defined than in Dr. A. E. Hancock's *The French Revolution and the English Poets*, New York, 1899.

American History since 1800
Book III. Chapter III.

Abundant references for the study of American history since 1800 will be found in Channing and Hart's *Guide*, pp. 329 ff. For the first twenty years of the century, see Henry Adams's *History of the United States*, New York, 1889–91 ; for the period between 1850 and 1863, J. F. Rhodes's *History of the United States*, New York, 1893–99, is the chief authority.

Literature in America since 1800
Book III. Chapter IV.

For literature in America since 1800, see the general authorities.

BOOK IV. LITERATURE IN THE MIDDLE STATES FROM 1798 TO 1857

Charles Brockden Brown
Book IV. Chapter I.

Brockden Brown's novels have been published at Philadelphia, 6 vols., 1857, and in a later and more sumptuous edition, 6 vols., Philadelphia, 1887, limited to 500 copies. Notable biographies of Brown are William Dunlap's *Life*, 2 vols., Philadelphia, 1815, and William H. Prescott's in Sparks's *Library of American Biography*, Vol. I. pp. 119–180, or in Prescott's *Biographical and Critical Miscellanies*, New York, 1845.

Washington Irving
Book IV. Chapter II.

Irving's works are published, in various editions, by the Putnams of New York. Standard biographies are the *Life and Letters of Wash-*

ington Irving, by his nephew, Pierre M. Irving, 4 vols., New York, 1862–64, and Mr. CHARLES DUDLEY WARNER'S *Washington Irving*, Boston, 1881, in the American Men of Letters series.

JAMES FENIMORE COOPER
Book IV. Chapter III.

Editions of COOPER'S novels abound; his other works are not in print. The best life of Cooper is that by Prof. T. R. Lounsbury, Boston, 1883, in the American Men of Letters series. It has a considerable bibliography. An excellent monograph on Cooper, by W. B. S. Clymer, is about to be published in the Beacon Biography series at Boston.

WILLIAM CULLEN BRYANT
Book IV. Chapter IV.

Of BRYANT'S works the standard edition is that of PARKE GODWIN: *Poetical Works*, 2 vols., New York, 1883 ; *Prose Writings*, 2 vols., New York, 1884. The best life of Bryant is PARKE GODWIN'S, in two volumes, New York, 1883.

Griswold's collections and Duyckinck's Cyclopædia have already been referred to in the list of general references. Drake and Halleck are generously represented in Stedman and Hutchinson's *Library* and in the collections of Griswold.

EDGAR ALLAN POE
Book IV. Chapter V.

Stedman and Woodberry's edition of Poe, in 10 vols., Chicago, 1894–95, is admirable. The best biography of Poe is Professor Woodberry's, Boston, 1885, in the American Men of Letters series. For Poe bibliography, see Stedman and Woodberry's tenth volume, pp. 267–281.

THE KNICKERBOCKER SCHOOL
Book IV. Chapter VI.

On American periodical publication between 1815 and 1833, see Dr. W. B. Cairns : *On the Development of American Literature from 1815 to 1833, with Especial Reference to Periodicals*, Madison, Wisconsin, 1898.

For the Knickerbocker writers in general, one should glance, if possible, at *The Knickerbocker Gallery: a Testimonial to the Editor of the Knickerbocker Magazine from its Contributors. . . . New York: Samuel Hueston, MDCCCLV.*

On WILLIS, Professor Beers writes : " Of the various collective editions of his [Willis's] verse, published since 1844, . . . the final and most complete is . . . the Clark and Maynard edition of 1868.   No really complete edition of Willis's writings has ever been printed.   The first collective edition which laid claim to being complete was entitled *The Complete Works of N. P. Willis,* 1 vol., 895 pp., New York, J. S. Redfield, 1846.   The thirteen volumes in uniform style, issued by Charles Scribner from 1849 to 1859, form as nearly a complete edition of Willis's prose as is ever likely to be made." (Beers's *Willis*, p. 353.)   A volume of selections from Willis's prose writings appeared at New York in 1885, under the editorship of Prof. H. A. Beers.   The best biography of Willis is that by Professor Beers, Boston, 1885, in the American Men of Letters series.

Willis.

Mrs. Kirkland's books, originally published by Francis, of New York and Boston, seem to be no longer in print ; they are chiefly *A New Home : Who 'll Follow ?* 1839 ; *Forest Life*, 1842 ; *Western Clearings*, 1846.

Melville.   Hermann Melville's best-known stories are: *Typee*, 1846 ; *Omoo*, 1847 ; *Moby Dick, the White Whale*, 1851.

Standard biographies of Bayard Taylor are his *Life and Letters,* edited by Marie Hansen-Taylor and Horace E. Scudder, 2 vols., Boston, 1884, and ALBERT H. SMYTH's *Bayard Taylor*, Boston, 1896, in the American Men of Letters series.

Taylor.

The principal writings of George William Curtis, with their dates of publication, are: *Nile Notes of a Howadji*, 1851 ; *Lotus Eating : A Summer Book*, 1852; *The Potiphar Papers*, 1853 ; *Prue and I*, 1856 ; *Works ; Collected and Newly Revised by the Author*, 5 vols., 1856 ; *Essays from the Easy Chair,* three series, 1892–'93–'94.   Mr. Edward Cary has written a life of Curtis for the American Men of Letters series, Boston, 1894.

Curtis.

BOOK V. THE RENAISSANCE OF NEW ENGLAND

SOME GENERAL CHARACTERISTICS OF NEW ENGLAND
Book V. Chapter I.

The outlines of New England history in the colonial period are well depicted in JOHN FISKE's *The Beginnings of New England*, Boston, 1889, which has a good bibliography, and in BROOKS ADAMS's *The Emancipation of Massachusetts*, Boston, 1887. WINSOR's *America*, Vol. III., and CHANNING AND HART's *Guide*, § 109 ff., contain extensive bibliographic notes on New England colonial history.

Of the later records of New England life mentioned in the text, Mrs. STOWE's *Oldtown Folks*, originally published at Boston in 1869, where also her *Uncle Tom's Cabin* appeared in two volumes in 1852, may be found in the lately published Riverside edition of her works; WHITTIER's *Snow Bound*, first printed at Boston in 1866, is prominent in any edition of his poems; LOWELL's *Cambridge Thirty Years Ago* (1854) is in the first volume of the Riverside edition of his works, and his *A Great Public Character* (1867) is in the second volume of the same edition; Miss LARCOM's chief works, with the dates of publication, are: *Ships in the Mist and Other Stories*, 1859; *Poems*, 1868; *Childhood Songs*, 1874; *An Idyl of Work*, 1875; *Wild Roses of Cape Ann, and Other Poems*, 1881; *A New England Girlhood*, 1889; Miss JEWETT's principal works up to 1895 may be found in Foley's *American Authors*, pp. 158-9; since 1895 she has published *The Country of the Pointed Firs*, 1896, and *The Queen's Twin, and Other Stories*, 1900; Dr. EDWARD EVERETT HALE's *New England Boyhood*, first published at Boston in 1893, may be found in the sixth volume of his lately collected works, Boston, 1900; Miss WILKINS has written *The Adventures of Ann*, 1886; *A Humble Romance and Other Stories*, 1887; *A New England Nun and Other Stories*, 1891; *Young Lucretia and Other Stories*, 1892; *The Pot of Gold and Other Stories* [1892]; *Jane Field. A Novel*, 1893; *Giles Cory, Yeoman. A Play*, 1893; *Pembroke: A Novel*, 1894; *Madelon. A Novel*, 1896; *Jerome, A Poor Man. A Novel*, 1897; Miss ALCOTT's *Little Women* was published at Boston, 1868-69. On the literary history of New England, see W. C. LAWTON's *New England Poets*, New York, 1898.

The New England Orators
Book V. Chapter II.

Webster's *Works*, in 6 vols., were published at Boston in 1851; for select speeches, see E. P. Whipple's *The Great Speeches and Orations of Daniel Webster, with an Essay on Daniel Webster as a Master of English Style*, Boston, 1879.
Webster.
Good biographies of Webster are George Ticknor Curtis's *Life of Daniel Webster*, 2 vols., New York, 1870, and Henry Cabot Lodge's *Daniel Webster*, Boston, 1883.

Edward Everett's *Orations and Speeches on Various Occasions*, in 4 vols., were published in Boston, 1853–68. On the renascent influence of Everett's teaching, one should read Emerson's
Everett. "Historic Notes of Life and Letters in New England," *Works*, Riverside edition, Vol. X. pp. 307 ff.

Rufus Choate's *Works, with Memoir by S. G. Brown*,
Choate. were published in Boston, 1862.

Robert Charles Winthrop's *Addresses and Speeches on Various Occasions* were published, in 4 vols., Boston, 1852–86.
Winthrop. The standard life of Winthrop is the *Memoir* by his son, Robert C. Winthrop, Jr., Boston, 1897.

The New England Scholars and Historians
Book V. Chapter III.

For an article on "Libraries in Boston" by the late Justin Winsor, see his *Memorial History of Boston*, Vol. IV. pp. 235 ff.
Prince. Prince's *Chronological History of New England* may be conveniently found in Arber's *English Garner*, Vol. II. pp. 287 ff., London, 1879.

George Ticknor's *History of Spanish Literature* was published in three volumes at New York, 1849; his *Life of William Hickling Prescott* appeared at Boston in 1864. The best biography
Ticknor. of Ticknor is *The Life, Letters, and Journals of George Ticknor*, by Miss Anna Ticknor, 2 vols., Boston, 1876.

Sparks's historical labours may be suggested by these chief titles: *Library of American Biography*, first series, 10 vols., Boston, 1834–
Sparks. 38; 2d series, 15 vols., Boston, 1844–48; *Washington's Writings*, 12 vols., Boston, 1834–37; *Franklin's Works*, 10 vols., Boston, 1836–40; *Correspondence of the American Revo-*

lution, 4 vols., Boston, 1853; *The Diplomatic Correspondence of the American Revolution*, 12 vols., Boston, 1829–30. For further detail, both biographical and bibliographical, see HERBERT B. ADAMS's *The Life and Writings of Jared Sparks*, 2 vols., Boston, 1893. Sparks's MSS. may be seen in the reading room of Harvard College Library.

PRESCOTT's *History of the Reign of Ferdinand and Isabella, the Catholic*, 3 vols., appeared at Boston in 1838; his *History of the Conquest of Mexico*, etc., in 3 vols., at New York in 1843; **Prescott.** his *Biographical and Critical Miscellanies*, at New York in 1845; the *History of the Conquest of Peru*, etc., 2 vols., New York, 1847; and the *History of the Reign of Philip the Second, King of Spain*, 3 vols., Boston, 1855–58. The best biography of Prescott is GEORGE TICKNOR's *Life of William Hickling Prescott*, Boston, 1864.

MOTLEY's *Merry-Mount; A Romance of the Massachusetts Colony*, 2 vols., appeared at Boston and Cambridge, in 1849; *The Rise of the Dutch Republic. A History*, 3 vols., New York, 1856; *History of the United Netherlands*, etc., 4 vols., New **Motley.** York, 1861–68; *The Life and Death of John of Barneveld*, etc., 2 vols., New York, 1875. Motley's letters have been edited by George William Curtis, in 2 vols., New York, 1889. See also the *Memoir* by Dr. HOLMES, Boston, 1879.

GEORGE BANCROFT's *A History of the United States*, etc., in 10 vols., was published at Boston and London, 1834–74; "The Author's Last Revision," in 6 vols., was published **Bancroft.** at New York, 1883–85.

RICHARD HILDRETH's *The History of the United States of America* was published, in 6 vols., at New York, 1851–56. **Hildreth.**

PALFREY's *History of New England*, in 5 vols., Boston, 1858–90. Palfrey died in 1881; the fifth volume was **Palfrey.** edited by his son, F. W. Palfrey.

FRANCIS PARKMAN's works, of which he personally retained the copyright, are published, in various editions, by Little, Brown & Co., of Boston. For accounts of Parkman's life and estimates of his work, see JOHN FISKE's *A Century of Science and* **Parkman.** *Other Essays*, Boston, 1899; and Mass. Hist. Soc. *Proceedings* for 1893, 2d series, Vol. VIII. pp. 349–369. The authorized biography of Parkman, by C. H. Farnham, has just been published in Boston.

UNITARIANISM
Book V. Chapter IV.

On Unitarianism in general, see the article by Dr. Andrew P. Peabody in WINSOR's *Memorial History of Boston*, Vol. VIII. Chap. XI.

CHANNING's works may be found in a convenient one-volume edition published at Boston in 1886. For his life, see WILLIAM H. CHANNING's *Memoirs of William Ellery Channing*, 3 vols., Boston, 1848, also published in one volume called the " Century Memorial Edition," at Boston in 1880.

The biography of George Ripley has been written by O. B. Frothingham for the series of American Men of Letters, Boston, 1882.

TRANSCENDENTALISM
Book V. Chapter V.

On Transcendentalism in general one should consult O. B. FROTH-

Transcendentalism. INGHAM's *Transcendentalism in New England : A History*, New York, 1876 ; and, if possible, *The Dial : A Magazine for Literature, Philosophy, and Religion*, 4 vols., Boston, 1840–44.

Margaret Fuller. The life of Margaret Fuller Ossoli has been written by Col. Thomas Wentworth Higginson for the series of American Men of Letters, Boston, 1884.

Brook Farm. Of several books on Brook Farm, the best is Mr. LINDSAY SWIFT's *Brook Farm : Its Members, Scholars, and Visitors*, New York, 1900.

RALPH WALDO EMERSON
Book V. Chapter VI.

The standard edition of Emerson's works is the Riverside, in 12 vols. See also the two volumes of Carlyle-Emerson letters, edited by Prof. Charles Eliot Norton. The standard biography of Emerson is the *Memoir*, in two volumes, by JAMES ELLIOT CABOT, Boston, 1887. HOLMES's *Ralph Waldo Emerson*, Boston, 1884, in the American Men of Letters series, is valuable. GARNETT's *Life of Ralph Waldo Emerson*, London, 1888, in the Great Writers series, has a considerable bibliography. Important critical estimates of Emerson are Matthew Arnold's *Emerson*, in his *Discourses in America;* Lowell's *Emerson the Lecturer*, in his Works, Riverside edition, Vol. I. pp. 349 ff.; and John Jay Chapman's *Emerson, Sixty Years After*, originally published in the *Atlantic Monthly* for January and February, 1897, and since reprinted in *Emerson and Other Essays*, New York, 1898.

THE LESSER MEN OF CONCORD
Book V. Chapter VII.

Bronson Alcott's chief works, with their dates of publication, are : *Observations on the Principles and Methods of Infant Instruction*, 1830; *The Doctrine and Discipline of Human Culture*, 1836; *Conversations with Children on the Gospels*, 2 vols., 1836–37 ; *Tablets*, 1868 ; *Concord Days*, 1872; *Table Talk*, 1877 ; *New Connecticut. An Autobiographical Poem*, 1881 ; *Sonnets and Canzonets*, 1882; *Ralph Waldo Emerson*, . . . *An Estimate of his Character and Genius*, etc., 1882. There is a *Memoir* of Alcott, in 2 vols., by Messrs. F. B. SANBORN and WILLIAM T. HARRIS, Boston, 1893.

The standard collection of Thoreau's works is the Riverside edition, in 10 vols., published at Boston. With Mr. F. B. SANBORN's *Henry David Thoreau*, Boston, 1882, and EMERSON's *Thoreau*, in the Riverside edition of his works, Vol. X. **Thoreau.** pp. 421–452, compare LOWELL's *Thoreau*, in his Works, Riverside edition, Vol. I. pp. 361 ff. See also STEVENSON's essay on Thoreau, in his *Familiar Studies in Men and Books* (Works, Thistle edition, Vol. XIV. pp. 116–149). Mr. H. S. SALT's *Life of Thoreau*, London, 1896, contains a bibliography.

Theodore Parker's collected works, in 14 vols., were published at London, 1863–65; his *Speeches, Addresses, and Occasional Sermons* were published in 2 vols., Boston, 1852. For the life of Parker, see JOHN WEISS: *Life and Correspondence of* **Parker.** *Theodore Parker*, 2 vols., New York, 1864, and O. B. FROTHINGHAM's *Theodore Parker : a Biography*, Boston, 1874.

THE ANTISLAVERY MOVEMENT
Book V. Chapter VIII.

On the Abolition movement in general, see WINSOR's *Memorial History of Boston*, Vol. III. Chap. VI., and Col. Thomas Wentworth

Higginson's *Contemporaries*, Boston, 1899 ; for bibliographic notes on the subject, consult Channing and Hart's *Guide*, § 187 ff.

Garrison. *Selections from Writings and Speeches of William Lloyd Garrison* were published at Boston, in 1852. The best biography of Garrison is that by Wendell Phillips Garrison and Francis Jackson Garrison, 4 vols., New York, 1885–89.

Sumner. Charles Sumner's works, in 15 vols., were published at Boston in 1874–83. The most complete biography is Edward L. Pierce's *Memoir and Letters of Charles Sumner*, 4 vols., Boston, 1879–93 ; a shorter book is Mr. Moorfield Storey's *Charles Sumner*, Boston, 1900, in the American Statesmen series. On the Sumner-Brooks affair, see J. F. Rhodes's *History of the United States*, Vol. II. Chap. VII.

Mrs. Stowe. The standard collections of Mrs. Stowe's writings is the lately published Riverside edition in 16 vols. Mrs. J. T. Fields has written *The Life of Harriet Beecher Stowe*, Boston, 1897.

John Greenleaf Whittier
Book V. Chapter IX.

The standard collection of Whittier's writings is the Riverside edition in 7 vols. The best biography is Samuel T. Pickard's *Life and Letters of John Greenleaf Whittier*, 2 vols., Boston, 1894. William J. Linton's *Life of Whittier* (London, 1893, in the Great Writers series) contains a bibliography. For a more extended expression of the views set forth in this chapter, see B. Wendell : *Stelligeri*, New York, 1893, pp. 149–201.

The "Atlantic Monthly"
Book V. Chapter X.

One gets an interesting impression of the general temper of the early "Atlantic Monthly" by glancing over *The Atlantic Index, 1857–88*, published at Boston in 1889.

Fields. The writings of James T. Fields are chiefly : *Poems*, 1849 ; *Yesterdays with Authors*, 1872 ; *Hawthorne*, 1876 ; *Old Acquaintance. Barry Cornwall and Some of his Friends*, 1876 ; *In and Out of Doors with Charles Dickens*, 1876 ; *Underbrush*, 1877 ; *Ballads and Other Verses*, 1881.

HENRY WADSWORTH LONGFELLOW
Book V. Chapter XI.

The standard collection of Longfellow's works is the Riverside edition in 11 vols. Samuel Longfellow's *Life*, etc., 3 vols., Boston, 1891, includes all the materials in the *Life* of 1886 and in the *Final Memorials* of 1887. Eric S. Robertson's *Life of Henry Wadsworth Longfellow*, London, 1887, in the Great Writers series, has a bibliography.

JAMES RUSSELL LOWELL
Book V. Chapter XII.

Lowell's works are collected in the Riverside edition, 11 vols., Boston. See also the *Last Poems*, edited by Prof. Charles Eliot Norton. *Lowell's Letters*, also edited by Professor Norton, were published in 2 vols., at New York, 1894. For the facts of Lowell's life see the memoir by A. Lawrence Lowell, in Mass. Hist. Soc. *Proceedings*, 2d series, Vol. XI. pp. 75 ff., and Dr. Edward Everett Hale's *James Russell Lowell and his Friends*, Boston, 1899. Mr. Horace E. Scudder is preparing a biography of Lowell for the American Men of Letters series. For a sketch of Lowell as a teacher, see B. WENDELL : *Stelligeri*, pp. 205–217.

OLIVER WENDELL HOLMES
Book V. Chapter XIII.

The standard collection of the writings of Dr. Holmes is the Riverside edition in 13 vols. ; the best biography is that by Mr. John T. Morse, Jr., the *Life and Letters of Oliver Wendell Holmes*, 2 vols., Boston, 1896.

NATHANIEL HAWTHORNE
Book V. Chapter XIV.

HAWTHORNE's works are collected in the Riverside edition, 12 vols., Boston. Perhaps the most notable biographies are JULIAN HAWTHORNE's *Nathaniel Hawthorne and his Wife*, 2 vols., Boston, 1885, and Mr. HENRY JAMES's *Hawthorne*, London, 1879, in the English Men of Letters series.

THE DECLINE OF NEW ENGLAND
Book V. Chapter XV.

E. P. WHIPPLE published : *Essays and Reviews,* 2 vols., 1848–49 ; *Lectures on Subjects connected with Literature and Life,* 1849 ;

Whipple. *Character and Characteristic Men,* 1866 ; *The Literature of the Age of Elizabeth,* 1869 ; *Success and Its Conditions,* 1871 ; *American Literature, and Other Papers,* 1887 ; *Outlooks on Society, Literature, and Politics,* 1888.

R. H. DANA is chiefly known for his *Two Years before the Mast,*

Dana. 1840, and his *To Cuba, and Back: A Vacation Voyage,* 1859.

The writings of Bishop Brooks are published at New York, by Messrs. E. P. Dutton & Co. Prof. A. V. G. ALLEN is said to be preparing an exhaustive *Life and Letters of Phillips Brooks,* to be published probably in 2 vols. ; meanwhile, Mr. M. A. DEW. HOWE's *Phillips Brooks,* Boston, 1899, is useful.

The Letters and Recollections of John Murray Forbes, edited by his daughter, Sarah Forbes Hughes, were published in 2 vols. at Boston, 1899.

BOOK VI. THE REST OF THE STORY

NEW YORK SINCE 1857
Book VI. Chapter I.

For BAYARD TAYLOR, see p. 544.

For a list of the writings of RICHARD GRANT WHITE see Foley's

Rich'd Grant White. *American Authors,* pp. 304–307 ; for the publications of
Holland. Dr. HOLLAND, *ibid.,* pp. 127–129 ; for the work of the
Roe. Rev. E. P. ROE, *ibid.,* pp. 241–242. The late HENRY
Bunner. BUNNER published : *A Woman of Honor,* 1883 ; *Airs from Arcady and Elsewhere,* 1884 ; *The Midge,* 1886 ; *The Story of a New York House,* 1887 ; *Short Sixes, Stories to be Read while the Candle burns,* 1891 ; *Zadoc Pine and Other Stories,* 1891 ; *The Runaway Browns,* 1892 ; *Rowen. "Second-Crop" Songs,* 1892 ; *Made in France : French Tales re-told with a U. S. Twist,* 1893 ; *More Short Sixes,* 1895.

WALT WHITMAN
Book VI. Chapter II.

WHITMAN'S *Complete Prose Works*, Boston, 1898, and his *Leaves of Grass*, Boston, 1898, together contain most of his work. Of the writings about Whitman one should note *Whitman : A Study*, by John Burroughs, Boston, 1896, which forms the tenth and last volume of the "New Riverside edition" of Burroughs's works ; and Mr. John Jay Chapman's essay (pp. 111–128) in *Emerson and Other Essays*, New York, 1898. Much of the other writing on Whitman is collected in a volume called *In Re Walt Whitman*, edited by Horace L. Traubel and others, and published at Philadelphia in 1893.

LITERATURE IN THE SOUTH
Book VI. Chapter III.

PROF. WILLIAM P. TRENT'S *William Gilmore Simms*, Boston, 1892, besides being an excellent biography of its subject, is a fairly sufficient guide to the literature of the South. Simms's works, in 10 vols., were published at New York in 1882 ; his *Poems*, 2 vols., at New York in 1853.

PAUL H. HAYNE'S *Poems, Complete*, etc., were published in Boston, 1882. See SIDNEY LANIER'S *Paul H. Hayne's Poetry* in his *Music and Poetry*, New York, 1898, pp. 197–211.

The latest collection of TIMROD'S work, a handsome "Memorial Edition" with memoir and portrait, was published at Boston in 1899.

The chief writings of SIDNEY LANIER are : *Poems*, 1877 ; *The Science of English Verse*, 1880 ; *The English Novel and the Principle of Its Development*, 1883 ; *Poems*, edited by **Lanier.** his wife, 1884 ; *Music and Poetry*, 1898 ; *Retrospects and Prospects*, 1899 ; *Letters* [1866–1881], 1899.

THE WEST
Book VI. Chapter IV.

For a note on Mrs. KIRKLAND'S writings, see p. 544.

CHARLES FARRAR BROWNE ("A. Ward") published : **Browne** *Artemus Ward : his Book*, 1862 ; *Artemus Ward : his* **(A. Ward.)** *Travels*, 1865 ; *Artemus Ward in London, and Other Papers*, 1867 ;

Complete Works, with Memoir by E. P. Hingston, London [1869] ; *Sandwiches,* 1870. The last two appeared after his death (1867).

DAVID ROSS LOCKE's (Petroleum V. Nasby's) writings are chiefly : *The Nasby Papers,* etc., 1864 ; *Divers Views, Opinions, and Prophe-*

Locke *cies,* 1866 ; *Swingin' round the Cirkle,* 1867 ; *Ekkoes*
(Nasby). *from Kentucky,* 1868 ; *Struggles, Social, Political, and Financial,* 1873 ; *The Moral History of America's Life-Struggle,* 1874 ; *The Morals of Abou Ben Adhem : Eastern Fruit on Western Dishes,* 1875 ; *Inflation at the Cross Roads,* 1875 ; *A Paper City,* 1879 ; *Hannah Jane,* 1881; *Nasby in Exile ; or Six Months of Travel,* 1882 ; *The Demagogue. A Political Novel,* 1891.

NOTE

To any one who knows the admirable books of Prof. Moses Coit Tyler, the obligation under which he has placed all future students of literature in America must be obvious. So far as his work has proceeded, it leaves little to be done by others. The best short and popular book on the subject is Mr. Pancoast's. Stedman and Hutchinson's "Library of American Literature" is an excellent anthology, supplemented by a trustworthy biographical dictionary, and exhaustively indexed. Mr. Stedman's "American Anthology" has admirable biographic notes.

Among those who have been helpful in the preparation of this book, it seems proper to mention Messrs. Philip Jacob Gentner, Chester Noyes Greenough, and George Stockton Wills, of Harvard University. Mr. Greenough has rendered great assistance in the preparation of the bibliographical notes. Particular acknowledgment is also due to Col. Thomas Wentworth Higginson, whose constant interest and kindness have been equalled only by his tolerance of occasional difference of opinion.

INDEX

INDEX

ABBOTT, Jacob, his "Rollo," 237, 302, 337.
Abbott, John S. C., 378.
Absolute Truth, devotion to, in New England, 238, 240, 241, 244, 294, 297, 299, 309, 446, 523, 524, 529.
Abstract Principles, American Devotion to, 63, 109–110, 115–116, 523, 525. *See* Revolution, in general; Right and Rights.
Adams, Charles Francis, 438.
Adams, Henry, his "History of the United States," 117, 149.
Adams, John, 7, 76, 117, 120, 247–248, 260, 437.
Adams, John Quincy, 437.
Adams, Samuel, 77, 120, 247, 260.
Addison, Joseph, 40, 65, 66, 68, 69, 95, 101, 136, 167, 248, 484, 524.
Africans, Native, 342, 482. *See* Slavery.
Agassiz, Louis, 376, 438.
Ainsworth, Harrison, 211.
Albany, New York, 451.
Albemarle, George Monk, Duke of, 19, 32.
Alcott, Amos Bronson, 328–332; 302, 303, 333, 337, 372.
Alcott, Louisa May, her "Little Women," 237, 337.
Alertness of Mind, as a national trait, 22, 100.
Almanacs in America, 36, 79.
America, defined, 6. *See* History, Literature, National Traits, United States.
America, Literary History of, 6, 9, 10, 521–530.
American Academy of Arts and Sciences, 261, 262.

"American Brag," 160, 445.
American Philosophical Society, 79, 93, 261.
Ames, Fisher, 120, 248.
Anarchy, 478.
Andover Theological Seminary, 192, 282, 415; Phillips Academy, 224, 348, 408.
Andrew, John Albion, 438.
Anne, Queen, 59, 65, 66, 67, 68, 119, 484, 524.
Anniversary Week in Boston, 420.
Anthology Club in Boston, 261, 291.
Antiquity, American delight in, 178, 271, 432.
Antislavery Movement, 339–357; 80, 131, 304, 305, 338, 369, 387–389, 401. *See* Reformers, Whittier.
Appleton, Thomas Gold, 438–439.
Aristocracy, tacit in New England, 71–73, 76, 235, 237, 242, 352, 356.
Armada, the Invincible, 26.
Arnold, Matthew, 526, 528.
Artistic Conscience of Americans, 177, 179, 217–218, 432–434, 477, 517, 527, 529.
Artistic Expression in the history of peoples, 462.
Artistic Temperament, 427–428, 430, 433, 471.
Assimilation, American power of, 28, 70, 77, 523.
"Atlantic Monthly," the, 370–377; 229, 378, 404, 410, 417, 436, 443–444, 449, 453.
Audubon, John James, 486.
Augustine, Saint, 16, 17, 89, 279, 298.
Austen, Jane, 193.
Australia, 104, 143.

BACON, Francis, 4, 22, 32, 37, 77.
Baltimore, 205, 233, 267, 284, 481.
Bancroft, George, 271–272.
Barlow, Joel, 126–128; 123, 129, 165.
Barnum, P. T., 511.
Bartlet, Phebe, 87–88.
Bartlett, Sidney, 415.
Bay Psalm Book, 36–38.
Beaumont and Fletcher, 22, 25, 298.
Beecher, Henry Ward, 353.
Beecher, Lyman, 352–353.
Beers, Henry Augustin, his Life of Willis, 226.
Bellows Falls, Vermont, 157.
Bethlehem, the Moravians of, 72.
Bible, the English, 5, 8, 16, 22, 30, 38, 46, 47, 70, 82, 190, 246, 248, 283, 292, 298, 373, 521.
Bible, Eliot's Indian, 51.
Bishoprics proposed in the American Colonies, 111.
Blackstone's "Commentaries," 76, 118.
Blenheim, Battle of, 60, 61.
"Bohemia" in America, 206, 229, 516–517.
Boone, Daniel, 500.
Boston, 26, 47, 55, 71, 76, 78, 92, 94, 95, 105, 120, 121, 122, 124, 193, 194, 201, 204, 223–225, 229, 233–234, 236, 237, 240–248, 253, 261–262, 264–266, 271, 275, 281, 287, 291, 292, 295, 297, 311, 317, 329, 351, 352, 353, 357, 360, 365, 370, 374, 375, 376, 389, 393, 402, 407–410, 412, 415, 416, 418, 420, 423, 426, 436–440, 450, 451, 453–454, 505.
Boston Athenæum, 261, 262, 291.
Boston Museum, 247.
Boston Public Library, 265–266.
Bowdoin College, 354, 378–380, 425, 426.
Braddock's Defeat, 73, 74.
Bradford, William, 26, 32, 50. His "History of Plymouth Plantation," 31, 263.
Bradstreet, Anne, 36, 40, 78, 119.
Brattle Street Church in Boston, 253, 288, 442.

British Classics published in America, 157.
Brook Farm, 305–309; 304, 324, 331, 333, 426, 429, 455.
Brooklyn, New York, 353, 465, 472, 478–479.
Brooks, Phillips, Bishop of Massachusetts, 122, 287, 438, 439, 443.
Brooks, Preston, his assault on Sumner, 351, 483.
Brown, Charles Brockden, 157–168; 169, 175, 181, 184, 185, 189, 190, 192, 194, 203, 219, 228, 230, 269, 280, 290, 335, 374, 432, 433, 449, 488, 527.
Browne, Charles Farrar, 511.
Browne, Sir Thomas, 23.
Browning, Elizabeth Barrett, 147, 209, 526, 528.
Browning, Robert, 147, 475–476, 526, 528.
Bryant, William Cullen, 192–203; 204, 205, 206, 207, 219, 221, 228, 229, 230, 244, 280, 288, 290, 338, 360, 433, 449, 527; his Translations from the Spanish, 391, 394.
Bulwer-Lytton, 161, 228.
Bunker Hill, Battle of, 76, 247, 250. Monument, 250, 403.
Bunner, Henry Cuyler, 461.
Bunyan, John, 20, 40.
Burke, Edmund, 65, 67, 68, 69, 76, 77, 108, 141, 524.
Burns, Robert, 67, 68, 119, 123, 136, 524.
Burton's "Anatomy of Melancholy," 23, 54, 400.
Butler, Samuel, 126, 400. His "Hudibras," 38, 40, 124, 125, 126.
Byles, Mather, 442.
Byrd, William, 484.
Byron, Lord, 145, 146, 174, 192, 196, 526, 527.

CABOT, James Elliot, his Life of Emerson, 309–310, 431.
Cairns, W. B., his monograph on American Literature, 219.
Calhoun, John Caldwell, 485.

Calvin, 14, 16, 89, 279.

Calvinism, summarized, 15, 16; in New England, 28, 34–40, 74, 80, 81, 84–91, 103, 121, 122, 180, 224, 238, 240, 241, 277, 280–283, 286, 287, 353, 359, 372, 385, 400, 407, 408, 409, 414, 418–423, 523, 528. *See* Puritanism.

Cambridge, Massachusetts, 71, 381, 393, 395, 396. Church of, 52, 288, 407. *See* Harvard College.

Campbell, Thomas, 132, 134, 196.

Canada, 30, 62, 73, 104, 105, 142, 143.

Carlyle, Thomas, 147, 206, 272, 296, 313, 475–476, 526, 528.

Centuries, in American history, 6–7; in general: the Seventeenth, 13–55, 136, 522–523; the Eighteenth, 59–136; 30, 357, 417, 423, 524–525; the Nineteenth, 139–154, 518, 525–530. *See* History, Literature.

"Century Magazine," the, 453, 454, 459.

Channing, Edward Tyrrell, 194, 262.

Channing, William Ellery, 284–286; 122, 267, 277, 279, 280, 291, 292, 293, 294, 296, 303, 338, 341, 379, 437, 442.

Character, the Development of American National, 7, 9, 33, 34, 74–76, 80, 102–103, 109–111, 136, 160, 162, 169, 186, 202, 238–245, 355, 523–530.

Characteristics of New England, 233–245.

Characters, in American fiction, 165, 184, 185–186, 188, 189, 354, 488.

Charles I., 13, 26, 79, 107.

Charles II., 13, 19, 90.

Charleston, South Carolina, 486, 487, 488, 491, 492.

"Charlotte Temple," Mrs. Rawson's, 219.

Charters of Massachusetts, 45.

Chatham, William Pitt, Earl of, 77, 108.

Chaucer, 4, 5.

Chicago, 73, 233, 451, 505–507.

Choate, Rufus, 106, 257, 371, 439, 485.

Church of England, *see* Episcopal.

Church and State in America, 70, 83. *See* Theocracy.

Churchill, Charles, 119.

Cincinnati, 353.

Civil War, the American, 73, 104, 105, 151–152, 256, 351, 357, 365–366, 368, 378, 398, 440, 450, 459, 461, 463, 466, 474, 478, 480, 481, 484, 487, 488, 489–499, 503, 511, 513, 514.

Civil Wars of England, 17, 18, 23, 29, 104, 107, 112, 346, 522.

Clark, Lewis Gaylord, 208, 220–223, 226.

Clarke, James Freeman, 438.

Class of 1829 at Harvard, 408, 414.

Classical Temper in American Writings, 201, 315–316, 431, 432.

Classics, study and influence of, in America, 247, 253–254, 257, 258–259, 260, 274, 292, 298, 325, 373, 483.

Clay, Henry, 485, 486.

Clemens, Samuel Langhorne, 513.

Clergy of New England, 71, 72, 75, 83, 235, 238–240, 246, 247, 258, 260, 281, 287, 292, 308, 311, 318, 325, 347, 439, 441–442, 465. *See* Orthodoxy, Puritanism, Theocracy, Unitarianism.

Cleveland, Ohio, 511, 512.

Coats of Arms, in New England, 71, 243.

Coleman, Benjamin, 442.

Coleridge, Samuel Taylor, 67, 69, 145, 146, 193, 296, 526, 527.

Columbia College, 79, 461, 480.

Commerce of New England, 244, 425, 440.

Common-sense in American Men of Letters, 98–101, 324–325, 328, 471, 527.

Commonwealth, the English, 13, 20, 21, 29, 42, 483, 523. *See* Cromwell.

Concord, Massachusetts, 328–338; 76, 315, 317, 403, 426, 429.

Congregations in New England, 239–240, 246.

Connecticut, 78, 83, 110, 123, 126, 329, 332, 352, 353, 407. *See* Hartford, New Haven.

Conservatism in America, 527 ; in New England, 243, 259, 302, 326–327, 343–346, 350, 356, 371, 442 ; in the South, 482–483, 487 ; in England, 59, 60, 62, 63, 64, 68, 139–141.

Constitution, the English, 16, 18, 19, 33, 140–141. *See* Reform Bill.

Constitution of the United States, 6, 29, 76, 93, 118, 149, 345, 346, 359, 366, 502.

Cooke, John Esten, 486, 487.

Cooper, James Fenimore, 181–191 ; 176, 194, 203, 207, 228, 230, 280, 290, 338, 449, 462, 488, 489, 500, 527.

Cooperstown, New York, 181, 182, 187.

Copley, John Singleton, 71, 76, 240–242.

" Copperheads," 459, 512.

Cotton, John, 26, 32, 42, 44, 235, 288, 311. John, the younger, 240.

Cowper, William, 67, 201, 228, 508.

Crèvecœur, 114, 115.

Criticism, Literary, in America, 187, 208–211, 400–401, 438, 458, 507.

Cromwell, Oliver, 13, 14, 17, 18, 19, 21, 24, 29, 31, 53, 107, 523.

Cross, Dr. Arthur Lyons, 111 *n.*

" Culture " in New England, 373.

Curtis, George William, 222, 229, 309, 455.

Custom, *see* Law, Rights.

Dana, Charles Anderson, 305, 308, 455.

Dana, Richard Henry, 194.

Dana, Richard Henry, Jr., 438.

Dartmouth College, 248, 257, 264, 408.

Darwin, Charles, 148.

Davies, Sir John, 41.

" Decadence," in contemporary literature, 189, 217, 477–479.

Declaration of Independence, 76, 93, 106, 113, 115, 275, 437, 485.

Decline of New England, 436–446, 453.

Defoe, Daniel, 20, 65, 66, 112. His " Robinson Crusoe," 387.

Democracy in America, 108, 203, 235, 236, 359, 362, 481, 509, 527–530 ; compared with European, 467–471, 529 ; in England, 148, 525, 527 ; imperial, 525. *See* Aristocracy, Equality, Excellence, Liberty.

Density of population, in its effect on character and history, 17, 33, 89, 152, 278, 281, 306, 384, 463, 529. *See* Inexperience, Retardation.

De Quincey, Thomas, 161, 193, 376.

Derby, George Horatio, 510.

Description, in American fiction, 164–166, 175, 186, 189, 354, 488.

" Dial," the, 300–305 ; 298, 308, 318, 330, 342, 347, 370, 373, 436, 443, 453.

" Dial," the Chicago, 507.

Dialect in American Writings, 401, 402, 477, 511–513.

Dialogue, as a literary form, 483–484.

Dicey, A. V., 18 *n.*

Dickens, Charles, 147, 171, 176, 206, 502, 526, 528.

Diplomacy, American Men of Letters in. *See* Everett, Irving, Lowell, Motley, Taylor, Willis.

Disraeli, Benjamin, 228.

Dissenters, English, 224, 288. *See* Methodism.

Distinction, Personal, of American Men of Letters, 201–202, 203, 229, 289, 315, 338, 509.

Disunion of National Temper, of America and England, 9, 105–116, 150, 153, 175, 182, 185, 187, 322–323, 525, 526 ; within America, 151, 351, 484, 505.

Divinity School at Cambridge, 314.

Dobson, Austin, 415.

" Dooley, Mr.," 173.

Drake, Joseph Rodman, 195–196.

Drama, the, 214; in America, 157–158, 204, 247, 301, 355, 517–518; in England, 20, 23, 24, 298, 302.

Dryden, John, 20, 21, 24, 25, 37, 38, 40, 42, 54, 55, 65, 68, 69, 136, 484, 523.

Dudley, Joseph, 41, 357.

Dudley, Thomas, 26, 32, 40.

Dunlap, William, 158. His Life of Brockden Brown, 158–160.

Dunster, Henry, President of Harvard College, 43, 240.

Duyckinck, Evert Augustus, his "Cyclopedia of American Literature," 195, 208, 462.

Dwight, John Sullivan, 305, 309, 438.

Dwight, Timothy, 120–123, 124, 129, 181, 352.

EAST RIVER, the, 465, 472, 478. Eaton, Theophilus, 50, 51.

Eccentricity in Literature, 466, 475–477.

Education, Development of, in America, 235, 253–254, 258, 260–261, 262, 264–266, 271, 306, 329–330, 394–395. See Classics, Harvard, Law, Modern Languages, Smith Professorship, Theology, Yale, etc.

Edwards, Jonathan, 83–91; 78, 80, 92, 93, 95, 99, 102, 103, 120, 136, 180, 240, 280, 285, 419, 422.

Election, the doctrine of, 15, 48, 49, 52, 84, 87–89, 100, 238, 239, 240, 279. See Calvinism.

Eliot, George, 147, 154, 176, 526, 528.

Eliot, John, 32, 37, 51.

Elizabeth, Queen, 13, 21, 25, 26, 31, 32, 53, 55, 59, 60, 65, 77, 126.

Elizabethan England, see National Traits.

Ellsler, Fanny, 209–210, 301.

Emancipation Proclamation, 356.

Embargo, Jefferson's, 193, 244, 429.

Emerson, Ralph Waldo, 311–327; 122, 206, 253–255, 260, 298, 300,

301, 302, 303, 304, 306, 308, 310, 328, 332, 335, 336, 337, 338, 371, 372, 373, 376, 379, 395, 412, 425, 426, 430, 432, 437, 438, 445, 469, 485, 489, 528.

Empire, the course of, 8–9, 30, 62, 106, 108, 142–144, 149–153, 525.

England, see History, Law, Literature, National Traits.

Enthusiasm, see National Traits.

Episcopal Church, the Protestant, of the United States, 79, 110, 111, 121, 184, 347, 442.

Equality, the Ideal of, 362, 468–469, 474, 529. See Democracy, Excellence, Right and Rights.

Essays, English, 67, 118, 174; in America, 120, 124, 170, 317, 417, 460, 498.

Essex, Earl of, 18, 32.

"Evening Post," the New York, 193, 196, 198, 230, 449.

Everett, Edward, 253–257; 170, 260, 264, 271, 280, 291, 311, 371, 437, 439, 485.

Evolution, philosophy of, 16, 293, 339.

Excellence, the Ideal of, 467–469, 471, 528, 530. See Democracy.

Expansion of the United States, 149.

Extracts from American writings: Barlow, 127–128; Bay Psalm Book, 37–38; Anne Bradstreet, 40–41; Brockden Brown, 162, 164; Bryant, 197–200; Channing, 277–278, 284–285, 341; W. G. Clark, 220; Crèvecœur, 114–115; Drake, 196; Dunlap, 158; Dwight, 120–123; Edwards, 84–89; Emerson, 253–254, 298, 312–314, 316, 320–324; Everett, 256–257; Fields, 375; Franklin, 94–99, 101–102; Freneau, 131–133; Halleck, 196; Hartford Wits, 128–129; P. H. Hayne, 492; Holland, 460; Holmes, 90–91, 222–223, 411–415, 419–422, 438, 444; Hopkinson, 113–114; Irving, 172, 175–176; Lanier, 496–498; Longfellow, 387–389, 391–392; Lowell,

186, 199, 339–340, 399, 402–403, 405; C. Mather, 44, 49, 51–52; Otis, 108–109; Poe, 209–210, 212–216; Stedman, 385; B. Taylor, 457; Thoreau, 335–336; F. O. Ticknor, 489–498; Timrod, 493–494; Trumbull, 124–126; Webster, 250–252; Whittier, 361–369; Whitman, 470–475; Wigglesworth, 39–40; Willis, 223, 227; Woolman, 80–81.

FAMILY Discipline in New England, 237.
Faneuil Hall in Boston, 255, 349.
Fashion in Boston, 225, 288.
"Federalist," the, 118, 120, 135, 136.
Felton, Cornelius Conway, 438, 439.
Fiction, in the Evolution of Literature, 5, 167, 190; in English Literature, 66, 68, 90, 147–148, 160–161, 176, 430–431, 477, 526–527; in America, 163–168, 179, 181–192, 271, 272, 354–356, 417, 426, 460–461, 486, 487, 488–489, 498. *See* Short Stories.
Fielding, Henry, 66, 68, 160, 171.
Fields, James Thomas, 375–377; 222, 438, 443–444.
Fine Arts, the, 5, 296, 385, 416, 476, 510.
First church of Boston, 42, 288, 311.
Fontenoy, Battle of, 60, 61.
Forbes, John Murray, 438, 439.
Form, Sense of, in American Writers, 166–167. *See* Artistic Conscience.
Fourier, 306–308.
Foxe, John, 26.
France, as enemy of England, 29–31, 60–63, 73–74, 272; as friend of America, 63, 115, 150. *See* Revolution, Revolutionary Spirit.
"Frankenstein," Mrs. Shelley's, 161, 193.
Franklin, Benjamin, 92–103; 79, 82, 120, 136, 173, 233, 245, 268, 437, 509; his Letter to a London newspaper, 173, 508.

"Fraser's Magazine," 187.
Freeman, James, 121–122, 281.
"Freeman's Oath," 36.
French and Indian Wars, 73, 274.
Freneau, Philip, 130–135, 136.
Fruitlands, Community at, 331, 333.
Fuller, Sarah Margaret, 300–301; 208, 229, 302, 304–306, 308, 331, 371, 386, 455.
Fuller, Thomas, 20, 23, 38, 54.

GARRISON, William Lloyd, 342–343, 348, 360.
Gayarré, Charles Étienne, 486.
Genealogy, American delight in, 264.
General Principles, American devotion to, *see* Abstract Principles.
George I., 59.
George II., 54, 59, 66, 68, 74, 75, 79, 524.
George III., 59, 60, 62, 105, 116, 126, 131, 139.
George IV., 139.
Georgia, 74, 481, 483, 484, 486, 489, 491, 492, 495.
German Learning, Influence of, in New England, 253, 264, 267, 268, 271, 272, 275, 295–296.
Gibbon, Edward, 67, 268, 275–276.
"Godey's Lady's Book," 204, 207, 219.
Godkin, Edwin Lawrence, 439, 454.
Godwin, Parke, 194.
Godwin, William, 67, 68, 160–162, 163, 184, 228, 488.
Goethe, Taylor's translation of, 456, 458.
Goldsmith, Oliver, 66, 160, 171, 173, 174, 184, 228, 276.
Gray, Thomas, 66, 200.
Great Awakening, the, 74–76, 110. *See* Whitefield.
Greeley, Horace, 454–455; 229, 300, 308.
Greenfield, Connecticut, 121, 123.
Griswold, Rufus Wilmot, 195, 199, 208, 455, 462.

HAKLUYT'S "Voyages," 20, 22, 37.

Hale, Edward Everett, 237.

Half-Way Covenant in the New England Churches, 86.

Halleck, Fitz-Greene, 195, 196–197, 208, 221.

Hamilton, Alexander, 117, 118, 120.

"Harper's Magazine," 453, 454.

"Harper's Weekly," 229, 449, 453, 454.

Hartford, Connecticut, 52, 84, 123, 124, 127, 360.

Hartford Wits, the, 119–130, 135, 136, 157.

Harvard College, 26, 42–43, 44, 46, 47, 48, 50, 75, 78, 79, 83, 93, 94, 119, 120, 122, 129, 224, 235, 240, 253, 255, 260, 261, 262, 264–265, 267, 269, 271, 272, 273, 281, 288, 311, 332, 346, 348, 350, 379–380, 381, 393, 394, 395, 396, 398, 404, 407, 408, 412–415, 443–445, 480.

Haverhill, Massachusetts, 358, 360.

Hawthorne, Nathaniel, 425–435, 163, 168, 176, 206, 240, 306, 308, 328, 376, 377, 379, 438, 445, 471, 477, 489, 516, 528.

Hayne, Paul Hamilton, 486, 490–492, 499.

Hayne, Robert Young, 252, 485, 490.

Henry, Patrick, 112, 120.

Herbert of Cherbury, Lord, 19, 32.

Herndon's Life of Lincoln, 503.

Hildreth, Richard, 272.

Historical Continuity, 18, 29.

Historical literature in America, 31, 36, 42, 43, 78, 81, 119, 136, 171–173, 178–179, 245, 263–276, 338, 378, 486, 528; in England, 37, 119, 275.

History, American, of the Seventeenth Century, 26–34; 42, 55, 70, 77, 357, 523; of the Eighteenth Century, 70–77, 524; of the Nineteenth Century, 149–153, 357, 525–526; in general, 530.

History, English, of the Seventeenth Century, 13–19, 20, 29, 55, 357,

522; of the Eighteenth Century, 59–64, 524; of the Nineteenth Century, 139–144, 525.

Hoar, Ebenezer Rockwood, 438.

Hoffman, Charles Fenno, 208, 220.

Holland, Josiah Gilbert, 459–461.

Hollis Professorship at Harvard College, 281.

Hollis Street Church in Boston, 442.

Holmes, Abiel, 288, 407.

Holmes, Oliver Wendell, 407–424; 65, 206, 221, 222, 229, 239, 376, 377, 425, 426, 430, 443, 489, 508–509, 511, 528; his "Autocrat," 241, 444; his "Mortal Antipathy," 222; his memoir of Motley, 437–438; his "One Hoss Shay," 90–91.

"Home Journal," the, 226.

Hooker, Richard, 4, 22, 37.

Hooker, Thomas, 26, 84.

Hopkinson, Francis, 112–115, 175, his "Battle of the Keys," 508.

"Hudibras," *see* Butler.

Human Nature, opposing views concerning; *see* Calvinism, Revolutionary Spirit, Unitarianism.

Humanism in New England, 406.

Humanity of Classical Literature, 315–316. *See* Popularity.

Hume, David, 66, 67.

Humor, American, 101, 173, 179, 507–513, 515, 518.

Hunt, Leigh, 174, 224, 228.

Hunt, William Morris, 438.

Hutchinson, Thomas, 77, 110, 120, 260; his "History of Massachusetts," 82, 263.

IDEALISM in America, 293–294, 304, 310, 319–323, 371–372, 417, 432, 524, 525, 529. *See* Mystery, Puritanism.

Ideals, American devotion to Abstract, *see* Abstract Principles.

Ideals, the National, of England and America, 8, 14, 18, 28, 46, 70, 82,

106, 190, 246, 521–530. *See* Bible, Democracy, Law, Right and Rights, Union.

Imitativeness in American Writings, 38, 41, 54, 119, 130, 135, 162, 167, 170, 173, 181, 184, 196, 224, 228, 247, 253, 258–259, 262, 272, 372, 386–387, 391, 480–481, 483, 489, 491. *See* Style.

Independence, Declaration of, *see* Declaration.

India, the Empire of, 62, 142, 143.

Indians, American, 31, 32, 73, 186, 274, 505.

Individualism, Growth of, in New England, 327, 330, 442–444. *See* Alcott, Emerson, Thoreau, Transcendentalism, Unitarianism.

Inexperience, the National of America, 34, 37, 55, 77, 116, 130, 136, 153, 218, 279, 287, 327, 359, 362, 384–385, 424, 446, 529. *See* Density, Retardation.

Innate ideas, 294, 300, 304.

Instrument of Government, the, 18, 28.

Insularity of Modern England, 62, 64, 69, 139–140. *See* John Bull.

Irving, Washington, 169–180 ; 168, 181, 184, 185, 189, 190, 191, 194, 195, 201, 203, 221, 228, 229, 230, 271, 276, 280, 290, 328, 432, 433, 449, 462, 477, 509, 511, 516, 527.

Isabella II., Queen, 169.

JAMES I., 13.
James II., 13, 59, 90.

James, Henry, 438.

Jamestown, Virginia, 28.

Jay, John, 117, 120.

Jefferson, Thomas, 106, 117, 120, 149, 193, 485.

Jewett, Sarah Orne, 237.

"John Bull," 64, 112, 140, 175, 403, 446, 524.

Johns Hopkins University, 495, 496.

Johnson, Samuel, 65, 66, 67, 68, 69, 112, 117, 136, 253, 524. Boswell's Life of, 67, 157.

Jonson, Ben, 20, 25.

Journalism in America, *see* Newspapers.

KEATS, John, 134, 145, 193, 195, 526.

Kennedy, John Pendleton, 486.

King's Chapel, in Boston, 105, 121–122, 178, 288 ; its "Liturgy," 281.

Kipling, Rudyard, 147, 516.

Kirkland, Caroline Matilda, 208, 229, 501–503.

"Knickerbocker Gallery," 237, 466.

"Knickerbocker Magazine," 374, 386, 459, 514.

"Knickerbocker School," the, 219–230; 280, 309, 338, 449, 465, 487, 513.

LAFAYETTE, 115–116.
Lamb, Charles, 67, 69.

Landor, Walter Savage, 67, 69, 197.

Language and Nationality, 3, 8, 18, 28, 82, 106, 521. *See* Ideals.

Language, the English, 3, 8.

Lanier, Sidney, 481, 486, 491, 495–499.

Larcom, Lucy, 237.

Law, the English or Common, 8, 14, 17, 18, 19, 30, 46, 61, 62, 63, 64, 70, 74, 82, 106, 108, 109, 116, 142–144, 150, 190, 246, 274, 292, 298, 325, 340, 373, 467, 521–522, 524, 530.

Law, the Profession of, in America, 236, 246, 248–249, 251, 258, 260, 274, 348, 350, 378, 408, 415, 441; American Men of Letters as Students of, 169, 194, 264, 380, 393, 408, 458, 485, 486, 487, 488, 491, 495.

Lectures in America, 247, 313, 314, 315, 317, 325, 330, 456, 459, 511.

Lee, Robert Edward, 151.

Leland, Charles Godfrey, 222.

Lewis, "Monk," 67, 68, 160, 163.

Liberalism, in New England, 42, 43, 46, 119, 122, 224, 442. *See* Transcendentalism, Unitarianism.

Liberty, the Ideal of, 273, 443, 467, 530.

"Liberty, Equality, and Fraternity," 467–468.

Lieber, Francis, 486.

Lincoln, Abraham, 151, 474, 503–504.

Literature defined, 1–3; evolution of, 5; motives of, 191, 228, 309; permanent, 315; study and influence of, in America. *See* Classics, Modern Languages.

Literature in America, 9–10, 405, 479; of the Seventeenth Century, 35–43; 55, 119, 190, 246, 523; of the Eighteenth Century, 78–82; 117–136; 190, 246, 525; of the Nineteenth Century, 154–518, 526–530.

Literature, Elizabethan, *see* English of the Seventeenth Century.

Literature, English, 4–6; of the Seventeenth Century, 20–25, 27, 37, 55, 65, 69, 136, 146, 523; of the Eighteenth Century, 65–69, 136, 146, 173–174, 200–201, 415–416, 524; of the Nineteenth Century, 145–148, 154, 201, 430–431, 526–529.

Literature, "Queen Anne." *See* English of the Eighteenth Century.

Literature of the Regency. *See* English of the Nineteenth Century.

Literature, Victorian. *See* English of the Nineteenth Century.

London, 25.

Longfellow, Henry Wadsworth, 378–392; 206, 209, 222, 296, 350, 376, 377, 393, 394, 395, 396, 397, 398, 406, 418, 425, 426, 430, 438, 489, 528.

Longstreet, Augustus Baldwin, 486.

Lord's Supper, in the New England Churches, 86, 312–313, 372, 379.

Lounsbury, Thomas Raynesford, his Life of Cooper, 182, 183.

Lowell, Abbott Lawrence, 149 *n.*

Lowell, Charles, 393, 442.

Lowell, James Russell, 393–406; 170, 206, 222, 237, 262, 296, 376, 377, 380–381, 414, 415, 418, 425, 426, 430, 438, 465, 489, 509, 528; his "Biglow Papers," 477, 508, 511; his "Fable for Critics," 185, 199, 222, 400, 508; his essay on "Thoreau," 339.

Lowell, John, 438.

Lower Classes of New England, 75–76, 102, 242, 332, 337–338, 348, 359, 362, 396, 402, 425, 427, 481; of the South. *See* Slavery; of the West, 501–502.

Loyalists, the American, 82, 107–108, 110, 125, 181, 241, 260, 381.

Lyric Quality in Literature, 216; in Southern poetry, 495, 498, 499.

"Lyrical Ballads," Wordsworth and Coleridge's, 68, 145, 159, 162, 189, 191, 290.

MACAULAY, Lord, 206, 268, 526.

Madison, James, 117, 118, 120, 150.

Magazines in America. *See* Periodicals.

Maine, woods of, 334, 425, 429.

Manufactures of New England, 152, 244, 245, 249, 440.

Marlborough, Duke of, 19, 21, 32, 61, 62.

Marlowe, Christopher, 207, 217.

Marshall, John, 118, 120, 485.

Mary Stuart, Queen, 26.

Massachusetts, 26, 27, 28, 31, 45, 78, 94, 110, 120, 122, 192, 193, 234, 253, 255, 262, 263, 278, 351, 356, 358, 360, 450, 459, 510.

Massachusetts Historical Society, 31, 261, 262, 263, 267, 274.

Materialism in New York, 451–454, 463; throughout America, 468, 505.

Mather, Cotton, 44–54; 33, 35, 42, 43, 70, 71, 75, 78, 82, 95, 136, 233,

245, 263, 279, 287, 288, 311, 313, 334, 409, 436–437, 439.

Mather, Increase, 32, 43, 44, 45, 46, 83, 95, 233, 261.

Mather, Richard, 27, 32, 37, 44.

Medicine, the Profession of, in America, 193, 236, 408–409.

Melodrama, 213–214, 432.

Melville, Hermann, 229.

Merchants of New England, 71–73, 76, 236, 237, 240–244, 439.

Methodism, 66, 74–75, 97, 374.

Mexican War, 401.

Middle States, or Colonies, 157–230; 36, 78, 79, 80, 154, 262, 291, 372, 449, 463–464, 480, 526, 527.

Milton, John, 20, 21, 23, 24, 37, 42, 55, 65, 68, 69, 136, 387, 523.

Minto, William, 206.

"Mirror," the New York, 223, 225, 226.

Mitchell, Donald Grant, 222.

Mitchill, Samuel Latham, his "Picture of New York," 171, 172.

Modern Languages and Literature, study and influence of, in America, 264–265, 292, 296–297, 379–385, 390, 393–396. *See* Smith Professorship.

Monroe Doctrine, the, 150–151.

Moore, Thomas, 69, 193.

Morris, George Pope, 225.

Morse, John Torrey, Jr., his life of Holmes, 438.

Motley, John Lothrop, 272–273; 170, 280, 371, 376, 437, 438.

Music, in New England, 296, 297, 309.

"Mutual Admiration" in Boston, 444.

Mystery, Sense of, in America, 163, 167, 179, 213, 214, 218, 418, 429, 432.

NAPOLEON, 61, 62, 128–129, 139, 140, 150.

Napoleon III., 151.

"Nasby, Petroleum V.," 512–513, 515.

"Nation," the, 453, 454.

Nationality, in general, 3. *See* Language; of America, 77. *See* Ideals.

National Traits of Elizabethan England (Spontaneity, Enthusiasm, and Versatility), 19, 21–24, 25, 27, 64, 67, 69, 522; evident in America, 28, 33, 53, 55, 75–77, 111, 112, 115, 131, 332, 445–446, 522–524, 529.

Nature, Sense of, in American Books, 273, 333–335, 361–363, 389, 493, 497–498. *See* Description.

Navy, the American, 181, 244.

Negro Minstrel Shows, 510.

Nelson, Lord, 62, 68, 139, 145.

Newburyport, 343, 360.

New England, 26, 27, 28–34, 35–43, 45–53, 55, 70–76, 78–79, 108, 152, 154, 190, 221, 226, 229, 230, 233–446, 449, 455, 462, 465, 471, 480, 489, 493, 501, 504, 513, 514, 523, 526, 528–530.

"New England Primer," 36.

New Hampshire, 248, 249, 253, 360, 455.

New Haven, 51, 84, 120, 124.

New Jersey, 80, 130, 181, 466.

Newman, Cardinal, 526, 528.

New Orleans, 73, 233, 486.

Newspapers in America, 79, 157, 183, 187, 193, 201, 202, 209, 211, 225–226, 229, 230, 309, 342, 360, 365, 400, 449, 455, 458, 507–513, 514–515, 517, 518.

Newton, Sir Isaac, 25, 32.

New York, 79, 114, 120, 130, 154, 157, 163, 182, 190, 191, 192–197, 201, 204, 205, 210, 219, 225, 226–230, 233, 234, 262, 280, 290, 308, 309, 338, 372, 374, 405, 449–464, 465–466, 472, 478–479, 489, 501, 504, 505, 513, 514, 515.

Nile, Battle of the, 60, 61, 62, 68, 139, 145, 146.

"North American Review," the, 194, 197, 255, 262, 267, 272, 291, 302, 370, 404, 436, 443, 453.

North and South, Divergence of, in America, 27–28, 151, 495. *See*

Antislavery Movement, Civil War, Disunion.

Northampton, Massachusetts, 83, 85, 86, 87, 240.

Norton, Charles Eliot, 262.

Nova Scotia, 29, 73.

Novel, the English. *See* Fiction.

ODYSSEY, the, 166, 477.
Old South Church in Boston, 224, 247, 263, 288.

Orations and Poems in New England, 412, 414.

Oratory in America, 108–109, 112, 135, 245, 246–259, 260, 262, 270, 275, 276, 277, 290, 291, 338, 346–351, 371, 372, 439, 443, 485, 486, 528.

"Orthodoxy" in New England, 120–123, 223–224, 288–289, 291, 318, 379, 407–408, 418–423. *See* Calvinism, Edwards, Mather, Puritanism, Unitarianism.

Osgood, Frances Sargent, 209–210, 301.

Otis, James, 108–109, 110, 112, 120, 247, 260.

Ovid. *See* Sandys.

PALFREY, John Gorham, 272.
Pamphleteering, 112, 119.

Pancoast, H. S., his "Introduction to American Literature," 485–487, 490.

Panic of 1857, 450.

Park Street Church in Boston, 224, 225.

Parker, Theodore, 346–348; 258, 302, 304, 308, 352, 366, 371, 439.

Parkman, Francis, 273–274; 29, 73, 280, 371, 438.

Patriotic verse in America, 120, 125, 127, 131, 193. *See* F. O. Ticknor, Timrod, Whittier.

Paulding, James Kirke, 195.

Payne, John Howard, 158.

Peabody, Andrew Preston, 262, 287.

Pearson, Eliphalet, 282.

Pedantry in New England, 326, 397.

Peirce, Benjamin, 438.

Pepys, Samuel, 19, 32.

Periodical Literature in America, 79, 157, 159, 205, 219, 262, 301–304, 370–377, 404, 449, 453–454, 515–517. *See* Newspapers.

Phi Beta Kappa Society of Harvard College, 194, 255, 313, 412.

Philadelphia, 78, 92, 93, 96, 97, 98, 112, 120, 130, 159, 165, 205, 233, 234, 261, 360, 451.

Phillips, Wendell, 348–350; 258, 352, 366, 371, 439.

Phillips, Willard, 194.

Philosophy in New England. *See* Idealism, Transcendentalism.

Phips, Sir William, 33, 45, 50, 73.

"Phœnix, John," 510–511, 512, 515.

Pierce, Franklin, 378, 425, 426.

Pierrepont, Sarah (Mrs. Edwards), 84–85.

Pinckney, Edward Coate, 486.

Pioneers, Western, 500–501.

Pitt. *See* Chatham.

Plan of this book, 10.

Plots in American Fiction, 185, 188, 189, 354, 488.

Plymouth Colony, 26, 28, 31, 240, 244, 255–256, 263, 288.

Poe, Edgar Allan, 204–218; 163, 168, 177, 219, 228, 230, 280, 301, 335, 338, 386, 432, 433, 449, 477, 486, 516; his "Literati," 220, 487, 501.

Poetry, in the Evolution of Literature, 5, 167; in America, 38–41, 90–91, 119–134, 186, 191, 192–203, 206, 209–210, 211–216, 220, 221, 223, 226, 227, 230, 304, 316, 317, 361–369, 375, 378–392, 398–403, 410–415, 443, 457–458, 461, 465–479, 481, 489–498, 516, 528; in England, 5, 21–24, 37, 38, 65, 66, 145–148, 154, 200, 291, 310, 526, 527, 528.

Poetry, Theories of, Bryant's, 198; Lanier's, 496; Poe's, 211.

Political Literature in America, 78, 81, 112, 117–119, 136, 180, 190, 209, 228, 245, 246, 247, 459, 485, 513, 525.

Pope, Alexander, 32, 65, 119, 136, 415.

Popularity, as a quality of Literature, 509–510. *See* Humanity.

Portland, Maine, 223, 378.

Portraits, family, 71, 76, 240–242.

Portsmouth, New Hampshire, 248, 375.

Precocity in literature, 197, 360.

Prescott, William Hickling, 268–271; 267, 272, 275, 280, 371, 438; his Life of Brockden Brown, 159, 160.

Present Time, the, 514–518.

Prince, Thomas, his "Annals," 263.

Princeton College, 79, 83, 85, 130.

Printing-presses in America about 1800, 157.

Prohibition in America, 103, 506.

Property, Right of, 340, 344, 345, 346, 356.

Prose, in the Evolution of Literature, 5, 167; in America, 44–52, 78–82, 84–89, 94–101, 162–164, 172–176, 191, 206–214, 216, 222–223, 226, 230, 246–276, 312–314, 320–324, 335–336, 353–355, 404–405, 417–420, 422, 425–435, 459–461, 466, 483, 488, 507–513, 514–518, 528; in England, 5, 22–25, 37, 53, 65, 66, 146–148, 154, 174, 184, 201, 206, 526, 527, 528.

Protestantism, 70. *See* Liberalism.

Public Speaking, Popularity of, in New England, 246–249, 255, 317.

"Puck," 453, 461.

Puritanism, in England, 14, 20, 24, 25, 29, 31, 33, 107, 517, 523; in New England, 28–31, 33, 38, 42, 44, 46, 48, 50, 52, 55, 70, 74, 75, 95, 102, 120, 163, 184, 294, 296, 299, 309, 310, 371–372, 416, 423, 429, 430, 432–433, 434, 446, 469, 523, 524, 525, 529. *See* Calvinism.

Purity of Temper, Instinctive in America, 189, 217, 218, 276, 307, 310, 327, 405, 424, 434, 445–446, 517.

QUAKERISM in America, 75, 80–81, 299, 341, 358, 365, 367, 455, 465.

"Quality" in New England. *See* Aristocracy.

"Quarterly Review," 192, 262.

Quebec, 73; Battle of, 60, 61, 62, 74.

RADCLIFFE, Mrs., 67; her "Mysteries of Udolpho," 68, 160, 161, 163.

Railways, transcontinental, 152, 440; in New England, 244, 440.

Ralegh, Sir Walter, 4, 18, 21, 22, 24, 27, 32, 37, 131.

Rationalism in New England, 417–420.

Raymond, Henry Jarvis, 455.

Refinement in American writings, 180, 203, 218, 228.

Reform Bill of 1832, 107, 140–141, 145, 146, 148, 198, 220, 290, 525, 526.

Reformers in New England, 229, 245, 300, 303, 304–305, 338, 339–340, 359, 371, 372, 398, 416, 441, 528. *See* Antislavery Movement, Brook Farm.

Regency, of George IV., 139, 147.

Relaxation of Social Pressure in America, 33, 53, 89, 102, 501. *See* Density, Inexperience.

Religion in New England. *See* Calvinism, Puritanism, Unitarianism.

Religion and Life, in America, 90, 95–100, 102–103.

Religious literature in America. *See* Theological.

Renaissance, of Europe, 17, 178, 245, 259, 297, 394.

Renaissance of New England, the, 233–446; 154, 206, 245, 258–259, 303, 372, 429–430, 469, 514, 528–530.

Representation, conflicting theories of, 107, 116.

Restoration, the, 13, 21, 24, 29, 31, 523.

Retardation of Development in America, 32, 123, 126, 130, 151, 174, 201, 275–276, 357, 416, 446, 483, 484, 489, 522–529. *See* Density, Inexperience.

Reversion, Social, in America, 504.

Revolution, the American, 104–116; 63, 67, 71, 73, 75, 76, 79, 81, 103, 117, 121, 130, 134, 152, 160, 169, 172, 175, 180, 185, 204, 240–242, 247, 253, 258, 260, 268, 346, 382, 437, 481, 484, 485, 524–525.

Revolution, the Constitutional, in England, 140, 144, 148. *See* Reform Bill.

Revolution, the French, 61, 63, 115–116, 140, 310, 345, 467, 471; its abstract philosophy, 63–64, 109, 467; its rationalism, 66, 161, 417, 423. *See* Revolutionary Spirit.

Revolution of 1688, the, 13, 21, 29, 523.

Revolutionary Spirit, its view of Human Nature, 102, 145–146, 186, 300, 332, 339, 443, 467, 500, 528–529; its contrasting manifestations, in England and France, 68, 145; in Europe and America, 290–293, 310. *See* Transcendentalism, Unitarianism.

Rhetoric in New England, 248, 253–257, 259, 270, 404.

Rhodes, James Ford, his "History of the United States," 351.

Richardson, Samuel, 66, 68, 160.

Richmond, Virginia, 204, 205, 341.

Right and Rights, English and American Ideal of, 8, 14, 64, 115–116, 467, 521, 524, 525, 529; Divergence of, *see* Disunion; American Revolution; French ideal of, 63, 109–110; *see* Revolutionary spirit.

Ripley, George, 229, 286, 302, 303, 305, 308, 455.

Roe, Edward Payson, 461.

Rogers, Samuel, 67, 69.

Romanticism, 431–432; in America, 162–163, 174–175, 177, 179, 195,

200, 203, 310, 334, 384–387, 390–391, 416–417, 432–434, 488–489, 496, 498, 529; in England, 145–146, 160–161, 174, 526, 527, 529.

Ross, David Locke, 512.

Rumford, Count, 261.

Ruskin, John, 147, 431, 526, 528.

Ryland's "Chronological Outlines of English Literature," 20 *n.*, 22, 35 *n.*, 60.

ST. LOUIS, 73, 233, 451.

Salem, 244, 251, 425, 426, 429. *See* Witchcraft.

San Domingo, Insurrection in, 345, 482.

Sandys, George, his translation of Ovid, 27, 36, 484.

San Francisco, 233, 451.

Satire in America, 90–91, 101, 113, 119, 122–126, 130, 193, 196, 400–403, 411, 420–421, 459, 508, 512–513.

Saturday Club of Boston, 376–377, 437–439, 444.

Scholarship in New England, 245, 260–276, 277, 290, 291, 295, 326, 338, 347, 371, 393–397, 443, 528.

Science, English, 25, 148; in America, *see* Cotton Mather, Franklin.

Scott, Sir Walter, 67, 134, 145, 146, 147, 148, 183, 184, 185, 189, 190, 191, 192, 193, 198, 220, 230, 290, 481, 488, 529; his "Waverley Novels," 146, 154, 174, 184, 526; his "Lady of the Lake," 389.

"Scribner's Magazine," 453, 454, 459.

"Scriptures" in New England, 303, 314, 318, 331, 372, 445.

Sea, American Books about the. *See* Cooper, Dana, Melville.

Seabury, Samuel, 110, 111.

Secession, 105, 255. *See* Civil War in America, Disunion.

Second Church of Boston, 44, 71, 288, 311–313, 326.

Sedgmoor, Battle of, 59.

Sentimentality in Literature, 200–201. *See* Romanticism.

Sewall, Samuel, 31, 32, 33, 246, 341; his Diary, 234, 236, 263.

Seward, William Henry, 222.

Shakspere, 4, 5, 20, 21, 22, 23, 24, 26, 27, 32, 37, 41, 42, 50, 55, 65, 68, 69, 136, 184, 217, 248, 253, 302, 315, 445, 458, 469, 523.

Shelley, Percy Bysshe, 146, 147, 160, 161, 165, 174, 193, 291, 526, 527.

Shepard, Thomas, 52.

Short Stories as a Form of Literature, 168, 174, 176–177, 191, 211–214, 226, 237, 430–434, 461, 477, 486, 506, 515–518. *See* Fiction.

Sibley, John Langdon, his "Harvard Graduates," 47.

Sidney, Sir Philip, 26.

Simms, William Gilmore, 480, 486, 487–489, 491, 492.

Slavery, Negro, 151, 340–346, 482. *See* Antislavery Movement.

Smith, Captain John, 35, 484.

Smith Professorship at Harvard College, 264–265, 266, 296, 379–381, 393, 406. *See* Longfellow, J. R. Lowell, George Ticknor.

Smollett, Tobias, 66, 68.

Socialism in New England. *See* Brook Farm.

Social Relations of American Men of Letters, Abroad, 170, 225, 264, 350, 396; at Home, 181, 188, 206, 228, 338, 376, 408–410, 465, 511–512. *See* Distinction.

Society, Structure of American, in New England, 71–73, 75, 92–94, 193, 224, 234–244, 248, 258, 266, 288, 326, 371, 378, 410, 436–441, 481; in the South, 206, 481–483, 487–488.

South, the, 151, 152, 341, 356–357, 480–499, 504, 513, 514. *See* North and South.

South Carolina, 234, 351, 489; Nullification in, 198, 487, 491. *See* Charleston.

"Southern Literary Messenger," 205, 219, 486.

Southey, Robert, 61, 67.

Spain, American delight in the romance of, 177–178, 270–271, 272; war with, in 1898, 150, 152.

Sparks, Jared, 262, 267–268, 270, 273, 284; his "Library of American Biography," 159, 268.

"Spectator," the, 66, 79, 94, 95, 118, 120, 124.

Spenser, 4, 5, 26, 27.

Spontaneity. *See* National Traits.

"Springfield Republican," the, 459.

Stedman, Edmund Clarence, his "Poets of America," 385, 415, 416, 417.

Stedman and Hutchinson's "Library of American Literature," 35 *n.*, 123, 157, 195, 208, 220, 341, 460, 461, 481, 492, 508.

Stedman and Woodberry's edition of Poe, 207, 208, 212.

Steele, Sir Richard, 65, 167.

Stelligeri, 414 *n.*

Stephens, Alexander Hamilton, 483–484.

Stevenson, Robert Louis, 147, 176, 229, 527.

Stoddard, Richard Henry, 222.

Stoddard, Solomon, 83, 86.

Stowe, Harriet Beecher, 352–356; 366, 371; her "Old Town Folks," 237; her "Uncle Tom's Cabin," 388.

Struggle for existence, 16, 17, 18, 33, 53.

Stuart, Gilbert, 64, 241–243, 248, 345.

Style, Literary, in America, 38, 41, 53, 95, 101, 162, 166, 173, 175, 177, 183, 193, 197, 199, 201, 211, 216, 226, 250–253, 257, 267, 269–270, 272, 274, 276, 323–324, 335–336, 354, 363, 390, 397, 404, 428, 459, 471, 473–478, 492, 495, 498, 507. *See* Dialect, Extracts.

Sumner, Charles, 170, 258, 348, 350–351, 352, 371, 387, 438, 483.

Surrey, Earl of, 38.
Survival of the fittest, 17.
Swift, Jonathan, 65, 112, 136, 172.

"TATLER," the, 66, 79, 118.
    "Taxation without Representation," 107.
Taylor, Bayard, 222, 229, 455-458.
Taylor, Father, 373.
Taylor, Jeremy, 20, 23.
Teaching, Professional, by Men of Letters, 380, 395, 397. *See* Longfellow, Lowell, Ticknor.
Temple, Sir William, 25, 40.
Tennyson, 147, 209, 526, 528.
Thackeray, William Makepeace, 147, 176, 206, 415, 526, 528.
Theocracy, in England, 17; in New England, 42, 44-46, 48, 70, 83, 95, 235. *See* Calvinism, Puritanism.
Theological literature in America, 36, 41, 43, 78, 80, 83-91, 110, 119, 121, 122, 123, 136, 180, 190, 209, 228, 246, 247, 263, 274, 292, 325, 437, 523, 525; in England, 37, 119.
Thoreau, Henry David, 332-337; 302, 328, 338, 339, 371, 376, 398, 489.
Ticknor, Francis Orrery, 489-490, 499.
Ticknor, George, 264-267; 170, 268, 270, 271, 280, 296, 371, 379-381, 393, 395, 406, 418, 437.
Timrod, Henry, 486, 491, 492-495, 497, 499.
Town Histories in New England, 264.
Tories, *see* Loyalists.
Trafalgar, Battle of, 62, 139.
Transcendentalism in New England, 290-310; 245, 311, 324, 330, 333, 338-340, 346, 347, 359, 371, 372, 379, 384, 386, 416, 418, 429, 432, 441, 485, 528. *See* Revolutionary Spirit.
Translations of American books, 183, 207.

Translations in Elizabethan literature, 5, 20, 22, 27, 484; in America, 198, 391, 456, 458.
Trent, W. P., 480, 487-488, 491.
"Tribune," the New York, 229, 230, 300, 308, 309, 449, 454-455, 456.
Trollope, Anthony, 176.
Trollope, Mrs., 502, 503.
Trumbull, John, 123-126; 120, 129.
Tudor, William, 262.
Twain, Mark, 101, 173, 271, 508, 513; his "Huckleberry Finn," 342, 477, 503.
Tyler, Moses Coit, 35 *n.*, 40; his "Literary History of the American Revolution," 104, 107, 112, 134, 485.

UNION, the ideal of, 105, 151, 345.
Unitarianism in New England, 277-289; 90, 122, 224, 245, 267, 273, 290, 291, 292, 295, 299, 303, 304, 308, 309, 311, 314, 326, 338, 341, 342, 346, 347, 353, 359, 371, 372, 379, 384, 393, 407-409, 418-419, 422, 441-442, 443, 528. *See* Revolutionary Spirit.
United States, 6, 7, 29, 127, 149-153, 169. *See* Constitution, Law.
Universities, the Office of, 383.
University of Pennsylvania, 79, 93.

VERSATILITY, *see* National Traits.
Victoria, Queen, 139, 141, 142, 144, 154, 169, 511, 525, 526.
Virginia, 26, 27, 35, 37, 108, 120, 152, 190, 204, 206, 234, 481, 484, 485, 487, 523; University of, 204.
Voltaire, 99, 115, 423.

WALTON, Izaak, 20, 23, 31, 37.
    War of 1812, 150, 160, 244.
" Ward, Artemus," 511-512, 515.

Ward, Nathaniel, his "Simple Cobbler of Agawam," 508.
Ware, Henry, 282.
Ware, Henry, Jr., 311.
Warren, Joseph, 247, 260.
Washington, George, 64, 76, 92, 117, 120, 151, 268, 357, 485; Weems's Life of, 159.
Washington, City of, 233, 451, 466.
Waterloo, Battle of, 61, 140, 145, 146, 525–526.
Wealth in New England, 71–73, 242, 248–249, 378, 440; in New York, 463; in the West, 441.
Webster, Daniel, 247–253, 255, 257, 280, 291, 354, 371, 437, 439, 485, 491; Whittier's poems on, 367–369.
Welde, Thomas, 37.
Wesley, John, 66, 74.
West, the, 500–513; 30, 152, 441, 514.
West Church of Boston, 442.
West Point Military Academy, 205.
Whigs of Massachusetts, 249, 255, 257.
Whipple, Edwin Percy, 438.
Whitcomb's "Chronological Outlines of American Literature," 35, 36, 78, 461.
White, Richard Grant, 458–459.
Whitefield, George, 74, 75, 97–99.
Whitman, Walt, 464, 465–479.
Whittier, John Greenleaf, 358–369, 388–389; 197, 237, 371, 376, 425, 426, 430, 438, 460, 465, 481, 489, 493, 495, 509, 528.

Wigglesworth, Michael, 36, 39, 78.
Wilkins, Mary Eleanor, 237.
William III., 7, 13, 25, 32, 33, 45, 53, 55, 59, 60, 79, 357.
William IV., 139, 140, 141, 143, 147.
Williams College, 193, 461.
Williams, Roger, 27, 32, 50, 77.
Willis, Nathaniel Parker, 222–230; 207, 208, 280, 288, 449.
Wills, George Stockton, 480.
Winslow, Edward, 26, 32.
Winsor, Justin, his "Memorial History of Boston," 287.
Winthrop, John, 26, 31, 32, 50, 77, 357; his History, 31, 263.
Winthrop, Professor John, 261.
Winthrop, Robert Charles, 258, 280, 439.
Wirt, William, 485.
Wister, Owen, 504.
Witchcraft at Salem, 33, 45–46.
Woodworth, Samuel, 195.
Woolman, John, 80–81, 299.
Wordsworth, William, 67, 69, 145, 146, 162, 174, 201, 228, 291, 399, 526, 527.
World's Fair of 1893, 505–506.

YALE COLLEGE, 75, 78, 79, 83, 120, 121, 122, 123, 124, 126, 129, 181, 224, 225, 352, 407, 486.
Yellow Fever in New York, 163–164.
"Youth's Companion," the, 224.

Date Due

	PRINTED	IN U. S. A.	